THE BIRDWATCHER'S YEARBOOK

AND DIARY 2000

GW00598053

Cover design: Sue Pemberton

Cover drawing: Rob Hume

The temperature is rising . . .

The indicators —

BTO

• Arrival date of the Swallow

The BTO can provide the huge data resource that will enable a serious study of the effects of earlier arrival on bird populations.

• Egg-laying dates of birds

Chaffinches along with a number of other species studied, showed significant long-term trends towards earlier laying in recent years. Are these changes good, bad or indifferent?

• Small bird population changes

Big population declines have occurred after severe winters. It is expected that Wren populations will not increase indefinitely if winters become progressively milder.

01842 750050

Find out more by calling our Membership Unit now for a FREE special issue of BTO News

THE
BIRDWATCHER'S
YEARBOOK
AND DIARY
2000

Edited by
John E Pemberton

BUCKINGHAM PRESS

Published in 1999 by
Buckingham Press
10 Raven Way
Christchurch
Dorset BH23 4BQ
England

01425 273632

© Buckingham Press 1999

ISBN 0 9533840 1 2
ISSN 0144-364 X

Printed and bound in Great Britain by
Redwood Books
Trowbridge, Wiltshire

CONTENTS

Bird Atlases/Avifaunas, Bird Recorders, Bird Reports, BTO Regional Representatives and Regional Development Officers, Clubs and Societies, Ringing Groups, RSPB County Youth Officers and Members' Groups, Wetland Bird Survey Count Organisers, Wildlife Hospitals and Wildlife Trusts

A comprehensive personal bird recording system. Species include all those on the British List, augmented by European breeding and regularly occurring species. BOU categories, BTO species codes and EURING numbers (for Voous order) are given, along with indications of rarities and rare breeding birds.

A collection of articles by the Director, a Council member and Staff of the British Trust for Ornithology, identifying major issues and objectives at the beginning of the 2000s.

CONTENTS 1981-1999

References consist of the year followed by the pages, eg.
99:240-242 = *The Birdwatcher's Yearbook 1999*, pages 240-242

1. FEATURES

2. SELECTED REFERENCE ITEMS

FOREWORD

In my former capacity as Species Officer for RSPB Wales over the past fifteen years, I was often asked how many Red Kites, Black Grouse, Hen Harriers, Golden Plover and many other species were nesting in the Principality. It saddened me that I was not only able to report almost exactly how many pairs there were, but that I also knew where each one was. In fact I was only one stage away from knowing every single individual by name, and that was simply because I was being asked to monitor populations of birds which were heading rapidly towards extinction.

Now don't get me wrong. I fully appreciate the excellent work of organisations such as the RSPB and the BTO with their dedicated staff and army of volunteers. The Breeding Bird Survey, for example, has proved to be an invaluable conservation tool and is now being replicated in other countries of the world. Thanks to a partnership of various organisations, the decline of the Corncrake has been reversed and the Red Kite is now seen in areas from which it was absent for more than a hundred years.

However, collating the data is only part of the answer to the ever increasing problem of declining bird populations against the backdrop of a rising human population with all its associated ills. Once you have the data, you often need to be able to respond quickly in order to conserve a species and prevent its extinction. This has always been one of the strengths of the RSPB in that it is not weighed down by bureaucracy and is therefore able to act immediately when a new crisis arises.

The one area where I believe we have been much less effective is in getting the urgency of our conservation message across in a simple and effective way to the general public.

How about the million and more members of the RSPB and the rising number of BTO members, you may ask. These, of course, are to be welcomed, as is the appearance of each new birdwatching magazine and the increasing awareness of conservation issues generally. Here, however, we are preaching to the converted. People who join a conservation organisation or who subscribe to a wildlife magazine do so because they already have an interest in the environment. But what about the other seventy per cent or so who fall outside this net? They number amongst their ranks Members of Parliament, industrialists, MEPs, huge landowners - all influential members of society - as well as the vast majority of the voting public. Environmental issues were high on the political agenda during the affluent Thatcherite years of the late 1980s, but since that time interest has waned.

The question we as conservationists must answer is how do we push the environment back up the rungs of the ladder of public awareness.

Articles in wildlife and countryside magazines are a useful way of getting messages across to targeted audiences, but the public at large need their messages packaged in a particular way. Most will read newspapers such as *The Sun*, *The Star* or *The Mirror*, and when was the last time you read a meaningful article on the reasons behind the decline of farmland birds or the loss of moorland in any of these? Apart from one memorable article about feeding garden birds entitled 'Get your lard out for the tits' in one of the tabloids some years ago, birdwatching articles in these papers tend to be rather derogatory references to twitchers, often comparing them to train spotters, or about Robins that have set up home in ladies' underwear.

It has always astounded me how many people have never heard of the RSPB or the BTO, or any conservation organisation for that matter. On television, nature programmes with a useful conservation message just don't make it to the primetime viewing slots on BBC 1. They are generally pushed to a Sunday afternoon on that channel or to a quieter viewing time on BBC 2; and the reason is that few people will watch them compared to programmes such as soap operas.

So what is the answer? Well, I don't have a book of magic tricks to solve the problem, but it is clear that we must all work to make wildlife an important but 'sexy' issue. If it takes a headline like the one above to get a lengthy article published, so be it; but we must always attempt to ensure that a serious conservation message is carried on the back of the piece. There have been some good examples of TV programmes that popularise birdwatching in a fun way while tackling serious issues, and without being demeaning to birdwatchers.

The messages need to be simple but thought-provoking. Do you remember hay meadows full of wild flowers, roadside verges a chorus of grasshoppers, gardens alive with Song Thrushes and telegraph wires heavy with Swallows and House Martins preparing to depart? It is questions like these that lead people to ask why such things, that once they took for granted, have disappeared from our countryside. And it is only when they do this that the hitherto disinterested public, and hence MPs and all those other influential people will sit up and take notice.

If we are to achieve this goal, however, we need to take action very soon. Otherwise programmes on the wildlife of Britain will be relegated to the archives alongside *Pathé News*.

Iolo Williams, July 1999

PREFACE

The year 2000 not only marks the start of a new millennium, it also sees the 20th anniversary of the Birdwatcher's Yearbook. To celebrate these events, *The Birdwatcher's Yearbook and Diary 2000* has been designated its "Millennium Edition".

As the 1900s draw to a close there are welcome signs of a new awareness that birds are important. Not only recognised as indicators of the health of the environment, they have also been included by the Government in its measures of the nation's quality of life. This progress is coupled with a fresh impetus in the drive to convince the wider public of the urgency of taking action to right the wrongs that are decimating the populations of many of our familiar birds like the Skylark and Song Thrush.

Iolo Williams, who for many years monitored the fortunes of birds in Wales for the RSPB, has now left that employment so as to devote himself to campaigning through the media for a reversal of their declines. His TV 'Birdman' series brought the plight of birds into the public's drawing room. His personal commitment to promoting the defence of wild birds in the face of adverse environmental impacts provides a rallying call for action in the new millennium. I invited Iolo to write the first Foreword to appear in the *Birdwatcher's Yearbook*. He readily accepted, and I urge you to read it.

To be successful, lobbying and campaigning must be based on sound scientific research. Here, the British Trust for Ornithology plays a vital role. There exists a unique partnership between birdwatchers and BTO scientists which, through carefully formulated censuses and surveys, has amassed over many years an invaluable fund of data. Fieldwork for these projects is both enjoyable and of crucial importance. Birdwatchers who join in get immense satisfaction from knowing that they are doing something of real value. Without their input, I doubt very much if the BTO would be able to produce the science that Iolo Williams and others - the Government included - so urgently require.

It helps all parties to know how the BTO works: how it gathers the sort of raw data that all scientific research requires, how it analyses and interprets that information and then makes it available for conservation action. I therefore commissioned a collection of articles, written by the Director, a member of Council and members of staff of the BTO to provide this authoritative picture in a special Millennium Feature for our 2000 edition. It shows in a realistic and sometimes quite dramatic way what can be achieved and how birdwatchers underpin the achievement.

Many birdwatchers are concerned about the direct or indirect effects of pesticides and herbicides on birds. These, however, are not something that amateurs can easily measure, unlike the recording of nests or the counting of wildfowl, for example. Consequently, this subject can not be part of the BTO's work. The nature and extent of such research is more befitting the Ministry of Agriculture and the best recourse for birdwatchers is probably to lobby their MP.

PC Paul Henery, adviser to the makers of a recent fictional TV series based on the work of police wildlife liaison officers, was the author of an article on this subject in our 1996 edition. In the last two editions we have listed PWLOs in the County Directory. Most officers with this title carry out the duties alongside their regular duties. It is always stressed that wildlife crime, like any other crime, can be reported to any officer or police station, and it is now felt unnecessary to continue listing individual officers.

This year the number of national projects has grown and particulars of more reserves have been included. In response to requests, details of national and regional birdlines are also given (see Quick Reference). Not surprisingly, there are many more e-mail addresses than hitherto, and as they proliferate they add to the pressures on space.

As always, the directory sections have been thoroughly updated and augmented where necessary. This requires a great deal of co-operation on the part of recipients of the large number of data forms we send out for checking and approval. Despite the high response rate, for which I am most grateful, there is also a good deal of chasing and double-checking to be done. The assistance provided by individuals in the major organisations is worthy of special acknowledgement, and I record here my thanks to Jeff Baker, Derek Toomer and their colleagues at BTO, Ian Dawson and Hazel Jones at RSPB, Bev Childs at BirdLife International, Steve Dudley at BOU, Mark Pollitt and Nikki Straughan at WWT, Bob Bleakley at EHS (NI) and Neil Willcox at SWT.

Not least, I thank my wife Joyce for her active participation in this task of information gathering and checking. Absolute accuracy, however, has an elusive quality and I must therefore make the disclaimer that no responsibility can be accepted for the consequences of any action based on the contents of this book.

John E Pemberton
16 September 1999

PART ONE
COUNTY DIRECTORY

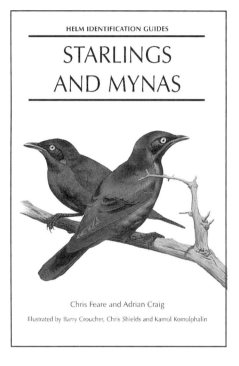

(Actual size 240 x 160 mm)

Starlings and Mynas, by Chris Feare and Adrian Craig, illustrated by Barry Shields and Kamol Komolphalin, Helm (A&C Black), 1998, 285p. £32.00. ISBN 0 7136 3961 X. Hbk.

Many people in Britain look on their local Starlings as something of a pest. Not so, Chris Feare. He has studied the common Starling for a quarter of a century and his monograph, *The Starling* (OUP, 1984) is a much quoted classic. His co-author has researched African starlings for two decades. Their combined efforts, along with those of the talented illustrators, have produced a book that is both authoritative and fascinating. The starling family, comprising 114 species, in fact includes some of the world's rarest birds and some of the most colourful. This volume depicts and describes them all. It is a work that wonderfully informs and delights.

Directory contents
The directory is a systematic listing of Bird Atlases/Avifaunas, Bird Recorders, Bird Reports, British Trust for Ornithology (BTO) Regional Representatives and Regional Development Officers, Clubs and Societies, Ringing Groups, Royal Society for the Protection of Birds (RSPB) County Youth Officers and Members' Groups, Wetland Bird Survey (WeBS) Count Organisers, Wildlife Hospitals and Wildlife Trusts.

Clubs: year founded and members
Figures appearing in brackets following the names of clubs, etc. indicate the date of formation and the current number of members, for example:

DORSET BIRD CLUB (1987; 560) means that the DBC was
formed in 1987 and that its current membership is 560.

Note that in the case of RSPB Members' Groups where a very high membership is shown this may be the number of RSPB members in that Group's catchment area rather than members of the Group itself.

Telephone number changes
Under the banner of 'The Big Number' the telephone companies are in the process of bringing in wide-ranging changes to telephone numbers. Old and new numbers will run in parallel for some time. In case of difficulty, information can be obtained by calling 'The Big Number' helpline free on 0808 22 4 2000, by visiting their website at www.numberchange.org, or by writing to National Code & Number Change, Dept C, PO Box 6929, London E3 3NX.

Sources
The information in the directory has been obtained either from the persons listed or from the appropriate national or other bodies. In some cases, where it has not proved possible to verify the details directly, alternative responsible sources have been relied upon. When no satisfactory record was available, previously included entries have sometimes had to be deleted.

Readers are requested to advise the editor of any errors or omissions, at the address given on the reverse of the title page.

ABBREVIATIONS

BC	Bird Club	RR	Regional Representative
BTO	British Trust for Ornithology	RS	Ringing Station
		RSPB	Royal Society for the Protection of Birds
BWI	BirdWatch Ireland		
NHS	Natural History Society	SOC	Scottish Ornithologists' Club
OC	Ornithological Club		
OS	Ornithological Society	TNC	Trust for Nature Conservation
RDO	Regional Development Officer	WT	Wildlife Trust
RG	Ringing Group		

ENGLAND

BEDFORDSHIRE

Bird Atlas/Avifauna
An Atlas of the Breeding Birds of Bedfordshire 1988-92 by R A Dazley and P Trodd (Bedfordshire Natural History Society, 1994).

Bird Recorders
Dave Odell, The Hobby, 74 The Links, Kempston, Bedford MK42 7LT. 01234 857149. Bedfordshire Bird Club Records & Research Committee. Phil Cannings, 30 Graham Gardens, Luton LU3 1NQ. Home 01582 400394; Work 01234 842220.

Bird Report
BEDFORDSHIRE BIRD REPORT (1946-). From Gill Dickens, 9 Ullswater Road, Dunstable, Beds LU6 3PX.

BTO Regional Representative & Regional Development Officer
RR. Phil Cannings, 30 Graham Gardens, Luton, Beds LU3 1NQ. Home 01582 400394; Work 01234 842220.
RDO. Judith Knight, 381 Bideford Green, Linslade, Leighton Buzzard, Beds LU7 7TY. 01525 378161.

Club
BEDFORDSHIRE BIRD CLUB. (1992; 234). Miss Sheila Alliez, Flat 67 Adamson Court, Hillgrounds Road, Kempston, Bedford MK42 8QT.

Ringing Groups
IVEL RG. Errol Newman, 29 Norse Road, Goldington, Bedford MK41 0NR. 01234 343119.
RSPB. Dr A D Evans, 6 Jennings Close, Potton, Sandy, Beds SG19 2SE.

RSPB Members' Groups
BEDFORD. (1970; 80). Barrie Mason, 6 Landseer Walk, Bedford MK41 7LZ. 01234 262280.
EAST BEDFORDSHIRE. (1973; 75). Terry Park, 8 Back Street, Biggleswade, Beds SG18 8JA. 01767 221363.
SOUTH BEDFORDSHIRE. (1973; 133). Brian Payne, 13A Sowerby Avenue, Luton LU2 8AF. 01582 723330.

Wetland Bird Survey Organiser
Kevin Sharpe, 22 Russet Close, Stewartby, Beds MK43 9LG. 01234 765070.

Wildlife Trust see Cambridgeshire.

BERKSHIRE

Bird Atlas/Avifauna
The Birds of Berkshire by P E Standley *et al* (Berkshire Atlas Group/Reading Ornithological Club, 1996).

Bird Recorder
Peter Standley, Siskins, 7 Llanvair Drive, South Ascot, Berks SL5 9HS. 01344 623502.

Bird Reports
BERKSHIRE BIRD BULLETIN (Monthly, 1986-). From Brian Clews, 118 Broomhill, Cookham, Berks SL6 9LQ. 01628 525314.
BIRDS OF BERKSHIRE (1974-). From Recorder.
BIRDS OF THE THEALE AREA (1988-). From Secretary, Theale Area Bird Conservation Group.
NEWBURY BIRD REPORT (1959-). From Secretary, Newbury District Ornithological Club.

BTO Regional Representative & Regional Development Officer
EAST & WEST RR. Chris Robinson, 2 Beckfords, Upper Basildon, Reading RG8 8PB. 01491 671420.
MAIDENHEAD RDO. Jeremy Langham, 23 Gorse Road, Cookham, Maidenhead, Berks SL6 9LL. 01628 526552.

Clubs
BERKSHIRE BIRD BULLETIN GROUP. (1986; 100). Berkshire Bird Bulletin Group, PO Box 680, Maidenhead, Berks SL6 9ST. 01628 525314.
NEWBURY DISTRICT ORNITHOLOGICAL CLUB. (1959; 120). Jim Burnett, 44 Bourne Vale, Hungerford, Berks RG1 0LL. 01488 681344.
READING ORNITHOLOGICAL CLUB. (1945; 225). Mike Smith, 5 Nabbs Hill Close, Tilehurst, Reading RG31 4SG. Home 0118 941 3365; Work 0118 950 0336; fax (evg) 0118 960 7703; email MSmith8741@aol.com.
THEALE AREA BIRD CONSERVATION GROUP. (1988; 75). Mike Smith, 5 Nabbs Hill Close, Tilehurst, Reading RG31 4SG. Home 0118 941 3365; Work 0118 950 0336; fax (evg) 0118 960 7703; email MSmith8741@aol.com.

Ringing Groups
NEWBURY RG. J Legg, 1 Malvern Court, Old Newtown Road, Newbury, Berks RG14 7DR.
RUNNYMEDE RG. K J Herber, Laleham, 60 Dale End, Brancaster Staithe, King's Lynn, Norfolk PE31 8DA.

RSPB Members' Groups
EAST BERKSHIRE. (1974; 250). Brian Clews, 118 Broomhill, Cookham, Maidenhead, Berks SL6 9LQ. 01628 525314.
READING. (1986; 80). David Mortlock, 267 Wensley Road, Reading RG1 6EE. 0118 961 2695.

WOKINGHAM & BRACKNELL. (1979; 180). Patrick Crowley, 56 Ellis Road, Crowthorne, Berks RG45 6PT. 01344 776473.

Wetland Bird Survey Organiser
Neil Bucknell, 10 Cleeve Court, Streatley, Reading RG8 9PS.

Wildlife Hospitals
KESTREL LODGE. D J Chandler, 101 Sheridan Avenue, Caversham, Reading RG4 7QB. 01189 477107. Birds of prey, ground feeding birds, waterbirds, seabirds. Temporary homes for all except large birds of prey. Veterinary support. Small charge.
SWAN LIFELINE. Chairman and Co-ordinator, Tim Heron, Swan Treatment Centre, Cuckoo Weir Island, South Meadow Lane, Eton, Berks SL4 6SS. 01753 859397; fax 01753 622709. Registered charity. Thames Valley 24-hour swan rescue and treatment service. Veterinary support. Operates membership scheme.

Wildlife Trust see Oxfordshire.

BUCKINGHAMSHIRE

Bird Atlas/Avifauna
The Birds of Buckinghamshire ed by P Lack and D Ferguson (Buckinghamshire Bird Club, 1993).

Bird Recorder
Andy Harding, 15 Jubilee Terrace, Stony Stratford, Milton Keynes MK11 1DU. Home 01908 565896; Work 01908 653328.

Bird Reports
AMERSHAM BIRDWATCHING CLUB ANNUAL REPORT (1975-). From Secretary.
BUCKINGHAMSHIRE BIRD REPORT (1980-). From Rob Andrews, 56 Copes Shroves, Hazlemere, High Wycombe, Bucks HP15 7AH.
NORTH BUCKS BIRD REPORT (10 pa). From Recorder.

BTO Regional Representative & Regional Development Officer
RR. Mick A'Court, 29 Amersham Hill, High Wycombe, Bucks HP13 6NU. Home 01494 536734; Work 01494 462246; fax 01494 459920; e-mail mick@focusrite.com.
RDO. Peter Hearn, 160 High Street, Aylesbury, Bucks HP20 1RE. Tel/fax 01296 581520; Work 01296 424145.

Clubs
AMERSHAM BIRDWATCHING CLUB. (1973; 70). Cliff Robinson, 6 Howards Thicket, Gerrard's Cross, Bucks SL9 7NX. 01753 885779.
BUCKINGHAMSHIRE BIRD CLUB. (1981; 300). Graeme Taylor, Field House, 54 Halton Lane, Wendover, Aylesbury, Bucks HP22 6AU. 01296 625796.
NORTH BUCKS BIRDERS. (1977; 60). Andy Harding, 15 Jubilee Terrace, Stony Stratford, Milton Keynes MK11 1DU. Home 01908 565896; Work 01908 653328.

Ringing Groups
BBONT RG. J G Worgan, Decoy Cottage, Boarstall, Brill, Aylesbury, Bucks HP18 9UX. 01844 237488.

HUGHENDEN RG. P Edwards, 8 The Brackens, Warren Wood, High Wycombe, Bucks HP11 1EB. 01494 535125.

RSPB Members' Groups
See also Herts: Chorleywood.
AYLESBURY. (1981; 200). Barry Oxley, 3 Swan Close, Station Road, Blackthorn, Bicester, Oxon OX6 0TU. 01869 247780.
NORTH BUCKINGHAMSHIRE. (1976; 400). Jim Parsons, 8 The Mount, Aspley Guise, Milton Keynes MK17 8EA. 01908 582450.

Wetland Bird Survey Organiser
Graeme Taylor, Field House, 54 Halton Lane, Wendover, Aylesbury, Bucks HP22 6AU. 01296 625796.

Wildlife Hospitals
MILTON KEYNES WILDLIFE HOSPITAL. Mr & Mrs V Seaton, 150 Bradwell Common Boulevard, Milton Keynes MK13 8BE. 01908 604198. Registered charity. All species of British birds and mammals. Veterinary support.
WILDLIFE HOSPITAL TRUST. St Tiggywinkles, Aston Road, Haddenham, Aylesbury, Bucks HP17 8AF. 01844 292292; fax 01844 292640; e-mail tiggys@globalnet.co.uk; http://www.sttiggywinkles.org.uk. Registered charity. All species. Veterinary referrals and helpline for vets and others on wild bird treatments. Full veterinary unit and staff. Teaching courses on wildlife care. Pub: *Bright Eyes* (free to members - sae).

Wildlife Trust see Oxfordshire.

CAMBRIDGESHIRE

Bird Atlas/Avifauna
An Atlas of the Breeding Birds of Cambridgeshire (VC 29) by P M M Bircham *et al* (Cambridge Bird Club, 1994).

Bird Recorders
CAMBRIDGESHIRE. Richard Allison, 3 Vermuyden Way, Fen Drayton, Cambridge CB4 5TA. Tel/fax 01954 231217.
HUNTINGDON & PETERBOROUGH. John Clark, 7 Westbrook, Hilton, Huntingdon, Cambs PE18 9NW. 01480 830472.

Bird Report
CAMBRIDGESHIRE BIRD REPORT (1926-). From Secretary, Cambridge Bird Club.

BTO Regional Representatives
CAMBRIDGESHIRE. Dr Roger Clarke, New Hythe House, 12 The Hythe, Reach, Cambridge CB5 0JQ. 01638 742447.
HUNTINGDON & PETERBOROUGH. Bill Douglas, 21 Felix Road, Ramsay Forty Foot, Huntingdon, Cambs PE17 1HY. 01487 711071.

Clubs
CAMBRIDGE BIRD CLUB. (1925; 280). Bruce Martin, 178 Nuns Way, Cambridge CB4 2NS. 01223 363656.

 ST NEOTS BIRD & WILDLIFE CLUB. (1993; 150). Tim Watling, 39 Shakespeare Road, Eaton Socon, Huntingdon, Cambs PE19 3HG. 01480 212763; e-mail tim.j.watling @unilever.com.

Ringing Group
WICKEN FEN RG. Dr C J R Thorne, Norden House, 17 The Footpath, Coton, Cambs CB3 7PX. 01954 210566; e-mail cjrt@cam.ac.uk.

RSPB Members' Groups
CAMBRIDGE. (1977; 290). Robin Bailey, 11 St Mary's Walk, Fowlmere, Royston, Herts SG8 7TS. 01763 208605.
HUNTINGDON. (1982; 280). Pam Peacock, Old Post Office, Warboys Road, Pidley, Huntingdon, Cambs PE17 3DA. 01487 840615; e-mail ppekp@primex.co.uk.

Wetland Bird Survey Organisers
CAMBRIDGESHIRE (Old). Bruce Martin, 178 Nuns Way, Cambridge CB4 2NS. 01223 363656.
HUNTINGDONSHIRE. Graham Elliott, 3 Greenway, Buckden, Huntingdon, Cambs PE18 9TU.
NENE WASHES. Charlie Kitchin, 21a East Delph, Whittlesey, Peterborough PE7 1RH. 01733 205140.
OUSE WASHES. Cliff Carson, Ouse Washes Reserve, Welches Dam, Manea, March, Cambs PE15 0ND. 01354 680212.
PETERBOROUGH. John Redshaw, 7 Fennell Road, Pinchbeck, Spalding, Lincs PE11 3RP. 01775 768227.

Wildlife Trust
BEDS, CAMBS, NORTHANTS & PETERBOROUGH WILDLIFE TRUST. (1990; 12000). 3B Langford Arch, London Road, Sawston, Cambridge CB2 4EE. 01223 712400; fax 01223 712412; e-mail cambswt@cix.co.uk.

CHESHIRE

Bird Atlas/Avifauna
The Breeding Bird Atlas of Cheshire and Wirral by J Guest *et al* (Cheshire & Wirral Ornithological Society, 1992) out of print.

Bird Recorder (inc Wirral)
Tony Broome, 4 Larchwood Drive, Wilmslow, Cheshire SK9 2NU. 01625 540434.

Bird Report
CHESHIRE & WIRRAL BIRD REPORT (1969-). From K Sheel, 11 Bridgecroft Road, Wallasey, Wirral CH45 7WX.

BTO Regional Representatives & Regional Development Officer
MID RR. Roy Leigh, 10 Mere Road, Higher Marston, Northwich, Cheshire CW9 6DR. 01606 892032.

NORTH & EAST RR. David Jones, 8 Wey Gates Drive, Hale Barns, Cheshire WA15 0BW. 0161 980 5273; e-mail d.b.jones@lineone.net.
SOUTH RR & RDO. Charles Hull, Edleston Cottage, Edleston Hall Lane, Nantwich, Cheshire CW5 8PL. 01270 628194.

Clubs
CHESHIRE & WIRRAL ORNITHOLOGICAL SOCIETY. (1988; 352). David Cogger, 113 Nantwich Road, Middlewich, Cheshire CW10 9HD. 01606 832517.
CHESTER & DISTRICT ORNITHOLOGICAL SOCIETY. (1967; 60). David King, 13 Bennett Close, Willaston, South Wirral CH64 2XF. 0151 327 7212.
KNUTSFORD ORNITHOLOGICAL SOCIETY. (1974; 45). Roy Bircumshaw, 267 Longridge, Knutsford, Cheshire WA16 8PH. 01565 634193.
LANCASHIRE & CHESHIRE FAUNA SOCIETY. (1914; 99). Dave Bickerton, 64 Petre Crescent, Rishton, Lancs BB1 4RB. 01254 886257; e-mail DaveBickerton @compuserve.com.
LYMM ORNITHOLOGY GROUP. (1975; 65). Mrs Ann Ledden, 4 Hill View, Widnes WA8 9AL. 0151 424 0441.
MID-CHESHIRE ORNITHOLOGICAL SOCIETY. (1963; 80). Paul Kenyon, 196 Chester Road, Hartford, Northwich CW8 1LG. 01606 77960.
SOUTH EAST CHESHIRE ORNITHOLOGICAL SOCIETY. (1964; 70). Colin Lythgoe, 11 Waterloo Road, Haslington, Crewe CW1 5TF. 01270 582642.
WILMSLOW GUILD ORNITHOLOGICAL SOCIETY. (1965; 60). Mrs Brenda Webb, 26 Lowfield Road, Shaw Heath, Stockport, Cheshire SK2 6RN. 0161 480 5855.

Ringing Groups
MERSEYSIDE RG. P Slater, 45 Greenway Road, Speke, Liverpool L24 7RY.
SOUTH MANCHESTER RG. C M Richards, Fairhaven, 13 The Green, Handforth, Wilmslow, Cheshire SK9 3AG. 01625 524527.

RSPB County Youth Officer
Mrs Jean Crouch, 4 Blenheim Close, Poynton, Stockport, Cheshire SK12 1DN. 01625 873147.

RSPB Members' Groups
CHESTER. (1987; 408). Bernard Wright, Carden Smithy, Clutton, Chester CH3 9EP. 01829 782243.
MACCLESFIELD. (1979; 360). Peter Kirk, Field Rise, Dumbah Lane, West Bollington, Macclesfield, Cheshire SK10 5AB. 01625 829119.
NORTH CHESHIRE. (1976; 160). Steve Kemp, 7 Denehurst Close, Penketh, Warrington WA5 2ES. 01925 723835.

Wetland Bird Survey Organisers
DEE ESTUARY. Colin Wells, Burton Point Farm, Station Road, Burton, Nr Neston, South Wirral CH64 5SB. 0151 336 7681.
MERSEY ESTUARY. Graham Thomason, 110 Coroners Lane, Widnes, Cheshire WA8 9HZ. 0151 424 7257.
INLAND. Tony O'Neill, 742 Hyde Road, Gorton, Manchester M18 7EF.

Wildlife Hospitals
RSPCA STAPELEY GRANGE WILDLIFE HOSPITAL. London Road, Stapeley, Nantwich, Cheshire CW5 7JW. 01270 610347. All wild birds. Oiled bird wash facilities and pools. Veterinary support.
SWAN SANCTUARY. Mrs C Clements, 24 St David's Drive, Callands, Warrington WA5 5SB. 01925 636245.

Wildlife Trust
CHESHIRE WILDLIFE TRUST. (1962; 3600). Grebe House, Reaseheath, Nantwich, Cheshire CW5 6DG. 01270 610180; fax 01270 610430; e-mail cheshirewt @cix.co.uk.

CORNWALL

Bird Recorders
CORNWALL. A R Pay, Salena Cottage, Wendron, Helston, Cornwall TR13 0EA. 01326 561628
ISLES OF SCILLY. Will Wagstaff, 42 Sally Port, St Mary's, Isles of Scilly TR21 0JE. 01720 422212.

Bird Reports
BIRDS IN CORNWALL (1931-). From Recorder.
ISLES OF SCILLY BIRD REPORT (1969-). From Martin Scott, 6 Museum Flats, Church Street, St Mary's, Isles of Scilly TR21 0JU.

BTO Regional Representatives & Regional Development Officers
CORNWALL RR & RDO. Paul Stubbs, 1 Gulveal Villas, Penmenner Road, The Lizard, Helston, Cornwall TR12 7NW. Tel/fax 01326 290404; e-mail paulstubbs @lineone.net.
ISLES OF SCILLY RR & RDO. Will Wagstaff, as above (Bird Recorders).

Club
CORNWALL BIRDWATCHING & PRESERVATION SOCIETY. (1931; 900). Steve Rogers, Roseland, Cyril Road, Truro TR1 3TA. 01872 273004.

Ringing Group
SCILLONIA SEABIRD GROUP. Peter Robinson, Riviera House, Parade, St Mary's, Isles of Scilly TR21 0LP. 01720 423057; e-mail pjrobinson2 @compuserve.com.

RSPB Members' Group
CORNWALL. (1972; 550). Michael Lord, Gue Gassel, Church Cove, The Lizard, Cornwall TR12 7PH. 01326 290981.

Wetland Bird Survey Organisers
TAMAR COMPLEX. Gladys Grant, 32 Dunstone Close, Plymstock, Plymouth PL9 8SG.
CORNWALL (excl Tamar complex). Dave Conway, Tregenna, Cooksland, Bodmin, Cornwall PL31 2AR. 01208 77686.

Wildlife Hospitals
MOUSEHOLE WILD BIRD HOSPITAL & SANCTUARY ASSOCIATION LTD. Mrs Jane Bennett, Raginnis Hill, Mousehole, Penzance, Cornwall TR19 6SR. 01736 731386. All species. No ringing.
RSPCA PERRANPORTH. Warden, Animal Welfare Centre, Blowing House Road, Higher Penwartha, Perranporth, Cornwall TR6 0BA. 01872 573856. All species. Oiled bird cleaning centre. Skilled bird vet available. Open each day 1600-1700 or by appointment (call 0990 555999). The Centre may close in October 1999 on retirement of Warden, Rex Harper.

Wildlife Trust
CORNWALL WILDLIFE TRUST. (1962; 6000). Five Acres, Allet, Truro, Cornwall TR4 9DJ. 01872 273939; fax 01872 225476; e-mail cornwt@cix.co.uk.

CUMBRIA

Bird Recorders
COUNTY. Tim Dean, Echna View, Burray, Orkney KW17 2SX. 01856 731204.
NORTH WEST (Allerdale & Copeland). J K Manson, Fell Beck, East Road, Egremont, Cumbria CA22 2ED. 01946 822947.
NORTH EAST (Carlisle & Eden). Michael F Carrier, Lismore Cottage, 1 Front Street, Armathwaite, Carlisle CA4 9PB. 01697 472218.
SOUTH (South Lakeland & Furness). Ronnie Irving, 24 Birchwood Close, Kendal, Cumbria LA9 5BJ. 01539 727523.

Bird Reports
BIRDS AND WILDLIFE IN CUMBRIA (1970-). From D Clarke, Tullie House Museum, Castle Street, Carlisle, Cumbria CA3 8TP.
WALNEY BIRD OBSERVATORY REPORT. From Tim Dean (as above).

BTO Regional Representatives
NORTH RR. John Callion, The Cherries, 2 Scawfield, Scaw Road, High Harrington, Workington, Cumbria CA14 4LZ. Home 01946 830651; Work 01946 830694.
SOUTH RR. Ian Kinley, 16 Underley Hill, Kendal, Cumbria LA9 5EX. 01539 727133.

Clubs
ARNSIDE & DISTRICT NATURAL HISTORY SOCIETY. (1967; 200). Mrs Margaret N Smith, Beachwood House, Redhills Road, Arnside, Carnforth, Lancs LA5 0AX. 01524 761853.
CUMBRIA BIRD CLUB. (1989; 215). Roy Atkins, 4 Garden Walk, Edmund Castle, Wetherall, Carlisle CA4 8QD. 01228 670661.

CUMBRIA RAPTOR STUDY GROUP. P N Davies, Snowhill Cottage, Caldbeck, Wigton, Cumbria CA7 8HL.

Ringing Groups
DUBBS RG. P N Davies, Snowhill Cottage, Caldbeck, Wigton, Cumbria CA7 8HL.
EDEN RG. G Longrigg, Mere Bank, Bleatarn, Warcop, Appleby, Cumbria CA16 6PX.
MORECAMBE BAY WADER RG. J Sheldon, 415 West Shore Park, Barrow-in-Furness, Cumbria LA14 3XZ. 01229 473102.
WALNEY BIRD OBSERVATORY. K Parkes, 176 Harrogate Street, Barrow-in-Furness, Cumbria LA14 5NA. 01229 824219.

RSPB Members' Groups
CARLISLE. (1974; 350). Michael F Carrier, as above (Bird Recorders).

SOUTH LAKELAND. (1973; 350). Ms Kathleen Atkinson, 2 Langdale Crescent, Windermere, Cumbria LA23 2HE. 01539 444254.
WEST CUMBRIA. (1986; 150). Neil Hutchin, Orchard House, Main Street, Greysouthen, Cockermouth, Cumbria CA13 0UG. 01900 825231.

Wetland Bird Survey Organisers
DUDDON ESTUARY. Bob Treen, 5 Rydal Close, Dalton-in-Furness, Cumbria LA15 8QU. 01229 464789.
IRT, MITE & ESK ESTUARIES. Gordon Steele, Holmside, Irton, Holmrook, Cumbria CA19 1YQ. 01946 724336.
MORECAMBE BAY. Jean Roberts, 11 St Paul's Drive, Brookhouse, Lancaster LA2 9PG. 01524 770295.
SOLWAY ESTUARY (Inner South). Norman Holton, North Plain Farm, Bowness-on-Solway, Carlisle CA5 5AG. Tel/fax 01697 351330 office hours only.
SOLWAY ESTUARY (Outer South). John C Callion, as page 26 (BTO Rep).
INLAND. Ms Kathleen Atkinson, 2 Langdale Crescent, Windermere, Cumbria LA23 2HE. 01539 444254.

Wildlife Trust
CUMBRIA WILDLIFE TRUST. (1962; 5000). Brockhole, Windermere, Cumbria LA23 1LJ. 01539 448280; fax 01539 448281; cumbriawt@cix.co.uk.

DERBYSHIRE

Bird Recorders
1. Rare breeding records. Roy A Frost, 66 St Lawrence Road, North Wingfield, Chesterfield, Derbyshire S42 5LL. 01246 850037. 2. Records Committee & rarity records. Rodney W Key, 3 Farningham Close, Spondon, Derby DE21 7DZ. 01332 678571. 3. Annual Report editor. Richard M R James, 10 Eastbrae Road, Littleover, Derby DE23 7WA. 01332 771787.

Bird Reports
BENNERLEY MARSH WILDLIFE GROUP ANNUAL REPORT. Secretary.
CARSINGTON BIRD CLUB ANNUAL REPORT. From Secretary.
DERBYSHIRE BIRD REPORT (1954-). From Recorder (Rodney W Key).
OGSTON BIRD CLUB REPORT (1970-). From Secretary.

BTO Regional Representatives
NORTH RR. Oly Biddulph, 75 Hemper Lane, Sheffield S8 7FA. Home 0114 237 6733; Work 0114 203 7718.
SOUTH RR. Dave Budworth, 121 Wood Lane, Newhall, Swadlincote, Derbys DE11 0LX. 01283 215188.

Clubs
BENNERLEY MARSH WILDLIFE GROUP. (1995; 135). Mark Keighley, 64 Highgate Drive, Ilkeston, Derbys DE7 9HU. 0115 944 4726.
BUXTON FIELD CLUB. (1946; 84). B Aries, 1 Horsefair Avenue, Chapel-en-le-Frith, High Peak, Derbys SK23 9SQ. 01298 815291.
CARSINGTON BIRD CLUB. (1992; 257). Mrs S Jackson, 2 Rothwell Road, Mickleover, Derby DE3 5PJ. 01332 511882.

DERBYSHIRE ORNITHOLOGICAL SOCIETY. (1954; 515). Steve Shaw, 84 Moorland View Road, Walton, Chesterfield, Derbys S40 3DF. 01246 236090; e-mail SteveShaw@ornsoc.freeserve.co.uk.
OGSTON BIRD CLUB. (1969; 480). T B Bingham, 1 Bevan Road, Danesmoor, Chesterfield S45 9RT. 01246 861213.

Ringing Groups
DARK PEAK RG. W M Underwood, 56 Bank Street, Hadfield, Glossop, Derbys SK13 1BB.
SORBY-BRECK RG. Geoff P Mawson, Moonpenny Farm, Farwater Lane, Dronfield, Sheffield S18 1RA. 01246 415097.
SOUDER RG. Dave Budworth, 121 Wood Lane, Newhall, Swadlincote, Derbys DE11 0LX. 01283 215188.

RSPB County Youth Officer
Miss Margaret Whitehead, 35 Shearwater Moor Road, Breadsall, Derby DE21 5LA. 01332 832434.

RSPB Members' Groups
CHESTERFIELD. (1987; 278). Peter Lowe, 117 Ashgate Road, Chesterfield, Derbys S40 4AH. 01246 205301.
DERBY. (1973; 3600). Brian Myring, 74 The Bancroft, Etwall, Derby DE65 6NF. 01283 734851.
HIGH PEAK. (1974; 250). Paul Reid, 14 Ashton Street, Woodley, Stockport SK6 1PB. 0161 494 7931.

Wetland Bird Survey Organiser
Chris Burnett, 23 The Potlocks, Willington, Derbys DE65 6YA. 01283 703634.

Wildlife Trust
DERBYSHIRE WILDLIFE TRUST. (1962; 4000). Elvaston Castle, Derby DE72 3EP. 01332 756610; fax 01332 758872; e-mail derbywt@cix.co.uk.

DEVON

Bird Atlas/Avifauna
Tetrad Atlas of Breeding Birds of Devon by H P Sitters (Devon Birdwatching & Preservation Society, 1988).

Bird Recorder
Mike Langman, 59 Sturcombe Avenue, Roselands, Paignton TQ4 7TD. 01803 528008.

Bird Reports
DEVON BIRD REPORT (1928-). From H Kendall, 33 Victoria Road, Bude, Cornwall EX23 8RJ. .
LUNDY FIELD SOCIETY ANNUAL REPORT (1946-). (Index on website). From Secretary.

BTO Regional Representative and Regional Development Officer
John Woodland, Glebe Cottage, Dunsford, Exeter EX6 7AA. 01647 252494.

Clubs

DEVON BIRDWATCHING & PRESERVATION SOCIETY. (1928; 1400). Mrs Joy Vaughan JP, 28 Fern Meadow, Okehampton, Devon EX20 1PB. 01837 53360.
KINGSBRIDGE & DISTRICT NATURAL HISTORY SOCIETY. (1989; 100). Martin Catt, Migrants Rest, East Prawle, Kingsbridge, Devon TQ7 2DB. 01548 511443.
LUNDY FIELD SOCIETY. (1946; 450). Chris Webster, 38 Greenway Avenue, Taunton, Somerset TA2 6HY. 01823 282889; e-mail chris@webster5.demon.co.uk; www.webster5.demon.co.uk/.
TOPSHAM BIRDWATCHING & NATURALISTS' SOCIETY. (1969; 119). Mrs Janice Vining, 2 The Maltings, Fore Street, Topsham, Exeter EX3 0HF. 01392 873514.

Ringing Groups

DEVON & CORNWALL WADER RG. R C Swinfen, 72 Dunraven Drive, Derriford, Plymouth PL6 6AT. 01752 704184.
LUNDY FIELD SOCIETY. A M Taylor, 26 High Street, Spetisbury, Blandford, Dorset DT11 9DJ. 01258 857336.
SLAPTON BIRD OBSERVATORY. Peter Ellicott, 10 Chapel Road, Alphington, Exeter EX2 8TB. 01392 277387.
SOUTH DEVON SEABIRD TRUST. Keith Grant, Whitcombe Farm, Kenn, Exeter EX6 7XQ. 01392 832795.

RSPB County Youth Officer

Mrs Sue Sykes, The Rectory, Mary Tavy, Tavistock, Devon PL19 9PP. 01822 810516.

RSPB Members' Groups

EXETER & DISTRICT. (1974; 680). Stan Handford, 5 Dunvegan Close, Exeter EX4 4AF. 01392 276083.
NORTH DEVON. (1970; 96). David Gayton, 29 Merrythorne Road, Fremington, Barnstaple, Devon EX31 3AL. 01271 371092.
PLYMOUTH. (1974; 850). Mrs Eileen Willey, 11 Beverstone Way, Roborough, Plymouth PL6 7DY. 01752 208996.

Wetland Bird Survey Organisers

TAMAR COMPLEX. Gladys Grant, 32 Dunstone Close, Plymstock, Plymouth PL9 8SG.
TAW & TORRIDGE ESTUARY. Tony Vickery, 4 Taw View, Bishop's Tawton, Barnstaple, Devon EX32 0AW.
OTHER SITES. Philip Stidwill, 80 Stuart Road, Pennycomequick, Plymouth PL1 5LP. 01752 559332.

Wildlife Hospitals

BIRD OF PREY CASUALTY CENTRE. Mrs J E L Vinson, Crooked Meadow, Stidston Lane, South Brent, Devon TQ10 9JS. 01364 72174. Birds of prey, with emergency advice on other species. Aviaries, releasing pen. Veterinary support.
BONDLEIGH BIRD HOSPITAL. Manager, Miss M Chetham, North Tawton, Devon EX20 2AJ. 01837 82328. All species. 14 aviaries, 2 aquapens. Veterinary support available, if requested, with payment of full charges.
CATT, Martin, as above (Clubs). Collects oiled birds and gives initial treatment before forwarding to cleaning station.
HURRELL, Dr L H. 201 Outland Road, Peverell, Plymouth PL2 3PF. 01752 771838. Birds of prey only. Veterinary support.
SUNNYDALE ANIMAL RESCUE. Roger Quaintance, 18 Queen Avenue, Ilfracombe, N Devon EX34 9LN. 01271 864855. All birds (esp raptors). Seabirds only for clean-ups. Veterinary support.

TORBAY WILDLIFE RESCUE CENTRE. Malcolm Higgs, 6A Gerston Place, Paignton, S Devon TQ3 3DX. 01803 557624. All wild birds, inc. oiled. Pools, aviaries, intensive care, washing facilities. Open at all times. 24-hr veterinary support. Holding areas off limits to public as all wildlife must be returned to the wild.

Wildlife Trust
DEVON WILDLIFE TRUST. (1962; 8000). Shirehampton House, 35-37 St David's Hill, Exeter EX4 4DA. 01392 279244; fax 01392 433221; e-mail devonwt@cix.co.uk.

DORSET

Bird Atlas/Avifauna
Dorset Breeding Bird Atlas (working title). In preparation.

Bird Recorder
Shaun Robson, 5 Pine Road, Corfe Mullen, Wimborne, Dorset BH21 3DW. 01202 886563.

Bird Reports
DORSET BIRDS (1977-). From Miss W Adams, 16 Sherford Drive, Wareham, Dorset BH20 4EN.
THE BIRDS OF CHRISTCHURCH HARBOUR (1959-). From General Secretary, Christchurch Harbour Ornithological Group.
PORTLAND BIRD OBSERVATORY REPORT. From Warden, see Reserves.

BTO Regional Representatives
Catherine and Graham Whitby, 2 Helston Close, Portisham, Weymouth, Dorset DT3 4EY. 01305 871301.

Clubs
CHRISTCHURCH HARBOUR ORNITHOLOGICAL GROUP. (1956; 150). John Hall, 15 Kingsbere Gardens, Haslemere Avenue, Highcliffe, Dorset BH23 5BQ. 01425 275610.
DORSET BIRD CLUB. (1987; 560). Mrs Eileen Bowman, 53 Lonnen Road, Colehill, Wimborne, Dorset BH21 7AT. 01202 884788.
DORSET NATURAL HISTORY & ARCHAEOLOGICAL SOCIETY. (1845; 2188). Kate Hebditch, Dorset County Museum, High West Street, Dorchester, Dorset DT1 1XA. 01305 262735.

Ringing Groups
CHRISTCHURCH HARBOUR RS. E C Brett, 3 Whitfield Park, St Ives, Ringwood, Hants BH24 2DX.
PORTLAND BIRD OBSERVATORY. Martin Cade, Old Lower Light, Portland Bill, Dorset DT5 2JT. 01305 820553.
STOUR RG. R Gifford, 62 Beacon Park Road, Upton, Poole, Dorset BH16 5PE.

RSPB Members' Groups
BLACKMOOR VALE. (1981; 120). Mrs Margaret Marris, 15 Burges Close, Marnhull, Sturminster Newton, Dorset DT10 1QQ. 01258 820091.
EAST DORSET. (1974; 310). Ken Baxter, 50 Littledown Avenue, Bournemouth BH7 7AR. 01202 257466.
POOLE. (1982; 305). John Derricott, 51 Dacombe Drive, Upton, Poole, Dorset BH16 5JJ. 01202 776312.

SOUTH DORSET. (1976; 400). Marion Perriss, Old Barn Cottage, Affpuddle, Dorchester, Dorset DT2 7HH. 01305 848268.

Wetland Bird Survey Organisers
EXCLUDING ESTUARIES. John Jones, Blackbird Cottage, 14 Church Lane, Sutton Waldron, Dorset DT11 8PA. 01747 811490.
CHRISTCHURCH HARBOUR and FLEET/WEY. Both vacant.
POOLE HARBOUR. Steve Smith, 7 South Road, Corfe Mullen, Wimborne, Dorset BH21 3HY.

Wildlife Hospital
SWAN RESCUE SANCTUARY. Ken and Judy Merriman, The Wigeon, Crooked Withies, Holt, Wimborne, Dorset BH21 7LB. 01202 828166; mobile 0385 917457. Swans. Hospital unit with indoor ponds and recovery pens. Outdoors: 35 ponds and lakes, and recovery pens. 24-hr veterinary support. Viewing by appointment only.

Wildlife Trust
DORSET WILDLIFE TRUST. (1961; 7000). Brooklands Farm, Forston, Dorchester, Dorset DT2 7AA. 01305 264620; fax 01305 251120; e-mail dorsetwt@cix.co.uk.

DURHAM

Bird Atlas/Avifauna
Durham Breeding Bird Atlas (working title). In preparation.

Bird Recorders
Tony Armstrong, 39 Western Hill, Durham City DH1 4RJ. 0191 386 1519.
CLEVELAND. Graeme Joynt, 3 Brigandine Close, Warrior Park, Seaton Carew, Hartlepool TS25 1ES. 01429 289968.

Bird Reports
BIRDS IN DURHAM (1971-). From Fred Milton, 16 Tyne View Place, Dunston, Gateshead NE38 2HR.
CLEVELAND BIRD REPORT (was Birds of Teesmouth 1962-). From Colin Dodsworth, 63 Stokesley Crescent, Billingham TS23 1NF. 01642 551223.

BTO Regional Representatives
David L Sowerbutts, 9 Prebends Field, Gilesgate Moor, Durham DH1 1HH. Home 0191 386 7201; Work 0191 374 3011.
CLEVELAND RR. Russell McAndrew, 5 Thornhill Gardens, Hartlepool TS26 0HX. 01429 277291.

Clubs
DURHAM BIRD CLUB. (1975; 233). Kevin Spindloe, 30 Swinburne Road, Hartlepool TS25 4JQ. 01429 292622.
TEESMOUTH BIRD CLUB. (1960; 220). Chris Sharp, 20 Auckland Way, Hartlepool TS26 0AN. 01429 865163.

Ringing Groups
DURHAM RG. S Westerberg, 32 Manor Road, Medomsley, Consett, Co Durham DH8 6QW. 01207 563862.
DURHAM DALES RG. J Barrett, Gale Cottage, Wolsingham, Bishop Auckland, Co Durham DL13 3LT.

RSPB Members' Group
DURHAM. (1974; 150). Joe Bray, 34 Langley Road, Newton Hall, Durham DH1 5LR. 0191 386 5838.

Wetland Bird Survey Organisers
TEES ESTUARY. Mike Leakey, English Nature, Visitor Centre, British Energy, Tees Road, Hartlepool TS25 2BZ. Tel/fax 01429 853325.
CLEVELAND (excl Tees Estuary). Graeme Joynt, 3 Brigandine Close, Warrior Park, Seaton Carew, Hartlepool TS25 1ES. 01429 289968.
DURHAM COAST. Robin Ward, Dept of Biological Sciences, University of Durham, South Road, Durham DH1 3LE. Home 0191 383 1259; Work 0191 374 3350; e-mail R.M.Ward@durham.ac.uk.
TYNE & WEAR SOUTH (Inland). Andrew Donnison, WWT Washington, District 15, Washington, Tyne & Wear NE38 8LE. 0191 416 5454 ext 222; fax 0191 416 5801.

Wildlife Trust
DURHAM WILDLIFE TRUST. (1971; 2500). Rainton Meadows, Chilton Moor, Houghton-le-Spring, Tyne & Wear DH4 6PU. 0191 584 3112; fax 0191 584 3934; e-mail durhamwt@cix.co.uk.

ESSEX

Bird Atlas/Avifauna
The Breeding Birds of Essex by M K Dennis (Essex Birdwatching Society, 1996).

Bird Recorders
1. Les Steward, 6 Creek View, Basildon, Essex SS16 4RU. 01268 551464; e-mail les.steward@btinternet.com. 2. Mike Dennis, 173 Collier Row Lane, Romford RM5 3ED. 01708 761865.

Bird Report
ESSEX BIRD REPORT (inc Bradwell Bird Obs records) (1950-). From Secretary, Essex Birdwatching Society.

BTO Regional Representatives
NORTH-EAST. Peter Dwyer, 48 Churchill Avenue, Halstead, Essex CO9 2BE. Tel/fax 01787 476524; Work 0171 558 3894; e-mail Petedwyer@aol.com.
NORTH-WEST. Geoff Gibbs, 72 Orchard Piece, Blackmore, Ingatestone, Essex CM4 0RZ. Home/work/fax:01277 823007; e-mail geoffg@essexwt.org.uk.
SOUTH. Jean Stone, Topcroft, 8 Hillview Road, Rayleigh, Essex SS6 7HX. 01268 775328.

Club
ESSEX BIRDWATCHING SOCIETY. (1949; 750). Maurice Adcock, The Saltings, 53 Victoria Drive, Great Wakering, Southend-on-Sea SS3 0AT. 01702 219437.

Ringing Groups
ABBERTON RG. C P Harris, Wlyandotte, Seamer Road, Southminster, Essex CM0 7BX.
BASILDON RG. B J Manton, 72 Leighcliff Road, Leigh-on-Sea, Essex SS9 1DN. 01702 475183; e-mail bjmanton@lineone.net.
BRADWELL BIRD OBSERVATORY. C P Harris, Wlyandotte, Seamer Road, Southminster, Essex CM0 7BX.

RSPB Members' Groups
CHELMSFORD. (1976; 5500). Michael Howard, 70 Longstomps Avenue, Chelmsford CM2 6LB. 01245 262020.
COLCHESTER. (1981; 350). Barry Jacobs, 140 Stourview Avenue, Mistley, Essex CO11 1UF. 01206 396043.
SOUTHEND. (1983; 400). Keith Crees, 178 Rawreth Lane, Rayleigh, Essex SS6 9RN. 01268 781843.

Wetland Bird Survey Organisers
STOUR ESTUARY. Russell Leavett, 24 Orchard Close, Great Oakley, Harwich, Essex CO12 5AX. Tel/fax 01255 886043.
THAMES ESTUARY (FOULNESS). Maurice Adcock, The Saltings, 53 Victoria Drive, Great Wakering, Southend-on-Sea SS3 0AT. 01702 219437.
INNER THAMES ESTUARY. Helen Baker, 60 Townfield, Rickmansworth, Herts WD3 2DD. 01923 772441.
LEE VALLEY GRAVEL PITS. Ian Kendall, Abbey Mills, Highbridge Street, Waltham Abbey, Essex EN9 1BZ.
OTHER SITES. Jeremy Alderton, 367 Baddow Road, Chelmsford CM2 7QF. 01245 471400.

Wildlife Trust
ESSEX WILDLIFE TRUST. (1959; 15500). Fingringhoe Wick Nature Reserve, South Green Road, Fingringhoe, Colchester CO5 7DN. 01206 729678; fax 01206 729298; e-mail admin@essexwt.org.uk.

GLOUCESTERSHIRE

Bird Atlas/Avifauna
Atlas of Breeding Birds of the North Cotswolds (North Cotswold Ornithological Society, 1990).

Bird Recorder
Andrew Jayne, 9 Hayes Court, Longford, Gloucester GL2 9AW. 01452 300035.

Bird Reports
GLOUCESTERSHIRE BIRD REPORT (1953-). From Peter Jones, 2 Beech Close, Highnam, Gloucester GL2 8EG. 01452 413561.
NORTH COTSWOLD ORNITHOLOGICAL SOCIETY ANNUAL REPORT (1983-). From Secretary.

BTO Regional Representative. Vacant.

Clubs
CHELTENHAM BIRD CLUB. (1976; 65). Mrs Frances Meredith, 14 Greatfield Drive, Charlton Kings, Cheltenham GL53 9BU. 01242 516393.
DURSLEY BIRDWATCHING & PRESERVATION SOCIETY. (1952; 403). Maurice Bullen, 20 South Street, Uley, Dursley, Glos GL11 5SP. 01453 860004.
GLOUCESTERSHIRE NATURALISTS' SOCIETY. (1948; 600). John McLellan, 15 Charlton Road, Tetbury, Glos GL8 8DX. 01666 504757.
NORTH COTSWOLD ORNITHOLOGICAL SOCIETY(1982; 40). T Hutton, 15 Green Close, Childswickham, Broadway, Worcs WR12 7JJ. 01386 858511.

Ringing Groups
SEVERN ESTUARY GULL GROUP. M E Durham, 6 Glebe Close, Frampton-on-Severn, Glos GL2 7EL. 01452 741312.
SEVERN VALE RG. Gordon Avery, 12 Hemmingsdale Road, Hempsted, Gloucester GL2 5HN.
WILDFOWL & WETLANDS TRUST. R Hearn, Wildfowl & Wetlands Trust, Slimbridge, Glos GL2 7BT. 01453 890333.

RSPB Members' Group
GLOUCESTERSHIRE. (1972; 700). Peter Jones, 2 Beech Close, Highnam, Gloucester GL2 8EG. 01452 413561.

Wetland Bird Survey Organisers
SEVERN ESTUARY. Mark Pollitt, Wildfowl & Wetlands Trust, Slimbridge, Glos GL2 7BT. 01453 890333.
INLAND. Dr Leslie Jones, Chestnut House, Water Lane, Somerford Keynes, Cirencester, Glos GL7 6DS. 01285 861545.
INLAND NORTH AVON. David Pryce, 5 The Knapp, Dursley, Glos GL11 4BT.

Wildlife Hospital
VALE WILDLIFE RESCUE. Ms Caroline Gould, Station Road, Beckford, Tewkesbury, Glos GL20 7AN. 01386 882288. All wild birds. Intensive care. Registered charity. Veterinary support.

Wildlife Trust
GLOUCESTERSHIRE WILDLIFE TRUST. (1961; 6200). Dulverton Building, Robinswood Hill Country Park, Reservoir Road, Gloucester GL4 6SX. 01452 383333; fax 01452 383334; e-mail info@gloucswt.cix.co.uk.

HAMPSHIRE

Bird Atlas/Avifauna
Birds of Hampshire by J M Clark and J A Eyre (Hampshire Ornithological Soc, 1993).

Bird Recorder
John Clark, 4 Cygnet Court, Old Cove Road, Fleet, Hants GU13 8RL. Tel/fax 01252 623397; e-mail johnclark@cygnetcourt.demon.co.uk.

Bird Reports
HAMPSHIRE BIRD REPORT (1955-). From Mrs Margaret Boswell, 5 Clarence Road, Lyndhurst, Hants SO43 7AL.
HANTS/SURREY BORDER BIRD REPORT (1971-). From John Clark, as above (Bird Recorder).

BTO Regional Representative
Glynne C Evans, Waverley, Station Road, Chilbolton, Stockbridge, Hants SO20 6AL. Home 01264 860697; Work 01962 847435.

Clubs
HAMPSHIRE ORNITHOLOGICAL SOCIETY. (1979; 955). Nigel Peace, 4 Wincanton Close, Alton, Hants GU34 2TQ. 01420 85496.

SOUTHAMPTON & DISTRICT BIRD GROUP. (1994; 120). Les Stride, 196 Calmore Road, Calmore, Southampton SO40 2RA. 01703 868058.

Ringing Groups
FARLINGTON RG. D A Bell, 38 Holly Grove, Fareham, Hants PO16 7UP.
ITCHEN RG. C R Cuthbert, 6 Jacklyns Close, Alresford, Hants SO24 9LL. 01962 734920.
LOWER TEST RG. J Pain, Owlery Holt, Nations Hill, Kingsworthy, Winchester SO23 7QY.

RSPB Members' Groups
BASINGSTOKE. (1979; 90). Peter Hutchins, 35 Woodlands, Overton, Whitchurch RG25 3HN. 01256 770831.
NORTH EAST HAMPSHIRE. (1976; 350). Graham Dumbleton, 28 Castle Street, Fleet, Hants GU13 9ST. 01252 622699.
PORTSMOUTH. (1974; 249). Gordon Humby, 19 Charlesworth Gardens, Waterlooville, Hants PO7 6AU. 01705 353949.
WINCHESTER & DISTRICT. (1974; 152). Maurice Walker, Jesmond, 1 Compton Way, Olivers Battery, Winchester SO22 4EY. 01962 854033.

Wetland Bird Survey Organisers
ESTUARIES & COASTAL SITES. Dave Unsworth, Flat 3, 142 Malmesbury Road, Shirley, Southampton SO15 5FQ.
INLAND. Keith Wills, 51 Peabody Road, Farnborough, Hants GU14 6EB. 01252 548408.

Wildlife Hospital
NEW FOREST OWL SANCTUARY. Bruce Berry, Crow Lane, Crow, Ringwood, Hants BH24 1EA. 01425 476487. All birds of prey, especially owls. Large aviaries, release scheme. Veterinary support.

Wildlife Trust
HAMPSHIRE WILDLIFE TRUST. (1960; 11,295). 8 Romsey Road, Eastleigh, Hants SO50 9AL. 02380 613636; fax 02380 612233; e-mail hampswt@cix.co.uk.

HEREFORDSHIRE

Bird Recorder
Paul H Downes, 450 Buckfield Road, Leominster HR6 8SD. 01568 611624.

Bird Report
HEREFORDSHIRE ORNITHOLOGICAL CLUB ANNUAL REPORT (1951-). From Ifor B Evans, 12 Brockington Drive, Tupsley, Hereford HR1 1TA. 01432 265509.

BTO Regional Representative
Steve Coney, Lion's Den, Bredwardine, Hereford HR3 6DE. 01981 500236.

Club
HEREFORDSHIRE ORNITHOLOGICAL CLUB. (1950; 382). C E Lankester, 6 Biddulph Way, Ledbury, Herefs HR8 2HN. 01531 633530.

Ringing Group
LLANCILLO RG. Dr G R Geen, 6 The Copse, Bannister Green, Felsted, Dunmow, Essex CM6 3NP. 01371 820189; e-mail thegeens@aol.com.

Wetland Bird Survey Organiser
Steve Coney, Lion's Den, Bredwardine, Hereford HR3 6DE. 01981 500236.

Wildlife Hospitals
ATHENE BIRD SANCTUARY. B N Bayliss, 61 Chartwell Road, Hereford HR1 2TU. 01432 273259. Birds of prey, ducks and waders, seabirds, pigeons and doves. Heated cages, small pond. Veterinary support.

Wildlife Trust
HEREFORDSHIRE NATURE TRUST. (1962; 1450). Lower House Farm, Ledbury Road, Tupsley, Hereford HR1 1UT. 01432 356872; fax 01432 275489; e-mail herefordwt@cix.co.uk.

HERTFORDSHIRE

Bird Atlas/Avifauna
Birds at Tring Reservoirs by R Young *et al* (Hertfordshire Natural History Society, 1996). *The Breeding Birds of Hertfordshire* by K W Smith *et al* (Herts NHS, 1993).

Bird Recorder
Rob Young, 37 Barkers Way, Stokenchurch, High Wycombe, Bucks HP14 3RD. 01494 485374; Mobile 0585 748223; http://fly.to/hertsbirdclub (incl electronic record submission).

Bird Report
HERTFORDSHIRE BIRD REPORT (1908-). From Secretary, Herts Bird Club.

BTO Regional Representative & Regional Development Officer
Chris Dee, 26 Broadleaf Avenue, Thorley Park, Bishop's Stortford, Herts CM23 4JY. Home 01279 755637; Work 01707 365815.

Clubs
FRIENDS OF TRING RESERVOIRS. (1993; 420). Judith Knight, 381 Bideford Green, Linslade, Leighton Buzzard, Beds LU7 7TY. 01525 378161.
HERTFORDSHIRE BIRD CLUB. (1971; 270). Ted Fletcher, Beech House, Aspenden, Herts SG9 9PG. 01763 272979; http://fly.to/hertsbirdclub.

Ringing Groups
AYLESBURY VALE RG (main activity at Marsworth). S M Downhill, 12 Millfield, Berkhamsted, Herts HP4 2PB.
MAPLE CROSS RG. P Delaloye, 34 Watford Road, Croxley Green, Herts WD3 3BJ. 01923 442182.
RYE MEADS RG. Chris Dee, as above (BTO Regional Rep).
TRING RG. J E Taylor, 4 Barbers Walk, Tring, Herts HP23 4DB. E-mail mick@focusrite.com.

RSPB Members' Groups
CHORLEYWOOD & DISTRICT. (1977; 99). Dennis A Spooner, Old Tannery House, 333 Uxbridge Road, Rickmansworth, Herts WD3 2DT. 01923 776854.

HARPENDEN. (1974; 900). Harry Simpson, 32 Battlefield Road, St Albans, Herts AL1 4DD. 01727 766887.

HEMEL HEMPSTEAD. (1973; 130). Ann Farrer, 38 Chipperfield Road, Kings Langley, Herts WD4 9JA. 01923 265337.

HITCHIN & LETCHWORTH. (1973; 109). Tim Goose, 45 Browning Drive, Hitchin, Herts SG4 0QR. 01462 435605; e-mail tim@twgoose.freeserve.co.uk.

POTTERS BAR & BARNET. (1977; 2000). Stan Bailey, 23 Bowmans Close, Potters Bar, Herts EN6 5NN. 01707 646073.

ST ALBANS. (1979; 1500). John Maxfield, 46 Gladeside, Jersey Farm, St Albans, Herts AL4 9JA. 01727 832688; e-mail peterantram@antram.demon.co.uk; http://www.antram.demon.co.uk/.

SOUTH EAST HERTS. (1971; 2000). Phil Blatcher, 3 Churchfields, Broxbourne, Herts EN10 7JU. 01992 441024.

STEVENAGE. (1982; 1000). Mrs Sue Pople, 633 Lonsdale Road, Stevenage, Herts SG1 5ED. 01438 232508.

WATFORD. (1974; 305). John Britten, Harlestone, 98 Sheepcot Lane, Garston, Watford WD2 6EB. 01923 673205; e-mail john.britten@btinternet.com; www.argonet.co.uk/users/jks.thompson/watrspb.html.

Wetland Bird Survey Organisers
EXCEPT LEE VALLEY. Jim Terry, 46 Manor Way, Borehamwood, Herts WD6 1QY. 0181 905 1461.

LEE VALLEY GRAVEL PITS. Ian Kendall, Abbey Mills, Highbridge Street, Waltham Abbey, Essex EN9 1BZ.

Wildlife Hospitals
SWAN CARE. Mrs Lis Dorer, 14 Moorland Road, Boxmoor, Hemel Hempstead, Herts HP1 1NH. 01442 251961. Swans. Sanctuary and treatment centre. Veterinary support.

Wildlife Trust
HERTS & MIDDLESEX WILDLIFE TRUST. (1964; 8500). Grebe House, St Michael's Street, St Albans, Herts AL3 4SN. 01727 858901; fax 01727 854542; e-mail hertswt@cix.co.uk.

ISLE OF WIGHT

Bird Recorder
John Stafford, Westering, Moor Lane, Brighstone, Newport, Isle of Wight PO30 4DL. 01983 740280.

Bird Reports
ISLE OF WIGHT BIRD REPORT (1996-) (various titles 1920-95). From IoW Ornithological Group, or Librarian of IoW Natural History Society.

BTO Regional Representative
James C Gloyn, 3 School Close, Newchurch, Isle of Wight PO36 0NL. 01983 865567.

Clubs
ISLE OF WIGHT NATURAL HISTORY & ARCHAEOLOGICAL SOCIETY. (1919; 500). Dr Margaret Jackson, The Fruitery, Brook, Newport, Isle of Wight PO30 6EP. 01983 740015.

ISLE OF WIGHT ORNITHOLOGICAL GROUP. (1986; 100). Dave Wooldridge, 2 Parkside, The Causeway, Freshwater, Isle of Wight PO40 9TN. 01983 753589.

RSPB Members' Group
ISLE OF WIGHT. (1979; 188). Revd Dennis Cox, 7 Upper Highland Road, Ryde, Isle of Wight PO33 1DZ. 01983 615613.

Wetland Bird Survey Organisers
ESTUARIES & COASTAL SITES. James C Gloyn, 3 School Close, Newchurch, Isle of Wight PO36 0NL. 01983 865567.
INLAND. John Stafford, Westering, Moor Lane, Brighstone, Newport, Isle of Wight PO30 4DL. 01983 740280.

Wildlife Trust
See Hampshire.

KENT

Bird Atlas/Avifauna
The Birds of Kent by D W Taylor *et al* (Kent Ornithological Society, 1981). *Kent Ornithological Society Winter Bird Survey* by N Tardivel (KOS, 1984).

Bird Recorder
Ian Hodgson, Whitgift House, Hardy Close, Canterbury, Kent CT2 8JJ. Tel/fax 01227 784303.

Bird Reports
DUNGENESS BIRD OBSERVATORY REPORT (1989-). From Warden, see Reserves.
KENT BIRD REPORT (1952-). From Steve Goode, 54 Essex Road, Longfield, Kent DA3 7QL.
SANDWICH BAY BIRD OBSERVATORY REPORT. From Warden, see Reserves.

BTO Regional Representative & Regional Development Officer
RR. Major Geoffrey F A Munns, Spring Place, St Aubyn's Close, Orpington, Kent BR6 0SN. 01689 835325.
RDO. Dr Grant Hazlehurst, 10 Apex Close, Beckenham, Kent BR3 5TU. Home 0181 650 7063; Work 0171 218 9048.

Club
KENT ORNITHOLOGICAL SOCIETY. (1952; 700). Kevin Thornton, 240 Wakeley Road, Rainham, Gillingham, Kent ME8 8NJ. 01634 233335.

Ringing Groups
ASHFORD RG. M J Palmer, 29 Hurst Road, Kennington, Ashford, Kent TN24 9PS. 01233 28547.

DARTFORD RG. P E Jones, Sheppards Barn, Hurst Green, Oxted, Surrey RH8 9BS.

DUNGENESS BIRD OBSERVATORY. David Walker, Dungeness Bird Observatory, Dungeness, Romney Marsh, Kent TN29 9NA. 01797 321309.

RECULVER RG. Chris Hindle, 42 Glenbervie Drive, Herne Bay, Kent CT6 6QL. 01227 373070.

SANDWICH BAY BIRD OBSERVATORY. Pete Findley, Sandwich Bay Bird Observatory, Guilford Road, Sandwich, Kent CT13 9PF. 01304 617341; e-mail sbbot@talk21.com.

SWALE WADER RG. Rod Smith, 67 York Avenue, Chatham, Kent ME5 9ES. 01634 865863; e-mail rodsmith@yendov99.freeserve.co.uk.

RSPB County Youth Officer
Mrs Ginny Duncanson, Pympes Court, Busbridge Road, Tovil, Maidstone, Kent ME15 0HZ. 01622 743193.

RSPB Members' Groups
CANTERBURY. (1973; 224). Alan Prior, 20 Shepherdsgate Drive, Herne Bay, Kent CT6 7TX. 01227 361362.

GRAVESEND. (1977; 240). Peter Heathcote, 9 Greenfinches, New Barn, Kent DA3 7ND. 01474 702498; www.gravesend-rspb.freeserve.co.uk.

MAIDSTONE. (1973; 250). Dick Marchese, 11 Bathurst Road, Staplehurst, Tonbridge, Kent TN12 0LG. 01580 892458.

MEDWAY. (1974; 230). Sue Carter, 31 Ufton Lane, Sittingbourne ME10 1JB. 01795 427854.

SEVENOAKS. (1974; 350). Bernard Morris, 16 Hever Avenue, West Kingsdown, Sevenoaks, Kent TN15 6HE. 01474 854055.

SOUTH EAST KENT. (1981; 260). Keith Shepherd, 311 Folkestone Road, Dover, Kent CT17 9LL. 01304 225757.

THANET. (1976; 283). Stephen Blaskett, Flat 2, 36 Connaught Road, Margate, Kent CT9 5TW. 01843 299212.

TONBRIDGE. (1975; 1350). Ms Gabrielle Sutcliffe, 1 Postern Heath Cottages, Postern Lane, Tonbridge, Kent TN11 0QU. 01732 365583.

Wetland Bird Survey Organisers
INNER THAMES ESTUARY. Jeremy Alderton, 367 Baddow Road, Chelmsford CM2 7QF. 01245 471400.

EAST. Ken Lodge, 14 Gallwey Avenue, Birchington, Kent CT7 9PA. 01843 843105.

MEDWAY ESTUARY & NORTH KENT MARSHES. Dave Jones, RSPB Bromhey Farm, Eastborough, Cooling, Rochester, Kent ME3 8DS.

PEGWELL BAY. Pete Findley, Sandwich Bay Bird Observatory, Guilford Road, Sandwich, Kent CT13 9PF. 01304 617341; e-mail sbbot@talk21.com.

SWALE ESTUARY. Bob Gomes, Kingshill Farm, Elmley, Sheerness, Kent ME12 3RW. 01795 665969.

DUNGENESS AREA. David Walker, Dungeness Bird Observatory, Dungeness, Romney Marsh, Kent TN29 9NA. 01797 321309.

WEST. Vacant.

Wildlife Hospital
RAPTOR CENTRE. Eddie Hare, Ivy Cottage, Groombridge Place, Groombridge, Tunbridge Wells, Kent TN3 9QG. 01892 861175; fax 01892 863761; www.raptorcentre.co.uk. Birds of prey. Veterinary support.

Wildlife Trust
KENT WILDLIFE TRUST. (1958; 10500). Tyland Barn, Sandling, Maidstone, Kent ME14 3BD. 01622 662012; fax 01622 671390; kentwildlife@cix.co.uk.

LANCASHIRE

Bird Atlas/Avifauna
An Atlas of Breeding Birds of Lancaster and District by Ken Harrison (Lancaster & District Birdwatching Society, 1995). *Breeding Birds of Lancashire and North Merseyside* (working title), sponsored by North West Water. Contact: Bob Pyefinch, 12 Bannistre Court, Tarleton, Preston PR4 6HA.

Bird Recorder (See also Manchester).
Inc North Merseyside. Maurice Jones, 31 Laverton Road, St Annes-on-Sea, Lancs FY8 1EW. 01253 721076.

Bird Reports
BIRDS OF LANCASTER & DISTRICT (1959-). From Secretary, Lancaster & District BWS.
EAST LANCASHIRE ORNITHOLOGISTS' CLUB BIRD REPORT (1998-). From Secretary.
BLACKBURN & DISTRICT BIRD CLUB ANNUAL REPORT (1992-). From Jim Bonner, 6 Winston Road, Blackburn BB1 8BJ.
FYLDE BIRD REPORT (1983-). From Secretary, Fylde Bird Club.
LANCASHIRE BIRD REPORT (1914-). From Secy, Lancs & Cheshire Fauna Soc.

BTO Regional Representatives & Regional Development Officer
EAST RR. A A Cooper, 28 Peel Park Avenue, Clitheroe, Lancs BB7 1ET. 01200 424577.
NORTH & WEST RR & RDO. Dave Sharpe, 17 Greenwood Avenue, Bolton-le-Sands, Carnforth, Lancs LA5 8AN. Home 01524 822492; Work 01524 64160; e-mail dave_s@airtime.co.uk.
SOUTH RR. Vacant.

Clubs
BLACKBURN & DISTRICT BIRD CLUB. (1991; 130). Dan Crowley, 32 Columbia Way, Lammack, Blackburn BB2 7DT. 01254 677614.
CHORLEY & DISTRICT NATURAL HISTORY SOCIETY. (1979; 170). Phil Kirk, Millend, Dawbers Lane, Euxton, Chorley, Lancs PR7 6EB. 01257 266783.
EAST LANCASHIRE ORNITHOLOGISTS' CLUB. (1955; 45). Doug Windle, 39 Stone Edge Road, Barrowford, Nelson, Lancs BB9 6BB. 01282 617401.

FYLDE BIRD CLUB. (1982; 60). Paul Ellis, 18 Staining Rise, Blackpool FY3 0BU. 01253 891281.

FYLDE NATURALISTS' SOCIETY. (1946; 140). Gerry Stephen, 10 Birch Way, Poulton-le-Fylde, Blackpool FY6 7SF. 01253 895195.
LANCASHIRE & CHESHIRE FAUNA SOCIETY. (1914; 99). Dave Bickerton, 64 Petre Crescent, Rishton, Lancs BB1 4RB. 01254 886257; e-mail DaveBickerton @compuserve.com.
LANCASHIRE BIRD CLUB. (1996). Dave Bickerton, 64 Petre Crescent, Rishton, Lancs BB1 4RB. 01254 886257; e-mail DaveBickerton@compuserve.com.
LANCASTER & DISTRICT BIRD WATCHING SOCIETY. (1959; 205). Andrew Cadman, 57 Greenways, Over Kellet, Carnforth, Lancs LA6 1DE. 01524 734462.
ROSSENDALE ORNITHOLOGISTS' CLUB. (1976; 35). Jim Ormerod, 785 Belmont Road, Bolton, Lancs BL1 7BY. 01204 598560.

Ringing Groups
FYLDE RG. G Barnes, 17 Lomond Avenue, Marton, Blackpool FY3 9QL.
MORECAMBE BAY WADER RG. J Sheldon, 415 West Shore Park, Barrow-in-Furness, Cumbria LA14 3XZ. 01229 473102.
NORTH LANCS RG. J Wilson BEM, 40 Church Hill Avenue, Warton, Carnforth, Lancs LA5 9NU.
SOUTH WEST LANCASHIRE RG. J D Fletcher, 4 Hawksworth Drive, Freshfield, Formby, Merseyside L37 7EZ. 01704 877837.

RSPB County Youth Officer
M T Graham, 90 Marsden Road, Burnley, Lancs BB10 2BL.

RSPB Members' Groups
BLACKPOOL. (1983; 170). Alan Stamford, 11 Sanderling Close, Anchors Holme, Blackpool FY5 3FN. 01253 859662.
LANCASTER. (1972; 210). J Wilson BEM, 40 Church Hill Avenue, Warton, Carnforth, Lancs LA5 9NU.

Wetland Bird Survey Organisers
MORECAMBE BAY. Mrs J Roberts, 11 St Paul's Drive, Brookhouse, Lancaster LA2 9PG. 01524 770295.
RIBBLE ESTUARY. Dick Lambert, 77 River View, Tarleton, Preston PR4 6ED. 01772 814230.
INLAND, NORTH. Dave Sharpe, 17 Greenwood Avenue, Bolton-le-Sands, Carnforth, Lancs LA5 8AN. Home 01524 822492; Work 01524 64160.
EAST. Stephen Dunstan, 29 Greenfinch Court, Herons Reach, Blackpool FY3 8FG. 01253 301009.
INLAND, WEST. Chris Tomlinson, WWT Martin Mere, Burscough, Ormskirk, Lancs L40 0TA. Home 01704 895181.

Wildlife Trust
LANCASHIRE WILDLIFE TRUST. (1962; 3500). Cuerden Park Wildlife Centre, Shady Lane, Bamber Bridge, Preston PR5 6AU. 01772 324129; fax: 01772 628849; e-mail lancswt@cix.co.uk; www.wildlifetrust.org.uk/lancashire.

LEICESTERSHIRE & RUTLAND

Bird Recorder
Rob Fray, 5 New Park Road, Aylestone, Leicester LE2 8AW. 0116 223 8491.

Bird Reports
LEICESTERSHIRE & RUTLAND BIRD REPORT (1941-). From Mrs S Graham, 5 Brading Road, Leicester LE3 9BG. 0116 262 5505.
RUTLAND NAT HIST SOC ANNUAL REPORT (1965-). From Secretary.

BTO Regional Representative & Regional Development Officer
Jim Graham, 5 Brading Road, Leicester LE3 9BG. Home 0116 262 5505; Work 0116 265 1227.

Clubs
BIRSTALL BIRDWATCHING CLUB. (1976; 50). Ken J Goodrich, 6 Riversdale Close, Birstall, Leicester LE4 4EH. 0116 267 4813.
LEICESTERSHIRE & RUTLAND ORNITHOLOGICAL SOCIETY. (1941; 430). Mrs Marion Vincent, 48 Templar Way, Rothley, Leicester LE7 7RB. 0116 230 3405.
MARKET HARBOROUGH & DISTRICT NATURAL HISTORY SOCIETY. (1971; 40). Mrs Sue Allibone, 20 Smyth Close, Market Harborough, Leics LE16 7NS. 01858 410385.
RUTLAND NATURAL HISTORY SOCIETY. (1964; 256). Mrs L Worrall, 6 Redland Close, Barrowden, Oakham, Rutland LE15 8ES. 01572 747302.

Ringing Groups
RUTLAND WATER RG. B Galpin, 15 Top Lodge, Fineshade, Corby, Northants NN17 3BB. E-mail barrie@fineshade.u-net.com
STANFORD RG. M J Townsend, 87 Dunton Rd, Broughton Astley, Leics LE9 6NA.

RSPB Members' Groups
LEICESTER. (1969, 900). Peter Kightley, 16 Barwell Road, Kirby Muxloe, Leics LE9 2AA. 0116 239 4271.
LOUGHBOROUGH. (1970; 300). Keith Freeman, 2 Leckhampton Road, Loughborough, Leics LE11 4TH. 01509 230908.

Wetland Bird Survey Organisers
EXCEPT RUTLAND WATER. Peter Harrop, Llansawel, 65 Merthyr Mawr Road, Bridgend CF31 3NN. 01572 757134; e-mail pandlhar@aol.com.
RUTLAND WATER. Tim Appleton, Fishponds Cottage, Stamford Road, Oakham, Rutland, Leics LE15 8AB. Home 01572 724101.

Wildlife Trust
LEICESTERSHIRE & RUTLAND WILDLIFE TRUST. (1956; 3000). 1 West Street, Leicester LE1 6UU. 0116 255 3904; fax 0116 254 1254; e-mail leicswt @cix.co.uk.

LINCOLNSHIRE

Bird Recorders
NORTH. Howard Bunn, 16 Vivian Avenue, Grimsby, N E Lincs DN32 8QF. 01472 600268.
SOUTH. Steve Keightley, Redclyffe, Swineshead Road, Frampton Fen, Boston PE21 0JR. 01205 290233.

Bird Reports
LINCOLNSHIRE BIRD REPORT (inc S Humb; Gib Point Obs) (1979-). From R K Watson, 8 High Street, Skegness, Lincs PE25 3NW. 01754 763481.

SCUNTHORPE & NORTH WEST LINCOLNSHIRE BIRD REPORT (1973-). From Secretary, Scunthorpe Museum Soc Orn Section.

BTO Regional Representatives & Regional Development Officer
EAST RR and NORTH RR. Both vacant.
SOUTH RR. Richard & Kay Heath, 56 Pennytoft Lane, Pinchbeck, Spalding, Lincs PE11 3PQ. 01775 767055; e-mail heathsrk@bigfoot.com.
WEST RR. Peter Overton, Hilltop Farm, Welbourn, Lincoln LN5 0QH. 01400 273323; fax 01400 273003; e-mail nyika@biosearch.datadata.net.
RDO. Nicholas Watts, Vine House Farm, Deeping St Nicholas, Spalding, Lincs PE11 3DG. 01775 630208.

Club
LINCOLNSHIRE BIRD CLUB. (1979; 220). John Mighell, 3 Church Walk, Metheringham, Lincoln LN4 3HA. 01526 321157.
SCUNTHORPE MUSEUM SOCIETY (Ornithological Section). (1973; 50). Craig Nimick, 115 Grange Lane South, Scunthorpe, N Lincs DN16 3BW. 01724 339659.

Ringing Groups
GIBRALTAR POINT BIRD OBSERVATORY. Adrian Blackburn, Suleska, 1 Richmond Road, Retford, Notts DN22 6SJ. 01777 706516.
MID LINCOLNSHIRE RG. S A Britton, 4 Anglian Way, Market Rasen, Lincs LN8 3RP. 01673 842899.
WASH WADER RG. P L Ireland, 27 Hainfield Drive, Solihull, W Midlands B91 2PL. 0121 704 1168; e-mail phil_ireland@bigfoot.com.

RSPB County Youth Officer
Jim Rance, 1 St Simons Drive, Cherry Willingham, Lincoln LN3 4LL. 01522 804799.

RSPB Members' Groups
GRIMSBY. (1986; 1467). Malcolm Crawford, 130 Chichester Road, Cleethorpes DN35 0JJ. 01472 509862.
LINCOLN. (1974; 250). Peter Skelson, 26 Parksgate Avenue, Lincoln LN6 7HP. 01522 695747.
SOUTH LINCOLNSHIRE. (1987; 200). Barry Hancock, The Limes, Mere Booth Road, Antons Gowt, Boston, Lincs PE22 7BG. 01205 280057.

Wetland Bird Survey Organisers
HUMBER, INNER SOUTH. Keith Parker, 20 Westwinds Road, Winterton, Scunthorpe, Lincs DN15 9RX. 01724 734261.
HUMBER, MID SOUTH SHORE. Ian Shepherd, 38 Lindsey Road, Cleethorpes DN35 8TN. 01472 697142.
HUMBER, OUTER SOUTH ESTUARY. John Walker, 3 Coastguard Cottages, Churchill Lane, Theddlethorpe, Mablethorpe, Lincs LN12 1PQ. Home 01507 338038.
MID & NORTH. John Hollis, c/o Hartsholme Country Park, Skellingthorpe Road, Lincoln LN6 0EY. Work 01522 686264; mobile 0771 2437426; e-mail jp_hollis @talk21.com.
SOUTH. John Redshaw, 7 Fennell Road, Pinchbeck, Spalding, Lincs PE11 3RP. 01775 768227.
WASH. Paul Fisher, 13 Beach Road, Snettisham, King's Lynn, Norfolk PE31 7RA.

Wildlife Hospital
FEATHERED FRIENDS WILD BIRD RESCUE. Colin Riches, 5 Blacksmith Lane, Thorpe-on-the-Hill, Lincoln LN6 9BQ. 01522 684874. All species. Purpose-built hospital unit. Heated cages, etc. Membership and adoption scheme available. Quarterly newsletter. Veterinary support.

Wildlife Trust
LINCOLNSHIRE TRUST FOR NATURE CONSERVATION. (1948; 10800). Banovallum House, Manor House Street, Horncastle, Lincs LN9 5HF. 01507 526667; fax 01507 525732; e-mail lincstrust@cix.co.uk; www.lincstrust.co.uk.

LONDON, GREATER

Bird Atlas/Avifauna
New Atlas of Breeding Birds of the London Area by Keith Betton (London Nat Hist Soc, in preparation).

Bird Recorder see also Surrey
Andrew Moon, 46 Highfield Way, Rickmansworth, Herts WD3 2PR. 01923 711927; fax 01923 776689.

Bird Report
LONDON BIRD REPORT (20-mile radius of St Paul's Cath) (1936-). From H M V Wilsdon, 79 Mill Rise, Westdene, Brighton BN1 5GJ. 01273 564715.

BTO Regional Representative & Regional Development Officer
LONDON & MIDDLESEX RR. Derek Coleman, Flat 9, 52 Nightingale Road, Carshalton, Surrey SM5 2EL. 0181 669 7421; e-mail d.coleman@icr.ac.uk.
SOUTH WEST RDO. Vacant.

Clubs
LONDON NATURAL HISTORY SOCIETY (Ornithology Section). (1858; 1100). Ms N Duckworth, 32 Blanchland Road, Morden, Surrey SM4 5ND. 0181 640 3927.
MARYLEBONE BIRDWATCHING SOCIETY. (1981; 95). Judy Powell, 7 Rochester Terrace, London NW1 9JN. 0171 485 0863.

Ringing Groups
ASHFORD RG. M J Palmer, 29 Hurst Road, Kennington, Ashford, Kent TN24 9PS. 01233 28547.
LONDON GULL STUDY GROUP. Mark Fletcher, 24 The Gowans, Sutton-on-the-Forest, York YO61 1DJ.

RSPB Members' Groups
BEXLEY. (1979; 4000). Mark Kelly, 59 College Road, Hextable, Swanley, Kent BR8 7LN. 01322 668140.
BROMLEY. (1972; 287). Bob Francis, 2 Perry Rise, Forest Hill, London SE23 2QL. 0181 669 9325.
CENTRAL LONDON. (1970; 250). Mrs Jill Aldred, 39 Ramillies Road, London W4 1JW. 0181 995 3450; www.janja.dircon.co.uk/rspb.
CROYDON. (1973; 4000). Sheila Mason, 5 Freshfields, Shirley, Croydon CR0 7QS. 0181 777 9370; http://hhwcomputing.freeserve.co.uk.
ENFIELD. (1971; 2700). Norman G Hudson, 125 Morley Hill, Enfield, Middx EN2 0BQ. 0181 363 1431.
HAVERING. (1972; 270). Eric Hammond, 33 Canterbury Avenue, Upminster, Essex RM14 3LD. 01708 222230.
NORTH LONDON. (1974; 3000). John Parsons, 65 Rutland Gardens, Harringay, London N4 1JW. 0181 802 9537.

NORTH WEST LONDON. (1983; 800). Bob Husband, The Firs, 49 Carson Road, Cockfosters, Barnet, Herts EN4 9EN. 0181 441 8742.
PINNER & DISTRICT. (1972; 300). Dennis Bristow, 118 Crofts Road, Harrow, Middx HA1 2PJ. 0181 863 5026.
RICHMOND & TWICKENHAM. (1979; 2300). Steve Harrington, 93 Shaftesbury Way, Twickenham TW2 5RW. 0181 898 4539.
WEST LONDON. (1973; 400). Alan Bender, 6 Allenby Road, Southall, Middx UB1 2HQ. 0181 571 0285.

Wetland Bird Survey Organiser
Helen Baker, 60 Townfield, Rickmansworth, Herts WD3 2DD. 01923 772441.

Wildlife Hospitals
ANDERSON, Miss E. 10 Barnstable House, Devonshire Drive, Greenwich, London SE10 8LD. 0181 692 7754. Able to take small birds only (no pigeons). Accommodation limited; always willing to give first aid and emergency advice. Veterinary support.
WILDLIFE RESCUE & AMBULANCE SERVICE. Barry and June Smitherman, 19 Chesterfield Road, Enfield, Middx EN3 6BE. 0181 292 5377. All categories of wild birds. Emergency ambulance with full rescue equipment, boats, ladders etc. Own treatment centre and aviaries. Veterinary support. Essential to telephone first.

Wildlife Trust
LONDON WILDLIFE TRUST. (1981; 6500). Harling House, 47-51 Great Suffolk Street, London SE1 0BS. 0171 261 0447; fax 0171 261 0538; e-mail londonwt @cix.co.uk.

MANCHESTER, GREATER

Bird Atlas/Avifauna
Breeding Birds in Greater Manchester by Philip Holland *et al* (1984).

Bird Recorders
Mrs A Judith Smith, 12 Edge Green Street, Ashton-in-Makerfield, Wigan WN4 8SL. 01942 712615; e-mail judith@gmbirds.freeserve.co.uk.

Bird Reports
BIRDS IN GREATER MANCHESTER (1976-). From Recorder.
LEIGH ORNITHOLOGICAL SOCIETY BIRD REPORT (1971-). From J Critchley, 2 Albany Grove, Tyldesley, Manchester M29 7NE. 01942 884644.

BTO Regional Representative and Regional Development Officer
RR. Mrs A Judith Smith, 12 Edge Green Street, Ashton-in-Makerfield, Wigan WN4 8SL. 01942 712615; e-mail judith@gmbirds.freeserve.co.uk.
RDO. Jim Jeffery, 20 Church Lane, Romiley, Stockport, Cheshire SK6 4AA. Home 0161 494 5367; Work 01625 522107 ext 112.

Clubs
GREATER MANCHESTER BIRD CLUB. (1954; 60). Roger Williams, 2 Milwain Road, Stretford, Manchester M32 9BY. 0161 865 1401.
HALE ORNITHOLOGISTS. (1968; 65). Ms Diana Grellier, 8 Apsley Grove, Bowdon, Altrincham, Cheshire WA14 3AH. 0161 928 9165.

LEIGH ORNITHOLOGICAL SOCIETY. (1971; 150). Mrs M Teresa Fayle, 9 Kirkham Road, Pennington, Leigh WN7 3UQ. 01942 606531; e-mail lowtonbirder @hotmail.com.
ROCHDALE FIELD NATURALISTS' SOCIETY. (1970; 87). Mrs J P Wood, 196 Castleton Road, Thornham, Royton, Oldham OL2 6UP. 0161 345 2012.
STOCKPORT BIRDWATCHING SOCIETY. (1972; 60). Dave Evans, 36 Tatton Road South, Stockport, Cheshire SK4 4LU. 0161 432 9513.

Ringing Groups
LEIGH RG. A J Gramauskas, 21 Elliot Avenue, Golborne, Warrington WA3 3DU. 01942 741543.
SOUTH MANCHESTER RG. C M Richards, Fairhaven, 13 The Green, Handforth, Wilmslow, Cheshire SK9 3AG. 01625 524527.

RSPB County Youth Officer
Brian Hallworth, 69 Talbot Street, Hazel Grove, Stockport SK7 4BJ. 0161 456 5328.

RSPB Members' Groups
BOLTON. (1978; 550). Tony Johnson, 65 Lever Park Avenue, Horwich, Bolton BL6 7LQ. 01204 468850.
MANCHESTER. (2000). Peter Wolstenholme, 31 South Park Road, Gatley, Cheshire SK8 4AL. 0161 428 2175.
STOCKPORT. (1979; 250). Brian Hallworth, 69 Talbot Street, Hazel Grove, Stockport SK7 4BJ. 0161 456 5328.
WIGAN. (1973; 130). Allan Rimmer, 206 Hodges Street, Wigan, Lancs WN6 7JG. 01942 241402.

Wetland Bird Survey Organiser
Robin Crompton, 56 Palmerston Road, Denton, Manchester M34 2NY. 0161 320 3048.

Wildlife Hospital
THREE OWLS BIRD SANCTUARY AND RESERVE. Trustee, Nigel Fowler, Wolstenholme Fold, Norden, Rochdale OL11 5UD. 01706 642162; 24-hr helpline 0973 819389. Registered charity. All species of wild bird. Rehabilitation and release on Sanctuary Reserve. Open every Sunday 1200-1700, otherwise visitors welcome by appointment. Bi-monthly newsletter. Veterinary support.

Wildlife Trust see Lancashire.

MERSEYSIDE & WIRRAL

Bird Atlas see Cheshire; **Bird Recorders** see Cheshire; Lancashire

Bird Reports see also Cheshire
HILBRE BIRD OBSERVATORY REPORT. From Warden, see Reserves.
NORTHWESTERN BIRD REPORT (1938- irregular). From Secretary, Merseyside Naturalists' Assoc.

BTO Regional Representatives
MERSEYSIDE RR. Vacant.
WIRRAL RR. Kelvin Britton, 9B Kingsmead Road South, Prenton, Birkenhead, Merseyside CH43 6TA. 0151 653 9751.

Clubs
LIVERPOOL ORNITHOLOGISTS' CLUB. (1953; 40). David J Low, 25 Heatherways, Freshfield, Liverpool L37 7HL. 01704 871115. (By invitation).
MERSEYSIDE NATURALISTS' ASSOCIATION. Joint Hon Secretaries: (1938; 250). Eric Hardy, 47 Woodsorrel Road, Liverpool L15 6UB. 0151 722 2819.
Mrs Eileen Houghton, 4 Willow Court, Valley View Park, Pentrebeirdd, Welshpool, Powys SY21 9DL. 01938 500768.
WIRRAL BIRD CLUB. (1977; 150). Mrs Hilda Truesdale, Cader, 8 Park Road, Meols, Wirral, CH47 7BG. 0151 632 2705.

Ringing Groups
HILBRE BIRD OBSERVATORY. John C Gittins, 17 Deva Road, West Kirby, Wirral CH48 4DB. 0151 625 5428.
MERSEYSIDE RG. P Slater, 45 Greenway Road, Speke, Liverpool L24 7RY.
SOUTH WEST LANCASHIRE RG. J D Fletcher, 4 Hawksworth Drive, Freshfield, Formby, Merseyside L37 7EZ. 01704 877837.

RSPB Members' Groups
LIVERPOOL. (1966; 162). Chris Tynan, 10 Barker Close, Huyton, Liverpool L36 0XU. 0151 480 7938.
SOUTH SEFTON. (1980; 175). Chris Sharratt, 22 Cecil Road, Seaforth, Liverpool L21 1DD. 0151 474 9129.
SOUTHPORT. (1974; 250). Mrs Brenda Nicholl, 24 Jubilee Road, Formby, Liverpool L37 2HT. 01704 872421.
WIRRAL. (1982; 160). Steve Woolfall, 85 Ridgemere Road, Pensby, Wirral, Merseyside CH61 8RR. 0151 648 6007.

Wetland Bird Survey Organisers
ALT ESTUARY. Dick Lambert, 77 River View, Tarleton, Preston PR4 6ED. 01772 814230.
DEE ESTUARY. Colin Wells, Burton Point Farm, Station Road, Burton, Nr Neston, South Wirral CH64 5SB. 0151 336 7681.
MERSEY ESTUARY. Graham Thomason, 110 Coroners Lane, Widnes, Cheshire WA8 9HZ. 0151 424 7257.
INLAND. Eric Hardy, 47 Woodsorrel Road, Liverpool L15 6UB. 0151 722 2819.

Wildlife Trust see Lancashire.

NORFOLK

Bird Atlas/Avifauna
Birds of Norfolk by M J Seago (Jarrolds, Norwich, 2nd edn 1997). New edition due in 2000.

Bird Recorder
Giles Dunmore, 49 Nelson Road, Sheringham, Norfolk NR26 8DA. 01263 822550.

Bird Reports
CLEY BIRD CLUB 10-KM SQUARE BIRD REPORT (1987-). From Secretary.
NAR VALLEY ORNITHOLOGICAL SOCIETY ANNUAL REPORT (1976-). From Secretary.

NORFOLK BIRD & MAMMAL REPORT (1953-). From Mrs M J Dorling, 6 New Road, Hethersett, Norwich NR9 3HH.
NORFOLK ORNITHOLOGISTS' ASSOCN ANNUAL REPORT (1961-). From Secretary.

BTO Regional Representatives
NORTH-EAST RR. Moss Taylor, 4 Heath Road, Sheringham, Norfolk NR26 8JH. 01263 823637.
NORTH-WEST RR. Vacant.
SOUTH-EAST RR. Graham Coxall, 4 Shirley Close, Frettenham, Norwich NR12 7LW. 01603 737486.
SOUTH-WEST RR. Vince Matthews, Rose's Cottage, The Green, Merton, Thetford, Norfolk IP25 6QU. 01953 884125; e-mail vam@vamatthews.u-net.com.

Clubs
CLEY BIRD CLUB. (1986; 300). Peter Gooden, 45 Charles Road, Holt, Norfolk NR25 6DA. 01263 712368.
GREAT YARMOUTH BIRD CLUB. (1989; 79). Keith R Dye, 104 Wolseley Road, Great Yarmouth, Norfolk NR31 0EJ. 01493 600705.
NAR VALLEY ORNITHOLOGICAL SOCIETY. (1976; 80). Ian Black, Three Chimneys, Tumbler Hill, Swaffham, Norfolk PE37 7JG. 01760 724092.
NORFOLK & NORWICH NATURALISTS' SOCIETY. (1869; 500). Dr Tony Leech, 3 Eccles Road, Holt, Norfolk NR25 6HJ. 01263 712282.
NORFOLK BIRD CLUB. (1992; 350). Vernon Eve, Pebble House, The Street, Syderstone, King's Lynn, Norfolk PE31 5SD. 01485 578121.

NORFOLK ORNITHOLOGISTS' ASSOCIATION. (1962; 1100). Jay Davidson, Broadwater Road, Holme-next-Sea, Hunstanton, Norfolk PE36 6LQ. 01485 525406.

Ringing Groups
BTO NUNNERY RG. Dawn Balmer, 39 Station Road, Thetford, Norfolk IP24 1AW.
HOLME BIRD OBSERVATORY. J M Reed, 21 Hardings, Panshanger, Welwyn Garden City, Herts AL7 2EQ. 01707 336351.
NORTH WEST NORFOLK RG. J M Reed, 21 Hardings, Panshanger, Welwyn Garden City, Herts AL7 2EQ. 01707 336351.
SHERINGHAM RG. D Sadler, Denver House, 25 Holt Road, Sheringham, Norfolk NR26 8NB. 01263 821904.
UEA RG. D Thomas, 11 Jessica Court, Orchard Street, Norwich NR2 4PB.
WASH WADER RG. P L Ireland, 27 Hainfield Drive, Solihull, W Midlands B91 2PL. 0121 704 1168; e-mail phil_ireland@bigfoot.com.
WISSEY RG. S J Browne, End Cottage, 24 Westgate Street, Hilborough, Norfolk IP26 5BN.

RSPB County Youth Officers
Mr & Mrs D Bedford. 23 Holway Close, Cromer, Norfolk NR27 9LH. 01263 510913; e-mail yoc@bedford41.freeserve.co.uk.

RSPB Members' Groups
NORWICH. (1971; 259). Percy Walker, 4 Bewit Road, Sprowston, Norwich NR7 8LB. 01603 460896.
WEST NORFOLK. (1977; 247). David Lake, 8 Ullswater Avenue, King's Lynn, Norfolk PE30 3NJ. 01553 673873.

Wetland Bird Survey Organisers
BREYDON WATER. Peter R Allard, 39 Mallard Way, Bradwell, Great Yarmouth, Norfolk NR31 8JY. 01493 657798.
NORTH NORFOLK COAST. Michael Rooney, English Nature, Hill Farm Offices, Main Road, Wells-next-the-Sea, Norfolk NR23 1AB. 01328 711866.
WASH. James Cadbury, RSPB, The Lodge, Sandy, Beds SG19 2DL. 01767 680551.
INLAND. Tim Strudwick, RSPB Strumpshaw Fen, Staithe Cottage, Low Road, Strumpshaw, Norfolk NR13 4HS. 01603 715191.

Wildlife Hospitals
RSPCA NORFOLK WILDLIFE HOSPITAL. Administrator: Mrs A Smith, Station Road, East Winch, King's Lynn, Norfolk PE32 1NR. 01553 842336. All species. Specialist treatment of oiled birds. Purpose-built surgery, x-ray, isolation, bird washing rooms, rehabilitation pools, aviaries. Group visits by appointment, with open days for the general public. Full-time veterinary surgeon and qualified staff.
SHAW, Mrs Brenda M. Fourways, Litcham, King's Lynn, Norfolk PE32 2NZ. 01328 701383. All species of wild bird. Veterinary support.

Wildlife Trust
NORFOLK WILDLIFE TRUST. (1926; 19,000). 72 Cathedral Close, Norwich NR1 4DF. 01603 625540; fax 01603 630593; e-mail nwt@cix.co.uk.

NORTHAMPTONSHIRE

Bird Recorder
Robert W Bullock, 81 Cavendish Drive, Northampton NN3 3HL. 01604 627262.

Bird Report
NORTHAMPTONSHIRE BIRD REPORT (1969-). From Recorder.

BTO Regional Representative & Regional Development Officer
RR. Phil W Richardson, 10 Bedford Cottages, Great Brington, Northampton NN7 4JE. 01604 770632.
RDO. Bill Metcalfe, 17 Culme Close, Oundle, Peterborough PE8 4QQ. 01832 274647.

Clubs
DAVENTRY NATURAL HISTORY SOCIETY. (1970; 20). Leslie G Tooby, The Elms, Leamington Road, Long Itchington, Rugby, Warks CV23 8PL. 0192 681 2269.
NORTHAMPTONSHIRE BIRD CLUB. (1973; 100). Mrs Eleanor McMahon, Oriole House, 5 The Croft, Hanging Houghton, Northants NN6 9HW. 01604 880009.

Ringing Group
NORTHANTS RG. D M Francis, 2 Brittons Drive, Billington Lane, Northampton NN3 5DP.

RSPB Members' Groups
MID NENE. (1975; 250). Michael Ridout, Melrose, 140 Northampton Road, Rushden, Northants NN10 6AN. 01933 355544.
NORTHAMPTON. (1978; 3000). Liz Wicks, 6 Waypost Court, Lings, Northampton NN3 8LN. 01604 408717.

Wetland Bird Survey Organiser
Phil Richardson, 10 Bedford Cottages, Great Brington, Northampton NN7 4JE. 01604 770632.

Wildlife Trust
See Cambridgeshire.

NORTHUMBERLAND

Bird Atlas/Avifauna
The Atlas of Breeding Birds in Northumbria edited by J C Day *et al* (Northumberland and Tyneside Bird Club, 1995).

Bird Recorder
Ian Fisher, 74 Benton Park Road, Newcastle upon Tyne NE7 7NB. 0191 266 7900.

Bird Reports
BIRDS IN NORTHUMBRIA (1970-). From Mike Carr, 100 Hollywood Avenue, Gosforth, Newcastle upon Tyne NE3 5BR.
BIRDS ON THE FARNE ISLANDS (1971-). From Secretary, Natural History Society of Northumbria.

BTO Regional Representative & Regional Development Officer
RR. Tom Cadwallender, 22 South View, Lesbury, Alnwick, Northumberland NE66 3PZ. Home 01665 830884; Work 01670 533039; e-mail tmcadwallender@lineone.net.
RDO. Muriel Cadwallender, 22 South View, Lesbury, Alnwick, Northumberland NE66 3PZ. 01665 830884.

Clubs
NATURAL HISTORY SOCIETY OF NORTHUMBRIA. (1829; 900). David C Noble-Rollin, Hancock Museum, Barras Bridge, Newcastle upon Tyne NE2 4PT. 0191 232 6386; e-mail david.noble-rollin@ncl.ac.uk.
NORTH NORTHUMBERLAND BIRD CLUB. (1984; 210). David Welch, 26 Armstrong Cottages, Bamburgh, Northumberland NE69 7BA. 01668 214403.
NORTHUMBERLAND & TYNESIDE BIRD CLUB. (1958; 270). Andrew Brunt, South Cottage, West Road, Longhorsley, Morpeth, Northumberland NE65 8UY. 01670 812166; www.netmarketing.co.uk/birdclub.

Ringing Groups
BAMBURGH RS. Mike S Hodgson, 31 Uplands, Monkseaton, Whitley Bay, Tyne & Wear NE25 9AG. 0191 252 0511.
NATURAL HISTORY SOCIETY OF NORTHUMBRIA. Dr C P F Redfern, Westfield House, Acomb, Hexham, Northumberland NE46 4RJ.
NORTHUMBRIA RG. Secretary. B Galloway, 34 West Meadows, Stamfordham Road, Westerhope, Newcastle upon Tyne NE5 1LS. 0191 286 4850.

Wetland Bird Survey Organisers
LINDISFARNE. Phil Davey, English Nature, Beal Station, Berwick-upon-Tweed TD15 2SP. 01289 381470.
COASTAL SITES & ESTUARIES (excl Lindisfarne). Dr Roger Norman, 1 Prestwick Gardens, Kenton, Newcastle upon Tyne NE3 3DN. Tel/fax 0191 285 8314.
INLAND. Mrs Margaret MacFarlane, 7 Wildshaw Close, Southfield Lea, Cramlington, Northumberland NE23 6LH.

Wildlife Hospitals
BERWICK SWAN & WILDLIFE TRUST. M L Allport, Keld, 4 Ryecroft Park, Wooler, Northumberland NE71 6AS. 01668 281249. Registered charity. All categories of birds. Indoor pool for swans. Veterinary support.
WILDLIFE IN NEED SANCTUARY. Mrs Lisa Bolton, Shepherds Cottage, Chatton, Alnwick, Northumberland NE66 5PX. 01668 215281. All categories of birds catered for. Number of gulls restricted. Oiled birds sent to Swan & Wildlife Trust, Berwick. Heated bird room. Aviaries. Veterinary support. Visiting strictly by appointment.

Wildlife Trust
NORTHUMBERLAND WILDLIFE TRUST. (1962; 5000). The Garden House, St Nicholas Park, Jubilee Road, Newcastle upon Tyne NE3 3XT. 0191 284 6884; fax 0191 284 6794; e-mail northwildlife@cix.co.uk.

NOTTINGHAMSHIRE

Bird Recorders
All sightings/records: Steve Keller, 17 Suffolk Avenue, Beeston Rylands, Notts NG9 1NN. 0115 917 1452.
Breeding birds: Chris Mills, 3 Brookside Close, Long Eaton, Nottingham NG10 4AQ. 0115 946 0107.

Bird Report
BIRDS OF NOTTINGHAMSHIRE (1943-). From Kevin Tomlinson, 20 Jackson Avenue, Ilkeston, Derbys DE7 8AD.

BTO Regional Rep and Regional Development Officer
RR. Mrs Lynda Milner, 6 Kirton Park, Kirton, Newark, Notts NG22 9LR. 01623 862025.
RDO. Reg Davis, 3 Windrush Close, Bramcote View, Nottingham NG9 3LN.

Nottinghamshire Birdwatchers

Clubs
COLWICK PARK WILDLIFE GROUP. (1994; 150). Michael Walker, 14 Ramblers Close, Colwick, Nottingham NG4 2DN. 0115 961 5494.
LOUND BIRD CLUB. (1991; 50). P Hobson, 23 Milne Road, Bircotes, Doncaster DN11 8AL. 01302 742779.
NOTTINGHAMSHIRE BIRDWATCHERS. (1935; 420). David P Goddard, 30 Cliffe Hill Avenue, Stapleford, Nottingham NG9 7HD. 0115 939 0334.
WOLLATON NATURAL HISTORY SOCIETY. (1976; 95). Mrs P Price, 33 Coatsby Road, Hollycroft, Kimberley, Nottingham NG16 2TH. 0115 938 4965.

Ringing Groups
BIRKLANDS RG. A D Lowe, 12 Midhurst Way, Clifton Estate, Nottingham NG11 8DY.
NORTH NOTTS RG. Adrian Blackburn, Suleska, 1 Richmond Road, Retford, Notts DN22 6SJ. 01777 706516.
SOUTH WEST NOTTINGHAMSHIRE RG. K J Hemsley, 8 Grange Farm Close, Toton, Beeston, Notts NG9 6EB. .
TRESWELL WOOD INTEGRATED POPULATION MONITORING GROUP. Chris du Feu, 66 High Street, Beckingham, Doncaster, S Yorks DN10 4PF.

RSPB Members' Groups
MANSFIELD. (1986; 255). Chris Watkinson, 9 Ash Ford Rise, Sutton-in-Ashfield, Notts NG17 2BB. 01623 517174.
NOTTINGHAM. (1974; 350). Tim Randall, 9 Oakmere Close, Edwalton, Nottingham NG12 4FJ. 0115 923 5211; tim randall@hotmail.com; www.notts-rspb.org.uk/.

Wetland Bird Survey Organiser
Mark Keighley, 64 Highgate Drive, Ilkeston, Derbys DE7 9HU. 0115 944 4726.

Wildlife Trust
NOTTINGHAMSHIRE WILDLIFE TRUST. (1963; 3500). The Old Ragged School, Brook Street, Nottingham NG1 1EA. 0115 958 8242; 0115 924 3175; e-mail nottswt@cix.co.uk.

OXFORDSHIRE

Bird Atlas/Avifauna
Birds of Oxfordshire by J W Brucker *et al* (Oxford, Pisces, 1992). *The New Birds of the Banbury Area* by T G Easterbrook (Banbury Ornithological Society, 1995).

Bird Recorder
Ian Lewington, 119 Brasenose Road, Didcot, Oxon OX11 7BP. 01235 819792.

Bird Reports
BIRDS OF OXFORDSHIRE (1920-). From Roy Overall, 30 Hunsdon Road, Iffley, Oxford OX4 4JE.
BANBURY ORNITHOLOGICAL SOCIETY ANNUAL REPORT (1952-). From P Douthwaite, Townsend Farm, Radway, Warwick.

BTO Regional Representatives
NORTH. Roger Evans, Hill View, Balscote, Banbury, Oxon OX15 6JN. 01295 730421.
SOUTH. Peter Abbott, The Mallards, 109 Brook Street, Benson, Oxon OX10 6LJ. 01491 837529.

Clubs
BANBURY ORNITHOLOGICAL SOCIETY. (1952; 100). Tony Clark, 11 Rye Close, Banbury, Oxon OX16 7XG. 01295 268900.
OXFORD ORNITHOLOGICAL SOCIETY. (1921; 235). David Hawkins, The Long House, Park Lane, Long Hanborough, Oxon OX8 8RD. 01993 880027; http://members.tripod.co.uk/OOS/index.htm.

Ringing Group
EDWARD GREY INSTITUTE. Dr A G Gosler, c/o Edward Grey Institute, Department of Zoology, South Parks Road, Oxford OX1 3PS. 01865 271158.

RSPB County Youth Officer
Mr P Parker, 29 Glebe Gardens, Grove, Wantage, Oxon OX12 7LX. 01235 768248.

RSPB Members' Groups
OXFORD. (1977; 100). Paul Mallett, 26 Cavendish Road, Summertown, Oxford OX2 7TW. 01865 511139; e-mail oxford.rspb@zoo.co.uk; http://www.zoo.co.uk/~z9001428.
VALE OF WHITE HORSE. (1977; 310). Margaret Meardon, 7 Tavistock Avenue, Didcot, Oxon OX11 8NA. 01235 210525.

Wetland Bird Survey Organisers
NORTH. Mrs Sandra Bletchly, 11 Orchard Grove, Bloxham, Banbury, Oxon OX15 4NZ. 01295 721048.
SOUTH. Mrs Catherine Ross, Duck End Cottage, Sutton, Witney, Oxford OX8 1RX. 01865 881552.

Wildlife Trust
BBONT. (1959; 11000). The Lodge, 1 Armstrong Road, Littlemore, Oxford OX4 4XT. 01865 775476; fax 01865 711301.

SHROPSHIRE

Bird Atlas/Avifauna
Atlas of the Breeding Birds of Shropshire (Shropshire Ornithological Society, 1996).

Bird Recorder
Geoff Holmes, 22 Tenbury Drive, Telford Estate, Shrewsbury SY2 5YF. 01743 364621.

Bird Report
SHROPSHIRE BIRD REPORT (1956-). Annual. From Secretary, Shropshire Ornithological Society.

BTO Regional Representative
Allan Dawes, Rosedale, Chapel Lane, Trefonen, Oswestry, Shrops SY10 9DX. 01691 654245.

Club
SHROPSHIRE ORNITHOLOGICAL SOCIETY. (1955; 680). John Turner, 1 Brookside Gardens, Yockleton, Shrewsbury SY5 9PR. 01743 821678.

RSPB County Youth Officer
Ms Y Blain, 6 Moorhead, Preston-upon-the-Wealdmoors, Telford, Shrops TF6 6DL. 01952 677123; e-mail yvonne.blain@virgin.net.

RSPB Members' Group
SHROPSHIRE. (1992; 320). Geoff Hall, Bank House, Woolston, Shrops SY6 6QB. 01694 781429.

Wetland Bird Survey Organiser
Bill Edwards, Hopton Villa, Maesbury Marsh, Oswestry, Shrops SY10 8JA. 01691
656679.

Wildlife Trust
SHROPSHIRE WILDLIFE TRUST. (1962; 2000). 167 Frankwell, Shrewsbury SY3
8LG. 01743 241691; fax 01743 366671; e-mail shropshirewt@cix.co.uk.

SOMERSET & BRISTOL

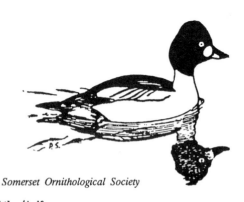

Somerset Ornithological Society

Bird Atlas/Avifauna
Atlas of Breeding Birds in Avon 1988-91 by R L Bland and John Tully (John Tully, 6
Falcondale Walk, Westbury-on-Trym, Bristol BS9 3JG, 1992).

Bird Recorders
Brian D Gibbs, 23 Lyngford Road, Taunton, Somerset TA2 7EE. 01823 274887;
e-mail brian.gibbs@virgin.net.
BATH, NE SOMERSET, BRISTOL, S GLOS. Harvey Rose, 12 Birbeck Road,
Bristol BS9 1BD. Home 0117 968 1638; Work 0117 928 7992; e-mail h.e.rose
@bris.ac.uk.

Bird Reports
AVON BIRD REPORT (1979-). From Harvey Rose, as above.
EXMOOR NATURALIST (1974-). From Secretary, Exmoor Natural History
Society.
SOMERSET BIRDS (1913-). From Secretary, Somerset Ornithological Society.

BTO Regional Representatives and Regional Development Officers
AVON RR. Richard L Bland, 11 Percival Road, Bristol BS8 3LN. Home/Work 0117
973 4828.
AVON RDO. John Tully, 6 Falcondale Walk, Westbury-on-Trym, Bristol BS9 3JG.
0117 950 0992.
SOMERSET RR. Eve Tigwell, Hawthorn Cottage, 3 Friggle Street, Frome, Somerset
BA11 5LP. 01373 451630.
SOMERSET RDO. Vacant.

Clubs

BRISTOL NATURALISTS' SOCIETY (Ornithological Section). (1936; 550). Dr Mary Hill, 15 Montrose Avenue, Redland, Bristol BS6 6EH. 0117 942 2193.
BRISTOL ORNITHOLOGICAL CLUB. (1966; 650). Mrs Judy Copeland, 19 St George's Hill, Easton-in-Gordano, North Somerset BS20 0PS. Tel/fax 01275 373554.
EXMOOR NATURAL HISTORY SOCIETY. (1974; 450). Miss Caroline Giddens, 12 King George Road, Minehead, Somerset TA24 5JD. 01643 707624.
MID-SOMERSET NATURALISTS' SOCIETY. (1949; 45). Roy Brearly, 2 Quayside, Bridgwater, Somerset TA6 3TA. 01278 427100.
SOMERSET ORNITHOLOGICAL SOCIETY. (1923; 350). Miss Sarah Beavis, The Old Surgery, 4 The Barton, Hatch Beauchamp, Somerset TA3 6SG. 01823 480948.

Ringing Groups

CHEW VALLEY RS. Dr M G Rowan, 22 Audley Park Road, Bath BA1 2XL.
GORDANO VALLEY RG. Lyndon Roberts, 20 Glebe Road, Long Ashton, Bristol BS18 9LH. 01275 392722.
RSPCA. C Seddon, RSPCA Wildlife Unit, West Hatch, Taunton TA3 5RT. 01823 480156.
STEEP HOLM RS. A J Parsons, Barnfield, Tower Hill Road, Crewkerne, Somerset TA18 8BJ. 01460 73640.

RSPB Members' Groups

BATH & DISTRICT. (1989; 240). Gordon Rich, 9 Cranwells Park, Bath BA1 2YD. 01225 422541.
CREWKERNE & DISTRICT. (1979; 325). Denise Chamings, Daniels Farm, Lower Stratton, South Petherton, Somerset TA13 5LP. 01460 240740.
TAUNTON. (1975; 148). Revd Keith Beck, 47 Scott Close, Taunton, Somerset TA2 6UL. 01823 327132.
WESTON-SUPER-MARE (N SOMERSET). (1977; 180). Don Hurrell, Freeways, Star, Winscombe BS25 1PS.

Wetland Bird Survey Organisers

BRIDGWATER BAY. Harvey Rose, 12 Birbeck Road, Bristol BS9 1BD. Home 0117 968 1638; Work 0117 928 7992; e-mail h.e.rose@bris.ac.uk.
SEVERN ESTUARY. Harvey Rose, 12 Birbeck Road, Bristol BS9 1BD. Home 0117 968 1638; Work 0117 928 7992; e-mail h.e.rose@bris.ac.uk.
SOMERSET LEVELS & MOORS. John Leece, RSPB, West Sedgemoor, Dewlands Farm, Redhill, Curry Rivel, Langport, Somerset TA10 0PH. Home 01823 698595; Work 01458 252805.
OTHER SITES. Keith Fox, Vernwood, 32 Ash Hayes Road, Nailsea, Bristol BS48 2LW.

Wildlife Hospital

RSPCA WILDLIFE HOSPITAL. C Seddon, West Hatch, Taunton TA3 5RT. 01823 480156. All species. National centre for the expert treatment of oiled seabirds. Veterinary support.

Wildlife Trusts

AVON WILDLIFE TRUST. (1980; 4500). Wildlife Centre, 32 Jacobs Wells Road, Bristol BS8 1DR. 0117 926 8018; fax 0117 929 7273; e-mail avonwt@cix.co.uk.
SOMERSET WILDLIFE TRUST. (1964; 8000). Fyne Court, Broomfield, Bridgwater, Somerset TA5 2EQ. 01823 451587; fax 01823 451671; e-mail somwt@cix.co.uk; http://wildlifetrust.org.uk/somerset.

STAFFORDSHIRE

Bird Recorder
Mrs Gilly Jones, 4 The Poplars, Lichfield Road, Abbots Bromley, Rugeley, Staffs
WS15 3AA. 01283 840555.

Bird Report See West Midlands

BTO Regional Representatives
NORTH. Alan Hancock, 12 Sparch Hollow, Newcastle-under-Lyme, Staffs ST5 9PA.
01782 615887.
SOUTH. Peter K Dedicoat, 232 Doxey, Stafford ST16 1EE. 01785 607620; e-mail
pdedicoat@argonet.co.uk.
CENTRAL. Frank C Gribble MBE, 22 Rickerscote Avenue, Stafford ST17 4EZ.
01785 254166.

Clubs
WEST MIDLAND BIRD CLUB (STAFFORD BRANCH). Andy Lawrence, 4
Ashlands Crescent, Harpfields, Stoke-on-Trent ST4 6QT. 01782 632586.
WEST MIDLAND BIRD CLUB (TAMWORTH BRANCH). Barbara Stubbs, 19
Alfred Street, Tamworth, Staffs B79 7RL. 01827 57865.

RSPB Members' Groups
BURTON-ON-TRENT. (1976; 40). Dave Lummis, 121 Wilmot Road, Swadlincote,
Derbys DE11 9EN. 01283 219902.
LICHFIELD & DISTRICT. (1977; 250). Ray Jennett, 12 St Margarets Road,
Lichfield, Staffs WS13 7RA. 01543 255195.
NORTH STAFFORDSHIRE. (1982; 211). John Booth, 32 St Margaret Drive, Sneyd
Green, Stoke-on-Trent ST1 6EW. 01782 262082.
SOUTH WEST STAFFORDSHIRE. (1972; 138). Mrs Theresa Dorrance, 39 Wilkes
Road, Codsall, Wolverhampton WV8 1RZ. 01902 847041.

Wetland Bird Survey Organiser
Maurice Arnold, 58 Overwoods Road, Hockley, Tamworth, Staffs B77 5LZ.

Wildlife Hospitals
BRITISH WILDLIFE RESCUE CENTRE. Alfred Hardy, Amerton Working Farm,
Stowe-by-Chartley, Stafford ST18 0LA. 01889 271308. On A518 Stafford/Uttoxeter
road. All species, including imprints and permanently injured. Hospital, large aviaries
and caging. Open to the public every day. Veterinary support.
GENTLESHAW BIRD OF PREY HOSPITAL. Robert A Smith, 5 Chestall Road,
Cannock Wood, Rugeley, Staffs WS15 4RB. 01543 676372. Registered charity. All
birds of prey (inc. owls). Hospital cages and aviaries; release sites. Veterinary
support. Also GENTLESHAW BIRD OF PREY AND WILDLIFE CENTRE,
Fletchers Country Garden Centre, Stone Road, Eccleshall, Stafford. 01785 850379
(1000-1700).
RAPTOR RESCUE (MID-STAFFS AREA). J M Cunningham, 8 Harvey Road,
Handsacre, Rugeley, Staffs WS15 4HF. 01543 491712; e-mail mickcunningham
@raptorrescue72.swinternet.co.uk. Birds of prey only. Heated hospital units. Indoor
flights, secluded aviaries, hacking sites, rehabilitation aviaries/flights. Falconry
rehabilitation techniques, foster birds for rearing young to avoid imprinting.
Veterinary support.

Wildlife Trust
STAFFORDSHIRE WILDLIFE TRUST. (1969; 4000). Coutts House, Sandon, Stafford ST18 0DN. 01889 508534; fax 01889 508422; e-mail staffswt@cix.co.uk.

SUFFOLK

Bird Atlas/Avifauna
Birds of Suffolk by S H Piotrowski (Suffolk Naturalists' Society, 1999).

Bird Recorders
NORTH EAST. Richard Walden, 21 Kilbrack, Beccles, Suffolk NR34 9SH. 01502 713521.
SOUTH EAST (inc. coastal region from Slaughden Quay southwards). Brian Thompson, 42 Dover Road, Ipswich IP3 8JQ. 01473 726771.
WEST (whole of Suffolk W of Stowmarket, inc. Breckland). Colin Jakes, 7 Maltward Avenue, Bury St Edmunds, Suffolk IP33 3XN. 01284 702215.

Bird Report
SUFFOLK BIRDS (inc Landguard Bird Observatory Report) (1950-). From Secretary, Suffolk Naturalists' Society.

BTO Regional Representative
Mick T Wright, 15 Avondale Road, Ipswich IP3 9JT. 01473 710032; e-mail mick.wright@btinternet.com.

Clubs
LAVENHAM BIRD CLUB. (1972; 50). Richard Michette, 7 Clopton Drive, Long Melford, Sudbury, Suffolk CO10 9LJ. 01787 377741 (day).
SUFFOLK ORNITHOLOGISTS' GROUP. (1973; 700). Andrew M Gregory, 1 Holly Road, Ipswich IP1 3QN. 01473 253816.

Ringing Groups
DINGLE BIRD CLUB. Dr D Pearson, 4 Lupin Close, Reydon, Southwold, Suffolk IP18 6NW.
LACKFORD RG. Dr Peter Lack, 11 Holden Road, Lackford, Bury St Edmunds, Suffolk IP28 6HZ.
LANDGUARD RG. M C Marsh, 5 Ennerdale Close, Felixstowe, Suffolk IP11 9SS. 01394 271757.
MARKET WESTON RG. Dr R H W Langston, Walnut Tree Farm, Thorpe Street, Hinderclay, Diss, Norfolk IP22 1HT.

RSPB Members' Groups
BURY ST EDMUNDS. (1982; 150). Trevor Hart, 9 Lime Walk, Felsham, Bury St Edmunds, Suffolk IP30 0QL. 01449 737983.
IPSWICH. (1975; 200). Mrs Glenda Sugars, 7 Colchester Road, Ipswich IP4 3BT. 01473 256198.
LOWESTOFT & DISTRICT. (1976; 170). Brian Sivyer, 39 Fern Avenue, Lowestoft, Suffolk NR32 3JF. 01502 560414; e-mail brian.sivyer@lineone.net.
WOODBRIDGE. (1986; 350). Colin Coates, 42A Bredfield Road, Woodbridge, Suffolk IP12 1JE. 01394 385209.

Wetland Bird Survey Organisers
ALDE COMPLEX. Rodney West, Flint Cottage, Stone Common, Blaxhall, Woodbridge, Suffolk IP12 2DP. 01728 689171; fax 01728 688044; e-mail rodwest@ndirect.co.uk.
BLYTH ESTUARY. Cliff Waller, Angel Cottage, Blythburgh, Halesworth, Suffolk IP19 9LQ. 01502 478239.
DEBEN ESTUARY. Nick Mason, Evening Hall, Hollesley, Woodbridge, Suffolk IP12 3QU.
ORWELL ESTUARY. Mick T Wright, 15 Avondale Road, Ipswich IP3 9JT. 01473 710032; e-mail mick.wright@btinternet.com.
STOUR ESTUARY. Russell Leavett, 24 Orchard Close, Great Oakley, Harwich, Essex CO12 5AX. Tel/fax 01255 886043.
INLAND. Rodney West, Flint Cottage, Stone Common, Blaxhall, Woodbridge, Suffolk IP12 2DP. 01728 689171; fax 01728 688044; e-mail rodwest@ndirect.co.uk.

Wildlife Trust
SUFFOLK WILDLIFE TRUST. (1961; 14,000). Brooke House, The Green, Ashbocking, Ipswich IP6 9JY. 01473 890089; fax 01473 890165; e-mail suffolkwt @cix.co.uk.

SURREY

Bird Atlas/Avifauna
Birds of Surrey (working title). In preparation.

Bird Recorder (inc London S of Thames & E to Surrey Docks)
Jeffery Wheatley, 9 Copse Edge, Elstead, Godalming, Surrey GU8 6DJ. 01252 702450.

Bird Report
SURREY BIRD REPORT (1952-). From J Gates, 159 Stoughton Road, Guildford, Surrey GU1 1LQ. 01483 573858.

BTO Regional Representative
Hugh Evans, 31 Crescent Road, Shepperton, Middx TW17 8BL. 01932 227781.

Clubs
SURBITON & DISTRICT BIRDWATCHING SOCIETY. (1954; 200). Paul Spencer, 2 King Edward Drive, Hook, Chessington, Surrey KT9 1DW. 0181 397 3770; e-mail http://www.ndirect.co.uk/norm2(sup 2)f/sdbws.
SURREY BIRD CLUB. (1957; 420). Mrs Jill Cook, Moorings, Vale Wood Drive, Lower Bourne, Farnham, Surrey GU10 3HW. 01252 792876; e-mail jilck@lineone.net; http://homepages.nildram.co.uk/~jhutch/sbc/.

Ringing Groups
HERSHAM RG. A J Beasley, 29 Selbourne Avenue, New Haw, Weybridge, Surrey KT15 3RB.
RUNNYMEDE RG. K J Herber, Laleham, 60 Dale End, Brancaster Staithe, King's Lynn, Norfolk PE31 8DA.

RSPB Members' Groups
DORKING & DISTRICT. (1982; 360). Peter H Crook, 33 The Park, Bookham, Surrey KT23 3LN. 01372 458175.

EAST SURREY. (1984; 2600). Elitta Fell, Surrey Beeches, Moorhouse, Westerham, Kent TN16 2EX. 01959 564060.

EPSOM & EWELL. (1974; 302). John Frost, 52 Ellesfield Drive, West Parley, Ferndown, Dorset BH22 8QW. 01202 873104.

GUILDFORD. (1971; 500). Peter Grundy, Garden Cottage, Albury, Guildford, Surrey GU5 9BE. 01483 202991.

NORTH WEST SURREY. (1973; 125). Mary Harris, 20 Meadway Drive, New Haw, Surrey KT15 2DT. 01932 858692.

Wetland Bird Survey Organiser
Seth Gibson, 22 Danetree Road, West Ewell, Surrey KT19 9RZ. 0181 786 8509.

Wildlife Hospitals
PIGEON RECOVERY. L & M Allen, 8 Vermont Road, Sutton, Surrey SM1 3EQ. 0280 644 7349. Any sick, injured or orphaned wild or domestic pigeon or dove. Accommodation for permanently disabled. Will collect where possible in London area, but not if bird is loose; no specialist equipment for rescue work. Veterinary support.

THE SWAN SANCTUARY. Dorothy Beeson BEM, The Swan Sanctuary, Field View, Egham, Surrey TW20 8AT. 01784 431667. All waterbirds. X-ray unit and fully equipped operating theatre. 24-hr veterinary support.

WILDLIFE AID. Simon Cowell, Randalls Farm House, Randalls Road, Leatherhead, Surrey KT22 0AL. 01372 377332; 24-hr emerg line 09061 800 132 (60p/min); fax 01372 375183; e-mail wildlife@pncl.co.uk; http://www.wildlife-aid.org.uk/wildlife. Registered charity. Operates a membership and fundraising scheme. All species. Most facilities; operating and intensive care unit; housing for all birds of prey. Veterinary support.

Wildlife Trust
SURREY WILDLIFE TRUST. (1959; 6000). School Lane, Pirbright, Woking, Surrey GU24 0JN. 01483 488055; fax 01483 486505; e-mail surreywt@cix.co.uk.

SUSSEX

Bird Atlas/Avifauna
Birds of Sussex ed by Paul James (Sussex Ornithological Society, 1996).

Bird Recorder
Until April 2000: Robin Pepper, Scobells Farm, Barcombe, Lewes, E Sussex BN8 5DY. 01273 400393; e-mail robinpepper@compuserve.com; www.sos-org.com.

Bird Reports
FRIENDS OF RYE HARBOUR NR ANNUAL REPORT (1977-). From Dr Barry Yates, see Clubs.

PAGHAM HARBOUR LOCAL NATURE RESERVE ANNUAL REPORT. From Warden, see Reserves.

SHOREHAM DISTRICT ORNITHOLOGICAL SOCIETY ANNUAL REPORT (1952-). From Secretary.

SUSSEX BIRD REPORT (1963-). From J E Trowell, Lorrimer, Main Road, Icklesham, Winchelsea, E Sussex TN36 4BS.

BTO Regional Representative
Dr A Barrie Watson, 83 Buckingham Road, Shoreham-by-Sea, W Sussex BN43 5UD.
01273 452472; e mail abwatson@mistral.co.uk.

Clubs
FRIENDS OF RYE HARBOUR NATURE RESERVE. (1973; 1600). Dr Barry
Yates, 2 Watch Cottages, Nook Beach, Winchelsea, E Sussex TN36 4LU. 01797
223862; e-mail yates@clara.net; www.yates.clara.net.
SHOREHAM DISTRICT ORNITHOLOGICAL SOCIETY. (1953; 120). Mrs B
Reeve, The Old Rectory, Coombes Lancing, W Sussex BN15 0RS. 01273 452497.
SUSSEX ORNITHOLOGICAL SOCIETY. (1962; 1465). Mrs V P Bentley,
Chetsford, London Road, Henfield, W Sussex BN5 9JJ. 01273 494723; www.sos-
org.com.

Ringing Groups
BEACHY HEAD RS. R D M Edgar, 6 Turnpike Close, Ringmer, Lewes, E Sussex
BN8 5PD.
CHICHESTER RG. Dr A Barrie Watson, 83 Buckingham Road, Shoreham-by-Sea,
W Sussex BN43 5UD. 01273 452472; e-mail abwatson@mistral.co.uk.
CUCKMERE RG. Tim Parmenter, 22 The Kiln, Burgess Hill, W Sussex RH15 0LU.
01444 236526.
RYE BAY RG. S J R Rumsey, Elms Farm, Pett Lane, Icklesham, Winchelsea,
E Sussex TN36 4AH. 01797 226137.
STEYNING RG. B R Clay, 30 The Drive, Worthing, W Sussex BN11 5LL.

RSPB Members' Groups
BATTLE. (1973; 100). Miss Lynn Jenkins, 61 Austen Way, Guestling, Hastings,
E Sussex TN35 4JH. 01424 432076.
BRIGHTON & DISTRICT. (1974; 780). Mrs Doris Kelly, 42 Downland Road,
Woodingdean, Brighton BN2 6DJ. 01273 685518; http://www.mistral.co.uk/phowes.
CHICHESTER & SW SUSSEX. (1979; 245). Dominic Carlton, Pipits Park Road,
Barnham, Bognor Regis, W Sussex PO22 0AQ. 01243 552716.
CRAWLEY & HORSHAM. (1978; 148). John Boulcott, 3 Holmbush Close,
Horsham, W Sussex RH12 5YB. 01403 255008.
EAST GRINSTEAD. (1998; 187). Roger Tremethick, 16 Wray Close, Ashurst Wood,
East Grinstead, W Sussex RH19 3QX. 01342 824143.
EASTBOURNE & DISTRICT. (1993; 520). Tony Aldridge, 39 Pashley Road,
Eastbourne, E Sussex BN20 8DY. 01323 724082.
HASTINGS & ST LEONARDS. (1983; 145). Richard Prebble, 1 Wayside, 490
Sedlescombe Road North, St Leonards-on-Sea, E Sussex TN37 7PH. 01424 751790.
HEATHFIELD. (1979; 75). Mrs Dorothy Cull, 33 Horam Park Close, Horam,
E Sussex TN21 0HW. 01435 812093.

Wetland Bird Survey Organisers
CHICHESTER HARBOUR. Anne de Potier, Chichester Harbour Conservancy, The
Harbour Office, Itchenor, Chichester, W Sussex PO20 7AW. 01243 512301; fax 01243
513026; e-mail anne@conservancy.co.uk
PAGHAM HARBOUR. Rob Carver, Nature Reserve Information Centre, Selsey
Road, Sidlesham, Chichester, W Sussex PO20 7NE. 01243 641508; fax 01243 641568;
e-mail pagham.nr@westsussex.gov.uk.
OTHER SITES. Chris Lowmass, 33 Barn Close, Seaford, E Sussex BN25 3EW. 01323
897758.

Wildlife Hospital
BRENT LODGE BIRD & WILDLIFE TRUST. Penny Cooper, Brent Lodge, Cow
Lane, Sidlesham, Chichester, West Sussex PO20 7LN. 01243 641672. All species of

wild birds. Full surgical and medical facilities (inc. X-ray). Purpose-built oiled bird washing unit. Can sometimes arrange collection in West Sussex. Veterinary support.

Wildlife Trust
SUSSEX WILDLIFE TRUST. (1961; 11000). Woods Mill, Shoreham Road, Henfield, W Sussex BN5 9SD. 01273 492630; fax 01273 494500; e-mail sussexwt@cix.co.uk.

TYNE & WEAR

Bird Recorders see Durham; Northumberland.

Bird Report See Durham; Northumberland.

Clubs
NATURAL HISTORY SOCIETY OF NORTHUMBRIA. (1829; 900). David C Noble-Rollin, Hancock Museum, Barras Bridge, Newcastle upon Tyne NE2 4PT. 0191 232 6386; e-mail david.noble-rollin@ncl.ac.uk.
NORTHUMBERLAND & TYNESIDE BIRD CLUB. (1958; 270). Andrew Brunt, South Cottage, West Road, Longhorsley, Morpeth, Northumberland NE65 8UY. 01670 812166; www.netmarketing.co.uk/birdclub.

RSPB Members' Groups
NEWCASTLE UPON TYNE. (1969; 255). John Evans, 21 Beacon Drive, Brunswick Green, Wideopen, Newcastle upon Tyne NE13 7HB. 0191 236 2369.
SUNDERLAND & SOUTH TYNESIDE. (1982; 35). Paul Metters, Almonte, 1 Bloomfield Drive, Elemore View, East Rainton, Houghton-le-Spring, Tyne & Wear DH5 9SF.

Wetland Bird Survey Organisers
NORTH COAST. Dr Roger Norman, 1 Prestwick Gardens, Kenton, Newcastle upon Tyne NE3 3DN. Tel/fax 0191 285 8314.
SOUTH COAST. Robin Ward, Dept of Biological Sciences, University of Durham, South Road, Durham DH1 3LE. Home 0191 383 1259; Work 0191 374 3350; e-mail R.M.Ward@durham.ac.uk.
INLAND, NORTH. Mrs Margaret MacFarlane, 7 Wildshaw Close, Southfield Lea, Cramlington, Northumberland NE23 6LH.
INLAND, SOUTH. Andrew Donnison, WWT Washington, District 15, Washington, Tyne & Wear NE38 8LE. 0191 416 5454 ext 222; fax 0191 416 5801.

WARWICKSHIRE

Bird Recorder
Jonathan Bowley, 17 Meadow Way, Fenny Compton, Southam, Warks CV47 2WD. 01295 770069.

Bird Report See West Midlands.

BTO Regional Representative
WARWICKSHIRE. Joe A Hardman, Red Hill House, Red Hill, Alcester, Warks B49 6NQ. 01789 763159; e-mail annandjoe.hardman@lineone.net.

Clubs
NUNEATON & DISTRICT BIRDWATCHERS' CLUB. (1950; 68). Alvin K Burton, 21 Barons Croft, Whittleford, Nuneaton, Warks CV10 9QQ. 01203 387061.
WEST MIDLAND BIRD CLUB (SOLIHULL BRANCH). George Morley, 64 Cambridge Avenue, Solihull, West Midlands B91 1QF.

Ringing Groups
ARDEN RG. Joe A Hardman, Red Hill House, Red Hill, Alcester, Warks B49 6NQ. 01789 763159; e-mail annandjoe.hardman@lineone.net.
BRANDON RG. David Stone, Overbury, Wolverton, Stratford-on-Avon, Warks CV37 0HG. 01789 731488.

RSPB Members' Groups
See West Midlands.

Wetland Bird Survey Organiser
Maurice Arnold, 58 Overwoods Road, Hockley, Tamworth, Staffs B77 5LZ.

Wildlife Trust
WARWICKSHIRE WILDLIFE TRUST. (1970; 5500). Andy Tasker, Director, Brandon Marsh Nature Centre, Brandon Lane, Coventry CV3 3GW. 01203 302912; fax 01203 639556; e-mail warkswt@cix.co.uk.

WEST MIDLANDS

Bird Atlas/Avifauna
The Birds of the West Midlands edited by Graham Harrison *et al* (West Midland Bird Club, 1982). Rev ed due 2000/2001.

Bird Recorder
Tim Hextell, 39 Windermere Road, Handsworth, Birmingham B21 9RQ. 0121 551 9997.

Bird Reports
THE BIRDS OF VALLEY PARK AND DUNSTALL PARK (1988-). From Secretary, Valley Park Bird Group.
WEST MIDLAND BIRD REPORT (inc Staffs, Warks, Worcs) (1934-). From Mrs D Dunstan, 4 Blossomfield Road, Solihull, West Midlands B91 1LD. 0121 705 1601.

BTO Regional Representative
BIRMINGHAM & WEST MIDLANDS. Jim R Winsper, 32 Links Road, Hollywood, Birmingham B14 4TP. Home/Work 0121 605 4163.

Clubs
SMESTOW VALLEY BIRD GROUP. (1988; 56). Frank Dickson, 11 Bow Street, Bilston, Wolverhampton WV14 7NB. 01902 493733.
WEST MIDLAND BIRD CLUB. (1929; 2000). Mrs Hilary Brittain, 13 Lawford Avenue, Lichfield, Staffs WS14 9XJ. 01543 254443.
WEST MIDLAND BIRD CLUB (BIRMINGHAM BRANCH). (1995; 800). John N Sears, 14 Ingram Street, Malmesbury, Wilts SN16 9BX. 01666 824417.

Ringing Groups
MERCIAN RG (Sutton Coldfield). R L Castle, 91 Maney Hill Road, Sutton Coldfield, West Midlands B72 1JT. 0121 686 5331.

RSPB Members' Groups
BIRMINGHAM. (1975; 70). John Bailey, 52 Gresham Road, Hall Green, Birmingham B28 0HY. 0121 777 4389.
COVENTRY & WARWICKSHIRE. (1969; 130). Alan King, 69 Westmorland Road, Coventry CV2 5BP. 024 767 27348.
SOLIHULL. (1983; 2350). John Roberts, 115 Dovehouse Lane, Solihull, West Midlands B91 2EQ. 0121 707 3101.
STOURBRIDGE. (1978; 150). Cathryn Pritchard, 249 Groveley Lane, West Heath, Birmingham B31 4PS. 0121 477 7710.
SUTTON COLDFIELD. (1986; 250). Paul Hobbs, 12 Hurlingham Road, Kingstanding, Birmingham B44 0LT. 0121 382 7154.
WALSALL. (1970; 80). Peter Hunt, 26 Dumblederry Lane, Aldridge, Staffs WS9 0DH. 01922 456908.
WOLVERHAMPTON. (1974; 100). E French, 10 Newey Road, Ashmore Park, Wednesfield, Wolverhampton WV11 2PU. 01902 738537.

Wetland Bird Survey Organiser
Maurice Arnold, 58 Overwoods Road, Hockley, Tamworth, Staffs B77 5LZ.

Wildlife Hospitals
KIDD, D J. 20 Parry Road, Ashmore Park, Wednesfield, Wolverhampton WV11 2PS. 01902 863971. All birds of prey, esp. owls. Aviaries, isolation pens. Veterinary support.
REPTILE & WILDLIFE RESCUE. Warren Davis, 103 Beauchamp Road, Billesley, Birmingham B13 0NN. 0121 444 3944; mobile 07979 370525. All species of wild birds. Full hand-rearing care. Veterinary support.
WEDNESFIELD ANIMAL SANCTUARY. Jimmy Wick, 92 Vicarage Road, Nordley, Wednesfield, Wolverhampton WV11 1SF. 01902 823064. Birds of prey, softbills, seed-eaters. Brooders, incubators, outdoor aviaries, heated accommodation. Telephone first. Veterinary support.

Wildlife Trust
BIRMINGHAM AND BLACK COUNTRY WILDLIFE TRUST. (1980; 900). Unit 310, Jubilee Trade Centre, 130 Pershore Street, Birmingham B5 6ND. 0121 666 7474; fax 0121 622 4443; e-mail urbanwt@cix.co.uk.

WILTSHIRE

Bird Recorder
Rob Turner, 14 Ethendun, Bratton, Westbury, Wilts BA13 4RX. 01380 830862.

Bird Report
Published in *Hobby* (journal of the Wiltshire OS) (1975-). From Nigel Pleass, The Curlews, 22 Ferrers Drive, Swindon SN5 6HJ.

BTO Regional Representatives
NORTH. Vacant.
SOUTH. Andrew Carter, Standlynch Farm, Downton, Salisbury SP5 3QR. 01722 710382.

Clubs
SALISBURY & DISTRICT NATURAL HISTORY SOCIETY. (1952; 168). G Nicholls, Mark House, Clarendon Road, Alderbury, Salisbury SP5 3AT. 01722 710260.
WILTSHIRE ORNITHOLOGICAL SOCIETY. (1974; 400). Miss Linda Cady, 12 Well Meadow, Burbage, Marlborough, Wilts SN8 3AD. 01672 810158.

Ringing Group
WEST WILTSHIRE RG. A J Rowe, Bozanti, Snappersnipes, Bratton Road, Westbury, Wilts BA13 3EW.

RSPB Members' Groups
NORTH WILTSHIRE. (1973; 130). Mrs Kathleen Wyatt, Lilacs, 29 Bouverie Avenue, Swindon SN3 1PZ. 01793 436909.
SOUTH WILTSHIRE. (1986; 938). Tony Goddard, Clovelly, Lower Road, Charlton All Saints, Salisbury SP5 4HQ. 01725 510309.

Wetland Bird Survey Organiser
Julian Rolls, 110 Beanacre, Melksham, Wilts SN12 7PZ. 01225 790495.

Wildlife Hospital
CALNE WILD BIRD AND ANIMAL RESCUE CENTRE. Tom and Caroline Baker, 2 North Cote, Calne, Wilts SN11 9DL. 01249 817893. All species of birds. Large natural aviaries (all with ponds), release areas, incubators, heated cages. Day and night collection. Veterinary support.

Wildlife Trust
WILTSHIRE WILDLIFE TRUST. (1962; 10000). 19 High Street, Devizes, Wilts SN10 1AT. 01380 725670; fax 01380 729017; e-mail wiltswt@cix.co.uk.

WORCESTERSHIRE

Bird Recorder
Richard Harbird, Flat 4, Buckley Court, 16 Woodfield Road, Moseley, Birmingham B13 9UJ. 0121 441 2459.

Bird Report See West Midlands.

BTO Regional Representative
G Harry Green, Windy Ridge, Pershore Road, Little Comberton, Pershore, Worcs WR10 3EW. 01386 710377.

Ringing Group
WYCHAVON RG. J R Hodson, 15 High Green, Severn Stoke, Worcester WR8 9JS. 01905 371333.

RSPB Members' Group
WORCESTER & MALVERN. (1980; 400). Garth Lowe, Sunnymead, Old Storridge, Alfrick, Worcester WR6 5HT. 01886 833362.

Wetland Bird Survey Organiser
Maurice Arnold, 58 Overwoods Road, Hockley, Tamworth, Staffs B77 5LZ.

Wildlife Hospital
NATIONAL BIRD OF PREY WELFARE TRUST. Co-ordinator, Steven David Wyton, 27 Barley Mow Lane, Catshill, Bromsgrove, Worcs B61 0LU. Tel/fax 01527 579113 24-hour. Registered charity. Birds of prey only. 46 indoor and outdoor rehabilitation units, fully equipped surgery, X-ray facilities, intensive care unit, incubators, brooders. Veterinary support. Mobile 0860 488800 or 0860 303638.

Wildlife Trust
WORCESTERSHIRE WILDLIFE TRUST. (1968; 8000). Lower Smite Farm, Smite Hill, Hindlip, Worcester WR3 8SZ. 01905 754919; fax 01905 755868; e-mail worcswt@cix.co.uk.

YORKSHIRE

Bird Atlas/Avifauna
Atlas of Breeding Birds in the Leeds Area 1987-1991 by Richard Fuller *et al* (Leeds Birdwatchers' Club, 1994). *The Birds of Yorkshire* by John Mather (Croom Helm, 1986). *Huddersfield Breeding Bird Atlas* (working title). In preparation. *Birds of Barnsley* by Nick Addey (Pub by author, 114 Everill Gate Lane, Broomhill, Barnsley S73 0YJ, 1998).

Bird Recorders
VC61 (East Yorkshire). Geoff Dobbs, 12 Park Avenue, Hull HU5 3ER. 01482 341524; e-mail geoffdobbs@aol.com.
VC62 (North Yorkshire East). David Bywater, 2 High Moor Way, Eastfield, Scarborough, N Yorks YO11 3LP. 01723 582619.
VC63 (South & West Yorkshire) to end 1999. John Dale, 158 Lindley Moor Road, Huddersfield HD3 3UE. 01484 652453.
VC64 (West Yorkshire). Vacant.
VC65 (North Yorkshire West). Nick Morgan, Linden, Church View, Ainderby Steeple, Northallerton, N Yorks DL7 9PU. 01609 770168; e-mail nick.morgan1 @virgin.net.

Bird Reports
BARNSLEY & DISTRICT BIRD STUDY GROUP REPORT (1971-). From Secretary.
BRADFORD NATURALISTS' SOCIETY ANNUAL REPORT. From I Hogg, 23 St Matthews Road, Bankfoot, Bradford BD5 9AB.
BRADFORD ORNITHOLOGICAL GROUP REPORT (1987-). From Shaun Radcliffe, Bradford Ornithological Group.
DONCASTER BIRD REPORT (1955-). From Mrs S Bird, 83 Ellers Avenue, Bessacar, Doncaster DN4 7DZ.
FILEY BRIGG BIRD REPORT (1976-). From John Harwood, 13 West Garth Gardens, Cayton, Scarborough, N Yorks YO11 3SF. 01723 584373.
FIVE TOWNS BIRD REPORT (1995-). From D Bacon, 18 Redhill Road, Airedale, Castleford, Yorkshire.
HALIFAX BIRDWATCHERS' CLUB ANNUAL REPORT (1991-). From Secretary.
HARROGATE & DISTRICT NATURALISTS' ORNITHOLOGY REPORT (1996-). From Secretary.
BIRDS IN HUDDERSFIELD (1967-). From Secretary, Huddersfield Bird Club.
LEEDS BIRDWATCHERS' CLUB ANNUAL REPORT. From Secretary.

BIRDS OF ROTHERHAM (1975-). From Secretary, Rotherham Orn Soc.
BIRDS IN THE SHEFFIELD AREA (1973-). From Tony Morris, 4A Raven Road,
Sheffield S7 1SB.
THE BIRDS OF SK58 (1993-). From Secretary, SK58 Birders.
SPURN BIRD OBSERVATORY ANNUAL REPORT. From Warden, see
Reserves.
TOPHILL LOW BIRD REPORT (1996-). From Recorder for VC61.
YORK ORNITHOLOGICAL CLUB ANNUAL REPORT (1970-). From Mrs D
Murfitt, 71 Moor Lane, Dringhouses, York YO3 2QX.
YORKSHIRE BIRD REPORT (1940-). From Secretary, Yorkshire Naturalists'
Union (Ornithological Section).

BTO Regional Representatives & Regional Development Officers
NORTH-EAST RR (Acting). Peter Ottaway, 7 Marshall Drive, Pickering, N Yorks
YO18 7JT. 01751 476714.
NORTH-WEST RR & RDO. Malcolm M Priestley, Havera Bank East, Howgill
Lane, Sedbergh, Cumbria LA10 5HB. Home 01539 620104; Work 01539 620535.
SOUTH RR. Chris Falshaw, 6 Den Bank Crescent, Sheffield S10 5PD. 0114 230 3857.
EAST RR. Vacant.
BRADFORD RR & RDO. Mike L Denton, 77 Hawthorne Terrace, Crosland Moor,
Huddersfield HD4 5RP. Home 01484 646990; Work 01484 650900.
HARROGATE RR. Mike Brown, 48 Pannal Ash Drive, Harrogate, N Yorks HG2
0HU. Home 01423 567382; Work 01423 507237.
HARROGATE RDO. Hamish Roberton, 2 Leadhall Avenue, Harrogate, N Yorks
HG2 9NH. Home 01423 879480; Work 01423 561614.
LEEDS & WAKEFIELD RR & RDO. Peter Smale, 2A Hillcrest Rise, Leeds LS16
7DL. 0113 226 9526; e-mail petersmale@cwcom.net.
RICHMOND RR. John Edwards, 7 Church Garth, Great Smeaton, Northallerton, N
Yorks DL6 2HW. Home 01609 881476; Work 01609 780780.
YORK RR. Peter Hutchinson, Rectory Corner, Brandsby, York YO6 4RJ. 01347
888601.

Clubs
BARNSLEY & DISTRICT BIRD STUDY GROUP. (1970; 35). Dave Pearce, 15
Bleakley Terrace, Notton, Wakefield WF4 2NS. 01226 723646.
BRADFORD NATURALISTS' SOCIETY. (1875; 50). D R Grant, 19 The
Wheatings, Ossett, W Yorks WF5 0QQ. 01924 273628.
BRADFORD ORNITHOLOGICAL GROUP. (1987; 150). Shaun Radcliffe, 8
Longwood Avenue, Bingley, W Yorks BD16 2RX. 01274 770960.
CASTLEFORD & DISTRICT NATURALISTS' SOCIETY. (1956; 30). Michael J
Warrington, 31 Mount Avenue, Hemsworth, Pontefract, W Yorks WF9 4QE. 01977
614954.
DONCASTER & DISTRICT ORNITHOLOGICAL SOCIETY. (1955; 60). Mrs C
McKee, 14 Poplar Close, Branton, Doncaster DN3 3QA. 01302 532454.
FILEY BRIGG ORNITHOLOGICAL GROUP. (1977; 35). Ian Robinson, 31
Wharfedale, Filey, N Yorkshire YO14 0DG. 01723 513991.
FIVE TOWNS BIRD GROUP. (1994; 26). Robert Knight, 2 Milnes Grove, Airedale,
Castleford, W Yorkshire WF10 3EZ. 0113 287 4285.
HALIFAX BIRDWATCHERS' CLUB. (1992; 33). Nick C Dawtrey, 14 Moorend
Gardens, Pellon, Halifax, W Yorks HX2 0SD. 01422 364228.
HARROGATE & DISTRICT NATURALISTS' SOCIETY. (1947; 410). Mrs J
McClean, 6 Rossett Park Road, Harrogate, N Yorks HG2 9NP. 01423 879095.
HORNSEA BIRD CLUB. (1967; 50). John Eldret, 44 Rolston Road, Hornsea HU18
1UN. 01964 532854.
HUDDERSFIELD BIRDWATCHERS' CLUB. (1966; 100). David Butterfield, 15
Dene Road, Skelmanthorpe, Huddersfield HD8 9BU. 01484 862006.

HULL VALLEY WILDLIFE GROUP. (1997; 175). F X Moffatt, 102 Norwood, Beverley, E Yorks HU17 9HL. 01482 882791; e-mail franki@xmoffatt.freeserve.co.uk; www.ashton34. freeserve.co.uk.

LEEDS BIRDWATCHERS' CLUB. (1949; 62). Mrs Shirley Carson, 2 Woodhall Park Gardens, Stanningley, Pudsey, W Yorks LS28 7XQ. 0113 255 2145.
NEW SWILLINGTON INGS BIRD GROUP. (1989; 20). Nick Smith, 40 Holmsley Lane, Woodlesford, Leeds LS26 8RN. 0113 282 6154.
PUDSEY ORNITHOLOGY GROUP. (1989; 22). Mrs Joan Thornes, 8 Newlands, Farsley, Leeds LS28 5BB. 0113 229 8356.
ROTHERHAM & DISTRICT ORNITHOLOGICAL SOCIETY. (1974; 80). Malcolm Taylor, 18 Maple Place, Chapeltown, Sheffield S35 1QW. 0114 246 1848.
SCALBY NABS ORNITHOL GROUP. (1993; 15). Ian Glaves, Halleykeld House, Chapel Lane, Sawdon, Scarborough, N Yorkshire YO13 9DZ. 01723 859766.
SHEFFIELD BIRD STUDY GROUP. (1972; 170). Chris Falshaw, 6 Den Bank Crescent, Sheffield S10 5PD. 0114 230 3857.
SK58 BIRDERS. (1993; 41). Andy Hirst, 15 Hunters Drive, Dinnington, Sheffield S25 2TG. 01909 560310; e-mail sk58birders@sk58.freeserve.co.uk.
SORBY NHS (ORNITHOL SECTION). (1918; 40). John Lintin Smith, 44 Southgrove Road, Sheffield S10 2NQ. 0114 266 4362.
WAKEFIELD NATURALISTS' SOCIETY. (1851; 40). Philip Harrison, 392 Dewsbury Road, Wakefield, W Yorks WF2 9DS. 01924 373604.
YORK ORNITHOLOGICAL CLUB. (1967; 75). Ian Traynor, The Owl House, 137 Osbaldwick Lane, York YO1 3AY.
YORKSHIRE NATURALISTS' UNION (Ornithological Section). (1940; 500). W F Curtis, Farm Cottage, Atwick, Driffield YO25 8DH. 01964 532477.

Ringing Groups
BARNSLEY RG. M C Wells, 715 Manchester Road, Stocksbridge, Sheffield S36 1DQ. 0114 288 4211.
DONCASTER RG. D Hazard, 41 Jossey Lane, Scawthorpe, Doncaster, S Yorks DN5 9DB. 01302 788044.
EAST DALES RG. S P Worwood, 18 Coltsgate Hill, Ripon, N Yorks HG4 2AB.
EAST YORKS RG. Peter J Dunn, 43 West Garth Gardens, Cayton, Scarborough, N Yorks YO11 3SF. 01723 583149; e-mail pjd@email.menet.net.
SORBY-BRECK RG. Geoff P Mawson, Moonpenny Farm, Farwater Lane, Dronfield, Sheffield S18 1RA. 01246 415097.
SOUTH CLEVELAND RG. W Norman, 2 Station Cottages, Grosmont, Whitby, N Yorks YO22 5PB. 01947 895226.
SPURN BIRD OBSERVATORY. D P Boyle, Spurn Bird Observatory, Kilnsea, Via Patrington, Hull HU12 0UG.
TEES RG. E Wood, Southfields, 16 Marton Moor Road, Nunthorpe, Middlesbrough, Cleveland TS7 0BH. 01642 323563.

WINTERSETT RG. P Smith, 16 Templar Street, Wakefield, W Yorks WF1 5HB. 01924 375082.

RSPB County Youth Officers

N YORKS. Ian Cresswell, Dove House, Skyreholme, Skipton, N Yorks BD23 6DE. 01756 720355; fax 01756 720407; e-mail IanCresswell@lentoid.com; http://www. airenct.co.uk/rspb.

S YORKS. K Burke, Woodlane House Farm, Woodlane, Stannington, Sheffield. 0114 233 5982.

W YORKS. Mrs V Langdale, 165 Whitehall Road, Wyke, Bradford BD12 9LN. 01274 600019; e-mail val@langdale.prestel.co.uk.

RSPB Members' Groups

AIREDALE AND BRADFORD. (1972; 3500). Peter Sutcliffe, 10 Southfield Mount, Riddlesden, Keighley, W Yorks BD20 5HS. 01535 600937.

CLEVELAND. (1974; 200). Mark Stokeld, 38 Ash Grove, Kirklevington, Cleveland TS15 9NQ. 01642 783819; e-mail mark@stokeld.demon.co.uk; www.stokeld. demon.uk.

CRAVEN & PENDLE. (1986; 250). Ian Cresswell, as above (RSPB County Youth Officers).

DONCASTER. (1984; 125). Sue Clifton, West Lodge, Wadworth Hall Lane, Wadworth, Doncaster DN11 9BH. Tel/fax 01302 854956.

EAST YORKSHIRE. (1986; 90). Trevor Malkin, 49 Taylors Fields, Kings Mill Road, Driffield, E Yorks YO25 6FQ. 01377 257325.

HUDDERSFIELD & HALIFAX. (1981; 200). David Hemingway, 267 Long Lane, Dalton, Huddersfield HD5 9SH. 01484 301920.

HULL & DISTRICT. (1983; 334). Derek Spencer, The Old Brewhouse, Main Road, Burton Pidsea, Hull HU12 9AX. 01964 670024.

LEEDS. (1975; 450). Linda Jenkinson, 112 Eden Crescent, Burley, Leeds LS4 2TR. 0113 230 4595.

SHEFFIELD. (1983; 500). Lyn Facer, 15 Hawthorne Avenue, South Anston, Sheffield S25 5GR. 01909 563108.

WAKEFIELD. (1987; 170). Paul Disken, 6 Northfield Road, Dewsbury, W Yorks WF13 2JX. 01924 456352.

WHITBY. (1977; 120). Fred Payne, 16 Hermitage Way, Eskdaleside, Sleights, Whitby, N Yorks YO22 5HG. 01947 810022.

YORK. (1973; 600). Don Hoad, Church Lodge, Overton, York YO30 1YL. 01904 470436; e-mail A1318534@infotrade.co.uk; http://www.tka.co.uk/YORKRSPB/.

Wetland Bird Survey Organisers

N YORKS, SCARBOROUGH. Mrs Shirley Pashby, 10 Ambrey Close, Hunmanby, Filey, N Yorks YO14 0LZ. 01723 891377.

HARROGATE & YORKSHIRE DALES. Bill Haines, 14 Railway Terrace, Knaresborough, N Yorks HG5 0JB. 01423 869789.

DONCASTER AREA. Hugh Parkin, 25 Hyman Close, Warmsworth, Doncaster, S Yorks DN4 9PB. 01302 857684.

SHEFFIELD AREA. David Adkin, Northfield House, Thorpe Road, Harthill, Sheffield S26 7YF. 01909 770368.

E YORKS (excl Humber estuary). Mrs Shirley Pashby, 10 Ambrey Close, Hunmanby, Filey, N Yorks YO14 0LZ. 01723 891377.

HUMBER, NORTH ESTUARY. Nick Cutts, 1 Castle Mews, West End, South Cave, E Yorks HU15 2EX.

BRADFORD/HUDDERSFIELD/HALIFAX AREA. Nick Carter, 72 Towngate, Midgley, Halifax, W Yorks HX2 6UJ. 01422 883923.

WAKEFIELD/BARNSLEY AREA. John Cudworth, 17A Prospect Road, Ossett, W Yorks WF5 8AE.

Wildlife Hospital
ANIMAL HOUSE WILDLIFE WELFARE. Mrs C Buckroyd, 14 Victoria Street, Scarborough YO12 7SS. 01723 371256; shop 01723 375162. All species of wild birds. Oiled birds given treatment before forwarding to cleaning stations. Incubators, hospital cages, heat pads, release sites. Birds ringed before release. Prior telephone call requested. Collection if required. Veterinary support.

Wildlife Trusts
TEES VALLEY WILDLIFE TRUST. (1979; 4000). Bellamy Pavilion, Kirkleatham Old Hall, Kirkleatham, Redcar, Cleveland TS10 5NW. 01642 759900; fax 01642 480401; e-mail teesvalleywt@cix.co.uk.
SHEFFIELD WILDLIFE TRUST. (1985; 132). Wood Lane House, 52 Wood Lane, Sheffield S6 5HE. Tel/fax 0114 231 0120; e-mail sheffieldwt@cix.co.uk.
YORKSHIRE WILDLIFE TRUST. (1946; 8000). 10 Toft Green, York YO1 6JT. 01904 659570; fax 01904 613467; e-mail yorkshirewt@cix.co.uk.

SCOTLAND

Please see note on page 290 regarding area headings for Scotland

Bird Report & Bird Club see Scottish Ornithologists' Club in National Directory.

BORDERS

Bird Atlas/Avifauna
The Breeding Birds of South-east Scotland, a tetrad atlas 1988-1994 by R D Murray *et al* (Scottish Ornithologists' Club, 1998).

Bird Recorder
Ray Murray, 4 Bellfield Crescent, Eddleston, Peebles EH45 8RQ. 01721 730677.

Bird Report
BORDERS BIRD REPORT (1979-). From Michael Bickmore, Moss Side, Hartwoodburn, Selkirk TD7 5EY. Tel/fax 01750 20022.

BTO Regional Representative & Regional Development Officer
RR. Alex Copland, 51A Clarendon Street, Bedford MK41 7SH. Home 01234 353756; Work 01767 680551; e-mail alex.copland@rsbp.org.uk.

RDO. Michael Bickmore, Moss Side, Hartwoodburn, Selkirk TD7 5EY. Tel/fax 01750 20022.

Bird Club
SOC BORDERS BRANCH. (90). Malcolm Ross, The Tubs, Dingleton Road, Melrose TD6 9QP. 01896 822132.

Ringing Group
BORDERS RG. Dr T W Dougall, 62 (1F2) Leamington Terrace, Edinburgh EH10 4JL. Fax 0131 469 5599.

RSPB Members' Group
BORDERS. (1995; 94). Nancy Marshall, The Birches, Leydon Grove, Clovenfords, Galashiels TD1 3NF. 01869 850564.

Wetland Bird Survey Organiser
Andrew Bramhall, 2 Abbotsferry Road, Tweedbank, Galashiels TD1 3RX.

CENTRAL

Bird Recorder
FORTH AREA. Dr C J Henty, Edgehill East, 7 Coneyhill Road, Bridge of Allan, Stirling FK9 4EL. 01786 832166.

Bird Report
CENTRAL REGION BIRD REPORT (1976-). From L Corbett, Library, University of Stirling, Stirling FK9 4LA. 01786 73171.

BTO Regional Representative
Neil Bielby, 56 Ochiltree, Dunblane, Perthshire FK15 0DF. 01786 823830.

Club
SOC STIRLING BRANCH. (1968; 90). Neil Bielby, 56 Ochiltree, Dunblane, Perthshire FK15 0DF. 01786 823830.

RSPB Members' Group
FORTH VALLEY. (1996; 150). Alex Downie, 2 St Lawrence Avenue, Dunblane, Perthshire FK15 9DE. 01786 825228.

Wetland Bird Survey Organisers
FORTH INNER ESTUARY (Blackness to Fallin). Professor David Bryant, Institute of Biological Sciences, University of Stirling, Stirling FK9 4LA. 01786 467755.
INLAND. Neil Bielby, 56 Ochiltree, Dunblane, Perthshire FK15 0DF. 01786 823830.

DUMFRIES & GALLOWAY

Bird Recorders
NITHSDALE, ANNANDALE & ESKDALE. Steve Cooper, Wildfowl & Wetlands Trust, Eastpark Farm, Caerlaverock, Dumfries DG1 4RS. 01387 770200; fax 01387 770539; e-mail mail@wwtck.idps.co.uk. 2. Paul N Collin, Gairland, Old Edinburgh Road, Minnigaff, Newton Stewart, Wigtownshire DG8 6PL. 01671 402861.

Bird Report
DUMFRIES & GALLOWAY REGION BIRD REPORT (1985-). From Recorder.

BTO Regional Representatives & Regional Development Officer
DUMFRIES RR. Richards Mearns, Connansknowe, Kirkton, Dumfries DG1 1SX. 01387 710031.
DUMFRIES RDO. Ken Bruce, Mallaig, Wellington Street, Glencaple, Dumfries DG1 4RA. 01387 770336.
KIRKCUDBRIGHT RR. Vacant.
WIGTOWN RR. Geoff Sheppard, The Roddens, Leswalt, Stranraer, Wigtownshire DG9 0QR. 01776 870685.

Clubs
SOC DUMFRIES BRANCH. (1961; 105). Brian Smith, Rockiemount, Colvend, Dalbeattie, Dumfries DG5 4QW. 01556 620617.
SOC STEWARTRY BRANCH. (1976; 76). Miss Joan Howie, 60 Main Street, St Johns Town of Dalry, Castle Douglas, Kirkcudbrightshire DG7 3UW. 01644 430226.
SOC WEST GALLOWAY BRANCH. (1975; 50). Geoff Sheppard, The Roddens, Leswalt, Stranraer, Wigtownshire DG9 0QR. 01776 870685.

Ringing Group
NORTH SOLWAY RG. Ken Bruce, Mallaig, Wellington Street, Glencaple, Dumfries DG1 4RA. 01387 770336.

RSPB Members' Group
GALLOWAY. (1985; 180). Mrs Pamela Pumphrey, Clonyard Farm, Colvend, Dalbeattie, Kirkcudbrightshire DG5 4QW. 01556 630246; e-mail pam@ppumph. prestel.co.uk.

Wetland Bird Survey Organisers
AUCHENCAIRN & ORCHARDTON ESTUARIES. Dr Bryan Nelson, Mine House, Auchencairn, Castle Douglas, Kirkcudbrightshire DG7 1RL. 01555 640320.
FLEET BAY. David Hawker, Windywalls, Upper Drumwall, Gatehouse of Fleet, Castle Douglas, Kirkcudbrightshire DG7 2DE. 01557 814249.
KIRKCUDBRIGHT BAY. Geoff Shaw, Kirriereoch, Bargrennan, Newton Stewart, Wigtownshire DG8 6TB. 01671 840288.
LOCH RYAN. Geoff Sheppard, The Roddens, Leswalt, Stranraer, Wigtownshire DG9 0QR. 01776 870685.
ROUGH FIRTH. Peter Norman, South Laundry Cottage, Cally, Gatehouse of Fleet, Castle Douglas DG7 2DJ. 01557 814738.
SOLWAY ESTUARY NORTH. Steve Cooper, WWT Caerlaverock, Eastpark Farm, Caerlaverock, Dumfries DG1 4RS. 01387 770200; fax 01387 770539; e-mail mail@wwtck.idps.co.uk
WIGTOWN BAY. Paul N Collin, Gairland, Old Edinburgh Road, Minnigaff, Newton Stewart, Wigtownshire DG8 6PL. 01671 402861.
OTHER SITES. Steve Cooper, WWT Caerlaverock, Eastpark Farm, Caerlaverock, Dumfries DG1 4RS. 01387 770200; fax 01387 770539; e-mail mail@wwtck.idps.co.uk

FIFE

Bird Recorders
FIFE REGION INC OFFSHORE ISLANDS (NORTH FORTH). Douglas Dickson, 2 Burrelton Court, Bankhead, Glenrothes, Fife KY7 4UN. 01592 774066.

ISLE OF MAY BIRD OBSERVATORY. Ian M Darling, 579 Lanark Road West, Balerno, Edinburgh EH14 7BL. Tel/fax 0131 449 4282.

Bird Reports
FIFE BIRD REPORT (1988-) (FIFE & KINROSS BR 1980-87). From W McBay, 41 Shamrock Street, Dunfermline, Fife KY12 0JQ.
ISLE OF MAY BIRD OBSERVATORY REPORT (1985-). From Isle of May Recorder.

BTO Regional Representative
FIFE & KINROSS RR. Norman Elkins, 18 Scotstarvit View, Cupar, Fife KY15 5DX. 01334 654348.

Clubs
FIFE BIRD CLUB. (1985; 287). FBC, 41 Shamrock Street, Dunfermline, Fife KY12 0JQ. 01383 723464.
SOC FIFE BRANCH. (1956; 190). Donald R Stewart, 18 Newmill Gardens, St Andrews, Fife KY16 8RY. 01334 475763.

Ringing Groups
ISLE OF MAY BIRD OBSERVATORY. Ian M Darling, as above.
SCOTTISH NATURAL HERITAGE. SNH, 48 Crossgate, Cupar, Fife KY15 5HS. 01334 654038; fax 01334 656924.
TAY RG. Ms S Millar, Edenvale Cottage, 1 Lydox Cottages, Dairsie, Fife KY15 4RN.

Wetland Bird Survey Organisers
EDEN ESTUARY. Les Hatton, Fife Ranger Service, Craigtoun Country Park, St Andrews, Fife KY16 8NX.
FORTH, NORTH ESTUARY. Mrs Bertha Govan, 12 McKane Place, Dunfermline, Fife KY12 7XD.
TAY ESTUARY (South). Norman Elkins, as above (BTO Regional Representative).
INLAND. Allan Brown, 61 Watts Gardens, Cupar, Fife KY15 4UG. 01334 656804.

Wildlife Hospital
SCOTTISH SPCA WILD LIFE REHABILITATION CENTRE. Middlebank Farm, Masterton Road, Dunfermline, Fife KY11 8QN. 01383 412520. All species. Open to visitors, groups and school parties. Veterinary support.

GRAMPIAN

Bird Recorders
NORTH-EAST SCOTLAND 1. Andy Thorpe, 30 M. Mearn Gardens, Milltimber, Aberdeen AB13 0EA. 01224 733296. 2. Andy Webb, 4 Morningside Place, Aberdeen AB10 7NG. 01224 312484.
MORAY & NAIRN. Martin J H Cook, Rowanbrae, Clochan, Buckie, Banffshire AB56 5EQ. 01542 850296.

Bird Reports
MORAY & NAIRN BIRD REPORT (1985-). From Moray & Nairn Recorder.
NORTH-EAST SCOTLAND BIRD REPORT (1974-). From Dave Gill, Drakemyre Croft, Methlick, Ellon, Aberdeenshire AB41 0JN. 01651 806252.
NORTH SEA BIRD CLUB ANNUAL REPORT (1979-). From NSBC Recorder, see over.

BTO Regional Representatives & Regional Development Officer
ABERDEEN RDO. Kath Hamper, 9 Mid Street, Inverallochy, Fraserburgh, Aberdeenshire AB43 8YA. 01346 583015.
ABERDEENSHIRE, BANFF & BUCHAN RR. Paul Doyle, South Meiklemoss, Collieston, Ellon, Aberdeenshire AB41 8SB. Home 01358 751365; Work 01224 493288; e-mail paul@meiklemoss.freeserve.co.uk.
ABERDEEN SOUTH RR. Graham Cooper, Westbank, Beltie Road, Torphins, Banchory, Aberdeen AB31 4JT. Home 01339 882706; Work 01224 205047.
KINCARDINE & DEESIDE. Graham Cooper, as previous entry.
MORAY RR. Bob Proctor, 94 Reid Street, Bishopmill, Elgin, Moray IV30 4HH. Home 01343 544874 (w/e); Work 01479 821409; fax 01479 821069.

Clubs
NORTH SEA BIRD CLUB. (1979; 300). Andrew Thorpe, (Recorder), Aberdeen University, Culterty Field Station, Newburgh, Ellon, Aberdeenshire AB41 0AA. 01358 789631; fax 01358 789214; e-mail nsbc@abdn.ac.uk.
SOC GRAMPIAN BRANCH. Alastair Duncan, 12 Cairncry Avenue, Aberdeen AB16 5DS. 01224 483717.

Ringing Groups
ABERDEEN UNIVERSITY RG. Andrew Thorpe, Culterty Field Station, Newburgh, Ellon, Aberdeenshire AB41 6AA. 01358 789631; e-mail a.thorpe @abdn.ac.uk.
GRAMPIAN RG. R Duncan, 86 Broadfold Drive, Bridge of Don, Aberdeen AB23 8PP.

RSPB Members' Group
ABERDEEN. (1977; 180). Bob Littlejohn, 28 Seafield Drive East, Aberdeen AB15 7UR. 01224 313576.

Wetland Bird Survey Organisers
ABERDEENSHIRE. Alistair Duncan, as above (Clubs).
LOSSIE ESTUARY. Bob Proctor, 94 Reid Street, Bishopmill, Elgin, Moray IV30 4HH. Home 01343 544874 (w/e); Work 01479 821409; fax 821069.
MORAY BASIN COAST. Bob Swann, 14 St Vincent Road, Tain, Ross-shire IV19 1JR. 01862 894329.
INLAND, MORAY. Martin Cook, Rowanbrae, Clochan, Buckie, Banffshire AB56 5EQ. 01542 850296.

Wildlife Hospital
GRAMPIAN WILDLIFE REHABILITATION TRUST. 40 High Street, New Deer, Turriff, Aberdeenshire AB53 6SX. 01771 644489. Veterinary surgeon. Access to full practice facilities. Will care for all species of birds.

HIGHLAND

Bird Atlas/Avifauna
The Birds of Sutherland by Alan Vittery (Colin Baxter Photography Ltd, 1997). *Birds of Skye* by Andrew Currie. In preparation.

Bird Recorders
CAITHNESS. Peter M Miller, 10 Harrold Cottages, Reiss, Wick, Caithness KW1 4RU. 01955 603665.

MORAY & NAIRN. Martin J H Cook, Rowanbrae, Clochan, Buckie, Banffshire AB56 5EQ. 01542 850296.
ROSS-SHIRE, INVERNESS-SHIRE, SUTHERLAND. Colin Crooke, RSPB, Etive House, Beechwood Park, Inverness IV2 3BW. 01463 715000. Home: 6 George Street, Avoch, Ross-shire IV9 8PU. 01381 620566.

Bird Reports
CAITHNESS BIRD REPORT (1983-). From Julian Smith, St John's, Brough, Dunnet, Caithness.
HIGHLAND BIRD REPORT (1991-). From Recorder.

BTO Regional Representatives & Regional Development Officers
CAITHNESS & SUTHERLAND RR. Neil Money, Heathfield House, Dunnet, Thurso, Caithness KW14 8XP. Tel/fax 01847 851346; Work 01847 805208; e-mail neil.money@zetnet.co.uk.
INVERNESS & SPEYSIDE. Hugh Insley, 1 Drummond Place, Inverness IV2 4JT. Home 01463 230652; Work 01463 232811.
NAIRN RR. Bob Proctor, 94 Reid Street, Bishopmill, Elgin, Moray IV30 4HH. Home 01343 544874 (w/e); Work 01479 821409; fax 821069.
RUM, EIGG, CANNA & MUCK RR & RDO. Bob Swann, 14 St Vincent Road, Tain, Ross-shire IV19 1JR. 01862 894329.
ROSS-SHIRE RR. Andrew Ramsay, Lower Courthill, Tain, Ross-shire IV19 1NE. Home tel/fax 01862 892361; work 01862 892121, fax 893334; e-mail adkr@infinnet.co.uk.
SKYE RR & RDO. Vacant.

Clubs
EAST SUTHERLAND BIRD GROUP. (1976; 80). Alan Vittery, Elmag Croft, 164 West Clyne, Brora, Sutherland KW9 6NH. 01408 621827.
SOC CAITHNESS BRANCH. (51). Pat Thompson, 9 Grant Crescent, Golspie, Sutherland KW10 6TS. Home 01408 633549; Work tel/fax 01408 634404.
SOC HIGHLAND BRANCH. (1955; 171). Janet Crummy, Coalhaugh, Tomatin, Inverness IV13 7YS. 01808 511261.

Ringing Groups
EAST ROSS RG. Ivan Brockway, Courthill, Tain, Ross-shire IV19 1NE. 01862 893193.
HIGHLAND RG. Bob Swann, 14 St Vincent Road, Tain, Ross-shire IV19 1JR. 01862 894329.

RSPB Area Youth Officer
CAITHNESS & SUTHERLAND. A J Davenport, The Neuk, Ladies Loch, Brora, Sutherland KW9 6NG. 01408 621968.

RSPB Members' Group
HIGHLAND. (1987; 250). Richard Prentice, Lingay, Lewiston, Drumnadrochit, Inverness IV63 6UW. 01456 450526.

Wetland Bird Survey Organisers
CAITHNESS. Stan Laybourne, Old School House, Harpsdale, Halkirk, Caithness KW12 6UN.
LOCHABER. John Dye, Toad Hall, Dalnabreac, Acharacle, Argyll PH36 4JX. 01967 431222.
MORAY BASIN COAST. Bob Swann, 14 St Vincent Road, Tain, Ross-shire IV19 1JR. 01862 894329.
WEST INVERNESS, LOCHALSH & WESTER ROSS. Vacant.

SKYE. Andrew Currie, Glaiseilean, Harrapool, Broadford, Isle of Skye IV49 9AQ. 01471 822344.
EAST INVERNESS, EASTER ROSS (Inland). Colin Crooke, RSPB, Etive House, Beechwood Park, Inverness IV2 3BW. 01463 715000.
INLAND, NAIRN. Martin Cook, Rowanbrae, Clochan, Buckie, Banffshire AB56 5EQ. 01542 850296.
INLAND, SPEYSIDE. Keith Duncan, SNH, Achantoul, Aviemore, Inverness-shire PH22 1QD. 01479 810477.
BADENOCH & STRATHSPEY. Keith Duncan, SNH, Achantoul, Aviemore, Inverness-shire PH22 1QD. 01479 810477.

LOTHIAN

Bird Atlas/Avifauna
The Breeding Birds of South-east Scotland, a tetrad atlas 1988-1994 by R D Murray *et al* (Scottish Ornithologists' Club, 1998).

Bird Recorder
Ian J Andrews, 39 Clayknowes Drive, Musselburgh, Midlothian EH21 6UW. 0131 665 0236. From 1 January 2000: David J Kelly, 149 High Street, Prestonpans, E Lothian EH32 9AX. Tel 01875 810827; e-mail david.kelly@easynet.co.uk.

Bird Reports
LOTHIAN BIRD REPORT (1979-). From Paul Speak, 49 Douglas Crescent, Longniddry, E Lothian EH32 0LH. 01875 852109.
WEST LOTHIAN BIRD CLUB REPORT (1991-). From Secretary, West Lothian Bird Club.

BTO Regional Representative
Alan Heavisides, 9 Addiston Crescent, Balerno, Edinburgh EH14 7DB. 0131 449 3816.

Clubs
EDINBURGH NATURAL HISTORY SOCIETY. (1869; 200). Mrs Mary Clarkson, 98 St Alban's Road, Edinburgh EH9 2PG. 0131 667 3815.
FOULSHIELS BIRD GROUP. (1991; 7). Frazer Henderson, 2 Elizabeth Gardens, Stoneyburn, W Lothian EH47 8BP. 01501 762972.
SOC LOTHIAN BRANCH. (1936; 440). Ian Thomson, 4 Craigielaw, Longniddry, E Lothian EH32 0PY. 01875 870588.

WEST LOTHIAN BIRD CLUB. (1990; 40). Secretary, W Lothian Bird Club, c/o Livingston Countryside Ranger Service, Bloom Farm, Livingston Village, W Lothian EH54 7AF. 01506 415441.

Ringing Group
LOTHIAN RG. A F Leitch, 2 Burgess Terrace, Edinburgh EH9 2BD.

RSPB Members' Group
EDINBURGH. (1974; 450). Michael Betts, 10 St Bernard's Row, Edinburgh EH4
1HW. 0131 332 1708; e-mail hmc@cee.hw.ac.uk; http://www.cee.he.ac.uk/~/hmc/
rspb.html.

Wetland Bird Survey Organisers
FORTH, OUTER SOUTH ESTUARY. Harry Dott, Stonecroft Cottage, Main
Street, West Linton, Peeblesshire EH46 7EE. 01968 661571.
TYNINGHAME ESTUARY. Bobby Anderson, John Muir Country Park, Town
House, Dunbar, East Lothian EH42 1ER. 01620 827318.
INLAND. Miss Joan Wilcox, 18 Howdenhall Gardens, Edinburgh EH16 6UN. 0131
664 8893.

ORKNEY

Bird Recorder
Tim Dean, Echna View, Burray, Orkney KW17 2SX. 01856 731204.

Bird Report
ORKNEY BIRD REPORT (inc North Ronaldsay Bird Report) (1974-). From Dr
Mildred F Cuthbert, Vishabreck, Evie, Orkney.

BTO Regional Representative & Regional Development Officer
Colin Corse, Garrisdale, Lynn Park, Kirkwall, Orkney KW15 1SL. Home 01856
874484; Work 01856 884156.

Club
SOC ORKNEY BRANCH. (1993; 15). Stuart Williams, Crafty, Firth, Orkney KW17
2ES. 01856 761742.

Ringing Groups
NORTH RONALDSAY BIRD OBSERVATORY. Ms A E Duncan, Twingness,
North Ronaldsay, Orkney KW17 2BE. 01857 633267.
ORKNEY RG. Colin J Corse, Garrisdale, Lynn Park, Kirkwall, Orkney KW15 1SL.
Home 01856 874484; Work 01856 884156.
SULE SKERRY RG. Dave Budworth, 121 Wood Lane, Newhall, Swadlincote,
Derbys DE11 0LX. 01283 215188.

RSPB Members' Group
ORKNEY. (1985; 250). Neil McCance, West End, Burray, Orkney KW17 2SS. 01856
731260.

Wetland Bird Survey Organisers
OPEN COASTAL SITES. Colin J Corse, Garrisdale, Lynn Park, Kirkwall, Orkney
KW15 1SL. Home 01856 874484; Work 01856 884156.
OTHER SITES. Eric Meek, RSPB, 12/14 North End Road, Stromness, Orkney
KW16 3AG. 01856 850176.

SHETLAND

Bird Recorders
FAIR ISLE. Deryk Shaw, Bird Observatory, Fair Isle, Shetland ZE2 9JU. 01595 760258; e-mail fairisle.birdobs@zetnet.co.uk.
SHETLAND. Kevin Osborn, 20 Nederdale, Lerwick, Shetland ZE1 0SA. 01595 695974.

Bird Reports
FAIR ISLE BIRD OBSERVATORY REPORT (1949-). From Scottish Ornithologists' Club, 21 Regent Terrace, Edinburgh EH7 5BT. 0131 556 6042.
SHETLAND BIRD REPORT (1969-). From Martin Heubeck, East House, Sumburgh Lighthouse, Virkie, Shetland ZE3 9JN.

BTO Regional Representative & Regional Development Officer
Dave Okill, Heilinabretta, Cauldhame, Trondra, Shetland ZE1 0XL. Home 01595 880450; Work 01595 696926.

Club
SHETLAND BIRD CLUB. (1973; 200). Wendy Dickson, Flat 4, Muckle Flugga Shore Station, Burrafirth, Unst, Shetland ZE2 9EQ. 01957 711275; www.zetnet.co.uk/sigs/birds/links.html.

Ringing Groups
FAIR ISLE BIRD OBSERVATORY. Deryk N Shaw, Bird Observatory, Fair Isle, Shetland ZE2 9JU. Tel/fax 01595 760258; e-mail fairisle.birdobs@zetnet.co.uk.
SHETLAND RG. Dave Okill, as above (BTO Regional Representative).

Wetland Bird Survey Organiser
David Eva, 6 Westerloch Brae, Lerwick, Shetland ZE1 0RP.

Wildlife Hospital
SSPCA. SSPCA, Gott, Shetland, Scotland.

STRATHCLYDE

Bird Atlas/Avifauna
Clyde Breeding Bird Atlas (working title). In preparation.

Bird Recorders
ARGYLL. Paul Daw, Tigh-na-Tulloch, Tullochgorm, Minard, Argyll PA32 8YQ. 01546 886260; e-mail monedula@globalnet.co.uk
AYRSHIRE. Angus Hogg, 11 Kirkmichael Road, Crosshill, Maybole, Ayrshire KA19 7RJ. 01655 740317; e-mail dcgos@globalnet.co.uk.
CLYDE ISLANDS. Bernard Zonfrillo, 28 Brodie Road, Glasgow G21 3SB. 0141 557 0791.
CLYDE. Iain P Gibson, 8 Kenmure View, Howwood, Johnstone, Renfrewshire PA9 1DR. 01505 705874.

Bird Reports
ARGYLL BIRD REPORT (1984-). From Bill Staley, 16 Glengilp, Ardrishaid, Argyll PA31 8LB.
AYRSHIRE BIRD REPORT (1976-). From Ayrshire Recorder.
CLYDE BIRDS (1973-). From Clyde Recorder.
MACHRIHANISH SEABIRD OBSERVATORY REPORT (1992-). From Observatory, see Reserves & Observatories.

BTO Regional Representatives
ARRAN, BUTE, CUMBRAES. Vacant.
AYRSHIRE RR. Paul Darnbrough, 65 Loreny Drive, Kilmarnock, Ayrshire KA1 4RH. Work 01563 528623.
ISLAY, JURA, COLONSAY RR. Dr Malcolm Ogilvie, Glencairn, Bruichladdich, Isle of Islay PA49 7UN. 01496 850218; e-mail MAOgilvie@indaal.demon.co.uk.
LANARK, RENFREW, DUMBARTON. Vacant.

Clubs
ARGYLL BIRD CLUB. (1983; 170). Peter Staley, Lincluden, Blairmore, Dunoon, Argyll PA23 8TL. 01369 840412.
SOC AYRSHIRE BRANCH. (1962; 100). Henry Martin, 9 Shawfield Avenue, Ayr, Ayrshire KA7 4RE. 01292 442086.
SOC CLYDE BRANCH. (300). Duncan Orr-Ewing, 4 Hall Lane, Doune, Perthshire FK16 6DQ. 01786 842019.

Ringing Groups
CLYDE RG. I Livingstone, 57 Strathview Road, Bellshill, Lanarkshire ML4 2UY.
GLASGOW UNIVERSITY RG. Prof P Monaghan, Dept of Zoology, University of Glasgow, Glasgow G12 8QQ.
TRESHNISH AUK RG. S W Walker, Snipe Cottage, Hamsterley, Bishop Auckland, Co Durham DL13 3NX.

RSPB County Youth Officer
Mrs H MacNaughton, 25 Woodvale Ave, Bearsden, Glasgow G61 2NS. 0141 942 1677.

RSPB Members' Groups
CENTRAL AYRSHIRE. (1978; 101). James Thomson, Sundrum Smithy, Ayr KA6 6LR. 01292 570351.
NORTH AYRSHIRE. (1976; 180). Duncan Macdonald Watt, Wildings Studio, 28 Greenbank, Dalry, Ayrshire KA24 5AY. 01294 832361.
GLASGOW. (1972; 146). Angus Gunn, 43 Dickens Avenue, Clydebank G81 3EP.
HAMILTON. (1976; 90). Mrs Isabel Crinean, 15A Central Avenue, Cambuslang, Glasgow G72 8AY. 0141 641 1292.
HELENSBURGH. (1975; 75). Alistair McIntyre, Craggan, Rosneath Road, Helensburgh, Dunbartonshire G84 0EJ. Work 01475 724433 ext 225.
RENFREWSHIRE. (1986; 200). Ms Alison Purssell, 2 Glencairn Place, High Street, Kilmacolm PA13 4BT. 01505 872576.

Wetland Bird Survey Organisers
ARGYLL & ISLANDS. Dr Malcolm Ogilvie, as above (BTO Regional Representative).
ARRAN. Peter Tupman, The Cottage, Porta Leacach, Kildonan, Isle of Arran KA27 8SD.
AYRSHIRE. Brian Orr, 14 Monach Gardens, Dreghorn, Irvine, Ayrshire KA11 4EB. 01294 216907; pager 01399 1133 quote 781406.
CLYDE ESTUARY. Jim & Valerie Wilson, 76 Laigh Road, Newton Mearns, Glasgow G77 5EQ. 0141 639 2516; e-mail jim.val@btinternet.com.

BUTE. Ian Hopkins, 2 Eden Place, High Street, Rothesay, Isle of Bute PA20 9BS.
GLASGOW, RENFREWSHIRE, DUMBARTONSHIRE & LANARKSHIRE. Jim
& Valerie Wilson, as above.
ISLE OF CUMBRAE. Professor John Allen, Drialstone, 21 Clyde Street, Millport,
Isle of Cumbrae KA28 0EG. 01475 530479.

Wildlife Hospital
HESSILHEAD WILDLIFE RESCUE CENTRE. Gay & Andy Christie, Gateside,
Beith, Ayrshire KA15 1HT. 01505 502415. All species. Releasing aviaries. Veterinary
support.

TAYSIDE

Bird Recorders
ANGUS & DUNDEE. Mike Nicoll, c/o Dundee Museum, Dundee DD1 1DA.
Home 01382 553266; Work 01382 432064.
PERTH & KINROSS. Ron Youngman, Blairchroisk Cottage, Ballinluig, Pitlochry,
Perthshire PH9 0NE. 01796 482324.

Bird Reports
ANGUS & DUNDEE BIRD REPORT (1974-). From Secretary, Angus & Dundee
BC.
PERTH & KINROSS BIRD REPORT (1974-). From Recorder.

BTO Regional Representatives & Regional Development Officer
ANGUS RR & RDO. Ken Slater, 19 Carnegie Street, Arbroath, Angus DD11 1TX.
01241 877073.
PERTHSHIRE RR. Vacant.

Clubs
ANGUS & DUNDEE BIRD CLUB. (1997; 68). Bob McCurley, 22 Kinnordy
Terrace, Dundee DD4 7NW. 01382 462944.
PERTHSHIRE SOCIETY OF NATURAL SCIENCE (Ornithological Section).
(1964; 61). Miss Esther Taylor, 23 Verena Terrace, Perth PH2 0BZ. 01738 621986.
SOC TAYSIDE BRANCH. (145). James Whitelaw, 36 Burn Street, Dundee DD3
0LB. 01382 819391.

Ringing Group
TAY RG. Ms S Millar, Edenvale Cottage, 1 Lydox Cottages, Dairsie, Fife KY15 4RN.

RSPB Members' Groups
DUNDEE. (1972; 110). Ron Downing, 3 Lynnewood Place, Dundee DD4 7HB. 01382
451987.
TAYSIDE. (1988; 160). Alan Davis, 6 Grey Street, Perth PH2 0JJ. 01738 622480.

Wetland Bird Survey Organisers
MONTROSE BASIN. Ian Hutchison, 13 Eddie Avenue, Brechin, Angus DD9 6YD.
TAY ESTUARY. Norman Elkins, 18 Scotstarvit View, Cupar, Fife KY15 5DX. 01334
654348.
ANGUS (excl Montrose Basin). Toby Green, Herdhill Cottage, Westmuir Road,
Kirriemuir, Angus DD8 5LG. 01575 575676.
PERTHSHIRE. Euan D Cameron, 3 Stormont Place, Scone, Perth PH2 6SR. 01738
552111.

Wildlife Hospital
SCOTTISH SPCA MIDDLEBANK WILDLIFE CENTRE. Masterton Road,
Dunfermline. 01383 412520. Rehabilitation of all species. Oiled bird cleaning unit.
Call SSPCA Control on 0131 339 0111.

WESTERN ISLES

Bird Recorder
Brian Rabbitts, 6 Carinish, Lochmaddy, North Uist HS6 5HL. 01876 580328;
brian.rabbitts@virgin.net.

Bird Report
OUTER HEBRIDES BIRD REPORT (1989-). From Recorder.

BTO Regional Representatives & Regional Development Officer
BENBECULA & THE UISTS RR & RDO. Paul R Boyer, 96 Carnan, South Uist,
Eochar, Lochboisdale, Western Isles HS8 5QX. Home 01870 610253; Work 01896
754333 & ask to bleep.
LEWIS & HARRIS RR. 1. Tony Pendle, 3 Linsiadar, Isle of Lewis HS2 9DR. 01851
621311. 2. Chris Reynolds, 50 Strouden Avenue, Bournemouth, Dorset BH8 9HX.
01202 528483.

Ringing Group
SHIANTS AUK RG. David Steventon, Welland House, 207 Hurdsfield Road,
Macclesfield, Cheshire SK10 2PX. 01625 421936.

Wetland Bird Survey Organisers
HARRIS & LEWIS. Peter Cunningham, Aros, 10 Barony Square, Stornoway, Isle of
Lewis HS1 2TQ. 01851 702423.
BENBECULA & THE UISTS. Paul R Boyer, 96 Carnan, Eochar, Lochboisdale,
South Uist, Western Isles HS8 5QX. 01870 610253.

WALES

Bangor Bird Group

Bird Report & Club see Welsh Ornithological Society in National Directory.

BTO Honorary Wales Officer
Dr Derek Thomas, Laburnum Cottage, 12 Manselfield Road, Murton, Swansea SA3
3AR. Home 01792 232623; Work 01792 205678 ext 4630.

NORTH WALES

Bird Atlas/Avifauna
The Birds of Caernarfonshire (1998, from Lionel Pilling, 51 Brighton Close, Rhyl LL18
3HL).

Bird Recorders
ANGLESEY. Stephen Culley, c/o 2 Gwelfor Estate, Cemaes Bay, Anglesey LL67
0NL.
CAERNARVON. John Barnes, Fach Goch, Waunfawr, Caernarfon, LL55 4YS.
01286 650362.
DENBIGHSHIRE & FLINTSHIRE. Norman Hallas, 63 Park Avenue, Wrexham
LL12 7AW. Tel/fax 01978 290522.
MERIONETH. D L Smith, 3 Smithfield Lane, Dolgellau, Gwynedd LL40 1BU. 01341
421064.

Bird Reports
BARDSEY BIRD OBSERVATORY ANNUAL REPORT. From Warden, see
Reserves.
CAMBRIAN BIRD REPORT (sometime Gwynedd Bird Report) (1953-). From
Rhion Pritchard, Pant Afonig, Hafod Lane, Bangor, Gwynedd LL57 4BU.
CLWYD BIRD REPORT. Latest published is 1992.
CONNAHS QUAY NATURE RESERVE REPORT (biennial). From Warden, see
Reserves.
DEESIDE NATURALISTS' SOCIETY BIRD REPORT 1992-96. From Mrs M
Dunne, 23 Larne Drive, Broughton, Chester.
MEIRIONNYDD BIRD REPORT. Published in Cambrian Bird Report (above).
WREXHAM BIRDWATCHERS' SOCIETY ANNUAL REPORT (1982-). From
Secretary, Wrexham Birdwatchers' Society.

BTO Regional Representatives & Regional Development Officer
ANGLESEY RR & RDO. Jim Clark, Glan Dwr, Llyn Traffwll, Caergeiliog, Holyhead LL65 3LR. Home 01407 741536; Work 01407 730762 fax 07070 711660.
CAERNARFON RR. John Barnes, Fach Goch, Waunfawr, Caernarfon, LL55 4YS. 01286 650362.
CLWYD EAST RR. Vacant.
CLWYD WEST RR (Acting). David Jones, Groesffordd Las, Maenan, Llanrwst, Conway LL26 0YR. 01492 660614.
MERIONETH RR. Peter Haveland, Ty Manceinion, Penmachno, Betws-y-Coed, Gwynedd LL24 0UD. Tel/fax 01690 760337; e-mail peter.haveland@tesco.net.

Clubs
BANGOR BIRD GROUP. (1947; 90). Secretary, Bangor Bird Group, Treborth Botanic Gardens, Bangor LL57 2RQ.
CAMBRIAN ORNITHOLOGICAL SOCIETY. (1952; 150). David Papworth, Llican Isa, Tyn y Groes, Conwy, N Wales LL32 8TA. 01492 650287.
CLWYD ORNITHOLOGICAL SOCIETY. (1956; 53). E E Jones, Sandiway, Llanasa, Holywell, Flints CH8 9NE. 01745 852984.
DEE ESTUARY CONSERVATION GROUP. (1973; 22 grps). A Gouldstone, RSPB, Maes y Ffynnon, Penrhosgarnedd, Bangor, Gwynedd.
DEESIDE NATURALISTS' SOCIETY. (1973; 400). R A Roberts, 38 Kelsterton Road, Connah's Quay, Flints CH5 4BJ.
WREXHAM BIRDWATCHERS' SOCIETY. (1974; 90). Miss Marian Williams, 10 Lake View, Gresford, Wrexham, Clwyd LL12 8PU. 01978 854633.

Ringing Groups
BARDSEY BIRD OBSERVATORY. Steven Stansfield, Bardsey Island, off Aberdaron, Pwllheli, Gwynedd LL53 8DE. 08312 55569.
MERSEYSIDE RG. P Slater, 45 Greenway Road, Speke, Liverpool L24 7RY.
SCAN RG. D Stanyard, Court, Groeslon, Caernarfon LL54 7UE.

RSPB Members' Group
NORTH WALES. (1986; 130). Maureen Douglas, 57 Penrhyn Beach East, Penrhyn Bay, Llandudno, Gwynedd LL30 3RW. 01492 547768.

Wetland Bird Survey Organisers
ANGLESEY & CAERNARFON (other sites). Jim Clark, Glan Dwr, Llyn Traffwll, Caergeiliog, Holyhead LL65 3LR. 01407 741536.
ARTRO, MAWDDACH & TRAETH BACH ESTUARIES. D L Smith, 3 Smithfield Lane, Dolgellau, Gwynedd LL40 1BU. 01341 421064.
CEFNI & BRAINT ESTUARIES. Will Sandison, CCW Hafod Elfyn, Penrhos, Bangor, Gwynedd.
CLWYD (coastal) & RIVER CLWYD. Peter Wellington, 4 Cheltenham Avenue, Rhyl, Denbighs LL18 4DN. 01745 354232.
CLWYD (INLAND). Dr Glenn Morris, 16 Cae'r Gog, Pantymwyn, Mold CH7 5EX.
CONWY ESTUARY. Ian Higginson, Conwy RSPB Nature Reserve, Llandudno Junction, Gwynedd LL31 9XZ. 01492 584091.
DEE ESTUARY. Colin Wells, Burton Point Farm, Station Road, Burton, Nr Neston, South Wirral CH64 5SB. 0151 336 7681.
DULAS BAY. David Wright, Graig Eithin, Mynydd Bodafon, Llanerchymedd, Anglesey LL71 8BG.
DYFI ESTUARY. Dick Squires, Cae'r Berllan, Eglwysfach, Machynlleth, Powys SY20 8TA. 01654 781265.
FORYD BAY. Simon Hugheston-Roberts, Oakhurst, St David's Road, Caernarfon LL55 1EL. 01286 672155.
INLAND SEA. Ivor McLean, 32 Lon-y-Bryn, Bangor LL57 2LD. 01248 362112.

MERIONETH, OTHER SITES. Trefor Owen, Crochendy Twrog, Maentwrog LL41 3YU. 01766 590302.
RED WHARF BAY. Dr Richard Arnold, Dept of Zoology, University College, Bangor LL57 2UW.

Wildlife Trust
NORTH WALES WILDLIFE TRUST. (1963; 2400). 376 High Street, Bangor, Gwynedd LL57 1YE. 01248 351541; fax 01248 353192; e-mail nwwt@cix.co.uk.

SOUTH WALES

Bird Atlas/Avifauna
An Atlas of Breeding Birds in West Glamorgan by David M Hanford *et al* (Gower Ornithological Society, 1992). *Birds of Glamorgan* by Clive Hurford and Peter Lansdown (Published by the authors, c/o National Museum of Wales, Cardiff, 1995).

Bird Recorders
GLAMORGAN (EAST). Steve Moon, 36 Rest Bay Close, Porthcawl, Bridgend CF36 3UN. Home 01656 786571; Work 01656 643170; pager 04325 235790.
GOWER (WEST GLAMORGAN). Robert Taylor, 285 Llangyfelach Road, Brynhyfryd, Swansea SA5 9LB.

Bird Reports
EASTERN GLAMORGAN BIRD REPORT (title varies 1963-95) 1996-. From Secretary, Glamorgan Bird Club.
GOWER BIRDS (1965-). From Secretary, Gower Ornithological Society.

BTO Regional Representatives & Regional Development Officer
EAST (former Mid & South Glam) RR. Rob Nottage, 32 Village Farm, Bonvilston, Cardiff CF5 6TY. 01446 781423.
WEST RR. Bob Howells, Ynys Enlli, 14 Dolgoy Close, West Cross, Swansea SA3 5LT. 01792 405363.
GLAMORGAN RDO. Dr Derek Thomas, 12 Manselfield Road, Murton, Swansea SA3 3AR. Home 01792 232623; Work 01792 205678 ext 4630.

Clubs
CARDIFF NATURALISTS' SOCIETY. (1867; 270). Stephen R Howe, Department of Geology, National Museum of Wales, Cardiff CF1 3NP. Work 01222 573363.
GLAMORGAN BIRD CLUB. (1990; 170). Steve Moon, as above (Bird Recorders).
GOWER ORNITHOLOGICAL SOCIETY. (1956; 120). Audrey Jones, 24 Hazel Road, Uplands, Swansea SA2 0LX. 01792 298859.

Ringing Groups
FLAT HOLM RG. Brian Bailey, Tamarisk House, Wards Court, Frampton-on-Severn, Glos GL2 7DY. E-mail brianhbailey98@freeserve.co.uk
KENFIG RG. Dave Bull, 1 Pantbach, Pentyrch, Cardiff CF4 8TG.

RSPB Members' Groups
CARDIFF & DISTRICT. (1973; 4500). Peter Elkington, 25 Wolfs Castle Avenue, Llanishen, Cardiff CF14 5JS. 01222 752523.
WEST GLAMORGAN. (1985; 421). Mark Johnson, 16 Pant y Telin Road, Portardulais, Swansea SA4 1PZ. 01792 882140.

Wetland Bird Survey Organisers
EAST (former Mid & South Glam). Rob Nottage, 32 Village Farm, Bonvilston, Cardiff CF5 6TY. 01446 781423.
SEVERN ESTUARY. Niall Burton, c/o BTO, The Nunnery, Thetford, Norfolk IP24 2PU. 01842 750050; fax 01842 750030.
WEST. Bob Howells, Ynys Enlli, 14 Dolgoy Close, West Cross, Swansea SA3 5LT. 01792 405363.

Wildlife Hospitals
GOWER BIRD HOSPITAL. Karen Kingsnorth and Simon Allen, Valetta, Sandy Lane, Parkmill, Swansea SA3 2EW. 01792 371630. All species. Prior telephone call requested. Veterinary support.
LLEWELLYN, Paul. 104 Manselfield Road, Murton, Swansea SA3 3AG. 01792 233712. All species of birds but specialist knowledge of raptors. Veterinary support.

Wildlife Trust
GLAMORGAN WILDLIFE TRUST. (1961; 1300). Fountain Road, Tondu, Bridgend CF32 0EH. 01656 724100; fax 01656 729880; e-mail glamorganwt@cix.co.uk.

EAST WALES

Bird Atlas/Avifauna
The Gwent Atlas of Breeding Birds by Tyler, Lewis, Venables & Walton (Gwent Ornithological Society, 1987).

Bird Recorders
BRECONSHIRE. Martin F Peers, Cyffylog, 2 Aberyscir Road, Cradoc, Brecon, Powys LD3 9PB. 01874 623774.
GWENT. Chris Jones, 22 Walnut Drive, Caerleon, Newport, Gwent NP6 1SB. 01633 423439.
MONTGOMERYSHIRE. Brayton Holt, Scops Cottage, Pentrebeirdd, Welshpool, Powys SY21 9DL. 01938 500266.
RADNORSHIRE. Pete Jennings, Penbont House, Elan Valley, Rhayader, Powys LD6 5HS. Home 01597 811522; Work 01597 810880.

Bird Reports
BRECONSHIRE BIRDS (1962-). From Brecknock Wildlife Trust.
GWENT BIRD REPORT (1964-). From Jerry Lewis, Y Bwthyn Gwyn, Coldbrook, Abergavenny, Monmouthshire NP7 9TD. Home 01873 855091; Work 01633 644856.
MONTOMERYSHIRE BIRD REPORT (1981-82-). From Montgomeryshire WT.
RADNOR BIRDS (1987/92-). From Radnorshire Recorder.

BTO Regional Representatives & Regional Development Officer
BRECKNOCK RR. John Lloyd, Cynghordy, Llandovery, Carms SA20 0LN. Home/Work/fax 01550 750202.
GWENT RR. Jerry Lewis, as above (Bird Reports).
MONTGOMERY RR. Brayton Holt, as above (Bird Recorders)
RADNORSHIRE RR & RDO. Pete Jennings, as above (Bird Recorders).

Clubs
BRECKNOCK WILDLIFE TRUST BIRD CLUB. (1993; 115). Jim Vale, Brecknock Wildlife Trust, Lion House, Bethel Square, Brecon, Powys LD3 7AY. 01874 625708.

GWENT ORNITHOLOGICAL SOCIETY. (1964; 350). T J Russell, The Pines, Highfield Road, Monmouth, Gwent NP5 3HP. 01600 716266; e-mail trus716266@aol.com.
MONTGOMERYSHIRE FIELD SOCIETY. (1946; 170). Mrs Hazel Formaggia, Dolfallen Newydd, Llawr-y-Glyn, Caersws, Powys SY17 5RJ. 01686 430674.
MONTGOMERYSHIRE WILDLIFE TRUST BIRD GROUP. (1997; 104). A M Puzey, Four Seasons, Arddleen, Llanymynech, Powys SY22 6RU. 01938 590578.
RADNOR BIRD GROUP. (1986; 600). Pete Jennings, Penbont House, as previous page (Bird Recorders).

Ringing Groups
GOLDCLIFF RG. Vaughan Thomas, Gilgal Cottage, Gilfach, Llanvaches, S Wales NP6 3AZ. 01633 400953.
LLANGORSE RG. Jerry Lewis, as previous page (Bird Reports).

RSPB Members' Group
RADNOR. (1977; 300). Mrs Linda Davies, White House, Aberedw, Builth Wells, Powys LD2 3UW. 01982 560490.

Wetland Bird Survey Organisers
SEVERN ESTUARY. Niall Burton, c/o BTO, The Nunnery, Thetford, Norfolk IP24 2PU. 01842 750050; fax 01842 750030.
GWENT (excl Severn Estuary). Chris Jones, as previous page (Bird Recorders).
POWYS. Martin F Peers, as previous page (Bird Recorders).

Wildlife Trusts
BRECKNOCK WILDLIFE TRUST. (1963; 1100). Lion House, Bethel Square, Brecon, Powys LD3 7AY. 01874 625708; fax 01874 610552; e-mail brecknockwt @cix.co.uk.
GWENT WILDLIFE TRUST. (1963; 1200). 16 White Swan Court, Church Street, Monmouth, Gwent NP5 3NY. 01600 715501; fax 01600 715832; e-mail gwentwildlife @cix.co.uk.
MONTGOMERYSHIRE WILDLIFE TRUST. (1982; 1000). Collot House, 20 Severn Street, Welshpool, Powys SY21 7AD. 01938 555654; fax 01938 556161; e-mail montwt@cix.co.uk.
RADNORSHIRE WILDLIFE TRUST. (1987; 789). Warwick House, High Street, Llandrindod Wells, Powys LD1 6AG. 01597 823298; fax 01597 823274; e-mail radnorshirewt@cix.co.uk.

WEST WALES

Bird Atlas/Avifauna
Birds of Pembrokeshire by Jack Donovan and Graham Rees (Dyfed WT, 1994).

Bird Recorders
CEREDIGION. Hywel Roderick, 32 Prospect Street, Aberystwyth, Ceredigion SY23 1JJ. 01970 617681.
CARMARTHENSHIRE. Rob Hunt, 9 Waun Road, Llanelli, Carmarthenshire SA15 3RS. 01554 778729.
PEMBROKESHIRE. 1. Jack Donovan MBE, The Burren, 5 Dingle Lane, Crundale, Haverfordwest, Pembrokeshire SA62 4DJ. 01437 762673. 2. Graham Rees, 22 Priory Avenue, Haverfordwest, Pembrokeshire SA61 1SQ. 01437 762877.

Bird Reports
CARMARTHENSHIRE BIRDS (1982-). From Carmarthenshire Recorder.
CEREDIGION BIRD REPORT (biennial 1982-87; annual 1988-) From Wildlife Trust West Wales.
PEMBROKESHIRE BIRD REPORT (1981-). From Wildlife Trust West Wales.

BTO Regional Representatives & Regional Development Officer
CARDIGAN RR. Moira Convery, 41 Danycoed, Aberystwyth, SY23 2HD.
CARMARTHEN. Vacant.
PEMBROKE RR & RDO. Vacant.

Clubs
LLANELLI NATURALISTS. (1971; 100). Richard Pryce, Trevethin, School Road, Pwll, Llanelli, Carmarthenshire SA15 4AL. 01554 775847.
PEMBROKESHIRE BIRD GROUP (Section of Dyfed WT). (1993; 60). Rod Hadfield, 104 Nun Street, St David's, Haverfordwest, Pembs SA62 6NX. 01437 720572.

Ringing Group
PEMBROKESHIRE RG. J Hayes, Lagan, 3 Wades Close, Pembroke SA71 4BN.

Wetland Bird Survey Organisers
BURRY, NORTH. Graham Rutt, c/o 13 St James Gardens, Uplands, Swansea SA1 6DY.
DYFI & DYSINNI ESTUARIES. Dick Squires, Cae'r Berllan, Eglwysfach, Machynlleth, Powys SY20 8TA. 01654 781265.
GWENDRAETH, TYWI & TAFF ESTUARIES. Gavin Hall, Visitor Centre, Pembrey Country Park, Pembrey, Carmarthenshire SA16 0EJ. 01269 871580.
NYFER ESTUARY. Vacant.
CARDIGAN (excl Dyfi Estuary). Peter Davis, Felindre, Aberarth, Aberaeron SA46 0LP. 01545 570870.
CARMARTHEN, INLAND. Vacant.
PEMBROKESHIRE. Ms Annie Poole, 1 Rushmoor, Martletwy, Narberth, Pembs SA67 8BB. 01834 891667; e-mail annie@clara.net.

Wildlife Hospitals
NEW QUAY BIRD HOSPITAL. Jean Bryant, Penfoel, Cross Inn, Llandysul, Ceredigion SA44 6NR. 01545 560462. All species of birds. Fully equipped for cleansing oiled seabirds. Veterinary support.
WEST WILLIAMSTON OILED BIRD CENTRE. Mrs J Hains, Lower House Farm, West Williamston, Kilgetty, Pembs SA68 0TL. 01646 651236. Facilities for holding up to 200 Guillemots, etc. for short periods. Initial treatment is given prior to despatch to other washing centres during *very* large oil spills; otherwise birds are washed at the Centre with intensive care and rehabilitation facilities. Also other species. Veterinary support.

Wildlife Trust
WILDLIFE TRUST WEST WALES. (1938; 3100). 7 Market Street, Haverfordwest, Pembrokeshire SA61 1NF. 01437 765462; fax 01437 767163; e-mail june@wildlife-wales.org.uk.

CHANNEL ISLANDS

BTO Regional Representative
Ian Buxton, Le Petit Huquet, La Rue du Hucquet, St Martin, Jersey JE3 6HU. Home
01534 855845; Work 01534 815544.

Ringing Group
The Channel Islands ringing scheme is run by the Société Jersiaise.

Wetland Bird Survey Organiser
INLAND. Glyn Young, Société Jersiase, The Museum, 9 Pier Road, St Helier, Jersey
JE2 4XW.

ALDERNEY

Bird Recorder
Mrs Jill Watson, Huitrier Pies, 9 Rue de Beaumont, Alderney GY9 3XU. Tel/fax
01481 822414.

Bird Report
ALDERNEY SOCIETY ORNITHOLOGY REPORT (1992-). From Recorder.

GUERNSEY

Bird Recorder
Barry Wells, Honeysuckle Cottage, Les Caches, St Martins, Guernsey GY4 6PL.
01481 35634.

Bird Reports
REPORT & TRANSACTIONS OF LA SOCIETE GUERNESIAISE (1882-). From
Recorder.
GUERNSEY BIRD REPORT. From Recorder.

Clubs
LA SOCIETE GUERNESIAISE (Ornithological Section). (1882; 55). Vic Froome, La Cloture, Coutil de Bas Lane, St Sampsons, Guernsey GY2 4XJ. 01481 54841.

RSPB Members' Group
GUERNSEY. (1975; 200). Anne Seebeck, Adelise, Ruette Saumarez, Catel, Guernsey GY5 7TJ. 01481 52884.

Wetland Bird Survey Organiser
COASTAL SITES. Tony Grange, 3/4 Market Street, St Peter Port, Guernsey GY1 1HF.

Wildlife Hospital
GUERNSEY. GSPCA ANIMAL SHELTER. Mrs Chris Guerin, Rue des Truchots, Les Fiers Moutons, St Andrews, Guernsey, Channel Islands GY6 8UD. 01481 57261. All species. Modern cleansing unit for oiled seabirds. 24-hour emergency service. Veterinary support.

JERSEY

Bird Recorder
Tony Paintin, 16 Quennevais Gardens, St Brelade, Jersey, Channel Islands JE3 8LH. 01534 741928.

Bird Report
JERSEY BIRD REPORT. From Secretary (Publications), Société Jersiaise.

Club
SOCIETE JERSIAISE (Ornithological Section). (1948; 40). Roger Noel, 7 Pier Road, St Helier, Jersey JE2 4XW. 01534 58314.

RSPB Members' Group
JERSEY. Robert Burrow, 1 Southlands, Green Road, St Clements, Jersey JE2 6QA. 01534 32167.

Wetland Bird Survey Organiser
COASTAL SITES. Roger Noel, 4 Le Petitte Piece, St Peters, Jersey JE3 7AE. 01534 481409.

Wildlife Hospital
JERSEY. JSPCA ANIMALS' SHELTER. Karen Hayes, 89 St Saviour's Road, St Helier, Jersey JE2 4GJ. 01534 724331; fax 01534 871797; e-mail jspca@super.net. All species. Expert outside support for owls and raptors. Oiled seabird unit. Veterinary surgeon on site. Educational Centre.

ISLE OF MAN

Bird Atlas/Avifauna
Manx Bird Atlas. 2000 is 3rd year of 5-yr research programme. Contact: Chris Sharpe, Greenbank, 33 Mines Road, Laxey, Isle of Man IM4 7NH. 01624 861130; e-mail manxbirdatlas@enterprise.net; http://www.enterprise.net/manxbirdatlas/wren.html.

Bird Recorder
Dr Pat Cullen, Troutbeck, Cronkbourne, Braddan, Isle of Man IM4 4QA. Home: 01624 623308; Work 01624 676774.

Bird Reports
MANX BIRD REPORT (1947-) published in *Peregrine*. From G D Craine, 8 Kissack Road, Castletown, Isle of Man IM9 1NP.
CALF OF MAN BIRD OBSERVATORY ANNUAL REPORT. From Secretary, Manx National Heritage, Manx Museum, Douglas, Isle of Man IM1 3LY.

BTO Regional Representative & Regional Development Officer
RR. Dr Pat Cullen, Troutbeck, Cronkbourne, Braddan, Isle of Man IM4 4QA. Home: 01624 623308; Work 01624 676774.
RDO. Aron Sapsford, 3 Higher Main Road, Upper Foxdale, Isle of Man IM4 3EH. Home 01624 801716; Work 01624 861130.

Club
MANX ORNITHOLOGICAL SOCIETY. (1967; 170). Mrs A C Kaye, Cronk Ny Ollee, Glen Chass, Port St Mary, Isle of Man IM9 5PL. 01624 834015.

Ringing Groups
CALF OF MAN BIRD OBSERVATORY. Tim Bagworth, Calf of Man, c/o Kionslieu, Plantation Hill, Port St Mary, Isle of Man IM14 3DS.
ISLE OF MAN RINGING GROUP. Aron Sapsford, 3 Higher Main Road, Upper Foxdale, Isle of Man IM4 3EH. Home 01624 801716; Work 01624 861130.

Wetland Bird Survey Organiser
Dr Pat Cullen, Troutbeck, Cronkbourne, Braddan, Isle of Man IM4 4QA. Home: 01624 623308; Work 01624 676774.

Wildlife Trust
MANX NATURE CONSERVATION TRUST. (1973; 900). Nature Conservation Centre, Tynwald Mills, St Johns, Isle of Man IM4 3AE. 01624 801985; fax 01624 801022; e-mail manxwt@cix.co.uk.

NORTHERN IRELAND

Bird Recorder
George Gordon, 2 Brooklyn Avenue, Bangor, Co Down BT20 5RB. 01247 455763;
e-mail gordon@ballyholme2.freeserve.co.uk.

Bird Reports
NORTHERN IRELAND BIRD REPORT. From John O'Boyle, 3 Killeen Park,
Belfast BT11 8HH.
IRISH BIRD REPORT. Included in *Irish Birds*, see BirdWatch Ireland in National
Directory.
COPELAND BIRD OBSERVATORY REPORT. From Warden, see Reserves.

BTO Regional Representatives
BTO IRELAND OFFICER. Ken Perry, 43 Portstewart Road, Coleraine, Co
Londonderry BT52 1RW. 028 703 42985; 028 703 328053; e-mail KWPerry
@compuserve.com.
ANTRIM & BELFAST. Vacant.
ARMAGH. David W A Knight, 20 Mandeville Drive, Tandragee, Craigavon, Co
Armagh BT62 2DQ. 01762 840658.
DOWN. Vacant.
LONDONDERRY. Charles Stewart, Bravallen, 18 Duncrun Road, Bellarena,
Limavady, Co Londonderry BT49 0JD.
TYRONE SOUTH & FERMANAGH. Philip S Grosse, 30 Tullybroom Road,
Clogher, Co Tyrone BT76 0UW. 016625 48606; e-mail phigro@aol.com.
TYRONE NORTH. Mary Mooney, 20 Leckpatrick Road, Ballymagorry, Strabane,
Co Tyrone BT82 0AL.

Clubs
NORTHERN IRELAND BIRDWATCHERS' ASSOCIATION See National
Directory.
NORTHERN IRELAND ORNITHOLOGISTS' CLUB See National Directory.
CASTLE ESPIE BIRDWATCHING CLUB. (1995; 59). Dot Blakely, 31 Clandeboye
Way, Bangor, Co Down BT19 1AD. 01247 450784.

Ringing Groups
ANTRIM & ARDS RG. M McNeely, 17 Lower Quilly Road, Dromore, Co Down
BT25 1NL.
COPELAND BIRD OBSERVATORY. C W Acheson, 28 Church Avenue,
Dunmurry, Belfast BT17 9RS.
NORTH DOWN RG. J Forsyth MBE, 24 Malone Park, Belfast BT9 6NJ. 01232
665534; e-mail forsyth.i@btinternet.com.

RSPB Members' Groups

ANTRIM. (1977; 23). Agnes Byron, 59 Tirgracey Road, Mucamore, Co Antrim BT41 4PS. 01849 462207.

BANGOR. (1973; 45). Fulton Somerville, 48 Gortland Park, Belfast BT5 7NU. 01232 794045.

BELFAST. (1970; 130). Ron Houston, 7 Kingsdale Park, Belfast BT5 7BY. 01232 796188.

COLERAINE. (1978; 45). John Clarke, 48 Shelbridge Park, Coleraine, Co Londonderry BT52 2HP. 0780 3427424.

FERMANAGH. (1977; 28). Doreen Morrison, 91 Derrin Road, Cornagrade, Enniskillen, Co Fermanagh BT74 6BA. 01365 326654.

LARNE. (1974; 55). Jimmy Christie, 254 Coast Road, Ballygally, Larne, Co Antrim BT40 2QL. 01574 583223.

LISBURN. (1978; 31). John Scott, 22 Whitla Road, Lisburn, Co Antrim BT28 3PP. 01846 601864.

Wetland Bird Survey Organisers

ANTRIM, BELFAST LOUGH. Ian Enlander, Environment & Heritage Service, Commonwealth House, 35 Castle Street, Belfast BT1 1GU. 01232 251477.

ANTRIM, LARNE LOUGH. Billy Hilditch, 18 McCrea's Brae, Whitehead, Carrickfergus, Co Antrim BT38 9NZ. 01960 372488.

ANTRIM, LOUGHS NEAGH & BEG. Warden, Lough Neagh Nature Reserves, Oxford Island, Craigavon, Co Armagh BT66 6NJ. 028 383 22398; fax 028 383 29027.

ANTRIM, OTHER SITES. Jim Wells, 16 Bridge Road, Lurgan, Co Armagh BT67 9LA. 01762 321837.

ARMAGH, LOUGHS NEAGH & BEG. Warden, Lough Neagh Nature Reserves, as above.

DOWN, BELFAST LOUGH. Ian Enlander, as above.

DOWN, CARLINGFORD LOUGH. Frank Carroll, 292 Barcroft Park, Newry, Co Down BT35 8ET. 01693 68015.

DOWN, DUNDRUM BAY. Hugh Thurgate, Murlough Stables, Keel Point, Dundrum, Co Down BT33 0NQ.

DOWN, LOUGHS NEAGH & BEG. Warden, Lough Neagh Nature Reserves, as above.

DOWN, OUTER ARDS. Ian Enlander, as above.

DOWN, STRANGFORD LOUGH. Paddy Mackie, Mahee Island, Comber, Newtownards, Co Down BT23 6EP.

FERMANAGH. Ian Enlander, as above.

LONDONDERRY, BANN ESTUARY. Hill Dick, 33 Hopefield Avenue, Portrush, Co Antrim BT56 8HB.

LONDONDERRY, LOUGH FOYLE. Dave Allen, RSPB, Belvoir Park Forest, Belfast BT8 4QT. 01232 491547.

LONDONDERRY, LOUGHS NEAGH & BEG. Warden, Lough Neagh Nature Reserves, as above.

TYRONE, LOUGHS NEAGH & BEG. Warden, Lough Neagh Nature Reserves, as above.

Wildlife Hospital

TACT WILDLIFE CENTRE. Mrs Patricia Nevines, 2 Crumlin Road, Crumlin, Co Antrim BT29 4AD. 028 944 22900. All categories of birds treated and rehabilitated; released where practicable, otherwise given a home. Visitors (inc. school groups and organisations) welcome by prior arrangement. Veterinary support.

Wildlife Trust

ULSTER WILDLIFE TRUST. (1978; 2100). 3 New Line, Crossgar, Co Down BT30 9EP. 028 44 830282; fax 028 44 830888; e-mail ulsterwt@cix.co.uk.

REPUBLIC OF IRELAND

Bird Recorders
1. Oran O'Sullivan, BirdWatch Ireland, Ruttledge House, 8 Longford Place, Monkstown, Co Dublin. +353 (0)1 2804322; fax +353 (0)1 2844407. 2. Rarities. Paul Milne, 62 The Village, Bettyglen, Raheny, Dublin 5. +353 (0)1 8317925; e-mail paulm@ionasoft.com; http://homepage.tinet.ie/~birdwatch.

Bird Reports
IRISH BIRD REPORT. Included in *Irish Birds* (see BirdWatch Ireland in National Directory).
CORK BIRD REPORT (1963-71; 1976-). From IWC Cork Branch secretary.
EAST COAST BIRD REPORT (1980-). From Tom Cooney, 42 All Saints Road, Raheny, Dublin 5.

BTO Regional Representative
BTO IRELAND OFFICER. Ken Perry, 43 Portstewart Road, Coleraine, Co Londonderry BT52 1RW. From Ireland: 08 028 703 42985; fax 08 028 703 328053; e-mail KWPerry@compuserve.com. From UK: 028 703 42985; fax 028 703 328053.

BirdWatch Ireland Branches
Branches may be contacted in writing c/o BirdWatch Ireland, Ruttledge House, 8 Longford Place, Monkstown, Co Dublin.

Ringing Groups
CAPE CLEAR BIRD OBSERVATORY. M E O'Donnell, 4 Ballyfree, Glenealy, Co Wicklow. E-mail modonnell@oceanfree.net.
GREAT SALTEE RS. O J Merne, National Parks & Wildlife, 7 Ely Place, Dublin 2. +353 (0)1 6472389; fax +353 (0)1 6620283.
MUNSTER RG. K P Collins, 35 Tower House, New Quay, Clonmel, Co Tipperary, Ireland. E-mail kevcoll@indigo.ie.
SHANNON WADER RG. P A Brennan, The Crag, Stonehall, Newmarket-on-Fergus, Co Clare.

Wildlife Hospital
MONARD GLEN SANCTUARY. Tom O'Byrne, Monard Glen, Rathpeacon, Co Cork, Ireland. Tel/fax +353 (0)21 385564. All bird species. Aviaries and enclosures. Veterinary support.

PART TWO
NATIONAL DIRECTORY

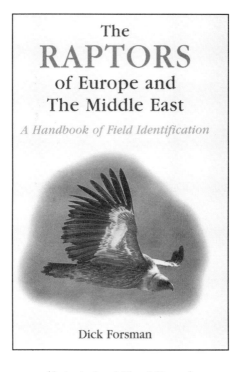

(Actual size 240 x 160 mm)

The Raptors of Europe and the Middle East: a handbook of field identification, by Dick Forsman. T & AD Poyser, 1999, 589p. £29.95. ISBN 0 85661 098 4. Hbk.

As befits a study of raptors, this volume concentrates on field characters and impressions rather than in-depth plumage descriptions. The principal illustrations are photographs - a wonderful collection of invaluable references. They are augmented by 'close-ups' of such as head patterns and wing profiles. Extensive field experience illuminates the species texts, which begin with an identification summary and go into detail of near and distant views, age and sex, confusion species, variations, moult, hunting and prey, distribution and movements. An essential book that prepares you for encounters with the birds and puts order into your field notes in a very helpful and reassuring way.

NATIONAL ORGANISATIONS

Figures appearing in brackets following the names of organisations indicate the date of formation and, if relevant, the current membership. Alternatively this information may appear in the descriptive notes.

ARMY ORNITHOLOGICAL SOCIETY. (1960; 250). Hon Secretary, Lt Col P S Bennett, SO1 DEF LOG(OPS/EX), ACDS(L), Room 7261, MOD Main Building, Whitehall, London SW1 2HB. 0171 218 6750; mobile 07771 614225. Activities include field meetings, expeditions, the preparation of checklists of birds on Ministry of Defence property, conservation advice and an annual bird count. Publishes an annual journal called *The Adjutant* and bulletins/newsletters twice a year. Open to MOD employees and civilians who have an interest in their local MOD estate.

ASSOCIATION FOR THE PROTECTION OF RURAL SCOTLAND. (1926). Director, Mrs Joan Geddes, Gladstone's Land, 3rd Floor, 483 Lawnmarket, Edinburgh EH1 2NT. 0131 225 7012; fax 0131 225 6592; e-mail aprs@aprs.org.uk; http://www.aprs.org.uk/. Works to protect Scotland's countryside from unnecessary or inappropriate development, recognising the needs of those who live and work there and the necessity of reconciling these with the sometimes competing requirements of recreational use.

ASSOCIATION OF COUNTY RECORDERS AND EDITORS. (1993; 120). Secretary, M J Rogers, 2 Churchtown Cottages, Towednack, St Ives, Cornwall TR26 3AZ. 01736 796223. The basic aim of ACRE is to promote best practice in the business of producing county bird reports, in the work of Recorders and in problems arising in managing record systems and archives. Organises periodic conferences and publishes *newsACRE*.

BARN OWL TRUST. Senior Conservation Officer, David Ramsden, Waterleat, Ashburton, Devon TQ13 7HU. 01364 653026; e-mail barnowl@eclipse.co.uk; http://www.eclipse.co.uk/barnowl. Registered charity. Aims to conserve the Barn Owl and its environment through conservation, education, research and information. Free leaflets on all aspects of Barn Owl conservation. Educational material inc. video and resource pack. Book 'Barn Owls on Site' (guide for planners and developers, priced). Works with and advises landowners, farmers, planners, countryside bodies and others to promote a brighter future for Britain's Barn Owls. Currently pursuing proactive conservation schemes in SW England to secure breeding sites and form a stable basis for population expansion. Phone on Tu and Thu only; send SAE for information.

BIRD OBSERVATORIES COUNCIL. Secretary, Peter Howlett, c/o Dept of Biodiversity, National Museums & Galleries, Cardiff CF10 3NP. 0292 057 3233; fax 0292 023 9009; e-mail peter.howlett@nmgw.ac.uk. The BOC replaced the Bird Observatories Committee in 1970. Its objectives are to provide a forum for establishing closer links and co-operation between individual autonomous observatories and to help co-ordinate the work carried out by them. All accredited bird observatories affiliated to the Council undertake a ringing programme and provide ringing experience to those interested; most also provide accommodation for visiting birdwatchers.

BIRD STAMP SOCIETY. (1986; 250). Secretary, Graham Horsman, 9 Cowley Drive, Worthy Down, Winchester, Hants SO21 2QW. 01962 889381; fax 01962 887423. Quarterly journal *Flight* contains philatelic and ornithological articles. Lists all new issues and identifies species.

BIRDWATCH IRELAND. Oran O'Sullivan, Ruttledge House, 8 Longford Place, Monkstown, Co Dublin, Ireland. (01) 2804322; fax (01) 2844407; e-mail bird@indigo.ie. The trading name of the Irish Wildbird Conservancy, a voluntary body founded in 1968 by the amalgamation of the Irish Society for the Protection of Birds, the Irish Wildfowl Conservancy and the Irish Ornithologists' Club. Now the BirdLife International partner in Ireland. Supported by over 5,000 members and 21 voluntary branches. Conservation policy is based on formal research and surveys of birds and their habitats. Owns or manages an increasing number of reserves (see Section 9: Reserves and Observatories) to protect threatened species and habitats. Publishes *Wings* quarterly and *Irish Birds* annually, in addition to annual project reports and survey results.

BRITISH BIRDS RARITIES COMMITTEE. Hon Secretary, M J Rogers, 2 Churchtown Cottages, Towednack, St Ives, Cornwall TR26 3AZ. 01736 796223. Set up in 1959, the Committee's function is to adjudicate records of species of rare occurrence in Britain (marked 'R' in the Log Charts). Its annual report, which includes records accepted by the Northern Ireland Birdwatchers' Association, is published in *British Birds*. As from 1981, the BBRC also assesses records from the Channel Islands and includes them in its report. In the case of rarities trapped for ringing, records should be sent to the Ringing Office of the British Trust for Ornithology, who will in turn forward them to the BBRC.

BRITISH FALCONERS' CLUB. (1927; 1200). Director, John R Fairclough, Home Farm, Hints, Tamworth, Staffs B78 3DW. Tel/fax 01543 481737; e-mail falconers @zetnet.co.uk; www.users.zetnet.co.uk/BFC. A national body with regional branches. Largest falconry club in Europe. Its aim is to encourage falconers in the responsible practice of their sport and in their efforts to conserve birds of prey by breeding, holding educational meetings and providing facilities, guidance and advice to those wishing to take up the sport. Publishes *The Falconer* annually.

BRITISH MUSEUM (NATURAL HISTORY) see Walter Rothschild Zoological Museum

BRITISH ORNITHOLOGISTS' CLUB. (1892; 600). Hon Secretary, Cdr M B Casement OBE RN, Dene Cottage, West Harting, Petersfield, Hants GU31 5PA. 01730 825280; e-mail mbcasement@aol.com.uk. Membership open only to members of the British Ornithologists' Union. A registered charity, the Club's objects are 'the promotion of scientific discussion between members of the BOU, and others interested in ornithology, and to facilitate the publication of scientific information in connection with ornithology'. About eight evening dinner meetings are held each year. Publishes the *Bulletin of the British Ornithologists' Club* quarterly, also (since 1992) a continuing series of Occasional Publications.

BRITISH ORNITHOLOGISTS' UNION. Administrator, Steve Dudley, c/o Natural History Museum, Akeman Street, Tring, Herts HP23 6AP. 01442 890080; fax 01442 890693; e-mail bou@bou.org.uk. The BOU, founded in 1858 by Professor Alfred Newton FRS, is one of the world's oldest and most respected ornithological societies. With a membership over 2,000 worldwide, its aim is to promote ornithology within the scientific and birdwatching communities, in Britain and around the world. This is largely achieved by the publication of its quarterly international journal, *Ibis* (1859-), one of the world's leading ornithological journals featuring work at the cutting edge of our understanding of the world's birdlife. The BOU also has an active programme of meetings, seminars and conferences at which birdwatchers and other ornithologists can learn more about work being undertaken both in this country and overseas. This often includes research projects that have received financial assistance from the BOU's ongoing programme of Ornithological Research Grants, which includes student sponsorship. Part of the BOU Library is housed at the Linnean Society, whilst copies of exchange journals, books reviewed in *Ibis* and offprints are held as part of the Alexander Library in the Zoology Department of the University of Oxford (see Edward Grey Institute).

BRITISH ORNITHOLOGISTS' UNION RECORDS COMMITTEE. Secretary, Dr Tim Melling, c/o The Natural History Museum, Akeman Street, Tring, Herts HP23 6AP. 01442 890080; fax 01442 890693; e-mail bourc.sec@bou.org.uk. The BOURC is a standing committee of the British Ornithologists' Union. Its function is to maintain the British List, the official list of birds recorded in Great Britain. Up-to-date versions are published annually as *The British List* which is distributed free to British birdwatchers via the popular birdwatching magazines. Where vagrants are involved it is concerned only with those which relate to potential additions to the British List (ie first records). In this it differs from the British Birds Rarities Committee (qv). In maintaining the British List, it also differs from the BBRC in that it examines, where necessary, pre-1958 records, monitors introduced species for possible admission to or deletion from the List, and reviews taxonomy and nomenclature generally. BOURC reports are published in the BOU's journal, *Ibis*. Decisions contained in these reports which affect the List are also announced via the popular birdwatching press and incorporated in *The British List*.

British Trust for Ornithology

Director, Dr Jeremy J D Greenwood, National Centre for Ornithology, The Nunnery, Thetford, Norfolk IP24 2PU. 01842 750050; fax 01842 750030; e-mail btostaff@bto.org. A registered charity formed in 1933, the BTO is financed by membership subscriptions, by a partnership contract from the Joint Nature Conservation Committee on behalf of English Nature, Scottish Natural Heritage and the Countryside Council for Wales; under a contract from the Environment and Heritage Service in Northern Ireland; and by contracts from other Government organisations, industry and voluntary conservation bodies. Governed by an elected Council, it has a rapidly growing membership of over 10,500 birdwatchers and enjoys the support of a large number of county and local birdwatching clubs and societies through the BTO/Bird Clubs Partnership. Its aims are: 'To promote and encourage the wider understanding, appreciation and conservation of birds through scientific studies using the combined skills and enthusiasm of its members, other birdwatchers and staff.'

The Populations Research Department incorporates the National Ringing Scheme, the Nest Record Scheme, the Breeding Bird Survey (in collaboration with JNCC and RSPB), the Common Birds Census, and the Waterways Bird Survey - all contributing to an integrated programme of population monitoring. The Habitats Research Department runs projects on the birds of farmland and woodland, also (in collaboration with WWT, RSPB and JNCC) the Wetland Bird Survey. Garden Birdwatch, which started in 1995, now has approximately 10,000 participants. The Trust has 140 voluntary regional representatives (see County Directory) who organise fieldworkers for the BTO's programme of national surveys in which members participate. The results of these co-operative efforts are communicated to government departments, local authorities, industry and conservation bodies for effective action. For details of current activities see National Projects. Members receive *BTO News* six times a year and have the option of subscribing to the thrice-yearly journal, *Bird Study* and twice yearly *Ringing & Migration*. Local meetings are held in conjunction with bird clubs and societies; there are regional and national birdwatchers' conferences, and specialist courses in modern censusing techniques. Grants are made for research, and members have the use of a lending and reference library at Thetford and the Alexander Library at the Edward Grey Institute of Field Ornithology (qv).

BRITISH WATERFOWL ASSOCIATION. Evelyn Van Vliet, Olney Park Cottage, Yardley Road, Olney, Bucks MK46 5EJ. 01234 713947. The BWA is an association of enthusiasts interested in keeping, breeding and conserving all types of waterfowl, including wildfowl and domestic ducks and geese. It is a registered charity, without trade affiliations, dedicated to educating the public about waterfowl and the need for conservation as well as to raising the standards of keeping and breeding ducks, geese and swans in captivity.

BRITISH WILDLIFE REHABILITATION COUNCIL. Secretary, Tim Thomas, Wildlife Department, RSPCA, Causeway, Horsham, W Sussex RH12 1HG. Established in 1987. Supported by many national bodies including the Zoological

Society of London, the British Veterinary Zoological Society, the RSPCA, the SSPCA, and the Vincent Wildlife Trust. Its aim is to promote the care and rehabilitation of wildlife casualties through the exchange of information between people such as rehabilitators, zoologists and veterinary surgeons who are active in this field. Organises an annual symposium or workshop. Publications include a newsletter and a nationwide list of rehabilitators.

BTCV (formerly British Trust for Conservation Volunteers). Chief Executive, Tom Flood, 36 St Mary's Street, Wallingford, Oxon OX10 0EU. 01491 839766. Set up in 1959 to involve people of all ages in practical conservation work, much of which directly affects bird habitats. There are over 2000 local conservation groups affiliated to BTCV, which also provides a service to many other bodies including the JNCC, RSPB, WWT and county wildlife trusts, national parks, water authorities, local authorities and private landowners. Runs over 750 training courses annually and offers working holidays in UK and overseas. Publishes a quarterly newsletter, *The Conserver*, practical handbooks and other publications. Further information and a list of local offices is available from the above address.

CAMPAIGN FOR THE PROTECTION OF RURAL WALES. Director, Merfyn Williams, Ty Gwyn, 31 High Street, Welshpool, Powys SY21 7YD. 01938 552525/556212; fax 552741; e-mail director@cprw.org.uk; www.cprw.org.uk.

CANADA GOOSE STUDY GROUP. Dr C B Thomas, Dept of Chemistry, University of York, Heslington, York YO10 5DD. Fax 01904 432516; e-mail cbt1@york.ac.uk. No longer active in ringing, the Group still functions to monitor records.

COUNTRY LANDOWNERS' ASSOCIATION. Director-General, Julian Anderson, 16 Belgrave Square, London SW1X 8PQ. 0171 235 0511. The CLA is at the heart of rural life and is the voice of the countryside for England and Wales, campaigning on issues which directly affect those who live and work in rural communities. It represents the interests of 50,000 members who together manage 60% of the countryside. CLA members range from some of the largest landowners, with interests in forest, moorland, water and agriculture, to some of the smallest with little more than a paddock or garden.

COUNTRYSIDE AGENCY. Chief Executive, Richard Wakeford, John Dower House, Crescent Place, Cheltenham, Glos GL50 3RA. 01242 521381; fax 01242 584270. Established in April 1999, succeeding the Countryside Commission. The leading organisation concerned with landscape conservation and with informal recreation in and public access to the countryside in England. Among a wide-ranging remit, much of it affecting the birdwatcher, the Agency promotes understanding of the countryside among decision makers, landowners and managers, and the general public; advises the Government on countryside issues; designates national parks and areas of outstanding natural beauty, establishes national trails and defines heritage coasts; gives grants to promote countryside conservation and recreation and access projects; pioneers new techniques in conservation and recreation management; and undertakes research to establish the facts about landscape change and leisure needs.

Offices
North East Region. Warwick House, Grantham Road, Newcastle upon Tyne NE2 1QF. 0191 232 8252; fax 0191 222 0185

North West Region. Bridgewater House, Whitworth Street, Manchester M1 6LT. 0161 237 1061; fax 0161 237 1062

South West Region. Bridge House, Sion Place, Clifton Down, Bristol BS8 4AS. 0117 973 9966; fax 0117 923 8086

Yorkshire & The Humber Region. Victoria Wharf, Embankment IV, Sovereign Street, Leeds LS1 4BA. 0113 246 9222; fax 0113 246 0353

East Midlands Region. 18 Market Place, Bingham, Nottingham NG13 9AP. 01949 876200; fax 01949 876222

West Midlands Region. Vincent House, 92-93 Edward Street, Birmingham B1 2RA. 0121 233 9399; fax 0121 233 9286

Eastern Region. 110 Hills Road, Cambridge CB2 1LQ. 01223 354462, fax 01223 313850

South East Region. 4th Floor, 71 Kingsway, London WC2B 6ST, 0171 831 3510; fax 0171 831 1439.

COUNTRYSIDE COUNCIL FOR WALES. Plas Penrhos, Ffordd Penrhos, Bangor, Gwynedd LL57 2LQ. 01248 385500; fax 01248 355782. CCW is the Government's statutory adviser on wildlife, countryside and maritime conservation matters in Wales. It is the executive authority for the conservation of habitats and wildlife. Through partners, CCW promotes protection of landscape, opportunities for enjoyment, and support of those who live, work in, and manage the countryside. It enables these partners, including local authorities, voluntary organisations and interested individuals, to pursue countryside management projects through grant aid. CCW is accountable to the National Assembly for Wales which appoints its Council members and provides its annual grant-in-aid.

Area Offices

West Area Plas Gogerddan, Aberystwyth SY23 3EE. 01970 828551; fax 01970 828314

North West Area Bryn Menai, Holyhead Road, Bangor LL57 2EF. 01248 373100; fax 01248 370734

South Area Unit 4, Castleton Court, Fortran Road, St Mellons, Cardiff CF3 0LT. 01222 772400; fax 01222 772412

East Area First Floor, Ladywell House, Park Street, Newtown, Powys SY15 1RD. 01686 626799; fax 01686 629556

North East Area Victoria House, Grosvenor Street, Mold CH7 1EJ. 01352 754000; fax 01352 752346

CPRE (formerly Council for the Protection of Rural England). Director, Ms K Parminter, Warwick House, 25 Buckingham Palace Road, London SW1W 0PP. 0171 976 6433; fax 0171 976 6373; e-mail info@cpre.org.uk; www.greenchannel.com/cpre. Patron HM The Queen. Formed in 1926, CPRE now has 43 county branches, 200 local groups and 45,000 members. It seeks to provide well researched and practical solutions to problems affecting the English countryside. Membership open to all.

DEPARTMENT OF THE ENVIRONMENT FOR NORTHERN IRELAND. Bob Bleakley, Environment and Heritage Service, Commonwealth House, 35 Castle Street, Belfast BT1 1GU. 01232 546521. EHS is responsible for the declaration and management of National Nature Reserves, the declaration of Areas of Special Scientific Interest, the administration of Wildlife Refuges, the classification of Special Protection Areas under the EC Birds Directive, and the designation of Ramsar sites and of Special Areas of Conservation under the EC Habitats Directive. It administers the Nature Conservation and Amenity Lands (Northern Ireland) Order 1985, the

Wildlife (Northern Ireland) Order 1985, the Game Acts and the Conservation (Natural Habitats, etc) Regulations (NI) 1995.

 **EDWARD GREY INSTITUTE OF FIELD ORNITHOLOGY.** Director, Prof C M Perrins LVO, FRS, Department of Zoology, South Parks Road, Oxford OX1 3PS. 01865 271275. The EGI takes its name from Edward Grey, first Viscount Grey of Fallodon, a life-long lover of birds and former Chancellor of the University of Oxford, who gave his support to an appeal for its foundation capital. Formally set up in 1938, the Institute now has a permanent research staff; it usually houses some twelve to fifteen research students, two or three senior visitors and post-doctoral research workers. The EGI also houses Prof Sir John Krebs' Ecology & Behaviour Group, which has specialised in the study of the ecology, demography and conservation of declining farmland birds. Field research is carried out mainly in Wytham Woods near Oxford and on the island of Skomer in West Wales. In addition there are laboratory facilities and aviary space for experimental work; and members of the Institute have access to departmental and university computers. The Institute houses the Alexander Library, probably the largest collection of twentieth-century material on birds outside the USA. Included in its manuscript collection are the papers of W B Alexander, T A Coward, G Eliot Howard, and Edmund Selous. The library of the British Falconers' Club is also maintained there. Library open to staff and graduate students of the Zoology Department of the University, members of the British Ornithologists' Union, the British Trust for Ornithology and the Oxford Ornithological Society. Other *bona fide* ornithologists may use the library by prior arrangement. Normal opening hours are: 9.00 am to 5 pm, Monday to Friday, except during University breaks at Christmas and Easter.

ENGLISH NATURE. Northminster House, Peterborough PE1 1UA. 01733 455100; fax 01733 455103; e-mail enquiries@english-nature.org.uk; http://www.english-nature.org.uk. Established by Parliament in April 1991, English Nature advises Government on nature conservation in England. It promotes, directly and through others, the conservation of England's wildlife and natural features within the wider setting of the UK and its international responsibilities. It selects, establishes and manages National Nature Reserves (many of which are described in Part 9: Reserves and Observatories), and identifies and notifies Sites of Special Scientific Interest. It provides advice and information about nature conservation and supports and conducts research relevant to these functions. Through the Joint Nature Conservation Committee (qv), English Nature works with sister organisations in Scotland and Wales on UK and international nature conservation issues.

Local Teams
Bedfordshire, Cambridgeshire and Northamptonshire. Ham Lane House, Ham Lane, Nene Park, Orton Waterville, Peterborough PE2 5UR. 01733 405840; fax 01733 394093; e-mail beds.cambs.nhants@english-nature.org.uk.
Cornwall. Trevint House, Strangways Villas, Truro TR1 2PA. 01872 262550; fax 01872 262551; e-mail cornwall@english-nature.org.uk.
Cumbria. Juniper House, Murley Moss, Oxenholme Road, Kendal LA9 7RL. 01539 792800; fax 01539 792830; e-mail cumbria@english-nature.org.uk.

Devon. The Old Mill House, 37 North Street, Okehampton EX20 1AR. 01837 55045; fax 01837 55046; e-mail devon@english-nature.org.uk.

Dorset. Slepe Farm, Arne, Wareham, Dorset BH20 5BN. 01929 556688; fax 01929 554752; e-mail dorset@english-nature.org.uk.

East Midlands. The Maltings, Wharf Road, Grantham, Lincs NG31 6BH. 01476 568431; fax 01476 570927; e-mail ingridg@english-nature.org.uk.

Essex, London and Hertfordshire. Harbour House, Hythe Quay, Colchester CO2 8JF. 01206 796666; fax 01206 794466; e-mail essex.herts@english-nature.org.uk.

Hampshire and Isle of Wight. 1 Southampton Road, Lyndhurst, Hants SO43 7BU. 01703 283944; fax 01703 283834; e-mail hants.iwigt@english-nature.org.uk.

Humber to Pennines. Bullring House, Northgate, Wakefield, W Yorks WF1 3BJ. 01924 387010; fax 01924 201507; e-mail humber.pennines@english-nature.org.uk.

Kent. The Countryside Management Centre, Coldharbour Farm, Wye, Ashford, Kent TN25 5DB. 01233 812525; fax 01233 812520; e-mail donnah@english-nature.org.uk.

Norfolk. 60 Bracondale, Norwich NR1 2BE. 01603 620558; fax 01603 762552; e-mail norfolk@english-nature.org.uk.

North and East Yorkshire. Genesis 1, University Road, Heslington, York YO10 5ZQ. 01904 435500; fax 01904 435520; e-mail york@english-nature.org.uk.

North West (Lancashire, Merseyside, Greater Manchester, Wirral). Pier House, 1st Floor, Wallgate, Wigan WN3 4AL. 01942 820342; fax 01942 820364; e-mail northwest@english-nature.org.uk.

Northumbria. Archbold House, Archbold Terrace, Newcastle upon Tyne NE2 1EG. 0191 281 6316; fax 0191 281 6305; e-mail northumbria@english-nature.org.uk.

Peak District and Derbyshire. Manor Barn, Over Haddon, Bakewell, Derbyshire DE45 1JE. 01629 815095; fax 01629 815091; e-mail sues@english-nature.org.uk.

Somerset. Roughmoor, Bishop's Hull, Taunton, Somerset TA1 5AA. 01823 283211; fax 01823 272978; e-mail suef@english-nature.org.uk.

Suffolk. Regent House, 110 Northgate Street, Bury St Edmunds, Suffolk IP33 1HP. 01284 762218; fax 01284 764318; e-mail suffolk@english-nature.org.uk.

Sussex and Surrey. Howard House, 31 High Street, Lewes, E Sussex BN7 2LU. 01273 476595; fax 01273 483063; e-mail sussex.surrey@english-nature.org.uk.

Thames and Chilterns (Buckinghamshire, Berkshire and Oxfordshire). Foxhold House, Crookham Common, Thatcham, Berks RG19 8EL. 01635 268881; fax 01635 268940; e-mail thames.chilterns@english-nature.org.uk.

Three Counties (Gloucestershire, Hereford and Worcester). Bronsil House, Eastnor, Ledbury HR8 1EP. 01531 638500; fax 01531 638501; e-mail three.counties@english-nature.org.uk.

West Midlands (Ches, Shrops, Staffs, Warks, W Mid). Attingham Park, Shrewsbury SY4 4TW. 01743 709611; fax 01743 709303; e-mail adhewens@english-nature.org.uk.

Wiltshire. Prince Maurice Court, Hambleton Avenue, Devizes, Wilts SN10 2RT. 01380 726344; fax 01380 721411; e-mail wiltshire@english-nature.org.uk.

ENVIRONMENT AGENCY (THE). Rio House, Waterside Drive, Aztec West, Almondsbury, Bristol BS12 4UD. 01454 624400. A non-departmental body, created in 1996, sponsored by the Department of the Environment, Transport and the Regions, MAFF and the Welsh Office. Primary aim: to protect and improve the environment and to contribute towards the delivery of sustainable development through the integrated management of air, land and water. Functions include pollution prevention and control, waste minimisation, management of water resources, flood defence, improvement of salmon and freshwater fisheries, conservation of aquatic species, navigation and use of inland and coastal waters for recreation.

Regional Offices

Anglian. Kingfisher House, Goldhay Way, Orton Goldhay, Peterborough PE2 0ZR. 01733 371811; fax 01733 231840.

North East. Rivers House, 21 Park Square South, Leeds LS1 2QG. 0113 244 0191; fax 0113 246 1889.

North West. Richard Fairclough House, Knutsford Road, Warrington WA4 1HG. 01925 53999; fax 01925 415961.

Midlands. Sapphire East, 550 Streetsbrook Road, Solihull B91 1QT. 0121 711 2324; fax 0121 711 5824.

Southern. Guildbourne House, Chatsworth Road, Worthing, W Sussex BN11 1LD. 01903 820692; fax 01903 821832.

South West. Manley House, Kestrel Way, Exeter EX2 7LQ. 01392 444000; fax 01392 444238.

Thames. Kings Meadow House, Kings Meadow Road, Reading RG1 8DQ. 01734 535000; fax 01734 500388.

Welsh. Rivers House, St Mellons Business Park, St Mellons, Cardiff CF2 0LT. 01222 770088; fax 01222 798555.

FARMING AND WILDLIFE ADVISORY GROUP. Chief Executive, Robert Bettley-Smith, National Agricultural Centre, Stoneleigh, Kenilworth, Warwickshire CV8 2RX. 02476 696699; fax 02476 696760. National Technical Manager, Richard Knight. Founded in 1969, FWAG is an independent UK registered charity supported by farmers, government and leading countryside organisations. Its aim is to unite farming and forestry with wildlife and landscape conservation. Has FWAGs in most UK counties. There are 85 Farm Conservation Advisers who give practical advice to farmers and landowners to help them integrate environmental objectives with commercial farming practices.

FIELD STUDIES COUNCIL. Cathy Preston, Preston Montford, Montford Bridge, Shrewsbury SY4 1HW. 01743 850674; fax 01743 850178; e-mail fsc.headoffice @ukonline.co.uk. The Council was created in 1943 to establish Centres where students from schools, universities and colleges of education, as well as individuals of all ages, could stay and study various aspects of the environment under expert guidance. The courses include many for birdwatchers, from beginners to those with experience, providing opportunities to study birdlife on coasts, estuaries, mountains and islands. There are some courses demonstrating bird ringing and others for members of the YOC. The length of the courses varies: many are for a weekend, but there are some of 4, 5, 6 or 7 days' duration. Research workers and naturalists wishing to use the records and resources are welcome. FSC Overseas includes birdwatching in its programme of overseas courses.

The UK Centres are: Blencathra Field Centre (Threlkeld, Keswick, Cumbria CA12 4SG); Dale Fort Field Centre (Haverfordwest, Pembs SA62 3RD); Rhyd-y-creuau, the Drapers' Field Centre (Betws-y-coed, Conwy LL24 0HB); Flatford Mill Field Centre (East Bergholt, Colchester CO7 6UL); Juniper Hall Field Centre (Dorking, Surrey RH5 6DA); Nettlecombe Court, The Leonard Wills Field Centre (Williton, Taunton, Somerset TA4 4HT); Malham Tarn Field Centre (Settle, N Yorks BD24 9PU); Orielton Field Centre (Pembroke, Pembs SA71 5EZ); Preston Montford Field Centre (Montford Bridge, Shrewsbury SY4 1DX); Slapton Ley Field Centre (Slapton, Kingsbridge, Devon TQ7 2QP), Castle Head Field Centre, Grange-over-Sands, Cumbria LA11 6QT - and a Day Centre at Epping Forest Field Centre (High Beach, Loughton, Essex IG10 4AF). Course programmes from FSC Head Office.

FORESTRY COMMISSION. Information Branch, 231 Corstorphine Road, Edinburgh EH12 7AT. 0131 334 0303; fax 0131 334 4473. Forest Enterprise is the executive agency which manages the Commission's forest estate.

Forestry Commission National Offices
England. Great Eastern House, Tenison Road, Cambridge CB1 2DU. 01223 314546; fax 01223 460699
Scotland. As HQ above
Wales. North Road, Aberystwyth, Ceredigion SY23 2EF. 01970 625866; fax: 01970 626177

Forest Enterprise Territorial Offices
England. 340 Bristol Business Park, Coldhurst Lane, Bristol BS31 2BF. 0117 906 6000; fax 0117 931 2859
Scotland. *North.* 21 Church Street, Inverness IV1 1EL. 01463 232811; fax 01463 243846. *South.* 55/57 Moffat Road, Dumfries DG1 1NP. 01387 269171; fax 01387 251491
Wales. Victoria Terrace, Aberystwyth, Ceredigion SY23 2DQ. 01970 612367; fax 01970 625282

FRIENDS OF THE EARTH. (1971; 150,000). 26/28 Underwood Street, London N1 7JQ. 0171 490 1555; http://www.foe.co.uk. One of UK's leading pressure groups, campaigning on a wide range of local, national and international environmental issues. Local groups in England, Wales and Northern Ireland.

GAME CONSERVANCY TRUST. (1933; 27,000). Director General, Dr G R Potts, Fordingbridge, Hampshire SP6 1EF. 01425 652381; fax 01425 655848; e-mail info@game-conservancy.org.uk; http://www.game-conservancy.org.uk. A registered charity which promotes the conservation of game and other wildlife in the British countryside. Over 60 scientists are engaged in detailed research of game ecology and farmland wildlife. Using their results, Game Conservancy Limited advises government, landowners, farmers and conservationists on practical management techniques which will benefit game and wildlife.

GOLDEN ORIOLE GROUP. (1987). Sec. Jake Allsop, 5 Bury Lane, Haddenham, Ely, Cambs CB6 3PR. 01353 740540; e-mail jakeallsop@aol.com. Organises censuses of breeding Golden Orioles in parts of Cambridgeshire, Norfolk and Suffolk. Maintains contact with a network of individuals in other parts of the country where Orioles may or do breed. Studies breeding biology, habitat and food requirements of the species.

HAWK AND OWL TRUST. (1969). Director, Colin Shawyer, 23 High Street, Wheathampstead, Herts AL4 8BB. Tel/fax 01582 832182. (Membership administration: 41b Dartmouth Road, London NW2 4ET). Registered charity dedicated to the conservation and appreciation of all birds of prey including owls. The Trust achieves its major aim of creating and enhancing wild habitats for birds of prey through projects which involve practical research, creative conservation and education. Projects are often conducted in close partnership with landowners, farmers and other countrymen as well as in association with other like-minded organisations. Members are invited to take part in population studies, field surveys, etc. Studies of Barn and Little Owls, Hen Harrier, Hobby and Goshawk are in progress. In 1988 a major project, the Barn Owl Conservation Network was launched in an effort to implement a country-wide programme of habitat creation and enhancement, and provision of artificial nest sites which is achieving considerable success. Recently the Trust has undertaken research projects for the DETR and Highways Agency on the impact of raptor predation on domestic pigeons and the effects of road traffic mortality on Barn Owls and other birds of prey. The Trust's Education Officer manages its National Conservation and Education Centre at Newland Park, Chalfont St Giles, Buckinghamshire. It holds scientific conferences and publishes an annual journal *Raptor*, a newsletter *Peregrine*, and educational materials for all ages.

INSTITUTE OF TERRESTRIAL ECOLOGY. Director, Prof T M Roberts, Monks Wood, Abbots Ripton, Huntingdon PE17 2LS. 01487 773381. The work of the ITE, a component body of the Natural Environment Research Council, includes a range of ornithological research, covering population studies, habitat management and work on the effects of pollution. The Institute has a long-term programme to monitor pesticide and pollutant residues in the corpses of predatory birds sent in by birdwatchers, and carries out detailed studies on affected species (for fuller particulars, including species covered, see 'Predatory Birds Monitoring Scheme' in National Projects). The Biological Records Centre (BRC), which is part of the ITE, is responsible for the national biological data bank on plant and animal distributions (except birds).

IRISH RARE BIRDS COMMITTEE. (1985). Hon Secretary, Paul Milne, 62 The Village, Bettyglen, Raheny, Dublin 5. 01-8317925. Assesses records of species of rare occurrence in the Republic of Ireland. Details of records accepted and rejected are incorporated in the Irish Bird Report, published annually in *Irish Birds*. In the case of rarities trapped for ringing, ringers in the Republic of Ireland are required to send their schedules initially to the National Parks and Wildlife Service, 51 St Stephen's Green, Dublin 2. A copy is taken before the schedules are sent to the British Trust for Ornithology.

JOINT NATURE CONSERVATION COMMITTEE. Business Manager, Monkstone House, City Road, Peterborough PE1 1JY. 01733 562626; fax 01733 555948. Established under the Environmental Protection Act 1990, JNCC is a committee of the three country agencies (English Nature, Scottish Natural Heritage, and the Countryside Council for Wales), together with independent members and representatives from Northern Ireland and the Countryside Agency. It is supported by specialist staff. Its statutory responsibilities include the establishment of common standards for monitoring, the analysis of information and research; advising Ministers on the development and implementation of policies for or affecting nature conservation; the provision of advice and the dissemination of knowledge to any persons about nature conservation; and the undertaking and commissioning of research relevant to these functions. JNCC additionally has the UK responsibility for relevant European and wider international matters. The Species Team, located at the HQ address above, is responsible for terrestrial bird conservation. The Seabirds and Cetaceans Team, which manages the Seabird Colony Register and Monitoring Programme and the Seabirds at Sea Programme, is located at Dunnett House, 7 Thistle Place, Aberdeen AB10 1UZ, tel 01224 655703.

LINNEAN SOCIETY OF LONDON. (1788). Executive Secretary, Dr J C Marsden, Burlington House, Piccadilly, London W1V 0LQ. 020 7434 4479; fax 020 7287 9364; e-mail john@linnean.demon.co.uk; www.linnean.org.uk. Named after Carl Linnaeus, the eighteenth-century Swedish biologist, who created the modern system of scientific biological nomenclature, the Society promotes all aspects of pure and applied biology. It houses Linnaeus's collection of plants, insects and fishes, library and correspondence. The Society has a major reference library of some 100,000 volumes. Publishes the *Biological, Botanical* and *Zoological Journals*, and the *Synopses of the British Fauna*.

MANX NATURE CONSERVATION TRUST see County Directory

MANX ORNITHOLOGICAL SOCIETY see County Directory

NATIONAL BIRDS OF PREY CENTRE. (1967). Mrs J Parry-Jones MBE, Newent, Glos GL18 1JJ. 01531 820286; fax 01531 821389; e-mail jpj@nbpc.demon.co.uk; http://nbpc.co.uk. Concerned with the conservation and captive breeding of all raptors. Over 110 aviaries and 85 species. Birds flown daily. Open Feb-Nov.

NATIONAL SOUND ARCHIVE WILDLIFE SECTION. (1969). Curator, Richard Ranft, British Library, National Sound Archive, 96 Euston Road, London NW1 2DB. 0171 412 7402/3; e-mail nsa-wildsound@bl.uk; www.bl.uk/collections/sound-archive/. (Formerly BLOWS - British Library of Wildlife Sounds). The most comprehensive collection of bird sound recordings in existence: over 100,000 recordings of over 7000 species of birds worldwide, available for free listening. Copies or sonograms of most recordings can be supplied for private study or research and, subject to copyright clearance, for commercial uses. Contribution of new material and enquiries on all aspects of wildlife sounds and recording techniques are welcome. Publishes *Bioacoustics,* CD and cassette guides to bird songs.

NATIONAL TRUST. Head Office, 36 Queen Anne's Gate, London SW1H 9AS. 0171 222 9251. Head of Nature Conservation: Dr H J Harvey, Estates Dept, 33 Sheep Street, Cirencester, Glos GL7 1RQ. 01285 651818. Northern Ireland Office: Rowallane House, Saintfield, Ballynahinch, Co. Down BT24 7LH. 01238 510721. Charity depending on voluntary support of its members and the public. Largest private landowner with over 603,000 acres of land and 565 miles of coast, and conservation society with over 2,400,000 members, in Britain. Founded in 1895. Works for the preservation of places of historic interest or natural beauty, in England, Wales and N Ireland. Under Acts of Parliament it is empowered to declare its land and buildings inalienable and has a right to appeal to Parliament against compulsory orders affecting such land. NT coast and countryside properties are open to the public at all times, subject only to the needs of farming, forestry and the protection of wildlife. Over a quarter of the Trust's land and holding is designated SSSI or ASSI (N Ireland) and about 10% of SSSIs in England and Wales are wholly or partially owned by the Trust, as are 26 NNRs (eg Blakeney Point, Farne Islands, Wicken Fen and large parts of Strangford Lough, N Ireland). Twenty per cent of both Ramsar Sites and SPAs include land owned by the Trust and 71 of the 117 bird species listed in the UK Red Data Book are found on Trust land.

NATIONAL TRUST FOR SCOTLAND. Director, Trevor A Croft, 5 Charlotte Square, Edinburgh EH2 4DU. 0131 226 5922; www.nts.org.uk. An independent charity formed in 1931. 230,000 members. Its 120 properties are described in *Guide to Scotland's Best*.

NATURE PHOTOGRAPHERS' PORTFOLIO. (1944). Hon Secretary, A Winspear-Cundall, 8 Gig Bridge Lane, Pershore, Worcs WR10 1NH. 01386 552103. A small society for photographers of wildlife, especially birds. Circulates postal portfolios of prints and transparencies.

NORTHERN IRELAND BIRDWATCHERS' ASSOCIATION. (1991). Hon Secretary, Chris Murphy, Larches, 12 Belvoir Close, Belvoir Park, Belfast BT8 4PL. 01232 693232. The NIBA Records Committee, established in 1997, has full responsibility for the assessment of records in N Ireland. NIBA also publishes the *Northern Ireland Bird Report*. 'Flightline', Northern Ireland's daily bird news service, is run under the auspices of the NIBA. Contact: George Gordon, 2 Brooklyn Avenue, Bangor, Co Down BT20 5RB. 01247 467408.

NORTHERN IRELAND ORNITHOLOGISTS' CLUB. (1965; 150). Gary Wilkinson, The Roost, 139 Windmill Road, Hillsborough, Co Down BT26 6NP. 01846 639254. Operates two small reserves in Co Down. Co-ordinates Project Barn Owl in NI. Has a regular programme of lectures and field trips for members. Publishes *The Harrier* quarterly.

PEOPLE'S DISPENSARY FOR SICK ANIMALS. (1917). Director General, Mrs Marilyn Rydström, Whitechapel Way, Priorslee, Telford, Shrops TF2 9PQ. 01952 290999. Registered charity. Provides free veterinary treatment for sick and injured animals whose owners qualify for this charitable service. It is dependent entirely upon public support and receives no state aid.

RARE BREEDING BIRDS PANEL. Secretary, Dr Malcolm Ogilvie, Glencairn, Bruichladdich, Isle of Islay PA49 7UN. 01496 850218; e-mail RBBP@indaal.demon. co.uk. Originally formed as a sub-committee of the RSPB in 1968, the RBBP has since 1973 been an independent body funded and supported jointly by the JNCC, the RSPB, *British Birds*, and the BTO. It collects in a central file all information on rare breeding birds in the United Kingdom, so that changes in status can be monitored as an aid to present-day conservation and stored for posterity. Special forms are used (obtainable free from the secretary) and records should if possible be submitted via the county and regional recorders. Annual report published in *British Birds*. For details of species covered by the Panel see Log Charts.

ROYAL AIR FORCE ORNITHOLOGICAL SOCIETY. (1965; 480). General Secretary, RAFOS, MOD DEO (L) Conservation, Blandford House, Farnborough Road, Aldershot, Hants GU11 2HA. RAFOS organises regular field meetings for members, carries out ornithological census work on MOD properties and mounts major expeditions annually to various UK and overseas locations. Publishes a *Newsletter* twice a year, a *Journal* annually, and reports on its expeditions and surveys.

ROYAL NAVAL BIRDWATCHING SOCIETY. (1946). Hon Secretary, Col P J S Smith RM (Ret'd), 19 Downlands Way, South Wonston, Winchester, Hants SO21 3HS. 01962 885258. Members (196 full and 88 associate and library) cover all the main ocean routes, and the Society has developed a system for reporting the positions and identity of seabirds and landbirds at sea by means of standard sea report forms. Members are encouraged to photograph birds while at sea and a library of photographs and slides is maintained. Publishes a *Bulletin* and an annual report entitled *The Sea Swallow.*

ROYAL PIGEON RACING ASSOCIATION. (54,000). General Manager, RPRA, The Reddings, Cheltenham GL51 6RN. 01452 713529. Promotes the sport of pigeon racing and controls pigeon racing within the Association. Organises liberation sites, issues rings, calculates distances between liberation sites and home lofts, and assists in the return of strays. May be able to assist in identifying owners of ringed birds caught or found.

ROYAL SOCIETY FOR THE PREVENTION OF CRUELTY TO ANIMALS. (1824). Causeway, Horsham, West Sussex RH12 1HG. 01403 264181. In addition to its animal homes the Society also runs a woodland study centre and nature reserve at Mallydams Wood in East Sussex and specialist wildlife rehabilitation centres at West Hatch, Taunton, Somerset TA3 5RT (01823 480156), at Station Road, East Winch, King's Lynn, Norfolk PE32 1NR (01553 842336), and London Road, Stapeley, Nantwich, Cheshire CW5 7JW (01270 610347). Inspectors are contacted through their Regional Communications Centres, which can be reached via the Society's national telephone number: 08705 555 999.

ROYAL SOCIETY FOR THE PROTECTION OF BIRDS. Chief Executive, Graham Wynne, RSPB, The Lodge, Sandy, Beds SG19 2DL. 01767 680551; fax 01767 692365; e-mail (firstname.name) @rspb.org.uk; http://www.rspb.org.uk. UK partner of BirdLife International. The RSPB, founded in 1889, is Europe's largest voluntary wildlife conservation body. A registered charity, governed by an elected body, with a subscribing membership of 1,012,000 (see also RSPB Phoenix and YOC). Its work in the conservation of wild birds and habitats covers the acquisition and management of nature reserves; research and surveys; monitoring and response to development proposals, land use practices and pollution which threaten wild birds; protection of rare and endangered species, and the provision of an advisory service on wildlife law enforcement. Work in the education and information field includes formal education in schools and colleges, informal activities for children through the YOC; publications (including *Birds*, a quarterly magazine for members, *Bird Life*, a bi-monthly magazine for YOC members, and *Conservation Review*, published annually); displays and exhibitions; the distribution of moving images about birds; and the development of membership involvement through Members' Groups. The activities of sales and funding involve direct mail and sale of goods designed to promote an interest in birds and fund raising by appeals and other means.

The RSPB currently manages 158 reserves throughout Britain and Northern Ireland, covering over 250,000 acres. Sites are carefully selected, most being officially recognised as of national or international importance to nature conservation. The policy is to achieve a countrywide network of reserves with examples of all the main bird communities. Visitors are generally welcome to most reserves, subject to any restrictions necessary to protect the wildlife and habitat. Current national projects include campaigns to safeguard the marine environment, safeguard estuaries, and halt illegal persecution of birds of prey.

There is increasing involvement with agriculture, energy and transport, and with biodiversity conservation generally. The International Dept is much involved with projects overseas, esp in Europe and Africa, notably with BirdLife partners.

Regional Offices

RSPB North England, 4 Benton Terrace, Sandyford, Newcastle upon Tyne NE2 1QU. 0191 281 3366.

RSPB North West, Westleigh Mews, Wakefield Road, Denby Dale, Huddersfield HD8 8QD. 01484 861148.

RSPB Central England, 46 The Green, South Bar, Banbury OX16 9AB. 01295 253330.

RSPB East Anglia, Stalham House, 65 Thorpe Rd, Norwich NR1 1UD. 01603 661662.

RSPB South East, 2nd Floor, Frederick House, 42-46 Frederick Place, Brighton BN1 1AT. 01273 775333.

RSPB South West, 1st Floor, Keble House, Southernhay Gardens, Exeter EX1 1NT. 01392 432691.

RSPB Scotland HQ, 25 Ravelston Terrace, Edinburgh EH4 3TP. 0131 311 6500.

RSPB North Scotland, Etive House, Beechwood Park, Inverness IV2 3BW. 01463 715000.

RSPB East Scotland, 10 Albyn Terrace, Aberdeen AB1 1YP. 01224 624824.

RSPB South & West Scotland, Unit 3.1, West of Scotland Science Park, Kelvin Campus, Glasgow G20 0SP. 0141 576 4100.

RSPB Wales, Bryn Aderyn, The Bank, Newtown, Powys SY16 2AB. 01686 626678.

RSPB Northern Ireland, Belvoir Park Forest, Belfast BT8 4QT. 01232 491547.

RSPB PHOENIX. Principal Youth Officer, Youth Unit, The Lodge, Sandy, Beds SG19 2DL. 01767 680551. Offers publications and a programme of activities to teenage members of the RSPB.

SCOTTISH BIRDS RECORDS COMMITTEE. Secretary, R W Forrester, 31 Argyle Terrace, Rothesay, Isle of Bute PA20 0BD. Set up by the Scottish Ornithologists' Club in 1984 to consider records of species not deemed rare enough to be considered by the British Birds Rarities Committee but which are rare in Scotland; also maintains the official list of Scottish birds.

SCOTTISH CONSERVATION PROJECTS. Balallan House, 24 Allan Park, Stirling FK8 2QG. 01786 479697. Runs 7-14 day 'Action Breaks' in Scotland during which participants undertake conservation projects; weekend training courses in environmental skills; midweek projects in Edinburgh, Glasgow and Aberdeen.

SCOTTISH FIELD STUDIES ASSOCIATION. (1950). Director, SFSA, Kindrogan Field Centre, Enochdhu, Blairgowrie, Perthshire PH10 7PG. 01250 881286; fax 01250 881433. Offers residential courses on a variety of environmental subjects.

SCOTTISH NATURAL HERITAGE. Chief Executive, SNH, Roger Crofts, 12 Hope Terrace, Edinburgh EH9 2AS. 0131 446 2201; 0131 446 2278; www.snh.org.uk. SNH is a statutory body established by the Natural Heritage (Scotland) Act 1991, formed in April 1992 and responsible to the Secretary of State for Scotland. It took over the powers and responsibilities of the Nature Conservancy Council for Scotland and the

Countryside Commission for Scotland, with functions relating to landscape and nature conservation, promoting understanding and enjoyment of Scotland's natural heritage, and encouraging its sustainable use.

SCOTTISH ORNITHOLOGISTS' CLUB. (1936; 2500). 21 Regent Terrace, Edinburgh EH7 5BT. 0131 556 6042; fax 0131 558 9947. Each of the Club's fourteen branches (see County Directory) has a programme of meetings during the winter and field trips throughout the year. The Club organises an annual weekend conference in the autumn and a one-day birdwatchers' conference in the spring. Members receive the quarterly newsletter *Scottish Bird News*, the twice yearly *Scottish Birds*, the annual *Scottish Bird Report* and *Raptor Round Up*. The SOC's Waterston Library is the best ornithological reference library in Scotland. Membership of the Society is open to anyone interested in Scottish ornithology.

SCOTTISH SOCIETY FOR THE PREVENTION OF CRUELTY TO ANIMALS. Chief Executive, James Morris, Braehead Mains, 603 Queensferry Road, Edinburgh EH4 6EA. 0131 339 0222; fax 0131 339 4777. Founded in 1839. Represents animal welfare interests to Government, local authorities and others. Educates young people to realise their responsibilities. Maintains an inspectorate to patrol and investigate and to advise owners of their responsibility for the welfare of animals and birds in their care. Maintains 14 welfare centres, 2 of which include oiled bird cleaning centres. Bird species, including birds of prey, are rehabilitated and where possible released back into the wild.

SCOTTISH WILDLIFE TRUST. (1964; 15,000). Chief Executive, SWT, Steve Sankey, Cramond House, Kirk Cramond, Cramond Glebe Road, Edinburgh EH4 6NS. 0131 312 7765; fax 0131 312 8705; e-mail scottishwt@cix.co.uk. Has branches and members' groups throughout Scotland. Aims to conserve all forms of wildlife and has over 100 reserves, many of great birdwatching interest, covering some 45,000 acres. Acts for the Wildlife Trusts and organises Scottish Wildlife Watch. Publishes *Scottish Wildlife* three times a year.

SEABIRD GROUP. (1966; 350). John Uttley, c/o The Lodge, Sandy, Beds SG19 2DL. E-mail johnuttley@bigfoot.com. Concerned with conservation issues affecting seabirds. Co-ordinates census and monitoring work on breeding seabirds; has established and maintains the *Seabird Colony Register* in collaboration with the JNCC; organises triennial conferences on seabird biology and conservation topics. Small grants available to assist with research and survey work on seabirds. Publishes the *Seabird Group Newsletter* every four months, and the journal *Atlantic Seabirds* quarterly in association with the Dutch Seabird Group.

SOCIETY OF WILDLIFE ARTISTS. (1964). President, Bruce Pearson, Federation of British Artists, 17 Carlton House Terrace, London SW1Y 5BD. 0171 930 6844. Registered charity. Annual exhibitions held in July/August at the Mall Galleries, London.

UK400 CLUB. (1981). L G R Evans, 8 Sandycroft Road, Little Chalfont, Amersham, Bucks HP6 6QL. 01494 763010. Serves to monitor the nation's top twitchers and their life lists, and to keep under review contentious species occurrences. Publishes a bi monthly magazine *Rare Birds*. Membership open to all.

ULSTER WILDLIFE TRUST see County Directory

WADER STUDY GROUP. (1970; 600). Membership Secretary, c/o BTO, The Nunnery, Thetford, Norfolk IP24 2PU. E-mail: rodwest@thenet.co.uk. The WSG is an association of wader enthusiasts, both amateur and professional, from all parts of the world. The Group aims to maintain contact between them, to help in the organisation of co-operative studies, and to provide a vehicle for the exchange of information. Publishes the *Wader Study Group Bulletin* three times a year and holds annual meetings throughout Europe.

WALTER ROTHSCHILD ZOOLOGICAL MUSEUM. Akeman Street, Tring, Herts HP23 6AP. 01442 824181. Founded by Lionel Walter (later Lord) Rothschild, the Museum displays British and exotic birds (1500 species) including many rarities and extinct species. Galleries open all year except 24-26 Dec. Adjacent to the Bird Group of the Natural History Museum - with over a million specimens and an extensive ornithological library, an internationally important centre for bird research.

WELSH KITE TRUST. Tony Cross, The Stable Cottage, Doldowlod, Llandrindod Wells, Powys LD1 6HG.

WELSH ORNITHOLOGICAL SOCIETY. (1988; 250). Paul Kenyon, 196 Chester Road, Hartford, Northwich CW8 1LG. 01606 77960; http://members.aol.com/welshos/cac. Promotes the study, conservation and enjoyment of birds throughout Wales. Runs the Welsh Records Panel which adjudicates records of scarce species in Wales. Publishes the journal *Welsh Birds* twice a year, along with *Newsletters*, and organises an annual conference.

WETLAND TRUST. S J R Rumsey, Elms Farm, Pett Lane, Icklesham, Winchelsea, E Sussex TN36 4AH. 01797 226137. Set up to encourage conservation of wetlands and develop study of migratory birds, and to foster international relations in these fields. Destinations for recent expeditions inc. Senegal, The Gambia, Guinea-Bissau, Nigeria, Kuwait, Thailand. Large numbers of birds are ringed each year in Sussex and applications are invited from individuals to train in bird ringing or extend their experience.

WILDFOWL & WETLANDS TRUST. Managing Director, Tony Richardson, Slimbridge, Gloucester GL2 7BT. 01453 890333; fax 01453 890827. Founded in 1946 by the late Sir Peter Scott. Over 70,000 members and 57000 bird adopters. A registered charity. Has 8 Centres with reserves (see Arundel, Caerlaverock, Castle Espie, Llanelli, Martin Mere, Slimbridge, Washington, Welney in Reserves and Observatories). A new Centre, The Wetland Centre, is due to open in west London in spring 2000. The Centres are nationally or internationally important for wintering wildfowl; they also aim to raise awareness of and appreciation for wetland wildlife,

the problems they face and the conservation action needed to help them. Programmes of walks and talks are available for visitors with varied interests - resources and progammes are provided for school groups. Centres except Caerlaverock and Welney have wildfowl from around the world, inc. endangered species. Research Department works on population dynamics, species management plans and wetland ecology. The Wetland Advisory Service (WAS) undertakes contracts, and Wetland Link International promotes the role of wetland centres for education and public awareness globally. Co-organiser of the Wetland Bird Survey (see National Projects; for Regional Organisers see County Directory), also of the Irish Wetland Bird Survey (see National Projects). Publishes *Wildfowl & Wetlands* magazine for members quarterly, and *Wildfowl* (an annual collection of scientific papers on wildfowl, wetlands and conservation) in November.

WILDLIFE SOUND RECORDING SOCIETY. (1968; 327). Hon Membership Secretary, WSRS, Mike Iannantuoni, 36 Wenton Close, Cottesmore, Oakham, Rutland LE15 7DR. 01572 812447. Works closely with the Wildlife Section of the National Sound Archive. Members carry out recording work for scientific purposes as well as for pleasure. A field weekend is held each spring, and members organise meetings locally. Four circulating tapes of members' recordings are produced for members each year, and a journal, *Wildlife Sound*, is published twice a year.

WILDLIFE TRUSTS (THE). Director-General, Dr Simon Lyster, The Kiln, Waterside, Mather Road, Newark NG24 1WT. 01636 677711; fax 01636 670001; e-mail wildlifersnc@cix.co.uk; www.wildlifetrust.org.uk. A nationwide network of 46 local trusts and 100 urban wildlife groups which work to protect wildlife in town and country. The Wildlife Trusts manage more than 2300 nature reserves, undertake a wide range of other conservation and education activities, and are dedicated to the achievement of a UK richer in wildlife. Publ *Natural World*. See also Wildlife Watch.

WILDLIFE WATCH. Mary Cornwell, The Green, Witham Park, Waterside South, Lincoln LN5 7JR. 01636 677711; fax 01636 670001. Founded in 1971. With 20,000 members, 800 local groups and 1000 members of the Watch Education Service, it is the national environmental club for young people and the junior branch of The Wildlife Trusts (see previous entry). Publishes *Watchword*.

WWF-UK (WORLD WIDE FUND FOR NATURE). (1961). Director, Panda House, Weyside Park, Catteshall Lane, Godalming, Surrey GU7 1XR 01483 426444; fax 01483 426409; www.wwf-uk.org. WWF is the world's largest conservation organisation. It has a global network of 27 national organisations (of which WWF-UK is one). Its mission is to achieve the conservation of nature and ecological processes, including saving species and habitats. Publishes *WWF News* (quarterly magazine).

YOC (formerly Young Ornithologists' Club). (1965; 150,000). National Organiser, Peter Holden, Youth Unit, The Lodge, Sandy, Beds SG19 2DL. 01767 680551. Junior section of the RSPB. Membership mainly for 7-12 year olds (see RSPB Phoenix for teenage club). There are over 500 YOC Groups run by almost 1500 volunteers. Activities include projects, holidays, roadshows, competitions, and local events for children. Publishes a bi-monthly magazine, *Bird Life*.

ZOOLOGICAL PHOTOGRAPHIC CLUB. (1899). Hon Secretary, Martin B Withers, 93 Cross Lane, Mountsorrel, Loughborough, Leics LE12 7BX. 0116 230 2281. Circulates black and white and colour prints of zoological interest only, via a series of postal portfolios.

ZOOLOGICAL SOCIETY OF LONDON. (1826). Secretary, Professor R McNeill Alexander FRS, Regent's Park, London NW1 4RY. 0171 722 3333. Carries out research, organises symposia and holds scientific meetings. Manages the Zoological Gardens in Regent's Park (first opened in 1828) and Whipsnade Wild Animal Park near Dunstable, Beds, each with extensive collections of birds. Publications include the *Journal of Zoology* (three volumes pa), *Animal Conservation* (quarterly), the *Symposia* (irreg.), the *International Zoo Yearbook*, and the *Zoological Record* (an annual bibliography of zoological literature, inc. birds, which from Vol 115 is published in association with BIOSIS, Philadelphia). The Society's library has a large collection of ornithological books and journals.

NATIONAL PROJECTS

National ornithological projects depend for their success on the active participation of amateur birdwatchers. In return they provide birdwatchers with an excellent opportunity to contribute in a positive and worthwhile way to the scientific study of birds and their habitats, which is the vital basis of all conservation programmes.

The following entries provide a description of each particular project and a note of whom to contact for further information (full addresses in previous section). It is always appreciated if enquirers enclose a stamped, addressed envelope when writing.

BEWICK'S SWAN RESEARCH

A WWT project

Recognition of individual Bewick's Swans by their black and yellow bill markings has been used for an extensive study of the flock wintering at Slimbridge, Gloucestershire since 1964. The swans show a high level of mate fidelity; 10 to 50% of the birds identified each season have been recorded at Slimbridge in previous years. Factors affecting the life cycle of individual birds can therefore be analysed in detail. A regular ringing programme was introduced in 1967 to identify staging sites used during migration to and from the Russian breeding grounds, and to continue monitoring individuals that transferred to other wintering sites. Bewick's Swans have also been caught and ringed at Caerlaverock (Dumfries & Galloway) and Welney (Norfolk) since 1979, and at Martin Mere (Lancashire) since 1990. Since 1991 WWT staff have made one or two expeditions to the Russian arctic each summer, to study the swans' breeding biology in collaboration with scientists from Russia, the Netherlands and Denmark. Sightings of marked birds are invaluable for maintaining the life-history records of individual swans. Contact: Eileen Rees, WWT.

BREEDING BIRD SURVEY

Supported by the BTO, JNCC (on behalf of EN, SNH, CCW & EHS NI) and the RSPB

Begun in 1994, the BBS is designed to keep track of the changes in populations of our common breeding birds. It is dependent on volunteer birdwatchers throughout the country who can spare about five hours a year to cover a 1x1km survey square. There are just two morning visits to survey the breeding birds each year. Survey squares are picked at random by computer to ensure that all habitats and regions are covered, making BBS the most important new survey in many years. Since its inception it has been a tremendous success, with over 2,300 squares covered and over 200 species recorded. Contact: Richard Bashford, BTO, or your local BTO Regional Representative (see County Directory).

BREEDING WADERS OF WET MEADOWS
A BTO project funded by the RSPB
A repeat of the 1982 survey. Will probably involve three visits to selected sites, with the aim of covering as many as possible of the sites covered in 1982, but the exact scale of the project has yet to be finalised. Contacts: Phil Atkinson, Steve Holloway, Rob Fuller, BTO.

BTO/JNCC WINTER FARMLAND BIRDS SURVEYS
A BTO project funded by a partnership of the BTO and the JNCC (on behalf of EN, SNH, CCW, and also on behalf of the Environment & Heritage Service in Northern Ireland)
Three winters of full surveys 1999/2000, 2000/01, 2001/02. This survey will cover a suite of species found on farmland in winter including Tree Sparrow, Linnet, Bullfinch, Yellowhammer, Redwing and Fieldfare, Lapwing and Golden Plover. It will involve several components, probably including coverage of random squares, counts at important sites and casual records. Contact: Simon Gillings, e-mail wfbs@bto.org.

COMMON BIRDS CENSUS
A BTO project, supported by JNCC
Volunteer fieldworkers make ten breeding-season visits each year to a plot of ordinary farmland or woodland. Maps are prepared showing the locations of birds' territories on each plot. These are of value both locally and nationally. The BTO uses the data nationally to study bird population changes, the structure of bird communities, and the relationships of breeding birds with their habitats. Long-term population trends derived from CBC are used to assess bird conservation priorities. An annual report is published in *BTO News*. The results relating to bird population changes during the period 1962-88 were published in *Population Trends in British Breeding Birds* (BTO, 1990). Contact: Fiona Sanderson, BTO.

CONCERN FOR SWIFTS
A Concern for Swifts Group project
Endorsed by the BTO and the RSPB, the Group monitors Swift breeding colonies, especially where building restoration and maintenance are likely to cause disturbance. Practical information can be provided to owners, architects, builders and others, as well as advice on nest boxes and the use of specially adapted roof tiles. The help of interested birdwatchers is always welcome. Contact: Jake Allsop, 01353 740540; fax 01353 741585.

CONSTANT EFFORT SITES SCHEME
A BTO project for bird ringers, funded by a partnership of the BTO, the JNCC (on behalf of EN, SNH, CCW, and also on behalf of the Environment & Heritage Service in Northern Ireland), Duchas the Heritage Service - National Parks & Wildlife Service (Ireland) and the ringers themselves
Participants in the Scheme monitor common songbird populations by mist-netting and ringing birds throughout the summer at more than 120 sites across Britain and Ireland. Changes in numbers of adults captured provide an index of population changes between years, while the ratio of juveniles to adults gives a measure of productivity. Between-year recaptures of birds are used to study variations in adult survival rates. Information from CES complements that from other long-term BTO surveys. Contact: Dawn Balmer, BTO.

CORMORANT ROOST SITE INVENTORY AND BREEDING COLONY REGISTER
R Sellers in association with WWT and JNCC
Daytime counts carried out under the Wetland Bird Survey provide an index of the number of Cormorants wintering in Great Britain, but many birds are known to go

WWT, therefore established the Christmas Week Cormorant Survey which, through a network of volunteer counters, sought to monitor the numbers of Cormorants at about 70 of the most important night roosts in GB. In 1997, this project was extended, in collaboration with JNCC, to produce a comprehensive Cormorant Roost Site Inventory for GB to aid the statutory nature conservation agencies in their advice to government. Over 100 county bird recorders and local bird experts played an integral role in compiling the inventory, which currently lists 276 night roosts, mostly in England. In 1990, Robin Sellers also established the Cormorant Breeding Colony Survey to monitor numbers and breeding success of Cormorants in the UK at both coastal and inland colonies. Some 1200 pairs of Cormorants, representing perhaps 15% of the local UK population, now breed inland. New colonies are forming every year as the population inland increases annually by 17%. By 1997, breeding had been attempted at over 50 inland sites and colonies established at 11, mainly in SE England. Recent research has shown that a high proportion of these inland breeders are of the continental race *Phalacrocorax carbo sinensis*. Anyone wishing to take part in either roost or breeding surveys should contact Dr Baz Hughes at WWT on extension 226. Records of night time roost sites would also be greatly appreciated and individually acknowledged.

COVER CROPS AND SONGBIRDS
A BTO project with the Game Conservancy Trust, supported by MAFF
The purpose is to compare the use made by birds (including game birds) of different wild bird crop mixtures and game-cover crops. The survey aims to cover 200 farm plots across England over three winters (October and March) 1998/99, 1999/00 and 2000/01. About 140 sites were covered in 1998/99, and volunteers are required for additional sites for the following two winters. Contact: Ian Henderson.

GARDEN BIRD FEEDING SURVEY
A BTO project
The 1998/99 season completed 29 years of the GBFS. Each year 250 observers record the numbers and variety of garden birds fed by man in the 26 weeks between October and March. Gardens are selected by region and type, from city flats, suburban semis and rural houses to outlying farms. Contact: David Glue, BTO.

GARDEN BIRDWATCH
A BTO project, supported by C J Wildbird Foods
Started in January 1995, this project is a year-round survey that monitors the use that birds make of gardens. Approximately 10,500 participants from all over the UK and Ireland keep a weekly log of species using their gardens. The data collected are used to monitor regional, seasonal and year-to-year changes in the garden populations of our commoner birds. To cover costs there is an annual registration fee of £10.00. All registered participants receive a quarterly magazine as well as discount vouchers redeemable on purchases from C J Wildbird Foods. Contact: Jacky Prior/Carol Povey, BTO.

GOLDEN ORIOLE CENSUS
A Golden Oriole Group project
With support from the RSPB, the Golden Oriole Group has undertaken a systematic annual census of breeding Golden Orioles in the Fenland Basin since 1987. In recent years national censuses have been made, funded by English Nature and the RSPB, in which some sixty volunteer recorders have participated. The Group is always interested to hear of sightings of Orioles and to receive offers of help with its census work. Studies of breeding biology, habitat and food requirements are also carried out. Contact: Jake Allsop, Golden Oriole Group, see page 105.

GOOSE CENSUSES

A WWT project

Britain and Ireland support internationally important populations of geese. Since many of the goose species feed away from wetlands during daylight hours, resorting to agricultural land and pastures, their numbers and distribution cannot be monitored adequately by counts at wetlands alone (see Wetland Bird Survey). Consequently additional surveys are required, involving visits to both feeding and roosting areas. The frequency and geographical extent of these censuses varies according to species; most are censused just once or twice during the autumn and winter, and in the main resorts only. Further volunteers are always needed to keep pace with some expanding goose populations. Volunteer counters in Scotland are especially welcomed. For further information contact: Richard Hearn, WWT.

HERONRIES CENSUS

A BTO project

This survey started in 1928 and has been carried out under the auspices of the BTO since 1934. It represents the longest continuous series of population data for any European breeding bird. Counts are made at a sample of heronries each year, chiefly in England and Wales, to provide an index of the current population level; data from Scotland and Northern Ireland are scant and more contributions from these countries would be especially welcomed. Herons may be hit hard during periods of severe weather but benefit by increased survival over mild winters. Their position at the top of a food chain makes them particularly vulnerable to pesticides and pollution. Contact: John Marchant, BTO.

IRISH WETLAND BIRD SURVEY (I-WeBS)

A joint project of BirdWatch Ireland, the National Parks & Wildlife Service of the Dept of Arts, Culture & the Gaeltacht, and WWT, and supported by the Heritage Council and WWF-UK

Established in 1994, I-WeBS aims to monitor the numbers and distribution of waterfowl populations wintering in Ireland in the long term, enabling the population size and spatial and temporal trends in numbers to be identified and described for each species. Methods are compatible with existing schemes in the UK and Europe, and I-WeBS collaborates closely with the Wetland Bird Survey (WeBS) in the UK. Synchronised monthly counts are undertaken at wetland sites of all habitats during the winter. Counts are straightforward, and counters receive a newsletter and full report annually. Additional help is always welcome, especially during these initial years as the scheme continues to grow. Contact: Kendrew Colhoun, BirdWatch Ireland.

LOW TIDE COUNTS SCHEME see Wetland Bird Survey

MANX CHOUGH PROJECT

A Manx registered charitable trust

Established in 1990 to help the conservation of the Chough in the Isle of Man, leading to its protection and population increase. This is by the maintenance of present nest sites, provision of suitable conditions for the re-occupation of abandoned sites and the expansion of the range of the species into new areas of the Island. Surveys and censuses are carried out. Raising public awareness of and interest in the Chough are further objects. Contact: Allen S Moore, Lyndale, Derby Road, Peel, Isle of Man IM5 1HH. 01624 843798.

NEST RECORD SCHEME

A BTO project, funded by a partnership of the BTO, the JNCC (on behalf of EN, SNH, CCW, and also on behalf of the Environment & Heritage Service in Northern Ireland)

All birdwatchers can contribute to this scheme by completing easy-to-use Nest Record Cards for any nesting attempt they find. The aim is to provide a picture of how Britain's birds are faring in town and countryside, in a way that no single observer could ever do. Even *one* card is a useful addition. Prospective new participants can obtain a free introductory pack. Contact: Samantha Rider, BTO.

PREDATORY BIRDS MONITORING SCHEME

An Institute of Terrestrial Ecology project

This long-running scheme was set up to monitor the effects of pesticides on wildlife and is now largely concerned with checking on the effectiveness of restrictions that have been imposed on some uses of agricultural chemicals. The species at present studied are Peregrine, Sparrowhawk, Kestrel, Merlin, Long-eared Owl, Barn Owl, Heron, Kingfisher and Great Crested Grebe, and the Institute of Terrestrial Ecology would be grateful to receive specimens of these. They should be packed in a polythene bag (sealed in some way), then in a padded envelope or box. Mark the outside of the package 'Perishable Goods' and post first class to: Miss L Dale, Institute of Terrestrial Ecology, Monks Wood, Abbots Ripton, Huntingdon, Cambridgeshire PE17 2LS (01487 773381). The following information is required: name and address of finder, locality in which the bird was found, date collected and the circumstances (eg found dead on road). The whole specimen should be sent. If there is any delay before posting, the dead bird should be put in a plastic bag and stored in a freezer to delay decomposition. Birds which have been kept in captivity are not required. Postage costs are reimbursed in the form of stamps.

RAPTOR AND OWL RESEARCH REGISTER

A BTO project

The Register has helped considerably over the past 25 years in encouraging and guiding research, and in the co-ordination of projects. There are currently almost 500 projects in the card index file through which the Register operates. The owl species currently receiving most attention are Barn and Tawny; as to raptors, the most popular subjects are Kestrel, Buzzard, Sparrowhawk, Hobby and Peregrine, with researchers showing increasing interest in Red Kite, and fewer large in-depth studies of Goshawk, Osprey and Harriers. Contributing is a simple process and involves all raptor enthusiasts, whether it is to describe an amateur activity or professional study. The nature of research on record varies widely - from local pellet analyses to captive breeding and rehabilitation programmes. Birdwatchers in both Britain and abroad are encouraged to write for photocopies of cards relevant to the species or nature of their work. The effectiveness of the Register depends upon those running projects (however big or small) ensuring that their work is included. Contact: David Glue, BTO.

RED KITE RE-INTRODUCTION PROJECT

An English Nature/SNH/RSPB project, supported by Forest Enterprise, the British Airways Assisting Conservation Programme, Yorkshire Water and authorities in Germany and Spain

The project involves the translocation of birds from Spain, Germany and the expanding Chilterns population for release at sites in England and Scotland. Records of any wing-tagged Red Kites in England should be reported to Ian Carter at English Nature, Northminster House, Peterborough, PE1 1UA (tel 01733 455281). Scottish records should be sent to Brian Etheridge at RSPB's North Scotland Regional Office, Etive House, Beechwood Park, Inverness, IV2 3BW (tel 01463 715000). Sightings are of particular value if the letter/number code (or colour) of wing tags can be seen or if the bird is seen flying low over (or into) woodland. Records should include an exact location, preferably with a six figure grid reference, and as much detail as possible about the bird's behaviour.

RETRAPPING ADULTS FOR SURVIVAL PROJECT

A BTO project for bird ringers, funded by a partnership of the BTO, the JNCC (on behalf of EN, SNH, CCW, and also on behalf of the Environment & Heritage Service in Northern Ireland), Duchas the Heritage Service - National Parks & Wildlife Service (Ireland) and the ringers themselves

This project started in 1998 and is an initiative of the BTO Ringing Scheme. It aims to gather retrap information for a wide range of species, especially those of conservation concern, in a variety of breeding habitats, allowing the monitoring of survival rates. Detailed information about survival rates from the RAS Project will help in the understanding of changing population trends. Ringers choose a target species, decide on a study area and develop suitable catching techniques. The aim then is to catch all the breeding adults of the chosen species within the study area. This is repeated each breeding season for a minimum of five years. The results will be relayed to conservation organisations who can use the information to design effective conservation action plans. Contact: Dawn Balmer, BTO.

RINGING SCHEME

A BTO project for bird ringers, funded by a partnership of the BTO, the JNCC (on behalf of EN, SNH, CCW, and also on behalf of the Environment & Heritage Service in Northern Ireland), Duchas the Heritage Service - National Parks & Wildlife Service (Ireland) and the ringers themselves

The purpose of the Ringing Scheme is to study mortality, survival and migration by marking birds with individually numbered metal rings which carry a return address. About 2,000 trained and licensed ringers operate in Britain and Ireland, and together they mark around 800,000 birds each year. All birdwatchers can contribute to the scheme by reporting any ringed birds they find. On finding a ringed bird the information to note is the ring number, species (if known), when and where the bird was found, and what happened to it. If the bird is dead the ring should be removed, flattened and attached to the letter. Finders who send their name and address will be given details of where and when the bird was ringed. About 14,000 ringed birds are reported each year and an annual report is published. Contact: Jacquie Clark, BTO.

SEABIRD COLONY REGISTER, SEABIRD MONITORING PROGRAMME, AND SEABIRD 2000

JNCC projects in collaboration with the Seabird Group, RSPB and Shetland Oil Terminal Environmental Advisory Group

The SCR is a computer database of numbers of seabirds breeding at colonies throughout the British Isles. It includes records from the comprehensive surveys undertaken in 1969/70 and 1985/87 in addition to more recent records derived from the SMP and other sources. The SMP monitors seabird numbers and breeding success at a range of colonies each year. Outputs include an annual report *Seabird Numbers and Breeding Success in Britain and Ireland*. The aim of the Seabird 2000 project is to carry out a complete census of breeding seabirds in Britain and Ireland between 1999 and 2002. This will provide updated baseline population estimates against which future trends can be assessed. Anyone holding seabird colony counts not previously submitted to the SCR or interested in volunteering to assist in data collection for the SMP or Seabird 2000 should contact: Kate Thompson, JNCC, Dunnet House, 7 Thistle Place, Aberdeen AB10 1UZ. 01224 655703; fax 01224 621488; e-mail thomps_k@jncc.gov.uk; www.jncc.gov.uk.

SIGHTINGS OF COLOUR-MARKED BIRDS
Various bodies
Studies of movements of colour-marked birds depend heavily on the help of birdwatchers. On sighting a colour-marked bird full details should be sent to the appropriate contact below. The information will be passed on to the person who marked the bird, who will send details of marking to the observer. Unfortunately some birds cannot be traced, owing for example to loss of rings or the inadequacy of the central record.

Waders: Wader Study Group, c/o Stephen Browne, BTO.
Wildfowl: Richard Hearn, WWT, Slimbridge, Gloucester GL2 7BT.
Cormorant: Jenny Kent, 8 Manor Road, Collingham, Newark, Notts NG23 7PL.
Chough: Eric Bignal, Kindrochaid, Bruichladdich, Islay PA44 7PP.
Large gulls: Peter Rock, 59 Concorde Drive, Westbury-on-Trym, Bristol BS10 6PX.
Small gulls: K T Pedersen, Daglykkevej 7, DK-2650 Hridovre, Denmark.
All other species: Bridget Griffin, BTO.

SWIFTS see Concern for Swifts

2000 BREEDING FERAL GOOSE AND SWAN SURVEY
A BTO project
There is increased interest in feral birds both in the United Kingdom and internationally. It is important to keep monitoring these birds to ensure that they do not start impinging on our native fauna. As part of the enhanced awareness of this issue, the numbers of non-native and feral geese are to be reassessed for the first time since the summer of 1991. The survey will take place between May and July 2000. It is likely to be based on more than 1000 randomly selected tetrads (4km^2), each of which will be visited twice, each visit being of two hours. The greatest number of tetrads will be in an area from North Yorkshire to the Welsh Borders and down to the south coast of England. Contacts: Mark Rehfish, Stephen Holloway, BTO.

WATERWAYS BIRD SURVEY
A BTO project
From March to July each year participants survey linear waterways (rivers and canals) to record the position and activity of riparian birds. Results show both numbers and distribution of breeding territories for each waterside species at each site. An annual report on population change is published in *BTO News*. Full results from 1974 to 1988 were included in *Population Trends in British Breeding Birds* (BTO, 1990). WBS maps show the habitat requirements of the birds and can be used to assess the effects of waterway management. Coverage of new plots is always required, especially in poorly covered areas such as Ireland, Scotland, Wales, SW England and the North East. Contact: John Marchant or Fiona Sanderson, BTO.

WeBS PILOT DISPERSED WATERFOWL SURVEY
A WeBS project, funded by the BTO, WWT, RSPB and JNCC
Little is known about the numbers of dabbling ducks, Moorhen, Coot, Little Grebe, Heron, etc that winter on small water bodies, streams, flooded fields, ditches and dykes, away from Wetland Bird Survey (WeBS) sites. Furthermore, there are no reliable population estimates of wintering Ruff and both species of snipe. This survey aims to assess whether it is possible to estimate the size of these populations. The full survey, planned for 2002/03 winter, would estimate how many of these birds occur in UK habitats not completely covered at present by WeBS. The Pilot will test the value of a tetrad-based approach incorporating intensive coverage of one of the 1km^2 units within each tetrad (4km^2). It is impractical to get whole tetrads intensively covered, but a large count unit is essential for the larger less common species. Therefore, three quarters of each tetrad will be covered for such species as the plovers and herons,

which can often be counted from roads and farm tracks. In the intensively covered 1km² all species will be counted according to habitat. The tetrads will be selected by randon sampling. BTO Regional Representatives may be asked to help with this survey if it proves difficult to obtain sufficient counters from WeBS Local Organisers. Contacts: Mark Rehfisch, Stephen Holloway, BTO.

WETLAND BIRD SURVEY
A joint scheme of BTO, WWT, RSPB & JNCC
The Wetland Bird Survey (WeBS) is the monitoring scheme for non-breeding waterfowl in the UK. The principal aims are: 1. to determine the population sizes of waterfowl; 2. to determine trends in numbers and distribution; 3. to identify important sites for waterfowl; and 4. to conduct research which underpins waterfowl conservation. WeBS data are used to designate important waterfowl sites and protect them against adverse development, for research into the causes of declines, for determining conservation priorities and strategies and to determine management plans for wetland sites and waterfowl. Once monthly, synchronised Core Counts are made at as many wetland sites as possible. Low Tide Counts are made on about 20 estuaries each winter to determine important feeding areas. Counts take just a few hours and are relatively straightforward. The 3,000 participants receive regular newsletters and a comprehensive annual report. New counters are always welcome. Contact: WeBS Secretariat, WWT (for Core Counts and general enquiries) and Andy Musgrove, BTO (Low Tide Counts).

WHOOPER SWAN RESEARCH
A WWT/Icelandic Museum of Nature History project
WWT's long-term study of Whooper Swans commenced in 1979 with the completion of swan pipes at Caerlaverock (Dumfries & Galloway) and Welney (Norfolk) and the subsequent development of a ringing programme for this species. Whooper Swans have been ringed at Martin Mere (Lancashire) from 1990 onwards. Since 1988 staff have made regular expeditions to Iceland where they collaborate with Icelandic ornithologists in monitoring clutch and brood sizes, and in catching the families and non-breeding flocks. The study aims to determine factors affecting the reproductive success of the Icelandic-breeding Whooper Swan population which winters mainly in Britain and Ireland. Relocating the families in winter is important for assessing the number of cygnets that survive autumn migration. Efforts made by birdwatchers to read Whooper Swan rings, and to report the number of juveniles associated with ringed birds, are therefore particularly useful. The first and last dates on which ringed birds are seen at a site are also valuable for monitoring the movements of the swans in winter. Contact: Eileen Rees, WWT.

WILDFOWL COLOUR RINGING
A WWT project
The Wildfowl & Wetlands Trust acts as a clearing house for all colour ringing of swans, geese and ducks on behalf of the BTO. The use of unique coloured leg-rings enables the movements and behaviour of known individuals to be observed without recapture. The rings are usually in bright colours with engraved letters and/or digits showing as black or white, and can be read with a telescope at up to 200m. A few colour-marked neck-collars, and plumage dyes, have also been used on geese and swans. Any records of observations should include species, location, ring colour and mark, and which leg the ring was on. The main study species are Mute Swan, Bewick's Swan, Whooper Swan, Pink-footed Goose, Greylag Goose, Greenland White-fronted Goose, Barnacle Goose, Brent Goose, Shelduck and Wigeon. Records will be forwarded to the relevant study, and when birds are traced ringing details will be sent back to the observer. All sightings should be sent to: Research Dept (Colour-ringed Wildfowl), WWT.

PART THREE
INTERNATIONAL DIRECTORY

HELM IDENTIFICATION GUIDES

BIRDS OF THE INDIAN SUBCONTINENT

Richard Grimmett, Carol Inskipp and Tim Inskipp

(Actual size 246 x 172 mm)

Birds of the Indian Subcontinent, by Richard Grimmett, Carol Inskipp and Tim Inskipp, illustrated by Clive Byers *et al*, Helm (A&C Black), 1998, 888p, £55.00. ISBN 0 7136 4004 9. Hbk.

This weighty identification manual covers all the species (some 1,300) that make up the avifauna of India, Pakistan, Nepal, Bangladesh, Bhutan, Sri Lanka and the Maldives. All but three are illustrated in over 150 plates, with facing texts that highlight key features; fuller systematic accounts follow. Extensive first-hand knowledge of the birds of this vast region is combined with information gleaned from the considerable literature available. The publishers have also produced a concise paperback version which includes all the synoptic texts and the illustrations in reduced size (*Pocket Guide to the Birds of the Indian Subcontinent*, Helm, 1999, £17.99). Whichever you purchase, it will amply repay the investment.

INTERNATIONAL ORGANISATIONS

AFRICAN BIRD CLUB. c/o Birdlife International, as below.
BIRDLIFE INTERNATIONAL. Wellbrook Court, Girton Road, Cambridge CB3 0NA. +44 (0)1223 277318; fax +44 (0)1223 277200; birdlife@birdlife.org.uk
EAST AFRICA NATURAL HISTORY SOCIETY (Bird Committee). D A Turner, Box 48019, Nairobi, Kenya. E-mail eaos@africaonline.co.ke. Pub: *Journal of the EANHS*; *Scopus*.
EURING. Euring Data Bank, Netherlands Institute of Ecology, PO Box 40. NL-6666 ZG Heteren, Netherlands.
EUROPEAN WILDLIFE REHABILITATION ASSOCIATION (EWRA). Les Stocker MBE, c/o Wildlife Hospital Trust, Aston Road, Haddenham, Aylesbury, Bucks HP17 8AF. +44 (0)1844 292292; fax +44 (0)1844 292640.
FAUNA AND FLORA INTERNATIONAL. Great Eastern House, Tenison Road, Cambridge CB1 2DT. +44 (0)1223 571000; fax +44 (0)1223 461481; e-mail info@fauna-flora.org. Pub: *Oryx*.
NEOTROPICAL BIRD CLUB. As OSME below. Pub: *Cotinga*.
ORIENTAL BIRD CLUB. As OSME below. E-mail mail@orientalbirdclub.org. Pub: *The Forktail*; *Bull OBC*.

ORNITHOLOGICAL SOCIETY OF THE MIDDLE EAST (OSME). c/o The Lodge, Sandy, Beds SG19 2DL. E-mail ag@osme.org. Pub: *Sandgrouse*.

WEST AFRICAN ORNITHOLOGICAL SOCIETY. R E Sharland, 1 Fisher's Heron, East Mills, Fordingbridge, Hants SP6 2JR. Pub: *Malimbus*.
WETLANDS INTERNATIONAL. PO Box 471, 6700 AL Wageningen, Netherlands. +31 317 478854; fax +31 317 478850; e-mail icu@wetlands.agro.nl.
WILDLIFE TRADE MONITORING UNIT. As WCMC below.
WORLD CONSERVATION MONITORING CENTRE (WCMC). 219 Huntingdon Road, Cambridge CB3 0DL. +44 (0)1223 277314; fax +44 (0)1223 277136; e-mail info@wcmc.org.uk.
WORLD OWL TRUST. The Owl Centre, Muncaster Castle, Ravenglass, Cumbria CA18 1RQ. +44 (0)1229 717393; fax +44 (0)1229 717107; e-mail admin@owls.org.
WORLD PHEASANT ASSOCIATION. PO Box 5, Lower Basildon, Reading RG8 9PF. +44 (0)118 984 5140; fax +44 (0)118 984 3369; e-mail wpa@gn.apc.org.
WORLD WIDE FUND FOR NATURE. Avenue du Mont Blanc, CH-1196 Gland, Switzerland. +41 22 364 9111; fax +41 22 364 5468.

FOREIGN NATIONAL ORGANISATIONS

The organisations on this list are members of the growing BirdLife international network. They fall into four categories, indicated as follows:

P Partner **A** Associate
PD Partner Designate **R** Representative

Associates and Representatives are not generally included for countries which have an organisation of Partner status.

ALBANIA. PD Albanian Society for the Protection and Preservation of Birds. Faculty of Natural Sciences, Tirana University, Al-Tirana. Fax +355 42 29 028; entelac@ngoinfoc.trirana.al.

ANDORRA. R Associació per a la Defensa da la Natura. Apartado de Correus Espanyols No 96, Andorra La Vella. Fax 376 84 3868; adn@andorra.ad.

ARGENTINA. P Aves Argentinas/AOP. 25 de Mayo 749, 2° piso, oficina 6, 1002 Buenos Aires. Tel/fax +54 11 4312 1015; aop@aorpla.org.ar. Pub: *El Hornero*.

AUSTRALIA. P Birds Australia. 415 Riversdale Road, Hawthorn East, Victoria 3123. Fax +61 3 9882 2677; raou@raou.com.au. Pub: *Emu*.

AUSTRIA. P BirdLife Austria. Museumsplatz 1/10/8, A-1070 Wien. Fax +43 1 524 7040; birdlife@blackbox.at. Pub: *Egretta*; *Vogelschutz in Österreich*.

BAHAMAS. R Bahamas National Trust. PO Box 4105, Nassau. Fax +1 242 393 4978; bnt@bahamas.net.bs. Pub: *BNT Newsletter*; *Bahamas Naturalist*.

BELGIUM. P Les Réserves Naturelles et Ornithologiques de Belgique (RNOB). Rue Royale, Sainte-Marie 105, B-1030 Brussels. +32 2 245 43 00; fax +32 2 245 39 33; willem.nr@bitserve.com.

BELIZE. PD Belize Audubon Society. 12 Fort Street, PO Box 1001, Belize City. +501 2 34987; fax +501 2 34985; base@btl.net. Pub: *BAS Bull*.

BOLIVIA. P Associación Armonía. Casilla 3081, Santa Cruz de la Sierra. Tel/fax +591 3 371 005; armonia@scbbs-bo.com.

BULGARIA. P Bulgarian Society for the Protection of Birds. PO Box 50, BG-1111 Sofia. Fax +359 2 62 08 15; bspb_hq@mb.bia.bg.com. Pub: *Neophron*.

BURKINA FASO. R Fondation des Amis de la Nature (NATURAMA). 01 B.P. 6133, Ouagadougou 01. +226 36 4959; fax +226 36 5118; naturama@fasonet.bf.

CANADA. P Bird Studies Canada (BSC). PO Box 160, Port Rowan, Ontario N0E 1M0. Fax +1 519 586 3532; mbradstreet@bsc-eoc.org.
P Canadian Nature Federation. 1 Nicholas Street, Suite 606, Ottawa, Ontario K1N 7B7. Fax +1 613 562 3371; cnf@cnf.ca. Pub: *Nature Canada*.

CHILE. PD Unión de Ornitólogos de Chile. Casilla 13.183, Santiago 21. E-mail unorch@entelchile.net.

CROATIA. R Croatian Society for Bird and Nature Protection. Ilirski Trg 9, HR-10000 Zagreb. Fax +385 1 389 5445; jasmina@mahazu.hazu.hr. Pub: *Troglodytes*.

CZECH REPUBLIC. P Czech Society for Ornithology. Hornoměcholupská 34, CZ-102 Praha 10. Fax +42 2 78 66 700; cso.vorisek@bbs.infima.cz. Pub: *Sylvia*.

DENMARK. P Dansk Ornitologisk Forening. Vesterbrogade 140, DK-1620 Copenhagen V. +45 3331 0512; fax +45 3331 2435; dof@dof.dk. Pub: *DOF Tidsskrift*; *Fugle*.

ECUADOR. P Fundación Ornitológica del Ecuador. PO Box 17-17-906, La Tierra 203 y Av. de los Shyris, Quito. Fax +593 2 464 359; cecia@uio.satnet.net.

EL SALVADOR. R Asociación Audubon de El Salvador. Urb. Serramonte II, Av. Bernal Senda 2,76, San Salvador. Fax +503 274 9180; harrouch@es.com.sv.

ESTONIA. PD Estonian Ornithological Society. Baer House, Vesti Str. 4, EE-2400 Tartu. Fax +372 7 422 180; jaanus@linnu.tartu.ee. Pub: *Hirundo*.

ETHIOPIA. P Ethiopian Wildlife and Natural History Society. PO Box 13303, Addis Ababa. Fax +251 1 552350; ewnhs@telecom.net.et.

FALKLAND ISLANDS. R Falklands Conservation. PO Box 26, Stanley. Fax +522288; conservation@horizon.co.fk.

FAROE ISLANDS. R Faroese Ornithological Society. Postssmoga 1230, FR-110 Torshavn. Fax +298 18 589; doreteb@ngs.fo. Pub: *Frágreiding trá FF*.

FINLAND. P BirdLife Suomi-Finland. Finland. Annankatu 29A, PO Box 1285, FIN-00101 Helsinki. Fax +358 9 685 4722; toimisto@birdlife.fi.

FRENCH POLYNESIA. R. Société d'Ornithologie de Polynésie 'Manu'. BP 21 098, Papeete, Tahiti. Fax +689 42 58 32; dircab.mag@agriculture.gov.pf.

FRANCE. P Ligue pour la Protection des Oiseaux. La Corderie Royale, BP 263, F-17305 Rochefort CEDEX. Fax +33 546 83 95 86; lpo@lpo-birdlife.asso.fr. Pub: *L'Oiseau*.

GERMANY. A Deutscher Rat für Vogelschutz e.V (DRV). Vogelwarte Radolfzell, Am Obstberg 1, D-78315 Radolfzell. Fax +49 7732 150 142, bauer@vowa.ornithol.mpg.de.
P Naturschutzbund Deutschland. Herbert-Rabius-Str 26, D-53225 Bonn. Fax +49 228 975 6190; claus.mayr@nabu.de. Pub: *Naturschutz heute*.

GHANA. P Ghana Wildlife Society. PO Box 13252, Accra. Fax (public fax bureau) +233 21 777098; wildsoc@ighmail.com.

GIBRALTAR. PD Gibraltar Ornithological and Natural History Society. Field Centre, Jews' Gate, Upper Rock Nature Reserve, PO Box 843. Fax +350 74022; gonhs@gibnet.gi. Pub: *Alectoris*; *Strait of Gibraltar Bird Observatory Report*.

GREECE. P Hellenic Ornithological Society. 53 Emm. Benaki Str. GR-10681 Athens. +30 1 330 11 67; fax +30 1 38 11 271; birdlife-gr@ath.forthnet.gr.

HONG KONG. R Hong Kong Birdwatching Society. PO Box 12460, GPO, Hong Kong. hkbws@hkbws.org.hk.

HUNGARY. P Hungarian Ornithological & Nature Conservation Society. Költö u. 21, 391, H-1536 Budapest. Fax +36 1 275 6267; mme@c3.hu. Pub: *Ornis hungarica*.

ICELAND. R Icelandic Society for the Protection of Birds. PO Box 5069, IS-125 Reykjavík. Fax +354 562 0464; fuglavernd@simnet.is. Pub: *Bliki*.

INDIA. PD Bomaby Natural History Society, Hornbill House, Shaheed Bhagat Singh Road, Mumbai 400023. +91 22 2843421; fax +91 22 2837615; bhns@bom3.vsnl.net.in.

INDONESIA. R Ornithological Society of Indonesia. c/o Taman Burung 'TMII', Bird Park, TMII, Jakarta (Timur) 13560. +62 21 840 9282; fax +62 21 840 1722; msprana@hotmail.com.

ISRAEL. PD Society for the Protection of Nature in Israel. SPNI, Hashsela 4, Tel Aviv 66103. Fax +972 3 687 7695; ioc@netvision.net.il. Pub: *Torgos* (twice yearly).

ITALY. P Lega Italiana Protezione Uccelli. Via Trento 49, I-431Parma. +39 0521 273190; fax +39 0521 273419; lipupro@tin.it. Pub: *Uccelli*.

JAMAICA. PD BirdLife Jamaica. 2 Starlight Avenue, Kingston 6. Fax +1 876 927 1864; gosse@infochan.com.

JAPAN. P Wild Bird Society of Japan. International Centre-WING, 2-35-2 Minamidaira, Hino City, Tokyo 191-0041. Fax +81 425 936 873; int.center@wing-wbsj.or.jp. Pub: *Strix*, *Yacho*.

JORDAN. P Royal Society for the Conservation of Nature. Box 6354, Jubeiha-Abu-Nusseir Circle, Amman 11183. +962 6 533 7932; fax +962 6 534 7411; adminrscn@rscn.org.jo.

KENYA. P NatureKenya. PO Box 44486, Nairobi. Fax +254 2 741049; eanhs@africaonline.co.ke.

LATVIA. PD Latvijas Ornitologijas Biedriba. PO Box 1010, Riga 50, LV-1050. Fax +371 76 03 100; putni@lanet.lv. Pub: *Putni daba*.

LEBANON. PD Society for the Protection of Nature and Natural Resources in Lebanon. PO Box 11-8281, Beirut. Fax +961 1 822 639; r-jaradi@cyberia.net.lb.

LIECHTENSTEIN. R Botanisch-Zoologische Gesellschaft. Im Bretscha 22, FL-9494 Schaan. Fax +41 75 232 2819; broggi@pingnet.li.

LITHUANIA. PD Lithuanian Ornithological Society. Institute of Ecology, Akademijos 2, LT-26Vilnius. Fax +370 2 72 92 55; birdlife@post.5ci.lt. Pub: *Acta Ornitologia Lituania*; *Ciconia*.

LUXEMBOURG. P Letzebuerger Natur-A Vulleschutz-Liga. Kräizhaff, Rue de Luxembourg, L-1899 Kockelscheuer. Fax +352 29 05 04; secretary@luxnatur.lv. Pub: *Regulus*.

MACEDONIA. R Bird Study and Protection Society of Macedonia. Institute of Biology, Faculty of Sciences, MAC-910Skopje. Fax +389 91 117 055; brankom@iunona.pmf.ukim.edu.mk. Pub: *Sylcan*.

MALAYSIA. P Malaysian Nature Society. PO Box 10750, 50724 Kuala Lumpur. +60 3 287 3820; fax +60 3 287 8773; natsoc@po.jaring.my.

MALTA. P BirdLife Malta. 28 Marina Court, Triq Rigord, Ta'Xbiex MSD 12. Fax +356 34 32 39; blm@orbit.net.mt. Pub: *Il-Merill*; *Bird's Eye View*.

MEXICO. R CIPAMEX. Lab. de Ecología, UBIPRO-ENEP-Iztacala, Av. de los Barrios s/n, Los Reyes, 54090 Tlalnepantla. Fax +52 5 846 0078; coro@servidor.unam.mx.

NEPAL. R Bird Conservation Nepal. PO Box 12465, Kamaladi, Kathmandu. Fax +977 1 224 237; birdlife@mos.com.np.

NETHERLANDS. P Vogelbescherming Nederland. PO Box 925, NL-37AX Zeist. Fax +31 30 69 18844; birdlife@antenna.nl. Pub: *Vogels*; *Vrije Vogels*.

NEW ZEALAND. R Royal Forest and Bird Protection Society. PO Box 631, Wellington. Fax +64 4 385 7373; batesl@wn.forest-bird.org.nz.

NIGERIA. R Nigerian Conservation Foundation. PO Box 74638, Victoria Island, Lagos. Fax +234 1 2642497; esohe@compuserve.com.

NORWAY. P Norwegian Ornithological Society. Seminarplassen 5, N-7060 Klaebu. Fax +47 72 83 12 55; norornis@online.no. Pub: *Var Fuglefauna*; *Cinclus*.

PAKISTAN. R Ornithological Society of Pakistan. Block D Near Farawa Chowk, PO Box 73, Dera Ghazi Khan, 32200. Fax +92 641 62408; aleem01@paknet1.ptc.pk.

PANAMA. PD Panama Audubon Society. Apartado 2026, Balboa Ancón, Panamá. Fax +507 224 9371; audupan@pananet.com. Pub: *Toucan*.

PARAGUAY. PD Fundación Moisés Bertoni. Prócer Carlos Argüello 208, c/Quesada, Asunción. Fax +595 21 608 741; ayanosky@pla.net.py.

PHILIPPINES. P The Haribon Foundation. 9A Malingap Cor, Malumanay Streets, Teachers' Village, Diliman, Quezon City. +63 2 436 2756; fax +63 2 925 3331; birdlife@haribon.org.ph.

POLAND. PD Polish Society for the Protection of Birds. PO Box 335, PL-80-958 Gdansk 50. Fax +48 58 3412 693; office@otop.most.org.pl. Pub: *Ptaki*.

PORTUGAL. A Associaçao Cientifica para o Conservaçao das Aves de Rapina. Luis Filipe Oliveira, Apt 105, P-2775 Carcavelos.

ROMANIA. P Romanian Ornithological Society. Str Gheorghe Dima 49/2, RO-3400 Cluj. Fax 40 69 81 4036; sorcj@codec.ro. Pub: *Alcedo*.

RUSSIA. PD Russian Bird Conservation Union. Shosse Entuziastov 60, Building 1, Moscow 111123. Fax +7 095 176 1063; rbcu@glas.apc.org.

SEYCHELLES. R BirdLife Seychelles. Nirmal Jivan Shah, PO Box 1310, Suite 202, Aarti Chambers, Mont Fleuri, Mahe. Fax +248 225121; birdlife@seychelles.net.

SIERRA LEONE. P Conservation Society of Sierra Leone. PO Box 1292, Freetown. Fax (bureau) +232 22 224439; ddsiaffa@hotmail.com.

SINGAPORE. P The Nature Society. 601 Slims Drive, 04-04 Pan. I Complex, Singapore 387382. Tel +65 741 1071; natsoc@mbox2.singnet.com.sg.

SLOVAKIA. PD Society for the Protection of Birds in Slovakia. PO Box 71, SK-093 01 Vranov nad Topl'ou. Fax +421 93 4462120; sovs@changenet.sk.

SLOVENIA. PD Bird Watching and Bird Study Association of Slovenia. Langusova 10, SLO-61000 Ljubljana. +386 60 962 5210; fax +386 61 133 9516; borut.mozetic@uni-lj.si. Pub: *Acrocephalus*.

SOUTH AFRICA. P BirdLife South Africa. PO Box 515, Randburg, Johannesburg 2125. Fax +27 11 7895188; info@birdlife.org.za. Pub: *Ostrich*.

SPAIN. P Sociedad Española de Ornitología. Melquiades Biencinto 34, E-28053 Madrid. Fax +34 91 434 0911; asanchez@seo.org. Pub: *Ardeola*; *La Garcilla*.

SRI LANKA. R Field Ornithology Group of Sri Lanka. Sarath Kotagama, Dept of Zoology, University of Colombo, Colombo 03. Fax +94 1 75 337 644; fogsl@slt.lk.

SURINAME. R Foundation for Nature Preservation in Surinam. Harrold Sijlbing, PO Box 436, Paramaribo. Fax +597 422 555; stinasu@sr.net.

SWEDEN. P Swedish Ornithological Society. Ekhagsvägen 3, S-104 03 Stockholm. Fax +46 (0)8 612 2536; birdlife@sofnet.org. Pub: *Var Fagelvärld*; *Ornis Svecica*.

SWITZERLAND. P Swiss Association for the Protection of Birds. Wiedingstr 78, PO Box 8521, CH-9036 Zürich. Fax +41 1 461 4778; birdlife.svs@bluewin.ch. Pub: *Ornis*. A Société Romande pour l'Etude et la Protection des Oiseaux. 50 rue Achille-Merguin, CH-2900 Porrentuy. Fax +41 6655 3124. Pub: *Nos Oiseaux*.

TAIWAN. P Chinese Wild Bird Federation. 1F, No 34, Alley 119, Lane 30, Yung-Chi Road 106, 110 Taipei. Fax +886 2878 74547; cwbf@ms4.accmail.com.tw.

TANZANIA. P Wildlife Conservation Society of Tanzania. PO Box 70919, Dar es Salaam. +255 51 112496; fax +255 51 124572 or 112496; wcst@africaonline.co.tz.

THAILAND. P Bird Conservation Society of Thailand (BCST). 69/12 Ramindra 24, Jarakheebua, Ladprao, Bangkok 10230. +66 2943 5965; fax +66 2519 3385/5965; bcst@box1.a-net.net.th.

TUNISIA. PD Association 'Les Amis des Oiseaux', Immeuble CERES, 23 rue d'Espagne, 1000 Tunis. Fax +216 1 350 875; e-mail aao.bird@planet.tn.

TURKEY. P Society for the Protection of Nature. Büyük Postane Caddesi No. 43-45 Bahçekapi-Sirkeci, Istanbul. Fax +90 212 257 35 18; nergis.yazgan@dhkd.org. Pub: *Kelaynaktan Haberler* (newsletter, 6 pa).

UGANDA. P NatureUganda. c/o Dept of Zoology, Makerere University, PO Box 7062, Kampala. Fax +256 41 533528; eanhs@imul.com.

UKRAINE. PD Ukrainian Union for Bird Conservation. Mrs Lisa Kharchenko, PO Box 613, Kiev-103, UA-252103. Fax +380 44 294 7131; bird@utop.freenet.kiev.ua. Pub: *Life of Birds*.

UNITED STATES OF AMERICA. P American Bird Conservancy. 1250 24th Street NW, Suite 400, Washington DC 20037. +1 202 778 9666; fax +1 202 778 9778.

URUGUAY. R Grupo Uruguayo para el Estudio y la Conservación de las Aves. Adrián Stagi, Casilla de Correo 6955, Correo Central, Montevideo. Fax +598 2 908 5959; gual@fcien.edu.uy.

VENEZUELA. P Venezuelan Audubon Society. Apartado No. 80450, Caracas 1080-A. +58 2 922 812; fax +58 2 991 0716; edqcrodner@cantv.ve.

ZAMBIA. R Zambian Ornithological Society. Pete Leonard, PO Box 33944, Lusaka 10101. zos@zamnet.zm. Pub: *Bulletin*.

ZIMBABWE. R BirdLife Zimbabwe, John Paxton, PO Box 470, Harare. +263 4 884413 (home); fax +263 4 794614; birds@zol.co.zw. Pub: *Honeyguide*.

PART FOUR

QUICK REFERENCE

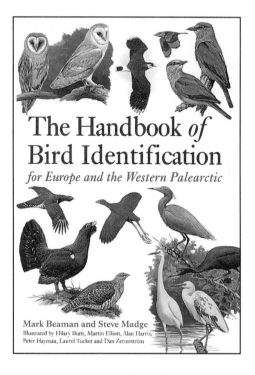

(Actual size 246 x 172 mm)

The Handbook of Bird Identification for Europe and the Western Palearctic, by Mark Beaman and Steve Madge, illustrated by Hilary Burn, Martin Elliott, Alan Harris, Peter Hayman, Laurel Tucker and Dan Zetterström, Helm (A&C Black), 1998, 868p, £65.00. ISBN 0 7136 3960 1. Hbk.

At well over 2kg this is not a fieldguide. Its size allows for *every* species recorded in the area to be included (close to 900) and for good-size illustrations. Often, however, the text is so dense that it is hard to follow. This isn't helped by being separated from the illustrations which, though excellent, are clustered in groups of plates. That said, this is a volume of undisputed quality, its comprehensive coverage contributing to its value. It is an affordable major reference work which may spend much of its time on the shelf but will prove invaluable in times of need.

TIDE TABLES 2000

(Tables for 2001 are not available at the time of going to press.)

British Summer Time

In 2000 BST applies from 0100 on 26 March to 0100 on 29 October.

Note that all the times in the following tables are GMT.
During British Summer Time one hour should be added.

Predictions are given for the times of high water at Dover throughout the year.

The times of tides at the locations shown on page 133 may be obtained by adding or subtracting their 'tidal difference' as shown on page 134 (subtractions are indicated by a minus sign).

Example 1
To calculate the time of first high water at Aberdeen on 5 March
1. Look up the time at Dover (10 42)*   = 10.42 am
2. Add the tidal difference for Aberdeen   = 2.30
3. Therefore the time of high water at Aberdeen   = 1.12 pm

Example 2
To calculate the time of second high water at Fishguard on 25 July
1. Look up the time at Dover (16 08)   = 4.08 pm
2. Add 1 hour for British Summer Time (17 08)   = 5.08 pm
3. Subtract the tidal difference for Fishguard   = -3.48
4. Therefore the time of high water at Fishguard = 1.20 pm

* All Dover times are shown on the 24-hour clock.
Thus, 10 42 = 10.42 am; 16 08 = 4.08 pm.

Heights of Tides

Following the time of each high water the height of the tide is given, in metres.

Tidal predictions for Dover have been computed by the Centre for Coastal and Marine Sciences - Proudman Oceanographic Laboratory

Time Zone GMT   Units METRES

Tidal Predictions : HIGH WATERS 2000
Datum of Predictions = Chart Datum : 3.67 metres below Ordnance Datum (Newlyn)
British Summer Time : 26th March to 29th October

DOVER — January

Date	Day	Morning hr min	m	Afternoon hr min	m
1	Sa	06 47	5.6	19 32	5.4
2	Su	07 53	5.7	20 30	5.6
3	M	08 48	5.8	21 00	5.8
4	Tu	09 34	6.0	22 00	6.0
5	W	10 13	6.1	22 38	6.2
6	Th	10 53	6.2	23 14	6.3
7	F	11 28	6.3	23 48	6.4
8	Sa	•• ••	• •	12 01	6.3
9	Su	00 20	6.4	12 32	6.2
10	M	00 54	6.4	13 04	6.2
11	Tu	01 26	6.3	13 41	6.1
12	W	02 00	6.2	14 16	6.0
13	Th	02 40	6.2	14 52	5.9
14	F	03 27	6.1	15 08	5.8
15	Sa	04 25	5.9	16 19	5.7
16	Su	05 37	5.9	18 19	5.7
17	M	06 49	6.1	19 29	5.8
18	Tu	08 07	6.3	20 37	6.1
19	W	08 59	6.6	21 36	6.4
20	Th	09 50	6.7	22 31	6.7
21	F	10 40	6.8	23 20	6.8
22	Sa	11 40	6.9	•• ••	• •
23	Su	00 08	6.9	12 29	6.8
24	M	00 51	6.9	13 14	6.6
25	Tu	01 34	6.8	13 56	6.4
26	W	02 16	6.6	14 38	6.2
27	Th	02 58	6.3	15 25	5.9
28	F	03 47	6.0	16 18	5.6
29	Sa	04 43	5.7	17 23	5.3
30	Su	05 54	5.4	18 40	5.2
31	M	07 11	5.3	19 53	5.3

DOVER — February

Date	Day	Morning hr min	m	Afternoon hr min	m
1	Tu	08 19	5.4	20 52	5.5
2	W	09 09	5.7	21 40	5.8
3	Th	09 58	5.9	22 19	6.0
4	F	10 35	6.0	22 55	6.2
5	Sa	11 07	6.2	23 27	6.4
6	Su	11 40	6.3	•• ••	• •
7	M	00 01	6.5	12 12	6.4
8	Tu	00 33	6.5	12 46	6.4
9	W	01 07	6.5	13 21	6.4
10	Th	01 41	6.4	13 56	6.3
11	F	02 16	6.3	14 38	6.1
12	Sa	02 59	6.1	15 29	6.0
13	Su	03 54	5.9	16 32	5.8
14	M	05 02	5.9	17 47	5.6
15	Tu	06 26	5.8	19 10	5.9
16	W	07 43	5.8	20 28	5.9
17	Th	08 55	6.1	21 30	6.2
18	F	09 54	6.4	22 29	6.5
19	Sa	10 45	6.6	23 22	6.8
20	Su	11 30	6.7	23 52	6.9
21	M	•• ••	• •	12 13	6.7
22	Tu	00 32	6.9	12 53	6.6
23	W	01 11	6.8	13 31	6.5
24	Th	01 48	6.7	14 07	6.3
25	F	02 26	6.4	14 47	6.0
26	Sa	03 06	6.1	15 30	5.7
27	Su	03 54	5.7	16 25	5.3
28	M	04 57	5.3	17 41	5.0
29	Tu	06 23	5.0	19 11	5.0

DOVER — March

Date	Day	Morning hr min	m	Afternoon hr min	m
1	W	07 48	5.1	20 21	5.3
2	Th	08 49	5.4	21 21	5.6
3	F	09 36	5.7	21 54	5.9
4	Sa	10 11	5.9	22 29	6.2
5	Su	10 42	6.2	23 02	6.4
6	M	11 14	6.4	23 34	6.6
7	Tu	11 48	6.5	•• ••	• •
8	W	00 08	6.7	12 23	6.6
9	Th	00 43	6.7	13 00	6.6
10	F	01 18	6.7	13 36	6.5
11	Sa	01 55	6.6	14 19	6.3
12	Su	02 38	6.4	15 08	6.1
13	M	03 33	6.1	16 11	5.8
14	Tu	04 41	5.8	17 30	5.5
15	W	06 11	5.5	19 03	5.6
16	Th	07 43	5.7	20 23	5.8
17	F	08 54	6.0	21 22	6.2
18	Sa	09 49	6.3	22 10	6.5
19	Su	10 34	6.5	22 52	6.7
20	M	11 14	6.6	23 31	6.8
21	Tu	11 52	6.6	•• ••	• •
22	W	00 09	6.8	12 29	6.6
23	Th	00 46	6.8	13 03	6.5
24	F	01 19	6.6	13 36	6.3
25	Sa	01 53	6.4	14 11	6.1
26	Su	02 28	6.1	14 48	5.8
27	M	03 05	5.7	15 34	5.4
28	Tu	04 05	5.2	16 42	5.1
29	W	05 30	4.9	18 16	4.9
30	Th	07 08	4.9	19 39	5.1
31	F	08 14	5.2	20 37	5.2

DOVER — April

Date	Day	Morning hr min	m	Afternoon hr min	m
1	Sa	09 02	5.6	21 20	5.9
2	Su	09 39	5.9	21 56	6.2
3	M	10 11	6.2	22 29	6.4
4	Tu	10 43	6.4	23 03	6.6
5	W	11 20	6.6	23 40	6.8
6	Th	11 58	6.7	•• ••	• •
7	F	00 18	6.9	12 39	6.7
8	Sa	00 56	6.8	13 19	6.6
9	Su	01 38	6.7	14 06	6.4
10	M	02 26	6.4	14 58	6.1
11	Tu	03 25	6.0	16 03	5.8
12	W	04 39	5.7	17 21	5.6
13	Th	06 11	5.5	18 53	5.8
14	F	07 39	5.7	20 07	5.8
15	Sa	08 44	6.0	21 04	6.1
16	Su	09 34	6.2	21 49	6.4
17	M	10 15	6.4	22 29	6.6
18	Tu	10 53	6.5	23 07	6.7
19	W	11 28	6.5	23 44	6.5
20	Th	•• ••	• •	12 04	6.5
21	F	00 20	6.6	12 37	6.4
22	Sa	00 54	6.5	13 11	6.3
23	Su	01 28	6.3	13 44	6.1
24	M	01 57	6.0	14 17	5.9
25	Tu	02 34	5.7	14 59	5.6
26	W	03 23	5.3	15 57	5.3
27	Th	03 39	5.0	17 16	5.1
28	F	04 39	4.9	18 41	5.4
29	Sa	06 07	5.2	19 46	5.5
30	Su	07 22	5.5	20 35	5.8

Time Zone GMT

Tidal Predictions : HIGH WATERS 2000

Datum of Predictions = Chart Datum : 3.67 metres below Ordnance Datum (Newlyn)

British Summer Time : 26th March to 29th October

Units METRES

DOVER — May

Date	Day	Morning hr min	m	Afternoon hr min	m
1	M	08 58	5.9	21 16	6.2
2	Tu	09 34	6.2	21 54	6.5
3	W	10 12	6.5	22 32	6.7
4	Th	10 53	6.7	23 11	6.9
5	F	**:**	6.8	23 54	6.9
6	Sa	**:**	6.8	12 20	6.8
7	Su	00 40	6.8	13 08	6.7
8	M	01 28	6.7	14 00	6.5
9	Tu	02 23	6.4	14 55	6.0
10	W	03 24	6.1	15 59	6.0
11	Th	04 36	5.8	17 09	5.7
12	F	06 01	5.7	18 30	5.7
13	Sa	07 18	5.7	19 41	5.9
14	Su	08 20	5.9	20 35	6.1
15	M	09 09	6.1	21 24	6.3
16	Tu	09 50	6.3	22 04	6.4
17	W	10 28	6.3	22 42	6.5
18	Th	11 04	6.4	23 18	6.5
19	F	11 41	6.4	23 58	6.4
20	Sa	**:**		12 16	6.4
21	Su	00 33	6.3	12 51	6.3
22	M	01 05	6.2	13 23	6.2
23	Tu	01 36	5.9	13 57	6.0
24	W	02 11	5.7	14 35	5.8
25	Th	02 55	5.5	15 26	5.6
26	F	03 56	5.2	16 26	5.4
27	Sa	05 10	5.3	17 40	5.4
28	Su	06 33	5.3	18 47	5.5
29	M	07 22	5.6	19 45	5.8
30	Tu	08 13	5.9	20 34	6.2
31	W	08 59	6.2	21 19	6.5

DOVER — June

Date	Day	Morning hr min	m	Afternoon hr min	m
1	Th	09 44	6.5	22 03	6.7
2	F	10 29	6.7	22 49	6.8
3	Sa	11 19	6.8	23 37	6.8
4	Su	**:**	**	12 09	6.8
5	M	00 29	6.8	13 01	6.7
6	Tu	01 19	6.7	13 53	6.6
7	W	02 13	6.4	14 45	6.4
8	Th	03 18	6.2	15 43	6.2
9	F	04 19	6.0	16 52	6.0
10	Sa	05 30	5.9	18 00	5.9
11	Su	06 41	5.7	19 01	5.7
12	M	07 43	5.7	20 00	5.9
13	Tu	08 37	6.0	20 52	6.0
14	W	09 23	6.1	21 37	6.1
15	Th	10 04	6.1	22 19	6.2
16	F	10 43	6.3	23 00	6.3
17	Sa	11 21	6.3	23 38	6.3
18	Su	11 58	6.3	**:**	**
19	M	00 15	6.2	12 34	6.3
20	Tu	00 49	6.1	13 08	6.2
21	W	01 21	6.0	13 41	6.1
22	Th	01 55	5.8	14 16	6.0
23	F	02 31	5.7	14 55	5.8
24	Sa	03 19	5.6	15 44	5.8
25	Su	04 18	5.5	16 45	5.7
26	M	05 24	5.6	17 49	5.7
27	Tu	06 29	5.8	18 54	5.9
28	W	07 31	6.1	19 53	6.1
29	Th	08 27	6.4	20 49	6.4
30	F	09 22	6.6	21 41	6.6

DOVER — July

Date	Day	Morning hr min	m	Afternoon hr min	m
1	Sa	10 14	6.6	22 34	6.8
2	Su	11 07	6.8	23 27	6.8
3	M	11 59	6.8	**:**	**
4	Tu	00 14	6.8	12 50	6.7
5	W	01 06	6.7	13 39	6.6
6	Th	01 56	6.5	14 27	6.5
7	F	02 56	6.3	15 15	6.3
8	Sa	03 46	6.0	16 08	6.1
9	Su	04 46	5.7	17 07	5.9
10	M	05 52	5.6	18 15	5.7
11	Tu	07 03	5.6	19 22	5.7
12	W	08 03	5.7	20 23	5.8
13	Th	08 58	5.9	21 16	6.0
14	F	09 44	5.9	22 01	6.1
15	Sa	10 25	6.1	22 40	6.1
16	Su	11 03	6.3	23 20	6.2
17	M	11 40	6.3	23 55	6.2
18	Tu	**:**	**	12 15	6.4
19	W	00 29	6.2	12 49	6.4
20	Th	01 01	6.1	13 21	6.3
21	F	01 32	6.1	13 52	6.3
22	Sa	02 06	6.0	14 26	6.2
23	Su	02 45	5.9	15 06	6.1
24	M	03 33	5.8	15 58	6.0
25	Tu	04 35	5.7	17 02	5.9
26	W	05 44	5.7	18 18	5.8
27	Th	06 56	6.0	19 31	6.0
28	F	08 06	6.3	20 34	6.4
29	Sa	09 11	6.4	21 32	6.4
30	Su	10 07	6.6	22 26	6.7
31	M	10 59	6.8	23 19	6.8

DOVER — August

Date	Day	Morning hr min	m	Afternoon hr min	m
1	Tu	11 48	6.9	**:**	**
2	W	00 09	6.8	12 34	6.9
3	Th	00 58	6.8	13 19	6.9
4	F	01 43	6.6	14 02	6.7
5	Sa	02 26	6.5	14 44	6.5
6	Su	03 11	6.1	15 29	6.2
7	M	04 00	5.8	16 22	5.9
8	Tu	04 59	5.5	17 27	5.6
9	W	06 12	5.3	18 44	5.4
10	Th	07 33	5.5	19 57	5.5
11	F	08 33	5.5	20 58	5.6
12	Sa	09 25	5.8	21 48	5.9
13	Su	10 05	6.1	22 25	6.0
14	M	10 43	6.3	23 00	6.2
15	Tu	11 17	6.4	23 33	6.3
16	W	11 49	6.5	**:**	*
17	Th	00 04	6.3	12 22	6.5
18	F	00 34	6.3	12 54	6.5
19	Sa	01 07	6.3	13 24	6.5
20	Su	01 39	6.3	13 56	6.4
21	M	02 14	6.2	14 33	6.3
22	Tu	02 59	6.0	15 25	6.1
23	W	03 57	5.6	16 25	5.9
24	Th	05 09	5.6	17 42	5.7
25	F	06 33	5.7	19 10	5.7
26	Sa	07 57	6.0	20 27	6.0
27	Su	09 05	6.2	21 29	6.4
28	M	10 00	6.6	22 21	6.6
29	Tu	10 46	6.8	23 09	6.8
30	W	11 31	7.0	23 52	6.8
31	Th	**:**	**	12 13	7.0

Time Zone GMT

Tidal Predictions : HIGH WATERS 2000
Datum of Predictions = Chart Datum : 3.67 metres below Ordnance Datum (Newlyn)
British Summer Time : 26th March to 29th October

Units METRES

DOVER — September

Date	Day	Morning hr min	m	Afternoon hr min	m
1	F	00 34	6.8	12 53	6.9
2	Sa	01 14	6.6	13 31	6.8
3	Su	01 52	6.4	14 09	6.6
4	M ⌒	02 30	6.1	14 49	6.3
5	Tu	03 13	5.8	15 39	5.9
6	W	04 08	5.5	16 39	5.4
7	Th	04 51	5.2	18 04	5.1
8	F	05 21	5.1	19 32	5.2
9	Sa	08 06	5.1	20 38	5.4
10	Su	09 01	5.7	21 27	5.8
11	M	09 43	6.0	22 04	6.0
12	Tu ○	10 18	6.3	22 35	6.2
13	W	10 50	6.5	23 04	6.4
14	Th	11 21	6.6	23 34	6.5
15	F	11 52	6.7	** **	6.7
16	Sa	00 05	6.6	12 23	6.7
17	Su	00 39	6.6	12 56	6.7
18	M ⌣	01 12	6.5	13 28	6.6
19	Tu	01 50	6.4	14 07	6.4
20	W	02 34	6.1	14 56	6.2
21	Th	03 33	5.9	16 03	5.8
22	F	04 56	5.5	17 11	5.6
23	Sa	06 26	5.5	19 11	5.6
24	Su	07 55	5.8	20 28	6.0
25	M ●	08 58	6.2	21 26	6.3
26	Tu	09 47	6.6	22 15	6.6
27	W	10 29	6.8	22 52	6.8
28	Th	11 07	6.9	23 31	6.8
29	F	11 48	7.0	** **	**
30	Sa	00 08	6.8	12 25	6.9

DOVER — October

Date	Day	Morning hr min	m	Afternoon hr min	m
1	Su	00 44	6.6	13 01	6.8
2	M	01 19	6.4	13 36	6.5
3	Tu	01 53	6.2	14 13	6.2
4	W ⌒	02 24	5.9	14 54	5.8
5	Th	03 20	5.6	15 51	5.3
6	F	04 01	5.2	17 17	5.0
7	Sa	06 28	5.2	18 57	5.0
8	Su	07 28	5.2	20 09	5.3
9	M	08 28	5.6	20 58	5.7
10	Tu	09 12	6.0	21 34	6.0
11	W ○	09 47	6.3	22 03	6.3
12	Th	10 18	6.5	22 32	6.5
13	F	10 48	6.7	23 03	6.6
14	Sa	11 20	6.8	23 37	6.7
15	Su	11 54	6.9	** **	**
16	M	00 13	6.7	12 30	6.8
17	Tu	00 51	6.5	13 08	6.7
18	W ⌣	01 34	6.5	13 50	6.1
19	Th	02 23	6.2	14 45	6.1
20	F	03 43	5.6	15 58	5.5
21	Sa	04 43	5.6	17 31	5.5
22	Su	06 18	5.6	19 08	5.7
23	M	07 39	5.8	20 19	6.0
24	Tu	08 40	6.2	21 54	6.3
25	W ●	09 27	6.5	21 31	6.5
26	Th	10 07	6.7	22 07	6.6
27	F	10 46	6.8	23 07	6.7
28	Sa	11 24	6.9	23 42	6.7
29	Su	11 59	6.8	** **	**
30	M	00 19	6.6	12 34	6.7
31	Tu	00 53	6.5	13 08	6.4

DOVER — November

Date	Day	Morning hr min	m	Afternoon hr min	m
1	W	01 28	6.3	13 43	6.1
2	Th	02 03	6.0	14 20	5.8
3	F ⌒	02 45	5.7	15 09	5.4
4	Sa	03 40	5.4	16 22	5.0
5	Su	04 57	5.1	17 56	4.9
6	M	06 27	5.2	19 17	5.1
7	Tu	07 36	5.4	20 10	5.5
8	W	08 26	5.8	20 51	5.9
9	Th ○	09 05	6.1	21 25	6.2
10	F	09 39	6.4	21 57	6.5
11	Sa	10 14	6.7	22 34	6.7
12	Su	10 50	6.9	23 11	6.8
13	M	11 28	6.9	23 54	6.8
14	Tu	** **	**	12 11	6.9
15	W	00 39	6.7	12 56	6.5
16	Th ⌣	01 26	6.6	13 46	6.5
17	F	02 05	6.3	14 45	6.1
18	Sa	03 05	6.1	15 57	5.8
19	Su	04 31	5.8	17 21	5.6
20	M	05 52	5.7	18 46	5.7
21	Tu	07 10	5.9	19 53	5.9
22	W	08 10	6.1	20 47	6.1
23	Th ●	08 59	6.3	21 30	6.3
24	F	09 43	6.5	22 08	6.5
25	Sa	10 22	6.6	22 46	6.5
26	Su	11 00	6.6	23 23	6.5
27	M	11 38	6.6	23 59	6.5
28	Tu	** **	**	12 15	6.5
29	W	00 34	6.4	12 50	6.3
30	Th	01 10	6.3	13 24	6.1

DOVER — December

Date	Day	Morning hr min	m	Afternoon hr min	m
1	F	01 43	6.1	13 59	5.8
2	Sa	02 21	5.9	14 40	5.5
3	Su ⌒	03 05	5.7	15 33	5.3
4	M	04 03	5.4	16 43	5.1
5	Tu	05 25	5.3	17 59	5.1
6	W	06 25	5.4	19 04	5.4
7	Th	07 25	5.7	19 56	5.7
8	F	08 14	6.0	20 41	6.0
9	Sa ○	08 59	6.3	21 25	6.3
10	Su	09 41	6.6	22 08	6.6
11	M	10 25	6.8	22 53	6.7
12	Tu	11 10	6.9	23 41	6.8
13	W	11 59	6.8	** **	**
14	Th	00 30	6.8	12 50	6.8
15	F	01 22	6.7	13 43	6.6
16	Sa ⌣	02 14	6.5	14 41	6.3
17	Su	03 08	6.3	15 41	6.0
18	M	04 07	6.1	16 49	5.8
19	Tu	05 14	5.9	18 02	5.6
20	W	06 25	5.9	19 11	5.7
21	Th	07 31	6.0	20 11	5.8
22	F	08 18	6.2	21 02	5.9
23	Sa ●	09 03	6.3	21 47	6.1
24	Su	10 03	6.3	22 28	6.2
25	M	10 43	6.4	23 06	6.4
26	Tu	11 23	6.4	23 44	6.4
27	W	11 59	6.3	** **	**
28	Th	00 34	6.4	12 34	6.2
29	F	00 54	6.4	13 08	6.1
30	Sa	01 26	6.3	13 39	6.0
31	Su	02 00	6.1	14 14	5.8

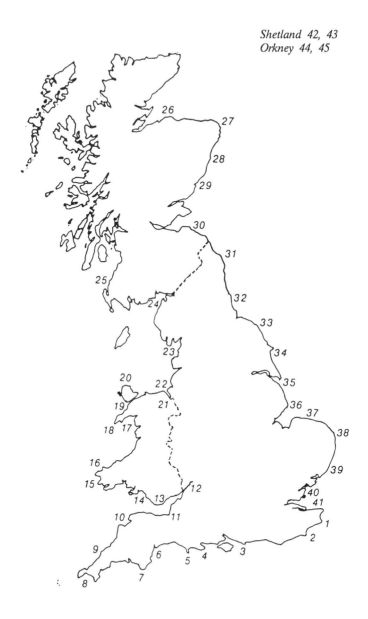

Shetland 42, 43
Orkney 44, 45

Map showing locations for which approximate tidal
differences are given on page 134

APPROXIMATE TIDAL DIFFERENCES

1	Dover	See pp	130-32
2	Dungeness	-0	12
3	Selsey Bill	0	09
4	Swanage (1st H. W. Springs)	-2	36
5	Portland	-4	23
6	Exmouth (Approaches)	-4	48
7	Salcombe	-5	23
8	Newlyn (Penzance)	5	59
9	Padstow	-5	47
10	Bideford	-5	17
11	Bridgwater	-4	23
12	Sharpness Dock	-3	19
13	Cardiff (Penarth)	-4	16
14	Swansea	-4	52
15	Skomer Island	-5	00
16	Fishguard	-3	48
17	Barmouth	-2	45
18	Bardsey Island	-3	07
19	Caernarvon	-1	07
20	Amlwch	-0	22
21	Connahs Quay	0	20
22	Hilbre Island (Hoylake/West Kirby)	-0	05
23	Morecambe	0	20
24	Silloth	0	51
25	Girvan	0	54
26	Lossiemouth	0	48
27	Fraserburgh	1	20
28	Aberdeen	2	30
29	Montrose	3	30
30	Dunbar	3	42
31	Holy Island	3	58
32	Sunderland	4	38
33	Whitby	5	12
34	Bridlington	5	53
35	Grimsby	-5	20
36	Skegness	-5	00
37	Blakeney	-4	07
38	Gorleston	-2	08
39	Aldeburgh	-0	13
40	Bradwell Waterside	1	11
41	Herne Bay	1	28
42	Sullom Voe	-1	34
43	Lerwick	0	01
44	Kirkwall	-0	26
45	Widewall Bay	-1	30

NB. Care should be taken when making calculations at the beginning and end of British Summer Time. See worked examples on page 129.

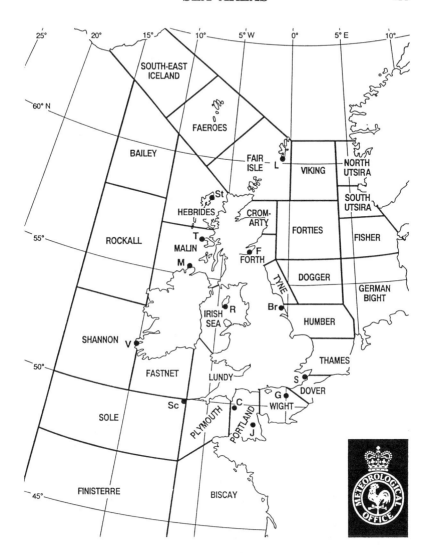

STATIONS WHOSE LATEST REPORTS ARE BROADCAST
IN THE 5-MINUTE FORECASTS

Br Bridlington; C Channel Light-Vessel Automatic; F Fife Ness; G Greenwich Light-Vessel Automatic; J Jersey; L Lerwick; M Malin Head; R Ronaldsway; S Sandettie Light-Vessel Automatic; Sc Scilly Automatic; St Stornoway; T Tiree; V Valentia

From information kindly supplied by the Meteorological Office

SUNRISE AND SUNSET TIMES 2000

Predictions are given for the times of sunrise and sunset on every Saturday throughout the year. For places on the same latitude as the following, add 4 minutes for each degree of longitude west (subtract if east).

26 Mar - 29 Oct times are British Summer Time
All other times are GMT

(In 2000 BST applies from 0100 on 26 March to 0100 on 29 October.)

	LONDON		MANCHESTER		EDINBURGH	
	Rise	Set	Rise	Set	Rise	Set
Jan 1	0806	1602	0825	1600	0844	1549
8	0805	1610	0823	1608	0841	1558
15	0800	1620	0818	1619	0835	1610
22	0753	1631	0810	1631	0826	1624
29	0744	1643	0800	1644	0814	1638
Feb 5	0734	1656	0748	1658	0801	1653
12	0722	1709	0735	1712	0746	1709
19	0708	1722	0721	1726	0730	1724
26	0654	1734	0705	1740	0714	1739
Mar 4	0639	1747	0649	1753	0656	1754
11	0623	1759	0633	1806	0638	1809
18	0607	1811	0616	1819	0620	1823
25	0551	1823	0559	1832	0601	1837
Apr 1	0636	1934	0642	1945	0643	1952
8	0620	1946	0625	1958	0625	2006
15	0605	1958	0609	2010	0607	2020
22	0550	2009	0553	2023	0550	2034
29	0536	2021	0538	2036	0533	2049
May 6	0523	2032	0524	2048	0518	2103
13	0512	2043	0511	2100	0504	2116
20	0502	2054	0500	2112	0451	2129
27	0453	2103	0451	2122	0441	2140

		LONDON		MANCHESTER		EDINBURGH	
		Rise	Set	Rise	Set	Rise	Set
Jun	3	0448	2111	0445	2130	0433	2150
	10	0444	2117	0441	2137	0428	2157
	17	0443	2121	0439	2141	0426	2202
	24	0444	2122	0441	2142	0427	2203
Jul	1	0448	2121	0445	2141	0432	2201
	8	0454	2117	0451	2137	0439	2156
	15	0501	2111	0459	2130	0448	2148
	22	0510	2103	0509	2121	0459	2138
	29	0520	2053	0520	2110	0512	2125
Aug	5	0531	2041	0532	2057	0525	2111
	12	0542	2028	0544	2043	0538	2056
	19	0553	2014	0556	2028	0552	2039
	26	0604	2000	0608	2012	0606	2022
Sep	2	0615	1944	0620	1956	0620	2004
	9	0626	1928	0632	1939	0633	1946
	16	0637	1912	0645	1922	0647	1927
	23	0649	1856	0657	1905	0700	1909
	30	0700	1840	0709	1847	0714	1850
Oct	7	0712	1824	0722	1831	0728	1832
	14	0723	1809	0735	1814	0742	1814
	21	0735	1754	0748	1759	0757	1757
	28	0748	1741	0801	1744	0812	1741
Nov	4	0700	1628	0714	1630	0727	1626
	11	0712	1617	0728	1618	0741	1612
	18	0724	1607	0741	1607	0756	1600
	25	0735	1600	0753	1559	0809	1550
Dec	2	0746	1554	0804	1553	0821	1543
	9	0754	1552	0813	1550	0832	1539
	16	0801	1552	0820	1550	0839	1538
	23	0805	1555	0824	1552	0843	1541
	30	0806	1600	0825	1558	0844	1547

COUNTY BIRDWATCH TALLIES

RULES

1. Teams shall comprise four members, all resident in the geographical area of the birdwatch, one of whom may be a driver and/or record-keeper.
2. Geographical areas shall generally be those used by the network of Bird Recorders.
3. A tally must be achieved on one calendar day.
4. No species shall be included in the tally unless seen or heard by at least three members of the team.
5. Team members and birds must be within the defined area at the time of recording.
6. Admitted species shall be those on the relevant official country list (eg. the British List for England, Scotland and Wales), plus Feral Pigeon; rarities must be accepted by the appropriate (county or national) Rarities Committee. Schedule D species shall be excluded.
7. Escapes, sick, injured or oiled birds shall not be admitted.
8. Attracting birds with a tape recording shall not be allowed.
9. The Birdwatchers' Code of Conduct shall be strictly observed.

NOTES

Tallies are accepted and published in good faith. A listing does not imply that the above rules have been adhered to, nor that any authentication or adjudication has been made.

A county or region's best record is used in determining its position in the table. If the same total has been reached in more than one year, only the first is given.

( ) Numbers within curved brackets indicate the latest known total number of species on the county or region's list. In order to ensure consistency as to which species should be included on the list, Rule 6 should be applied.

If the same total has been reached by more than one county or region the names are listed alphabetically and a joint position indicated by an 'equals' sign (=).

POSITION	COUNTY	SPECIES		YEAR
1	Norfolk	159	(401)	1990
2	Dorset	158	(396)	1989
3	Kent	153	(396)	1999
4	Hampshire	151	(352)	1994
5	Yorkshire	150	(428)	1992
6	Cheshire	149	(338)	1993
7 =	Grampian	148	(340)	1998
7 =	Suffolk	148	(371)	1992
9	Highland	146	(246)	1988
10 =	Cleveland	142	(349)	1994
10 =	Durham	142	(348)	1999
12	Lancs & N Merseyside	141	(346)	1996
13	Cumbria	140	(350)	1996
14	Northumberland	138	(384)	1988
15 =	Highland, NE Scotland	136	(?)	1993
15 =	Sussex	136	(382)	1996
17 =	Gwynedd (old county)	135	(349)	1989
17 =	Tayside, Angus/Dundee	135	(302)	1994
19	Highland, N Scotland	134	(?)	1988
20 =	Devon	133	(403)	1991
20 =	Northern Ireland	133	(309)	1993
22	Fife (excl May)	130	(300)	1996
23	Derbyshire	129	(304)	1998
24 =	Cornwall	128	(451)	1992
24 =	Lincolnshire	128	(369)	1988
24 =	Lothian	128	(343)	1994
27	Ayrshire	127	(287)	1991
28 =	Caernarfonshire	126	(347)	1993
28 =	Nottinghamshire	126	(308)	1991
30 =	Clwyd	125	(296)	1995
30 =	Staffordshire	125	(293)	1993
32	Yorkshire, East	124	(353)	1993
33 =	Anglesey	123	(304)	1999
33 =	Essex	123	(365)	1996
33 =	Somerset	123	(336)	1995
36 =	Carmarthenshire	122	(291)	1991
36 =	Gloucestershire	122	(307)	1998
38 =	Berkshire	121	(307)	1990
38 =	Caithness	121	(292)	1994
38 =	Moray & Nairn	121	(284)	1993
41 =	Republic of Ireland	119	(425)	1996
41 =	Wexford	119	(?)	1992
43 =	Manchester	118	(300)	1992
43 =	Wiltshire	118	(303)	1989
45 =	Cambridgeshire	117	(301)	1990
45 =	Merionethshire	117	(263)	1989

POSITION	COUNTY	SPECIES		YEAR
47 =	Cambs, Hunts/Peterbro	115	(294)	1989
47 =	Dumfries & Galloway	115	(279)	1986
47 =	Glamorgan (Old)	115	(300)	1986
47 =	Leics/Rutland	115	(302)	1997
47 =	Pembrokeshire	115	(353)	1995
47 =	Surrey	115	(322)	1995
53 =	Borders	114	(290)	1997
53 =	Northamptonshire	114	(309)	1998
53 =	Worcestershire	114	(285)	1995
56 =	Buckinghamshire	113	(276)	1990
56 =	Isle of Wight	113	(321)	1989
56 =	London	113	(348)	1994
59 =	Montgomeryshire	112	(217)	1991
59 =	Rutland	112	(272)	1994
61 =	Bedfordshire	111	(280)	1996
61 =	Glamorgan, East	111	(295)	1993
61 =	Gwent	111	(288)	1991
61 =	Warwickshire	111	(292)	1993
65 =	Glamorgan, West	110	(288)	1991
65 =	Oxfordshire	110	(296)	1995
67	Leicestershire	109	(290)	1998
68	Central	108	(248)	1996
69 =	Ceredigion	107	(282)	1986
69 =	Hertfordshire	107	(282)	1989
71 =	Merseyside	105	(?)	1993
71 =	Western Isles	105	(337)	1985
73 =	Avon	104	(320)	1993
73 =	Shetland	104	(415)	1988
75	Shropshire	103	(263)	1989
76	Radnorshire	97	(235)	1988
77	Guernsey	96	(296)	1992
78	Breconshire	95	(252)	1991
79	West Midlands	92	(273)	1995
80	Herefordshire	90	(245)	1994
81	Cornwall, Scilly	85	(402)	1992
	Alderney		(266)	
	Argyll		(313)	
	Fife, Isle of May		(251)	
	Highland, Sutherland		(268)	
	Isle of Man		(287)	
	Jersey		(299)	
	Orkney		(364)	
	Shetland, Fair Isle		(354)	

Note. The last eight do not have a one-day tally. They are included here solely to record the total number of species on each area's list.

BIRDWATCHERS' CODE OF CONDUCT

Today's birdwatchers are a powerful force for nature conservation. The number of those of us interested in birds rises continually and it is vital that we take seriously our responsibility to avoid any harm to birds. We must also present a responsible image to non-birdwatchers who may be affected by our activities and particularly those on whose sympathy and support the future of birds may rest. There are 10 points to bear in mind.

1. Welfare of birds must come first. Whether your particular interest is photography, ringing, sound recording, scientific study or just bird-watching, remember that the welfare of the bird must always come first.

2. Habitat protection. Its habitat is vital to a bird and therefore we must ensure that our activities do not cause damage.

3. Keep disturbance to a minimum. Birds' tolerance of disturbance varies between species and seasons. Therefore, it is safer to keep all disturbance to a minimum. No birds should be disturbed from the nest in case opportunities for predators to take eggs or young are increased. In very cold weather disturbance to birds may cause them to use vital energy at a time when food is difficult to find. Wildfowlers already impose bans during cold weather: birdwatchers should exercise similar discretion.

4. Rare breeding birds. If you discover a rare bird breeding and feel that protection is necessary, inform the appropriate RSPB Regional Office, or the Species Protection Department at the Lodge. Otherwise it is best in almost all circumstances to keep the record strictly secret in order to avoid disturbance by other birdwatchers and attacks by egg-collectors. Never visit known sites of rare breeding birds unless they are adequately protected. Even presence may give away the site to others and cause so many other visitors that the birds may fail to breed successfully.
   Disturbance at or near the nest of species listed on the First Schedule of the Wildlife and Countryside Act 1981 is a criminal offence.

5. Rare migrants. Rare migrants or vagrants must not be harrassed. If you discover one, consider the circumstances carefully before telling anyone. Will an influx of birdwatchers disturb the bird or others in the area? Will the habitat be damaged? Will problems be caused with the landowner?

6. The Law. The bird protection laws, as now embodied in the Wildlife and Countryside Act 1981, are the result of hard campaigning by previous generations of birdwatchers. As birdwatchers we must abide by them at all times and not allow them to fall into disrepute.

7. Respect the rights of landowners. The wishes of landowners and occupiers of land must be respected. Do not enter land without permission. Comply with permit schemes. If you are leading a group, do give advance notice of the visit, even if a formal permit scheme is not in operation. Always obey the Country Code.

8. Respect the rights of other people. Have proper consideration for other birdwatchers. Try not to disrupt their activities or scare the birds they are watching. There are many other people who also use the countryside. Do not interfere with their activities and, if it seems that what they are doing is causing unnecessary disturbance to birds, do try to take a balanced view. Flushing gulls when walking a dog on a beach may do little harm, while the same dog might be a serious disturbance at a tern colony. When pointing this out to a non-birdwatcher be courteous, but firm. The non-birdwatchers' goodwill towards birds must not be destroyed by the attitudes of birdwatchers.

9. Keeping records. Much of today's knowledge about birds is the result of meticulous record keeping by our predecessors. Make sure you help to add to tomorrow's knowledge by sending records to your county bird recorder.

10. Birdwatching abroad. Behave abroad as you would at home. This code should be firmly adhered to when abroad (whatever the local laws). Well behaved birdwatchers can be important ambassadors for bird protection.

COUNTRY CODE

Enjoy the countryside and respect its life and work

Guard against all risk of fire. Fasten all gates

Keep your dogs under close control

Keep to public paths across farmland

Use gates and stiles to cross fences, hedges and walls

Leave livestock, crops and machinery alone

Take your litter home. Help to keep all water clean

Protect wildlife, plants and trees

Take special care on country roads. Make no unnecessary noise

(Reproduced with the kind permission of the Countryside Agency)

SCHEDULE 1 SPECIES

Under the provisions of the Wildlife and Countryside Act 1981 the following bird species (listed in Schedule 1 - Part I of the Act) are protected by special penalties at all times.

Avocet
Bee-eater
Bittern
Bittern, Little
Bluethroat
Brambling
Bunting, Cirl
Bunting, Lapland
Bunting, Snow
Buzzard, Honey
Chough
Corncrake
Crake, Spotted
Crossbills (all species)
Curlew, Stone
Divers (all species)
Dotterel
Duck, Long-tailed
Eagle, Golden
Eagle, White-tailed
Falcon, Gyr
Fieldfare
Firecrest
Garganey
Godwit, Black-tailed
Goshawk
Grebe, Black-necked

Grebe, Slavonian
Greenshank
Gull, Little
Gull, Mediterranean
Harriers (all species)
Heron, Purple
Hobby
Hoopoe
Kingfisher
Kite, Red
Merlin
Oriole, Golden
Osprey
Owl, Barn
Owl, Snowy
Peregrine
Petrel, Leach's
Phalarope, Red-necked
Plover, Kentish
Plover, Little Ringed
Quail, Common
Redstart, Black
Redwing
Rosefinch, Scarlet
Ruff
Sandpiper, Green

Sandpiper, Purple
Sandpiper, Wood
Scaup
Scoter, Common
Scoter, Velvet
Serin
Shorelark
Shrike, Red-backed
Spoonbill
Stilt, Black-winged
Stint, Temminck's
Swan, Bewick's
Swan, Whooper
Tern, Black
Tern, Little
Tern, Roseate
Tit, Bearded
Tit, Crested
Treecreeper, Short-
   toed
Warbler, Cetti's
Warbler, Dartford
Warbler, Marsh
Warbler, Savi's
Whimbrel
Woodlark
Wryneck

The following species (listed in Schedule 1 - Part II of the Act) are protected by special penalties during the close season, which is 1 Feb to 31 Aug (21 Feb to 31 Aug below high water mark), but may be killed outside this period.

Goldeneye
Greylag Goose (in Outer Hebrides, Caithness, Sutherland, and Wester Ross only)
Pintail

NATIONAL & REGIONAL BIRDLINES

BIRDLINE	TO OBTAIN INFORMATION	TO REPORT SIGHTINGS (HOTLINES)
National		
Bird Information Service	09068 700222	01263 741140
Regional		
Northern Ireland	01247 467408	
Scotland	09068 700234	01293 611944
Wales	09068 700248	01492 544588
East Anglia	09068 700245	01603 763388
Midlands	09068 700247	01905 754154
North East	09068 700246	01426 983963
North West	09068 700249	0151 336 6188
South East	09068 700240	01426 933933
South West	09068 700241	01179 253320

Birdline South East

Charges

At the time of compilation, calls to 09068 numbers cost 60p per minute.

PART FIVE
DIARY 2000

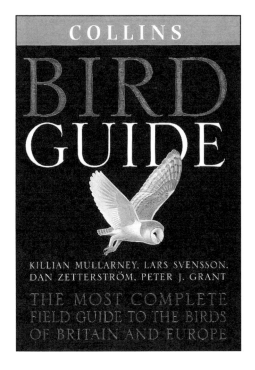

(Actual size 201 x 140 mm)

Collins Bird Guide, by Lars Svensson and Peter J Grant, illustrated by Killian Mullarney and Dan Zetterström, HarperCollins, 1999, 400p, £24.99. ISBN 0 00 219728 6. Hbk.

This near-pocket-size book is a masterpiece of planning and execution. Impeccable texts and maps for the 700+ species of Britain and Europe, plus vagrants, are on the left hand pages with immaculate static and action illustrations facing them. Authors and artists complement each other wonderfully to provide a vast and accessible body of information. The book abounds with practical guidance, including italic type in the text to highlight key features and Peterson-style pointers and captions in the plates - where all the seasonal, age, sex and other plumage variants are shown. This is a splendid volume, calculated to improve your ID skills and answer your most searching questions. Definitely one to get.

1 Sat	
2 Sun	
3 Mon	*New Year's Day Holiday (UK & R. of Ireland)*
4 Tue	
5 Wed	
6 Thu	
7 Fri	
8 Sat	
9 Sun	
10 Mon	
11 Tue	
12 Wed	
13 Thu	
14 Fri	
15 Sat	
16 Sun	
17 Mon	
18 Tue	
19 Wed	
20 Thu	
21 Fri	
22 Sat	
23 Sun	
24 Mon	
25 Tue	
26 Wed	
27 Thu	
28 Fri	
29 Sat	
30 Sun	
31 Mon	

1 Tue	
2 Wed	
3 Thu	
4 Fri	
5 Sat	
6 Sun	
7 Mon	
8 Tue	
9 Wed	
10 Thu	
11 Fri	
12 Sat	
13 Sun	
14 Mon	
15 Tue	
16 Wed	
17 Thu	
18 Fri	
19 Sat	
20 Sun	
21 Mon	
22 Tue	
23 Wed	
24 Thu	
25 Fri	
26 Sat	
27 Sun	
28 Mon	
29 Tue	

1 Wed	*St David's Day*
2 Thu	
3 Fri	
4 Sat	
5 Sun	
6 Mon	
7 Tue	
8 Wed	
9 Thu	
10 Fri	
11 Sat	
12 Sun	
13 Mon	
14 Tue	
15 Wed	
16 Thu	
17 Fri	*St Patrick's Day (Holiday in N. Ireland & R. of Ireland)*
18 Sat	
19 Sun	
20 Mon	
21 Tue	
22 Wed	
23 Thu	
24 Fri	
25 Sat	
26 Sun	*Start of British Summer Time*
27 Mon	
28 Tue	
29 Wed	
30 Thu	
31 Fri	

1 Sat	
2 Sun	
3 Mon	
4 Tue	
5 Wed	
6 Thu	
7 Fri	
8 Sat	
9 Sun	
10 Mon	
11 Tue	
12 Wed	
13 Thu	
14 Fri	
15 Sat	
16 Sun	
17 Mon	
18 Tue	
19 Wed	
20 Thu	
21 Fri	*Good Friday (Holiday in UK & R. of Ireland)*
22 Sat	
23 Sun	*St George's Day*
24 Mon	*Easter Monday (Holiday in R. of Ireland & UK except Scotland)*
25 Tue	
26 Wed	
27 Thu	
28 Fri	
29 Sat	
30 Sun	

1 Mon	*Early May Bank Holiday (UK & R. of Ireland)*
2 Tue	
3 Wed	
4 Thu	
5 Fri	
6 Sat	
7 Sun	
8 Mon	
9 Tue	
10 Wed	
11 Thu	
12 Fri	
13 Sat	
14 Sun	
15 Mon	
16 Tue	
17 Wed	
18 Thu	
19 Fri	
20 Sat	
21 Sun	
22 Mon	
23 Tue	
24 Wed	
25 Thu	
26 Fri	
27 Sat	
28 Sun	
29 Mon	*Spring Bank Holiday (UK)*
30 Tue	
31 Wed	

1 Thu	
2 Fri	
3 Sat	
4 Sun	
5 Mon	*June Holiday (R. of Ireland)*
6 Tue	
7 Wed	
8 Thu	
9 Fri	
10 Sat	
11 Sun	
12 Mon	
13 Tue	
14 Wed	
15 Thu	
16 Fri	
17 Sat	
18 Sun	
19 Mon	
20 Tue	
21 Wed	
22 Thu	
23 Fri	
24 Sat	
25 Sun	
26 Mon	
27 Tue	
28 Wed	
29 Thu	
30 Fri	

1 Sat	
2 Sun	
3 Mon	
4 Tue	
5 Wed	
6 Thu	
7 Fri	
8 Sat	
9 Sun	
10 Mon	
11 Tue	
12 Wed	*Holiday (N. Ireland)*
13 Thu	
14 Fri	
15 Sat	
16 Sun	
17 Mon	
18 Tue	
19 Wed	
20 Thu	
21 Fri	
22 Sat	
23 Sun	
24 Mon	
25 Tue	
26 Wed	
27 Thu	
28 Fri	
29 Sat	
30 Sun	
31 Mon	

1 Tue	
2 Wed	
3 Thu	
4 Fri	
5 Sat	
6 Sun	
7 Mon	*August Holiday (R. of Ireland)*
8 Tue	
9 Wed	
10 Thu	
11 Fri	
12 Sat	
13 Sun	
14 Mon	
15 Tue	
16 Wed	
17 Thu	
18 Fri	
19 Sat	
20 Sun	
21 Mon	
22 Tue	
23 Wed	
24 Thu	
25 Fri	
26 Sat	
27 Sun	
28 Mon	*Summer Bank Holiday (UK)*
29 Tue	
30 Wed	
31 Thu	

1 Fri	
2 Sat	
3 Sun	
4 Mon	
5 Tue	
6 Wed	
7 Thu	
8 Fri	
9 Sat	
10 Sun	
11 Mon	
12 Tue	
13 Wed	
14 Thu	
15 Fri	
16 Sat	
17 Sun	
18 Mon	
19 Tue	
20 Wed	
21 Thu	
22 Fri	
23 Sat	
24 Sun	
25 Mon	
26 Tue	
27 Wed	
28 Thu	
29 Fri	
30 Sat	

1 Sun	
2 Mon	
3 Tue	
4 Wed	
5 Thu	
6 Fri	
7 Sat	
8 Sun	
9 Mon	
10 Tue	
11 Wed	
12 Thu	
13 Fri	
14 Sat	
15 Sun	
16 Mon	
17 Tue	
18 Wed	
19 Thu	
20 Fri	
21 Sat	
22 Sun	
23 Mon	
24 Tue	
25 Wed	
26 Thu	
27 Fri	
28 Sat	
29 Sun	*End of British Summer Time*
30 Mon	*October Holiday (R. of Ireland)*
31 Tue	

1	Wed	
2	Thu	
3	Fri	
4	Sat	
5	Sun	
6	Mon	
7	Tue	
8	Wed	
9	Thu	
10	Fri	
11	Sat	
12	Sun	
13	Mon	
14	Tue	
15	Wed	
16	Thu	
17	Fri	
18	Sat	
19	Sun	
20	Mon	
21	Tue	
22	Wed	
23	Thu	
24	Fri	
25	Sat	
26	Sun	
27	Mon	
28	Tue	
29	Wed	
30	Thu	*St Andrew's Day*

1 Fri	
2 Sat	
3 Sun	
4 Mon	
5 Tue	
6 Wed	
7 Thu	
8 Fri	
9 Sat	
10 Sun	
11 Mon	
12 Tue	
13 Wed	
14 Thu	
15 Fri	
16 Sat	
17 Sun	
18 Mon	
19 Tue	
20 Wed	
21 Thu	
22 Fri	
23 Sat	
24 Sun	
25 Mon	*Christmas Day*
26 Tue	*Boxing Day Hol (UK); St Steven's Day Hol (R. of Ireland)*
27 Wed	
28 Thu	
29 Fri	
30 Sat	
31 Sun	

PLANNER 2001

JAN
FEB
MAR
APR
MAY
JUN
JUL
AUG
SEP
OCT
NOV
DEC

NOTES

PART SIX
LOG CHARTS

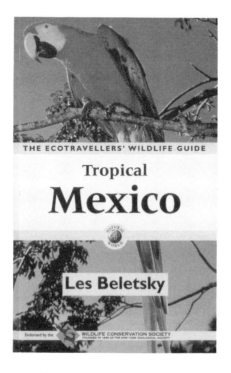

THE ECOTRAVELLERS' WILDLIFE GUIDE

Tropical

Mexico

Les Beletsky

Endorsed by the WILDLIFE CONSERVATION SOCIETY
FOUNDED IN 1895 AS THE NEW YORK ZOOLOGICAL SOCIETY

(Actual size 216 x 138 mm)

Where to Watch Birds in Mexico, by Steve N G Howell, Helm (A&C Black), 1999, 365p, £19.99. ISBN 0 7136 5087 7. Pbk.
Tropical Mexico: the ecotravellers' wildlife guide, by Les Beletsky, Academic Press, 1999, 498p, £29.95. ISBN 0 12 084812 0. Pbk.

The first of these is a collection of trips and site guides with species lists. All stem from first-hand experience and provide enough practical travel advice to ensure success. Beletsky does things very differently. First he gives 80 pages of bird-family profiles, taking in both ecology and behaviour, then follows with 50 pages of glorious plates, each with its facing page of synoptic information including identification and habitat notes. The big, big plus, however, is that he gives the same treatment to amphibians, reptiles and mammals. This should see to it that you do not miss out on the non-avian wonders that Mexico has to offer. Take both books with you.

SPECIES, CATEGORIES, CODES

AND GUIDE TO USE

Species list

The charts include all species on the British List (as determined by the British Ornithologists' Union), with the exception of the extinct Great Auk *Pinguinus impennis,* augmented by birds which breed or occur regularly in Europe - almost 600 altogether. They do not include vagrants which are not on the British List (see below) but which may have occurred in other parts of the British Isles. Readers who wish to record such species may use the extra rows provided at the end of the charts. In this connection it should be noted that separate lists exist for Northern Ireland (kept by the Northern Ireland Birdwatchers' Association) and the Isle of Man (kept by the Manx Ornithological Society), and that Irish records are assessed by the Irish Rare Birds Committee. Species are arranged here according to the sequence proposed by Professor K H Voous and recommended for general adoption by major ornithological bodies. Names of species are those most widely used in the relevant English-language field guides (with some proposed changes shown in parentheses); each is followed by its scientific name, printed in italics.

Species categories

The following categories are those promulgated by the British Ornithologists' Union.

A Species which have been recorded in an apparently natural state at least once since 1 January 1950.

B Species which would otherwise be in Category A but have not been recorded since 31 December 1949.

C Species that, although originally introduced by man, either deliberately or accidentally, have established breeding populations derived from introduced stock that maintain themselves without necessary recourse to further introduction. (This category has been subdivided to differentiate between various groups of naturalised species, but these subdivisions are outside the purpose of the log charts.)

D   Species that would otherwise appear in Categories A or B except that there is reasonable doubt that they have ever occurred in a natural state. (Species in this category are included in the log charts, though they do not qualify for inclusion in the British List, which comprises species in Categories A, B and C only. One of the objects of Category D is to note records of species which are not yet full additions, so that they are not overlooked if acceptable records subsequently occur. Bird report editors are encouraged to include records of species in Category D as appendices to their systematic lists.)

E   Species that have been recorded as introductions, transportees or escapees from captivity, and whose populations (if any) are thought not to be self-sustaining. They do not form part of the British List and are not included in the log charts.

EU Species not on the British List, or in Category D, but which either breed or occur regularly elsewhere in Europe.

BTO species codes

British Trust for Ornithology two-letter species codes are shown in brackets after the scientific name. They exist for many species, races and hybrids recorded in recent surveys. Readers should refer to the BTO if more codes are needed. In addition to those given in the charts, the following are available for some well-marked races or forms - Whistling Swan (WZ), European White-fronted Goose (EW), Greenland White-fronted Goose (NW), Dark-bellied Brent Goose (DB), Pale-bellied Brent Goose (PB), Black Brant (BB), Green-winged Teal (TA), Yellow-legged Gull (YG), Kumlien's Gull (KG), Feral Pigeon (FP), White Wagtail (WB), Black-bellied Dipper (DJ), Hooded Crow (HC), intermediate crow (HB).

Rarities

R   Rarities are indicated by a capital letter 'R' immediately preceding the 'Euring No.' column.

EURING species numbers

EURING species numbers are given in the third column. As they are taken from the full Holarctic bird list there are many apparent gaps. It is important that these are not filled arbitrarily by observers wishing to record species not listed in the charts, as this would compromise the integrity of the scheme. Similarly, the addition of a further digit to indicate sub-species is to be avoided, since EURING has already assigned numbers for this purpose. The numbering follows the Voous order of species.

Rare breeding birds
Species monitored by the Rare Breeding Birds Panel (see National Directory) comprise all those on Schedule 1 of the Wildfowl and Countryside Act 1981 (see Quick Reference) together with all escaped or introduced species breeding in small numbers. The following annotations in the charts reflect the RBBP's categories:

(b)[A]   Rare species. All breeding details requested.

(b)[B]   Less scarce species. Totals requested from counties with more than 10 pairs or localities; elsewhere all details requested.

(b)[C]   Less scarce species (specifically Barn Owl, Kingfisher, Crossbill). County summaries requested.

(b)[D]   Escaped or introduced species. Treated as less scarce species.

Life list
Ticks made in the 'Life List' column suffice for keeping a running personal total of species. However, added benefit can be obtained by replacing ticks with a note of the year of first occurrence. To take an example: one's first-ever Iceland Gull, seen on 27 April 2000, would be logged with '00' in the Life List and '27' in the April column (as well as a tick in the 2000 column). As Life List entries are carried forward annually, in years to come it would be a simple matter to relocate this record.

First and last dates of migrants
Arrivals of migrants can be recorded by inserting dates instead of ticks in the relevant month columns. For example, a Sandwich Tern on 15 March would be recorded by inserting '15' against Sandwich Tern in the March column. The same applies to departures, though dates of last sightings can only be entered at the end of the year after checking one's field notebook.

Unheaded columns
The three unheaded columns at the right hand end of each chart are for special (personal) use. This may be, for example, a second holiday, a particular county or a 'local patch'. Another use could be to indicate species on, for example, the Northern Ireland List or the Isle of Man List.

1	DIVERS - GREBES - ALBATROSS FULMAR - PETRELS - SHEARWATERS	Eur no.	Life list	2000 list	Jan	Feb	Mar	Apr	May	Jun	Jul	Aug	Sep	Oct	Nov	Dec	24 hr	Gar den	Holi -day		
A	Red-throated Diver *Gavia stellata* (RH) [B]	0002																			
A	Black-throated Diver *G. arctica* (BV) (b)[A]	0003																			
A	Great Northern Diver *G. immer* (ND)	0004																			
A	White-(Yellow-)billed Diver *G. adamsii* (WV) R	0005																			
A	Pied-billed Grebe *Podilymbus podiceps* (PJ) R	0006																			
A	Little Grebe *Tachybaptus ruficollis* (LG)	0007																			
A	Great Crested Grebe *Podiceps cristatus* (GG)	0009																			
A	Red-necked Grebe *P. grisegena* (RX) (b)[A]	0010																			
A	Slavonian Grebe *P. auritus* (SZ) (b)[A]	0011																			
A	Black-necked Grebe *P. nigricollis* (BN) (b)[A]	0012																			
A	Black-browed Albatross *Diomedea melanophris* (AA) R	0014																			
A	Fulmar *Fulmarus glacialis* (F)	0020																			
A	'Soft-plumaged Petrel' *Pterodroma mollis?* R	0026																			
B	Capped Petrel *P. hasitata* R	0029																			
B	Bulwer's Petrel *Bulweria bulwerii* R	0034																			
A	Cory's Shearwater *Calonectris diomedea* (CQ)	0036																			
A	Great Shearwater *Puffinus gravis* (GQ)	0040																			
A	Sooty Shearwater *P. griseus* (OT)	0043																			
A	Manx Shearwater *P. puffinus* (MX)	0046																			
A	Mediterranean Shearwater *P. yelkouan*	0046																			
A	Little Shearwater *P. assimilis* R	0048																			
A	Wilson's Petrel *Oceanites oceanicus* R	0050																			
B	White-faced Petrel *Pelagodroma marina* R	0051																			
A	Storm Petrel *Hydrobates pelagicus* (TM)	0052																			
	Sub-total																				

	PETRELS contd - GANNET - CORMORANTS PELICANS - HERONS - STORKS	Eur no.	Life list	2000 list	Jan	Feb	Mar	Apr	May	Jun	Jul	Aug	Sep	Oct	Nov	Dec	24 hr	Garden	Holiday
A	Leach's Petrel *Oceanodroma leucorhoa* (TL) (b)B	0055																	
A R	Swinhoe's Petrel *O. monorhis*	0056																	
B R	Madeiran Petrel *O. castro*	0058																	
A	Gannet *Morus bassanus* (GX)	0071																	
A	Cormorant *Phalacrocorax carbo* (CA)	0072																	
A R	Double-crested Cormorant *P. auritus*	0078																	
A	Shag *P. aristotelis* (SA)	0080																	
EU	Pygmy Cormorant *P. pygmeus*	0082																	
D R	Great White Pelican *Pelecanus onocrotalus* (YP)	0088																	
EU	Dalmatian Pelican *P. crispus*	0089																	
A R	Magnificent Frigatebird *Fregata magnificens*	0093																	
A	Bittern *Botaurus stellaris* (BI) (b)A	0095																	
A R	American Bittern *B. lentiginosus* (AM)	0096																	
A R	Little Bittern *Ixobrychus minutus* (LL)	0098																	
A R	Night Heron *Nycticorax nycticorax* (NT) (b)AD	0104																	
A R	Green Heron *Butorides virescens* (HR)	0107																	
A R	Squacco Heron *Ardeola ralloides* (QH)	0108																	
A R	Cattle Egret *Bubulcus ibis* (EC)	0111																	
A	Little Egret *Egretta garzetta* (ET) (b)A	0119																	
A R	Great White Egret *Ardea alba* (HW)	0121																	
A	Grey Heron *A. cinerea* (H)	0122																	
A	Purple Heron *A. purpurea* (UR)	0124																	
A R	Black Stork *Ciconia nigra* (OS)	0131																	
A	White Stork *C. ciconia* (OR)	0134																	
	Sub-total																		

3	IBIS - SPOONBILL - FLAMINGO SWANS - GEESE - DUCKS	Eur no.	Life list	2000 list	Jan	Feb	Mar	Apr	May	Jun	Jul	Aug	Sep	Oct	Nov	Dec	24 hr	Gar den	Holi-day	
A	Glossy Ibis Plegadis falcinellus (IB) R	0136																		
A	Spoonbill Platalea leucorodia (NB) (b)A	0144																		
D	Greater Flamingo Phoenicopterus ruber (FL) R	0147																		
AC	Mute Swan Cygnus olor (MS)	0152																		
A	Bewick's (Tundra) Swan C. columbianus (BS)	0153																		
A	Whooper Swan C. cygnus (WS) (b)AD	0154																		
A	Bean Goose Anser fabalis (BE) (b)D	0157																		
A	Pink-footed Goose A. brachyrhynchus (PG) (b)AD	0158																		
A	White-fronted Goose A. albifrons (WG) (b)D	0159																		
A	Lesser White-fr Goose A. erythropus (LC) (b)D R	0160																		
AC	Greylag Goose A. anser (GJ)	0161																		
A	Snow Goose A. caerulescens (SJ) (b)D	0163																		
AC	Canada Goose Branta canadensis (CG)	0166																		
A	Barnacle Goose B. leucopsis (BY) (b)D	0167																		
A	Brent Goose B. bernicla (BG) (b)D	0168																		
A	Red-breasted Goose B. ruficollis (EB) (b)D R	0169																		
C	Egyptian Goose Alopochen aegyptiacus (EG) (b)D	0170																		
B	Ruddy Shelduck Tadorna ferruginea (UD) (b)D	0171																		
A	Shelduck T. tadorna (SU)	0173																		
C	Mandarin Duck A. galericulata (MN)	0178																		
A	Wigeon Anas penelope (WN) (b)B	0179																		
A	American Wigeon A. americana (AW) R	0180																		
D	Falcated Duck A. falcata (FT) R	0181																		
AC	Gadwall A. strepera (GA) (b)B	0182																		
	Sub-total																			

4	DUCKS contd		Eur no.	Life list	2000 list	Jan	Feb	Mar	Apr	May	Jun	Jul	Aug	Sep	Oct	Nov	Dec	24 hr	Gar den	Holi -day			
D	Baikal Teal *A. formosa* (IK)	R	0183																				
A	Teal *A. crecca* (T)		0184																				
AC	Mallard *A. platyrhynchos* (MA)		0186																				
A	American Black Duck *A. rubripes* (BD)	R	0187																				
A	Pintail *A. acuta* (PT) (b)^A		0189																				
A	Garganey *A. querquedula* (GY) (b)^A		0191																				
A	Blue-winged Teal *A. discors* (TB) (b)^D	R	0192																				
A	Shoveler *A. clypeata* (SV)		0194																				
D	Marbled Duck *Marmaronetta angustirostris*	R	0195																				
A	Red-crested Pochard *Netta rufina* (RQ) (b)^D		0196																				
A	Canvasback *Aythya valisineria*	R	0197																				
A	Pochard *A. ferina* (PO) (b)^B		0198																				
A	Redhead *A. americana*	R	0199																				
A	Ring-necked Duck *A. collaris* (NG)		0200																				
A	Ferruginous Duck *A. nyroca* (FD)	R	0202																				
A	Tufted Duck *A. fuligula* (TU)		0203																				
A	Scaup *A. marila* (SP) (b)^A		0204																				
A	Lesser Scaup *A. affinis* (AY)	R	0205																				
A	Eider *Somateria mollissima* (E)		0206																				
A	King Eider *S. spectabilis* (KE)	R	0207																				
A	Steller's Eider *Polysticta stelleri* (ES)	R	0209																				
A	Harlequin *Histrionicus histrionicus* (HQ)	R	0211																				
A	Long-tailed Duck *Clangula hyemalis* (LN) (b)^A		0212																				
A	Common Scoter *Melanitta nigra* (CX) (b)^A		0213																				
	Sub-total																						

5	DUCKS contd / RAPTORS	Eur no.	Life list	2000 list	Jan	Feb	Mar	Apr	May	Jun	Jul	Aug	Sep	Oct	Nov	Dec	24 hr	Gar den	Holi-day	
A	Surf Scoter *M. perspicillata* (FS)	0214																		
A	Velvet Scoter *M. fusca* (VS)	0215																		
A	Bufflehead *Bucephala albeola* R	0216																		
A	Barrow's Goldeneye *B. islandica* R	0217																		
A	Goldeneye *B. clangula* (GN) (b)AD	0218																		
A	Hooded Merganser *Lophodytes cucullatus* (HO) R	0219																		
A	Smew *Mergellus albellus* (SY)	0220																		
A	Red-breasted Merganser *Mergus serrator* (RM)	0221																		
A	Goosander *M. merganser* (GD)	0223																		
C	Ruddy Duck *Oxyura jamaicensis* (RY)	0225																		
EU	White-headed Duck *O. leucocephala* (WQ)	0226																		
A	Honey Buzzard *Pernis apivorus* (HZ) (b)A	0231																		
EU	Black-winged Kite *Elanus caeruleus*	0235																		
A	Black Kite *Milvus migrans* (KB) R	0238																		
AC	Red Kite *M. milvus* (KT) (b)A	0239																		
A	White-tailed Eagle *Haliaeetus albicilla* (WE) (b)A	0243																		
D	Bald Eagle *H. leucocephalus* R	0244																		
EU	Lammergeier *Gypaetus barbatus*	0246																		
B	Egyptian Vulture *Neophron percnopterus* R	0247																		
B	Griffon Vulture *Gyps fulvus* R	0251																		
D	Black (Monk) Vulture *Aegypius monachus* R	0255																		
EU	Short-toed Eagle *Circaetus gallicus*	0256																		
A	Marsh Harrier *Circus aeruginosus* (MR) (b)A	0260																		
A	Hen Harrier *C. cyaneus* (HH) (b)B	0261																		
	Sub-total																			

6	RAPTORS contd	Eur no.	Life list	2000 list	Jan	Feb	Mar	Apr	May	Jun	Jul	Aug	Sep	Oct	Nov	Dec	24 hr	Gar den	Holi -day
A	Pallid Harrier C. macrourus R	0262																	
A	Montagu's Harrier C. pygargus (MO) (b)A	0263																	
AC	Goshawk Accipiter gentilis (GI) (b)B	0267																	
A	Sparrowhawk A. nisus (SH)	0269																	
EU	Levant Sparrowhawk A. brevipes	0273																	
A	Buzzard Buteo buteo (BZ)	0287																	
EU	Long-legged Buzzard B. rufinus	0288																	
A	Rough-legged Buzzard B. lagopus (RF)	0290																	
EU	Lesser Spotted Eagle Aquila pomarina	0292																	
B	Greater Spotted Eagle A. clanga R	0293																	
EU	Imperial Eagle A. heliaca	0295																	
A	Golden Eagle A. chrysaetos (EA) (b)B	0296																	
EU	Booted Eagle Hieraaetus pennatus	0298																	
EU	Bonelli's Eagle H. fasciatus	0299																	
A	Osprey Pandion haliaetus (OP) (b)A	0301																	
A	Lesser Kestrel Falco naumanni R	0303																	
A	Kestrel F. tinnunculus (K)	0304																	
A	American Kestrel F. sparverius R	0305																	
A	Red-footed Falcon F. vespertinus (FV) R	0307																	
A	Merlin F. columbarius (ML) (b)B	0309																	
A	Hobby F. subbuteo (HY) (b)B	0310																	
A	Eleonora's Falcon F. eleonorae R	0311																	
EU	Lanner F. biarmicus (FB)	0314																	
D	Saker F. cherrug (JF) R	0316																	
	Sub-total																		

7	RAPTORS contd - GAMEBIRDS RAILS - CRAKES - GALLINULES	Eur no.	Life list	2000 list	Jan	Feb	Mar	Apr	May	Jun	Jul	Aug	Sep	Oct	Nov	Dec	24 hr	Gar den	Holi -day		
A	Gyrfalcon *F. rusticolus* (YF) R	0318																			
A	Peregrine *F. peregrinus* (PE) (b)B	0320																			
EU	Hazel Grouse *Bonasa bonasia*	0326																			
A	Red (Willow) Grouse *Lagopus lagopus* (RG)	0329																			
A	Ptarmigan *L. mutus* (PM)	0330																			
A	Black Grouse *Tetrao tetrix* (BK)	0332																			
BC	Capercaillie *T. urogallus* (CP)	0335																			
EU	Rock Partridge *Alectoris graeca*	0357																			
C	Red-legged Partridge *A. rufa* (RL)	0358																			
EU	Barbary Partridge *A. barbara*	0359																			
AC	Grey Partridge *Perdix perdix* (P)	0367																			
A	Quail *Coturnix coturnix* (Q) (b)B	0370																			
C	Pheasant *Phasianus colchicus* (PH)	0394																			
C	Golden Pheasant *Chrysolophus pictus* (GF) (b)D	0396																			
C	Lady Amherst's Pheasant *C. amherstiae* (LM) (b)D	0397																			
EU	Andalusian Hemipode *Turnix sylvatica*	0400																			
A	Water Rail *Rallus aquaticus* (WA)	0407																			
A	Spotted Crake *Porzana porzana* (AK) (b)A	0408																			
A	Sora *P. carolina* R	0409																			
A	Little Crake *P. parva* (JC) R	0410																			
A	Baillon's Crake *P. pusilla* R	0411																			
A	Corncrake *Crex crex* (CE) (b)A	0421																			
A	Moorhen *Gallinula chloropus* (MH)	0424																			
B	Allen's Gallinule *Porphyrula alleni* R	0425																			
	Sub-total																				

8 GALLINULES contd - COOTS / CRANES - BUSTARDS - WADERS

	Species	R	Eur no.	Life list	2000 list	Jan	Feb	Mar	Apr	May	Jun	Jul	Aug	Sep	Oct	Nov	Dec	24 hr	Gar den	Holi -day
A	American Purple Gallinule *P. martinica*	R	0426																	
EU	Purple Gallinule *Porphyrio porphyrio*		0427																	
A	Coot *Fulica atra* (CO)		0429																	
A	American Coot *F. americana*	R	0430																	
EU	Crested Coot *F. cristata*		0431																	
A	Crane *Grus grus* (AN) (b)[A]		0433																	
A	Sandhill Crane *G. canadensis*	R	0436																	
A	Little Bustard *Tetrax tetrax*	R	0442																	
A	Houbara Bustard *Chlamydotis undulata*	R	0444																	
A	Great Bustard *Otis tarda* (US)	R	0446																	
A	Oystercatcher *Haematopus ostralegus* (OC)		0450																	
A	Black-winged Stilt *Himantopus himantopus* (IT)	R	0455																	
A	Avocet *Recurvirostra avosetta* (AV) (b)[A]		0456																	
A	Stone Curlew *Burhinus oedicnemus* (TN) (b)[A]		0459																	
A	Cream-coloured Courser *Cursorius cursor*	R	0464																	
A	Collared Pratincole *Glareola pratincola*	R	0465																	
A	Oriental Pratincole *G. maldivarum* GM)	R	0466																	
A	Black-winged Pratincole *G. nordmanni*	R	0467																	
A	Little Ringed Plover *Charadrius dubius* (LP) (b)[B]		0469																	
A	Ringed Plover *C. hiaticula* (RP)		0470																	
A	Semipalmated Plover *C. semipalmatus*	R	0471																	
A	Killdeer *C. vociferus* (KL)	R	0474																	
A	Kentish Plover *C. alexandrinus* (KP)		0477																	
A	Lesser Sand Plover *C. mongolus*	R	0478																	
	Sub-total																			

9	WADERS contd		Eur no.	Life list	2000 list	Jan	Feb	Mar	Apr	May	Jun	Jul	Aug	Sep	Oct	Nov	Dec	24 hr	Gar den	Holi -day	
A	Greater Sand Plover *C. leschenaultii* (DP)	R	0479																		
A	Caspian Plover *C. asiaticus*	R	0480																		
A	Dotterel *C. morinellus* (DO) (b)[B]		0482																		
A	American Golden Plover *Pluvialis dominica* (ID)	R	0484																		
A	Pacific Golden Plover *P. fulva* (IF)	R	0484																		
A	Golden Plover *P. apricaria* (GP)		0485																		
A	Grey Plover *P. squatarola* (GV)		0486																		
EU	Spur-winged Plover *Hoplopterus spinosus* (UW)		0487																		
A	Sociable Lapwing *Vanellus gregarius* (IP)	R	0491																		
A	White-tailed Lapwing *V. leucurus*	R	0492																		
A	Lapwing *V. vanellus* (L)		0493																		
A	Great Knot *Calidris tenuirostris*	R	0495																		
A	Knot *C. canutus* (KN)		0496																		
A	Sanderling *C. alba* (SS)		0497																		
A	Semipalmated Sandpiper *C. pusilla* (PZ)	R	0498																		
A	Western Sandpiper *C. mauri* (ER)	R	0499																		
A	Red-necked Stint *C. ruficollis*	R	0500																		
A	Little Stint *C. minuta* (LX)		0501																		
A	Temminck's Stint *C. temminckii* (TK) (b)[A]		0502																		
A	Long-toed Stint *C. subminuta*	R	0503																		
A	Least Sandpiper *C. minutilla*	R	0504																		
A	White-rumped Sandpiper *C. fuscicollis* (WU)	R	0505																		
A	Baird's Sandpiper *C. bairdii* (BP)	R	0506																		
A	Pectoral Sandpiper *C. melanotos* (PP)		0507																		
	Sub-total																				

10	WADERS contd		Eur no.	Life list	2000 list	Jan	Feb	Mar	Apr	May	Jun	Jul	Aug	Sep	Oct	Nov	Dec	24 hr	Gar den	Holi -day
A	Sharp-tailed Sandpiper *C. acuminata*	R	0508																	
A	Curlew Sandpiper *C. ferruginea* (CV)		0509																	
A	Purple Sandpiper *C. maritima* (PS) (b)A		0510																	
A	Dunlin *C. alpina* (DN)		0512																	
A	Broad-billed Sandpiper *Limicola falcinellus* (OA)	R	0514																	
A	Stilt Sandpiper *Micropalama himantopus*	R	0515																	
A	Buff-breasted Sandpiper *Tryngites subruficollis* (BQ)		0516																	
A	Ruff *Philomachus pugnax* (RU) (b)A		0517																	
A	Jack Snipe *Lymnocryptes minimus* (JS)		0518																	
A	Snipe *Gallinago gallinago* (SN)		0519																	
A	Great Snipe *G. media* (DS)	R	0520																	
A	Long-billed Dowitcher *L. scolopaceus* (LD)	R	0527																	
A	Woodcock *Scolopax rusticola* (WK)		0529																	
A	Black-tailed Godwit *Limosa limosa* (BW) (b)A		0532																	
A	Hudsonian Godwit *L. haemastica* (HU)	R	0533																	
A	Bar-tailed Godwit *L. lapponica* (BA)		0534																	
A	Little Whimbrel (Curlew) *Numenius minutus*	R	0536																	
B	Eskimo Curlew *N. borealis*	R	0537																	
A	Whimbrel *N. phaeopus* (WM) (b)A		0538																	
A	Curlew *N. arquata* (CU)		0541																	
A	Upland Sandpiper *Bartramia longicauda* (UP)	R	0544																	
A	Spotted Redshank *Tringa erythropus* (DR)		0545																	
A	Redshank *T. totanus* (RK)		0546																	
A	Marsh Sandpiper *T. stagnatilis* (MD)	R	0547																	
	Sub-total																				

11	WADERS contd SKUAS - GULLS	Eur no.	Life list	2000 list	Jan	Feb	Mar	Apr	May	Jun	Jul	Aug	Sep	Oct	Nov	Dec	24 hr	Gar den	Holi -day		
A	Greenshank *T. nebularia* (GK) (b)[B]	0548																			
A	Greater Yellowlegs *T. melanoleuca* (LZ) [R]	0550																			
A	Lesser Yellowlegs *T. flavipes* (LY) [R]	0551																			
A	Solitary Sandpiper *T. solitaria* (I) [R]	0552																			
A	Green Sandpiper *T. ochropus* (GE)	0553																			
A	Wood Sandpiper *T. glareola* (OD) (b)[A]	0554																			
A	Terek Sandpiper *Xenus cinereus* (TR) [R]	0555																			
A	Common Sandpiper *Actitis hypoleucos* (CS)	0556																			
A	Spotted Sandpiper *A. macularia* (PQ) [R]	0557																			
A	Grey-tailed Tattler *Heteroscelus brevipes* (YT) [R]	0558																			
A	Turnstone *Arenaria interpres* (TT)	0561																			
A	Wilson's Phalarope *Phalaropus tricolor* (WF) [R]	0563																			
A	Red-necked Phalarope *P. lobatus* (NK) (b)[A]	0564																			
A	Grey Phalarope *P. fulicarius* (PL)	0565																			
A	Pomarine Skua *Stercorarius pomarinus* (PK)	0566																			
A	Arctic Skua *S. parasiticus* (AC)	0567																			
A	Long-tailed Skua *S. longicaudus* (OG)	0568																			
A	Great Skua *Catharacta skua* (NX)	0569																			
B	Great Black-headed (Pallas's) Gull *Larus ichthyaetus* [R]	0573																			
A	Mediterranean Gull *L. melanocephalus* (MU) (b)[A]	0575																			
A	Laughing Gull *L. atricilla* (LF) [R]	0576																			
A	Franklin's Gull *L. pipixcan* (FG) [R]	0577																			
A	Little Gull *L. minutus* (LU)	0578																			
A	Sabine's Gull *L. sabini* (AB)	0579																			
	Sub-total																				

12 GULLS contd / TERNS

	Species		Eur no.	Life list	2000 list	Jan	Feb	Mar	Apr	May	Jun	Jul	Aug	Sep	Oct	Nov	Dec	24 hr	Gar den	Holi -day		
A	Bonaparte's Gull *L. philadelphia* (ON)	R	0581																			
A	Black-headed Gull *L. ridibundus* (BH)		0582																			
A	Slender-billed Gull *L. genei* (EI)	R	0585																			
EU	Audouin's Gull *L. audouinii*		0588																			
A	Ring-billed Gull *L. delawarensis* (IN)		0589																			
A	Common (Mew) Gull *L. canus* (CM)		0590																			
A	Lesser Black-backed Gull *L. fuscus* (LB)		0591																			
A	Herring Gull *L. argentatus* (HG)		0592																			
A	Iceland Gull *L. glaucoides* (IG)		0598																			
A	Glaucous Gull *L. hyperboreus* (GZ)		0599																			
A	Great Black-backed Gull *L. marinus* (GB)		0600																			
A	Ross's Gull *Rhodostethia rosea* (OG)	R	0601																			
A	Kittiwake *Rissa tridactyla* (KI)		0602																			
A	Ivory Gull *Pagophila eburnea* (IV)	R	0604																			
A	Gull-billed Tern *Sterna nilotica*	R	0605																			
A	Caspian Tern *S. caspia* (CJ)	R	0606																			
A	Royal Tern *S. maxima* (QT)	R	0607																			
A	Lesser Crested Tern *S. bengalensis* (TF) (b)[A]	R	0609																			
A	Sandwich Tern *S. sandvicensis* (TE)		0611																			
A	Roseate Tern *S. dougallii* (RS) (b)[A]		0614																			
A	Common Tern *S. hirundo* (CN)		0615																			
A	Arctic Tern *S. paradisaea* (AE)		0616																			
A	Aleutian Tern *S. aleutica*	R	0617																			
A	Forster's Tern *S. forsteri* (FO)	R	0618																			
	Sub-total																					

13		Eur no.	Life list	2000 list	Jan	Feb	Mar	Apr	May	Jun	Jul	Aug	Sep	Oct	Nov	Dec	24 hr	Gar den	Holi -day
	TERNS contd - AUKS - SANDGROUSE DOVES/PIGEONS - PARAKEET																		
A	R Bridled Tern *S. anaethetus*	0622																	
A	R Sooty Tern *S. fuscata*	0623																	
A	Little Tern *S. albifrons* (AF) (b)B	0624																	
A	R Whiskered Tern *Chlidonias hybridus* (WD)	0626																	
A	Black Tern *C. niger* (BJ)	0627																	
A	R White-winged Black Tern *C. leucopterus* (WI)	0628																	
A	Guillemot *Uria aalge* (GU)	0634																	
A	R Brünnich's Guillemot *U. lomvia* (TZ)	0635																	
A	Razorbill *Alca torda* (RA)	0636																	
A	Black Guillemot *Cepphus grylle* (TY)	0638																	
A	R Ancient Murrelet *Synthliboramphus antiquus*	0645																	
A	Little Auk *Alle alle* (LK)	0647																	
A	Puffin *Fratercula arctica* (PU)	0654																	
EU	Black-bellied Sandgrouse *Pterocles orientalis*	0661																	
EU	Pin-tailed Sandgrouse *P. alchata*	0662																	
A	R Pallas's Sandgrouse *Syrrhaptes paradoxus*	0663																	
AC	Rock Dove *Columba livia* (DV)	0665																	
A	Stock Dove *C. oenas* (SD)	0668																	
A	Woodpigeon *C. palumbus* (WP)	0670																	
A	Collared Dove *Streptopelia decaocto* (CD)	0684																	
A	Turtle Dove *S. turtur* (TD)	0687																	
A	R Rufous (Oriental) Turtle Dove *S. orientalis*	0689																	
A	R Mourning Dove *Zenaida macroura*	0695																	
C	Rose-ringed Parakeet *Psittacula krameri* (RI) (b)D	0712																	
	Sub-total																		

14	CUCKOOS - OWLS NIGHTJARS - SWIFTS		Eur no.	Life list	2000 list	Jan	Feb	Mar	Apr	May	Jun	Jul	Aug	Sep	Oct	Nov	Dec	24 hr	Gar den	Holi -day		
A	Great Spotted Cuckoo *Clamator glandarius* (UK)	R	0716																			
A	Cuckoo *Cuculus canorus* (CK)		0724																			
A	Black-billed Cuckoo *Coccyzus erythrophthalmus*	R	0727																			
A	Yellow-billed Cuckoo *C. americanus*	R	0728																			
A	Barn Owl *Tyto alba* (BO) (b)C		0735																			
A	Scops Owl *Otus scops*	R	0739																			
EU	Eagle Owl *Bubo bubo* (b)D		0744																			
A	Snowy Owl *Nyctea scandiaca* (SO) (b)A	R	0749																			
A	Hawk Owl *Surnia ulula*	R	0750																			
EU	Pygmy Owl *Glaucidium passerinum*		0751																			
C	Little Owl *Athene noctua* (LO)		0757																			
A	Tawny Owl *Strix aluco* (TO)		0761																			
EU	Ural Owl *S. uralensis*		0765																			
EU	Great Grey Owl *S. nebulosa*		0766																			
A	Long-eared Owl *Asio otus* (LE)		0767																			
A	Short-eared Owl *A. flammeus* (SE)		0768																			
A	Tengmalm's Owl *Aegolius funereus*	R	0770																			
A	Nightjar *Caprimulgus europaeus* (NJ)		0778																			
B	Red-necked Nightjar *C. ruficollis*	R	0779																			
A	Egyptian Nightjar *C. aegyptius*	R	0781																			
A	Common Nighthawk *Chordeiles minor*	R	0786																			
A	Chimney Swift *Chaetura pelagica*	R	0790																			
A	White-throated Needletail *Hirundapus caudacutus*	R	0792																			
A	Swift *Apus apus* (SI)		0795																			
	Sub-total																					

15 SWIFTS ctd - K'FISHERS - B-EATERS - ROLL'R HOOPOE - WOODPECK'RS - PHOEBE - LARKS

	Species	Eur no.	Life list	2000 list	Jan	Feb	Mar	Apr	May	Jun	Jul	Aug	Sep	Oct	Nov	Dec	24 hr	Gar den	Holi -day
A	Pallid Swift *A. pallidus* R	0796																	
A	Pacific Swift *A. pacificus* R	0797																	
A	Alpine Swift *A. melba* (AI) R	0798																	
EU	White-rumped Swift *A. caffer*	0799																	
A	Little Swift *A. affinis* R	0800																	
A	Kingfisher *Alcedo atthis* (KF) (b)C	0831																	
A	Belted Kingfisher *Ceryle alcyon* R	0834																	
EU	Blue-cheeked Bee-eater *Merops superciliosus* R	0839																	
A	Bee-eater *M. apiaster* (MZ)	0840																	
A	Roller *Coracias garrulus* R	0841																	
A	Hoopoe *Upupa epops* (HP)	0846																	
A	Wryneck *Jynx torquilla* (WY) (b)A	0848																	
EU	Grey-headed Woodpecker *Picus canus*	0855																	
A	Green Woodpecker *P. viridis* (G)	0856																	
EU	Black Woodpecker *Dryocopus martius*	0863																	
A	Yellow-bellied Sapsucker *Sphyrapicus varius* R	0872																	
A	Great Spotted Woodpecker *Dendrocopos major* (GS)	0876																	
EU	Syrian Woodpecker *D. syriacus*	0878																	
EU	Middle Spotted Woodpecker *D. medius*	0883																	
EU	White-backed Woodpecker *D. leucotos*	0884																	
A	Lesser Spotted Woodpecker *D. minor* (LS)	0887																	
EU	Three-toed Woodpecker *Picoides tridactylus*	0898																	
A	Eastern Phoebe *Sayornis phoebe* R	0909																	
EU	Dupont's Lark *Chersophilus duponti*	0959																	
	Sub-total																		

16		LARKS contd - MARTINS SWALLOWS - PIPITS		Eur no.	Life list	2000 list	Jan	Feb	Mar	Apr	May	Jun	Jul	Aug	Sep	Oct	Nov	Dec	24 hr	Gar den	Holi -day
A	Calandra Lark Melanocorypha calandra		R	0961																	
A	Bimaculated Lark M. bimaculata		R	0962																	
A	White-winged Lark M. leucoptera		R	0965																	
A	Short-toed Lark Calandrella brachydactyla (VL)			0968																	
A	Lesser Short-toed Lark C. rufescens		R	0970																	
A	Crested Lark Galerida cristata		R	0972																	
EU	Thekla Lark G. theklae			0973																	
A	Woodlark Lullula arborea (WL) (b)B			0974																	
A	Skylark Alauda arvensis (S)			0976																	
A	Shore (Horned) Lark Eremophila alpestris (SX)			0978																	
A	Sand Martin Riparia riparia (SM)			0981																	
A	Tree Swallow Tachycineta bicolor		R	0983																	
A	Crag Martin Pryonoprogne rupestris		R	0991																	
A	Swallow Hirundo rustica (SL)			0992																	
A	Red-rumped Swallow H. daurica (VR)		R	0995																	
A	Cliff Swallow H. pyrrhonota		R	0998																	
A	House Martin Delichon urbica (HM)			1001																	
A	Richard's Pipit Anthus novaeseelandiae (PR)			1002																	
A	Blyth's Pipit A. godlewskii		R	1004																	
A	Tawny Pipit A. campestris (TI)			1005																	
A	Olive-backed Pipit A. hodgsoni (OV)		R	1008																	
A	Tree Pipit A. trivialis (TP)			1009																	
A	Pechora Pipit A. gustavi		R	1010																	
A	Meadow Pipit A. pratensis (MP)			1011																	
		Sub-total																			

17	PIPITS contd - WAGTAILS - WAXWINGS / DIPPER - WREN - ACCENTORS - ROBINS	Eur no.	Life list	2000 list	Jan	Feb	Mar	Apr	May	Jun	Jul	Aug	Sep	Oct	Nov	Dec	24 hr	Gar den	Holi -day
A	R Red-throated Pipit *A. cervinus* (VP)	1012																	
A	Rock Pipit *A. petrosus* (RC)	1014																	
A	Water Pipit *A. spinoletta* (WI)	1014																	
A	R Buff-bellied Pipit *A. rubescens*	1014																	
A	Yellow Wagtail *Motacilla flava* (YW)	1017																	
A	R Citrine Wagtail *M. citreola*	1018																	
A	Grey Wagtail *M. cinerea* (GL)	1019																	
A	Pied (White) Wagtail *M. alba* (PW)	1020																	
A	R Cedar Waxwing *Bombycilla cedorum*	1046																	
A	(Bohemian) Waxwing *B. garrulus* (WX)	1048																	
A	Dipper *Cinclus cinclus* (DI)	1050																	
A	Wren *Troglodytes troglodytes* (WR)	1066																	
A	R Northern Mockingbird *Mimus polyglottos*	1067																	
A	R Brown Thrasher *Toxostoma rufum*	1069																	
A	Dunnock *Prunella modularis* (D)	1084																	
A	R Alpine Accentor *P. collaris*	1094																	
A	R Rufous-tailed Scrub Robin *Cercotrichas galactotes*	1095																	
A	Robin *Erithacus rubecula* (R)	1099																	
A	R Thrush Nightingale *Luscinia luscinia* (FN)	1103																	
A	Nightingale *L. megarhynchos* (N)	1104																	
A	R Siberian Rubythroat *L. calliope*	1105																	
A	Bluethroat *L. svecica* (BU)	1106																	
A	R Red-flanked Bluetail *Tarsiger cyanurus*	1113																	
A	R White-throated Robin *Irania gutturalis*	1117																	
	Sub-total																		

18	REDSTARTS - CHATS WHEATEARS - THRUSHES		Eur no.	Life list	2000 list	Jan	Feb	Mar	Apr	May	Jun	Jul	Aug	Sep	Oct	Nov	Dec	24 hr	Gar den	Holi -day
A	Black Redstart *Phoenicurus ochruros* (BX) (b)^A		1121																	
A	Redstart *P. phoenicurus* (RT)		1122																	
A	Moussier's Redstart *P. moussieri*	R	1127																	
A	Whinchat *Saxicola rubetra* (WC)		1137																	
A	Stonechat *S. torquata* (SC)		1139																	
A	Isabelline Wheatear *Oenanthe isabellina*	R	1144																	
A	Wheatear *O. oenanthe* (W)		1146																	
A	Pied Wheatear *O. pleschanka* (PI)	R	1147																	
A	Black-eared Wheatear *O. hispanica*	R	1148																	
A	Desert Wheatear *O. deserti*	R	1149																	
A	White-crowned(-tailed) Black Wheatear *O. leucopyga*	R	1157																	
EU	Black Wheatear *O. leucura*		1158																	
A	Rock Thrush *Monticola saxatilis* (OH)	R	1162																	
A	Blue Rock Thrush *M. solitarius*	R	1166																	
A	White's Thrush *Zoothera dauma*	R	1170																	
A	Siberian Thrush *Z. sibirica*	R	1171																	
A	Varied Thrush *Z. naevia* (VT)	R	1172																	
A	Wood Thrush *Hylocichla mustelina*	R	1175																	
A	Hermit Thrush *Catharus guttatus*	R	1176																	
A	Swainson's Thrush *C. ustulatus*	R	1177																	
A	Grey-cheeked Thrush *C. minimus*	R	1178																	
A	Veery *C. fuscescens*	R	1179																	
A	Ring Ouzel *Turdus torquatus* (RZ)		1186																	
A	Blackbird *T. merula* (B)		1187																	
	Sub-total																			

19			Eur no.	Life list	2000 list	Jan	Feb	Mar	Apr	May	Jun	Jul	Aug	Sep	Oct	Nov	Dec	24 hr	Gar den	Holi -day		
	THRUSHES contd WARBLERS																					
A	Eye-browed Thrush *T. obscurus*	R	1195																			
A	Dusky Thrush *T. naumanni*	R	1196																			
A	Dark-throated Thrush *T. ruficollis* (XC)	R	1197																			
A	Fieldfare *T. pilaris* (FF) (b)^A		1198																			
A	Song Thrush *T. philomelos* (ST)		1200																			
A	Redwing *T. iliacus* (RE) (b)^A		1201																			
A	Mistle Thrush *T. viscivorus* (M)		1202																			
A	American Robin *T. migratorius* (AR)	R	1203																			
A	Cetti's Warbler *Cettia cetti* (CW) (b)^A		1220																			
A	Zitting Cisticola (Fan-tailed Warbler) *Cisticola juncidis*	R	1226																			
A	Pallas's Grasshopper Warbler *Locustella certhiola*	R	1233																			
A	Lanceolated Warbler *L. lanceolata*	R	1235																			
A	Grasshopper Warbler *L. naevia* (GH)		1236																			
A	River Warbler *L. fluviatilis* (VW)	R	1237																			
A	Savi's Warbler *L. luscinioides* (VI) (b)^A	R	1238																			
A	Moustached Warbler *Acrocephalus melanopogon*	R	1241																			
A	Aquatic Warbler *A. paludicola* (AQ)		1242																			
A	Sedge Warbler *A. schoenobaenus* (SW)		1243																			
A	Paddyfield Warbler *A. agricola* (PY)	R	1247																			
A	Blyth's Reed Warbler *A. dumetorum*	R	1248																			
A	Marsh Warbler *A. palustris* (MW) (b)^A		1250																			
A	Reed Warbler *A. scirpaceus* (RW)		1251																			
A	Great Reed Warbler *A. arundinaceus* (QW)	R	1253																			
A	Thick-billed Warbler *A. aedon*	R	1254																			
	Sub-total																					

20	WARBLERS contd		Eur no.	Life list	2000 list	Jan	Feb	Mar	Apr	May	Jun	Jul	Aug	Sep	Oct	Nov	Dec	24 hr	Gar den	Holi -day
A	Olivaceous Warbler *Hippolais pallida*	R	1255																	
A	Booted Warbler *H. caligata*	R	1256																	
EU	Olive-tree Warbler *H. olivetorum*		1258																	
A	Icterine Warbler *H. icterina* (IC)		1259																	
A	Melodious Warbler *H. polyglotta* (ME)	R	1260																	
A	Marmora's Warbler *Sylvia sarda* (MM)	R	1261																	
A	Dartford Warbler *S. undata* (DW) (b)B		1262																	
A	Spectacled Warbler *S. conspicillata*	R	1264																	
A	Subalpine Warbler *S. cantillans*	R	1265																	
A	Sardinian Warbler *S. melanocephala*	R	1267																	
EU	Cyprus Warbler *S. melanothorax*		1268																	
A	Rüppell's Warbler *S. rueppelli*	R	1269																	
A	Desert Warbler *S. nana*	R	1270																	
A	Orphean Warbler *S. hortensis*	R	1272																	
A	Barred Warbler *S. nisoria* (RR)		1273																	
A	Lesser Whitethroat *S. curruca* (LW)		1274																	
A	Whitethroat *S. communis* (WH)		1275																	
A	Garden Warbler *S. borin* (GW)		1276																	
A	Blackcap *S. atricapilla* (BC)		1277																	
A	Greenish Warbler *P. trochiloides* (NP)	R	1293																	
A	Arctic Warbler *P. borealis* (AP)	R	1295																	
A	Pallas's Warbler *P. proregulus* (PA)		1298																	
A	Yellow-browed Warbler *P. inornatus* (YB)		1300																	
A	Hume's Leaf Warbler *P. humei*	R	1300																	
	Sub-total																			

21	WARBLERS contd - 'CRESTS' FLYCATCHERS - TITS		Eur no.	Life list	2000 list	Jan	Feb	Mar	Apr	May	Jun	Jul	Aug	Sep	Oct	Nov	Dec	24 hr	Gar den	Holi -day		
A	Radde's Warbler *P. schwarzi*	R	1301																			
A	Dusky Warbler *P. fuscatus* (UY)	R	1303																			
A	Western Bonelli's Warbler *P. bonelli* (IW)	R	1307																			
A	Eastern Bonelli's Warbler *P. orientalis* (IW)	R	1307																			
A	Wood Warbler *P. sibilatrix* (WO)		1308																			
A	Chiffchaff *P. colybita* (CC)		1311																			
EU	Iberian Chiffchaff *P. brehmii*	R	1311																			
A	Willow Warbler *P. trochilus* (WW)		1312																			
A	Goldcrest *Regulus regulus* (GC)		1314																			
A	Firecrest *R. ignicapillus* (FC) (b)[A]		1315																			
D	Asian Brown Flycatcher *Muscicapa dauurica*		1335																			
A	Spotted Flycatcher *M. striata* (SF)		1335																			
A	Red-breasted Flycatcher *Ficedula parva* (FY)		1343																			
D	Mugimaki Flycatcher *F. mugimaki*	R	1344																			
EU	Semi-collared Flycatcher *F. semitorquata*		1347																			
A	Collared Flycatcher *F. albicollis*	R	1348																			
A	Pied Flycatcher *F. hypoleuca* (PF)		1349																			
A	Bearded Tit *Panurus biarmicus* (BR) (b)[B]		1364																			
A	Long-tailed Tit *Aegithalos caudatus* (LT)		1437																			
A	Marsh Tit *Parus palustris* (MT)		1440																			
EU	Sombre Tit *P. lugubris*		1441																			
A	Willow Tit *P. montanus* (WT)		1442																			
EU	Siberian Tit *P. cinctus*		1448																			
A	Crested Tit *P. cristatus* (CI) (b)[B]		1454																			
			Sub-total																			

22		TITS contd - NUTHATCHES - 'CREEPERS ORIOLE - SHRIKES - CROWS	Eur no.	Life list	2000 list	Jan	Feb	Mar	Apr	May	Jun	Jul	Aug	Sep	Oct	Nov	Dec	24 hr	Gar den	Holi -day				
A		Coal Tit *P. ater* (CT)	1461																					
A		Blue Tit *P. caeruleus* (BT)	1462																					
A		Great Tit *P. major* (GT)	1464																					
EU		Krüper's Nuthatch *Sitta krueperi*	1469																					
EU		Corsican Nuthatch *Sitta whiteheadi*	1470																					
A	R	Red-breasted Nuthatch *S. canadensis*	1472																					
A		Nuthatch *S. europaea* (NH)	1479																					
EU		Rock Nuthatch *S. neumayer*	1481																					
A	R	Wallcreeper *Tichodroma muraria*	1482																					
A		Treecreeper *Certhia familiaris* (TC)	1486																					
A	R	Short-toed Treecreeper *C. brachydactyla* (TH)	1487																					
A	R	Penduline Tit *Remiz pendulinus* (DT)	1490																					
A		Golden Oriole *Oriolus oriolus* (OL) (b)A	1508																					
A	R	Brown Shrike *Lanius cristatus*	1513																					
A	R	Isabelline Shrike *L. isabellinus* (IL)	1514																					
A		Red-backed Shrike *L. collurio* (ED) (b)A	1515																					
A	R	Lesser Grey Shrike *L. minor*	1519																					
A		Great Grey Shrike *L. excubitor* (SR)	1520																					
A	R	Southern Grey Shrike *L. meridionalis*	1520																					
A		Woodchat Shrike *L. senator* (OO)	1523																					
EU		Masked Shrike *L. nubicus*	1524																					
A		Jay *Garrulus glandarius* (J)	1539																					
EU		Siberian Jay *Perisoreus infaustus*	1543																					
EU		Azure-winged Magpie *Cyanopica cyana*	1547																					
		Sub-total																						

	23 CROWS contd - STARLINGS SPARROWS - FINCHES		Eur no.	Life list	2000 list	Jan	Feb	Mar	Apr	May	Jun	Jul	Aug	Sep	Oct	Nov	Dec	24 hr	Gar den	Holi -day	
A	Magpie *Pica pica* (MG)		1549																		
A	Nutcracker *Nucifraga caryocatactes* (NC)	R	1557																		
EU	Alpine Chough *Pyrrhocorax graculus*		1558																		
A	Chough *P. pyrrhocorax* (CF) (b)B		1559																		
A	Jackdaw *Corvus monedula* (JD)		1560																		
A	Rook *C. frugilegus* (RO)		1563																		
A	Carrion (Hooded) Crow *C. corone* (C)		1567																		
A	Raven *C. corax* (RN)		1572																		
D	Daurian Starling *Sturnus sturninus*	R	1579																		
A	Starling *S. vulgaris* (SG)		1582																		
EU	Spotless Starling *S. unicolor*		1583																		
A	Rose-coloured (Rosy) Starling *S. roseus* (OE)	R	1584																		
A	House Sparrow *Passer domesticus* (HS)		1591																		
A	Spanish Sparrow *P. hispaniolensis*	R	1592																		
A	Tree Sparrow *P. montanus* (TS)		1598																		
A	Rock Sparrow *Petronia petronia*	R	1604																		
D	Snow Finch *Montifringilla nivalis*	R	1611																		
A	Yellow-throated Vireo *Vireo flavifrons*	R	1628																		
A	Philadelphia Vireo *V. philadelphicus*	R	1631																		
A	Red-eyed Vireo *V. olivaceus* (EV)	R	1633																		
A	Chaffinch *Fringilla coelebs* (CH)		1636																		
A	Brambling *F. montifringilla* (BL) (b)A		1638																		
A	Serin *Serinus serinus* (NS) (b)A		1640																		
A	Greenfinch *Carduelis chloris* (GR)		1649																		
	Sub-total																				

24	FINCHES contd NORTH AMERICAN WARBLERS		Eur no.	Life list	2000 list	Jan	Feb	Mar	Apr	May	Jun	Jul	Aug	Sep	Oct	Nov	Dec	24 hr	Gar den	Holi -day
A	Goldfinch *C. carduelis* (GO)		1653																	
A	Siskin *C. spinus* (SK)		1654																	
A	Linnet *C. cannabina* (LI)		1660																	
A	Twite *C. flavirostris* (TW)		1662																	
A	Redpoll *C. flammea* (LR)		1663																	
A	Arctic Redpoll *C. hornemanni* (AL)	R	1664																	
A	Two-barred Crossbill *Loxia leucoptera* (PD)	R	1665																	
A	Crossbill *L. curvirostra* (CR) (b)^C		1666																	
A	Scottish Crossbill *L. scotica* (CY) (b)^B		1667																	
A	Parrot Crossbill *L. pyyopsittacus* (PC) (b)^A	R	1668																	
A	Trumpeter Finch *Bucanetes githagineus*	R	1676																	
A	Common Rosefinch *Carpodacus erythrinus* (SQ) (b)^A		1679																	
A	Pine Grosbeak *Pinicola enucleator*	R	1699																	
A	Bullfinch *Pyrrhula pyrrhula* (BF)		1710																	
A	Hawfinch *Coccothraustes coccothraustes* (HF)		1717																	
A	Evening Grosbeak *Hesperiphona vespertina*	R	1718																	
A	Black-and-white Warbler *Mniotilta varia*	R	1720																	
A	Golden-winged Warbler *Vermivora chrysoptera*	R	1722																	
A	Tennessee Warbler *V. peregrina*	R	1724																	
A	Northern Parula *Parula americana*	R	1732																	
A	Yellow Warbler *Dendroica petechia*	R	1733																	
A	Chestnut-sided Warbler *D. pensylvanica*	R	1734																	
A	Blackburnian Warbler *D. fusca*	R	1747																	
A	Cape May Warbler *D. tigrina*	R	1749																	
	Sub-total																			

25	NORTH AMERICAN WARBLERS contd NEW WORLD SPARROWS - BUNTINGS		Eur no.	Life list	2000 list	Jan	Feb	Mar	Apr	May	Jun	Jul	Aug	Sep	Oct	Nov	Dec	24 hr	Gar den	Holi -day
A	Magnolia Warbler *D. magnolia*	R	1750																
A	Yellow-rumped Warbler *D. coronata*	R	1751																
D	Palm Warbler *D. palmarum*	R	1752																
A	Blackpoll Warbler *D. striata*	R	1753																
A	Bay-breasted Warbler *D. castanea*	R	1754																
A	American Redstart *Setophaga ruticilla* (AD)	R	1755																
A	Ovenbird *Seiurus aurocapillus*	R	1756																
A	Northern Waterthrush *S. noveboracensis*	R	1757																
A	Yellowthroat *Geothlypis trichas*	R	1762																
A	Hooded Warbler *Wilsonia citrina*	R	1771																
A	Wilson's Warbler *W. pusilla*	R	1772																
A	Summer Tanager *Piranga rubra*	R	1786																
A	Scarlet Tanager *P. olivacea*	R	1788																
A	Eastern Towhee *Pipilo erythrophthalmus*	R	1798																
A	Lark Sparrow *Chondestes grammacus*	R	1824																
A	Savannah Sparrow *Passerculus sandwichensis*	R	1826																
A	Song Sparrow *Melospiza melodia*	R	1835																
A	White-crowned Sparrow *Zonotrichia leucophrys*	R	1839																
A	White-throated Sparrow *Z. albicollis*	R	1840																
A	Dark-eyed Junco *Junco hyemalis* (JU)	R	1842																
A	Lapland Bunting *Calcarius lapponicus* (LA)		1847																
A	Snow Bunting *Plectrophenax nivalis* (SB) (b)A		1850																
A	Black-faced Bunting *Emberiza spodocephala*	R	1853																
A	Pine Bunting *E. leucocephalos* (EL)	R	1856																
	Sub-total																			

26	BUNTINGS contd NORTH AMERICAN GROSBEAKS etc		Eur no.	Life list	2000 list	Jan	Feb	Mar	Apr	May	Jun	Jul	Aug	Sep	Oct	Nov	Dec	24 hr	Gar den	Holi -day		
A	Yellowhammer *E. citrinella* (Y)		1857																			
A	Cirl Bunting *E. cirlus* (CL) (b)A		1858																			
A	Rock Bunting *E. cia*	R	1860																			
EU	Cinereous Bunting *E. cineracea*		1865																			
A	Ortolan Bunting *E. hortulana* (OB)		1866																			
A	Cretzschmar's Bunting *E. caesia*	R	1868																			
A	Yellow-browed Bunting *E. chrysophris*	R	1871																			
A	Rustic Bunting *E. rustica*	R	1873																			
A	Little Bunting *E. pusilla* (LJ)		1874																			
D	Chestnut Bunting *E. rutila*	R	1875																			
A	Yellow-breasted Bunting *E. aureola*	R	1876																			
A	Reed Bunting *E. schoeniclus* (RB)	R	1877																			
A	Pallas's Bunting *E. pallasi*	R	1878																			
D	Red-headed Bunting *E. bruniceps*		1880																			
A	Black-headed Bunting *E. melanocephala*	R	1881																			
A	Corn Bunting *Miliaria calandra* (CB)		1882																			
A	Rose-breasted Grosbeak *Pheucticus ludovicianus*	R	1887																			
D	Blue Grosbeak *Guriaca caerulea*	R	1891																			
A	Indigo Bunting *Passerina cyanea*	R	1892																			
A	Bobolink *Dolichonyx oryzivorus*	R	1897																			
A	Brown-headed Cowbird *Molothrus ater*	R	1899																			
A	Baltimore Oriole *Icterus galbula*	R	1918																			
X																						
X																						
	Sub-total																					

27		Eur no.	Life list	2000 list	Jan	Feb	Mar	Apr	May	Jun	Jul	Aug	Sep	Oct	Nov	Dec	24 hr	Gar den	Holi -day		
X																					
X																					
X																					
X																					
X																					
X																					
X																					
X																					
X																					
X																					
X																					
X																					
X																					
X																					
X																					
X																					
X																					
X																					
X																					
X																					
X																					
X																					
X																					
X																					
																					Sub-total

28		Eur no.	Life list	2000 list	Jan	Feb	Mar	Apr	May	Jun	Jul	Aug	Sep	Oct	Nov	Dec	24 hr	Gar den	Holi -day			
X																						
X																						
X																						
X																						
X																						
X																						
X																						
X																						
X																						
X																						
X																						
X																						
X																						
X																						
X																						
X																						
X																						
X																						
X																						
X																						
X																						
X																						
X																				TOTAL		

PART SEVEN

MILLENNIUM

FEATURE

A collection of articles by the Director, a Council member and Staff of the British Trust for Ornithology, identifying major issues and objectives at the beginning of the 2000s.

Bird ringing, photo courtesy Jeff Baker

PEOPLE POWER

PART 1

A NATIONAL PERSPECTIVE

by

Jeff Baker*

The articles written by BTO colleagues for this edition of the *Birdwatcher's Yearbook* highlight some very important environmental issues which have serious long-term implications, not only for British wildlife but perhaps also for mankind as a whole. The piece on climate change is a chilling reminder to us all that the planet we live on is very sensitive to the activities of Man. Monitoring the effects of changes and producing the hard evidence to demonstrate them is a very difficult science, and there are few methods that are unequivocally acknowledged by scientists as being totally without flaw. However, the use of fauna and flora as indicators of environmental change is rapidly gaining currency in the scientific community. This acceptance has recently been strengthened by the results from the Nest Records Scheme, which clearly demonstrate that some bird species are now nesting earlier than they were in the 1940s and 1950s.

The climate debate is, of course, a global one and the solutions to the problems more difficult to resolve given the socio-economic considerations of each country. However, looking nearer to home, and of equal importance in a parochial sense is the changing face of farming and the impact this is having on wildlife. The evidence from bird data gathered over many years strongly suggests a close link between farmland bird declines and the intensification of farming practices,

---

* Jeff Baker is Head of Membership in the Membership and Development Department of the BTO. Before taking up this post in 1998 he worked as Licensing Officer in the BTO's Ringing Unit for over 25 years. He has written and illustrated several books, mostly concerning identification of birds in the hand (for bird ringers) and in the field.

largely brought about by the Common Agricultural Policy. Data from the Common Bird Census, with supplementary information from other BTO monitoring schemes such as the Constant Effort Ringing Sites and the Breeding Bird Survey, have without question been the major source of identifying these declines.

These examples of how BTO information can be used to identify environmental problems, along with others explored in later articles, show just how valuable and unique the national data set is. Monitoring of common bird populations in a variety of ways has been the BTO's forte

Counting estuarine birds as part of the Wetland Bird Survey
(photograph BTO collection)

for over 60 years. The seeds of national censusing were sown as far back as 1928 when Max Nicholson, with the backing of Harry Witherby, realised the opportunities of systematic recording year on year and launched a national census of Heronries. This was also the first survey of its kind that involved the deployment of hundreds of volunteers in the field. It is a fitting tribute to the vision and foresight of these pioneering ornithologists that the Heronries Census survives to this day and is the BTO's longest surviving survey, closely followed by the Rookeries Census.

This national treasure trove has now been recognised by the Government. In 1998, John Prescott, the Deputy Prime Minister, announced that some of the BTO's bird monitoring data would be used as one of the measures in a set of 'Quality of Life' indicators.

In the grand scheme of things the role of the BTO's work is undoubtedly more pertinent now than it ever has been. The bulk of the data collected over the years derives from the massive contribution made by volunteer fieldworkers. As the Director, Jeremy Greenwood, points out later, there are few other countries that can match our record in bird population monitoring because of this fact! The power of the organisation, then, lies first and foremost in its volunteer workforce and then in its ability to deliver the goods, in other words providing sound, robust science.

It follows that in the relationship between scientist and volunteer it is of the utmost importance that the BTO gets its level of appeal right when 'selling' surveys to birdwatchers. Complicated and time-consuming survey methods can be an uninviting prospect to many people, even a complete 'turn-off'. Yet, for the BTO to push back the boundaries of science and enter new fields of investigation it is sometimes inevitable that the design of a survey is going to be more questioning and, consequently, more demanding of the volunteer. Getting the balance right is a difficult exercise, though the numbers of volunteers participating in the Breeding Bird Survey, Wetland Bird Survey and many of the single species surveys the BTO carries out suggests it has succeeded in getting it just about right so far. To enable it to overcome some of the problems associated with more complex survey methods, the BTO is now entering a phase where it believes some form of training should be offered to fieldworkers. This can take the very simple form of supplying audio tapes of calls or songs of birds to hone identification skills, to more intensive methods such as practical field days for recording habitat types or transect work.

Much of the survey co-ordination work is conducted through a volunteer network of Regional Representatives. Again, this is a unique partnership between HQ and regional organisers, the origins of which date back to 1948. The very important role of the RRs is to recruit and mobilise the volunteer workforce to undertake surveys. Without their input the prospect of running surveys from HQ would be a vastly more difficult task. The network has served the BTO very well over the years, but the Trust must be vigilant in these times of long working hours to make sure it does not overstretch its network co-ordinators by asking too much of them.

There is no doubt that from the year 2000 and beyond the BTO will need to strengthen this collaborative part of its operation if it is to carry out all the projects it hopes to. An increasingly important element will be to engage more actively in recruiting young birdwatchers into its ranks. Signs across the birdwatching community at present are not encouraging in this respect, with an ageing membership in many local bird clubs, county trusts and natural history societies. It has never been more important to offer young people the opportunity of getting involved in fieldwork so that they can make a real contribution to conservation and thereby benefit their own future.

With public attention focusing more and more on environmental matters and world leaders being forced to sit up and take notice, the future is likely to be a very busy one for the BTO and its members.

PART 2

A LOCAL PERSPECTIVE

by

John Tully*

It was Gilbert White who described the natural history of Selborne in Hampshire in great detail. This cleric in the second half of the 18th century took care to describe the natural happenings over many years in his letters and diary. *The Natural History of Selborne* has been in print for over two hundred years and is second only to the Bible in its number of editions. His ornithological observations include everyday descriptions of birds feeding and breeding in and around the village. Numbers are not accurately recorded but some quantitative data are contained in terms like 'multitudes of swifts' and 'rarities', like Peregrine, which were only examined after being shot. We have moved on since that time but interest in the birds of our surroundings still persists. How many of us keep a garden list?

---

* John Tully is a Council member of the BTO and Regional Development Officer for the old Avon area (Bristol, Bath and Weston-super-Mare). Apart from his interest in local surveys, he and Richard Bland are carrying out a pilot national survey into birds breeding in gardens.

Nowadays, information on populations of our bird species is mainly produced by surveys organised by the British Trust for Ornithology. Their object is generally to provide a nationwide picture of the state of this species or that. Large surveys of *all* species have led to two breeding atlases, one winter atlas and a migration atlas which is about to be published. The information on a national scale is fascinating but many readers will also note the part of the map which relates to their local area. We are all interested in our own backyard.

The observers for most surveys are organised on a county basis and thankfully more and more birdwatchers are willing to spend some of their time on BTO surveys. The last breeding atlas involved between 10,000 and 15,000 observers, a testimony to their dedication to birdwatching. In Avon about 300 people submitted records and the interest was such that a county breeding atlas was produced which provided a finer grid of local information. Our area is not exceptional, most counties have either produced a breeding atlas or are in the process of publishing one.

One function of the BTO surveys is to stimulate local interest and to give the local observers a reliable and standardised method of collecting data. Another feature of the method is that it is repeatable for future years and will give reliable data for the long-term trends of the species. The collection of habitat information has highlighted the relation each species has to its environment. If we want to preserve species in our local area and maintain or improve biodiversity then we must pay careful attention to retaining or restoring local habitat.

The local results of the recent BTO Lapwing survey indicated a very low population. The results were not surprising but the small breeding numbers concentrated everyone's mind. The disappearance of wet meadows has been alarming. The local Wildlife Trust together with the co-operation of the local authorities and other bodies are now involved in restoring higher water levels to some of our low-lying farmland. There are signs that the decline of breeding Lapwing has been halted but only future local monitoring will tell if the scheme has been a success.

Perhaps it was the start of the Breeding Bird Survey (BBS) in 1994 which started our local continuous study of breeding birds in Avon. The BBS is based on 1km squares and involves observers in only three morning visits in the breeding season. The small time requirement has enabled more participation by those birdwatchers who have a lot of business or family commitments. All observations are based on two 1km walks in the square. The first visit is used to detail the habitat covered on the walks which are divided up into ten 200m sections. The other two visits are bird recording visits when all birds seen and heard are noted.

The results give a record of the birds using the square in the breeding season *and* their relationship to the habitat. Most observers are now attached to their survey area and have stayed with their squares over the first six years of the scheme. If the dates of the visits are within a week of the previous year then the collective national figures will give an indication of year-on-year change for most of our bird species.

The BBS covers all habitats and for the first time urban and moorland areas are getting regular coverage. The squares are selected nationally to represent a sample of habitats in proportion to the regional distribution of the major habitats. Here in Avon about 70% of the land is farmland and 20% urban, so 70% of the selected squares are farmland and 20% urban.

One local problem in finding observers was due to the squares being pre-selected, as observers were saying 'Can I do my square? It is more interesting than the one you have given me'. This led to the opportunity to use the BBS method on their own square *as well as* the given square. We can use these additional results locally. This approach has meant that over 100 squares are covered in Avon which is 7% of the county area. 75% of the squares are national BBS and the remainder only used locally. Additionally, many observers make counts on their square during the winter months and this continues the run of local winter information. Winter records have been kept since the winter atlas in the mid 1980s.

Recruiting was helped a great deal by the discovery of six Bee-eaters on a habitat visit early in 1994 in a square considered boring. The word soon

A Bee-eater would enliven any survey
(photograph by B Turner)

got around that rarities can turn up anywhere and while the BBS counts mainly common species, Bee-eaters and their like are a welcome addition and a useful recruiting sergeant.

The current situation is that six years' data are available for most squares. Analysis of some red-listed species like Skylark gives the patterns of abundance over our area. We have found unsuspected peaks and troughs which need further investigation. Local trends for Skylark are becoming available but short-term trends need to be treated with caution. In the long term of 20, 50 or 100 years the method can be repeated to put details on our bird numbers in a way that has not been possible before. If only we had information from Gilbert White of the habitat details and bird counts for Selborne in 1770!

Summing the cumulative species in a square is a crude measure of biodiversity. The larger numbers reflect the range of habitats and their richness in the 1km square. There is a danger of just using simple numbers and perhaps we should weight such values so that red-listed species have a weighting of three, amber two and others one. The result would be to highlight local areas of special conservation need and act as a useful tool for discussion of our local priorities. All records are submitted to our local Environmental Record Office and copies are supplied to the ecologists in each of our four local authorities.

The BBS also makes it possible to compare numbers of similar species. Blue Tit is in a 2:1 ratio to Great Tit. There are seven Blackbirds to every one Song Thrush on the latest figures. The relative scarcity of species can be put in context from the counting. Tree Sparrows are locally declining and their latest statistic is that only three birds were counted in the 42,000 birds of the 1998 BBS. Yellow Wagtail was equally worrying with four birds counted. Hopefully this latter species will benefit from the measures taken to benefit Lapwings.

The obvious way of raising the numbers of certain species is to increase their habitat. However, in our area of high human population the problem is often to safeguard the loss of wildlife to inappropriate development. Making planning decisions is always difficult and sometimes the best habitats are threatened. The decision may go to appeal and the case for the environment needs to be argued with strong evidence. The records of quantitative data on the bird species over a number of years will be an important part of that case.

I hope that local records will continue to be expanded and that fifty years into the new millennium our knowledge will extend to accurate numbers, distribution and variation of numbers of each species. Such a goal relies on birdwatchers committed to spending some of their valuable leisure time on providing the information.

BIRDS AS INDICATORS

OF THE HEALTH OF
THE ENVIRONMENT

by

David Noble*

The silent spring in the title of Rachel Carson's famous book is an evocative example of how birds can warn us about serious dangers in our environment. Poisoned by the accumulation of DDT and other organochlorine pesticides, songbirds and their avian predators were succumbing to the insidious effects of virtually undetectable compounds previously considered quite safe. At the same time, biologists were starting to report eggs of Gannets and other fish-eating species so thin-shelled that they broke when the birds tried to incubate them.

Like canaries taken down into mines to act as early warning devices of dangerous gases, birds have long been used by humans as indicators of the health of our surroundings. The canaries and Gannet eggs warn us of the presence of toxic substances, but the information provided by indicators can be much more subtle. The quality of our water, for example, is revealed by its effects on the waterfowl that live there. One of the best documented cases of this connection is the change in distribution of the Tufted Duck in central Europe in response to eutrophication (action causing water to become rich in plant nutrients), which reduces the availability of its main food, the zebra mussel. Not only is the health of an ecosystem reflected by the presence or abundance of particular species, but by a greater diversity of species. Eutrophication adversely affected Tufted Ducks, but it can cause large increases in the number of individuals of less ecologically specialized species such as Mallard and Coot. This means that species richness can be used to evaluate the health of an ecosystem, as well as identify areas of ecological importance.

---

* Dr David Noble is the Head of the Census Unit at the BTO. His main ornithological interests are conservation, seabird ecology and evolutionary ecology, particularly brood parasitism.

Why use birds as indicators rather than a more direct measure? The main reason is that they are easier to count and study. It is much easier to record a Kingfisher perched above a stream than sample for the presence of small fish, although both tell you the same thing. The second point is that by virtue of their trophic level and longevity, birds integrate the effects over time of a number of potential hazards. And, because birds are a relatively well known group, they can be used as surrogates for other taxa for which information is scarce. The diversity of restricted-range bird species in terrestrial tropic regions, for example, corresponds well with taxa such as flowering plants or butterflies, although not unexpectedly, the correspondence with fish diversity is less reliable.

Another advantage of using birds as indicators is their strong appeal to the general public. Species (such as Peregrine Falcon) adopted as flagships for conservation programmes are typically large, majestic or particularly colourful birds. This is not always the case: during campaigns to clean up the North American Great Lakes in the 1980s, the ubiquitous Herring Gull was promoted by the slogan 'healthy gulls mean healthy lakes' despite having a somewhat tarnished reputation as a pest. In this case, the indicator is not the presence or even abundance of a particular species, but its breeding success.

Ideally, species selected as indicators should be resident and obtain the majority of their food in the target habitat. Dippers and Grey Wagtails both live along upland streams, feeding on insects that are sensitive to acidification. Studies in Wales revealed that because Dippers spend almost 100% of their time foraging there, breeding success in acidic streams was significantly reduced, whereas wagtails, which sometimes forage in other habitats, cope with acidification. Selection of an appropriate indicator for broad-scale monitoring of acidification of waterways gives an idea of the complexity. Ospreys are very sensitive to acidification, but the density of breeding pairs in most of Europe is too sparse to use this species for monitoring. On the other hand, although the density of the relatively abundant Goldeneye is related to acidification (through its effect on fish densities), this species is strongly affected by the availability of nest sites in tree holes, and that would have to be taken into account in any monitoring scheme.

Current threats to Britain's birds

Many of the examples above involve pollutants. In fact, mainly in response to their effects on birds, organochlorines have been largely banned, and today's pesticides should have undergone more rigorous environmental health testing before release. Increased conservation efforts, particularly those directed at rare species or important habitats, appear to have been successful in reversing the bad fortunes of a number of species such as Red Kite, Avocet and Buzzard. This has been achieved by a variety of measures including introducing controls of hunting or disturbance at breeding sites, captive breeding and re-introductions, and protection of important breeding areas.

Despite these successes - achieved through concerted effort by conservationists - urban development, agricultural intensification and increasing human demands for resources continue to threaten natural environments. Not only habitat loss but fragmentation and disturbance can have profound effects on birds. A general deterioration of the countryside may seem obvious to anyone having trouble trying to get away from it all and find truly natural areas, but how serious is this for birds? After all, lots of birds seem perfectly happy in urban parks and gardens.

Bird censuses conducted by Britain's volunteer birdwatchers may provide the answer. Many common countryside birds frequent a mixture of farmland, woodland and urban environments that is often extremely fragmented. These are the species monitored best by the British Trust for Ornithology's terrestrial bird survey schemes such as the Breeding Bird Survey (BBS) and the Common Bird Census (CBC). Moreover, because plots and birds can be categorized by habitat or habitat preferences, we can monitor particular components of the environment.

The Government's 'Indicators of Sustainability'

The idea that bird numbers provide an important indicator of the health of the environment became widely appreciated last year with the launch of the Government's 'Indicators of Sustainability'. Populations of wild birds, dubbed the 'Skylark index', was one of thirteen headline indicators of the state of the nation, and featured prominently in the media. These new statistics were meant to provide a broader picture of the quality of life in modern Britain than that given by economic indicators alone, by reflecting people's concerns about health, housing, jobs and the environment.

The index for wild bird populations was the result of co-operation between the British Trust for Ornithology, the Royal Society for the Protection of Birds, and the Department of the Environment, Transport and the Regions. Population trends of 186 species of wild breeding birds in the UK were compiled for the period 1970-1997. Exclusion of introduced and alien species and 33 rare species (populations less than 500 pairs) yielded the headline indicator based on numbers of 139 common breeding species. The largest source of data for the index was the CBC, with additional information from the Waterways Bird Survey, the Wetlands Birds Survey, the New Atlas, the Seabird Monitoring Programme/Seabird Colony Register, the Rare Breeding Birds Panel, the RSPB Statutory Conservation Agencies' surveys of red data birds, and a range of single-species surveys.

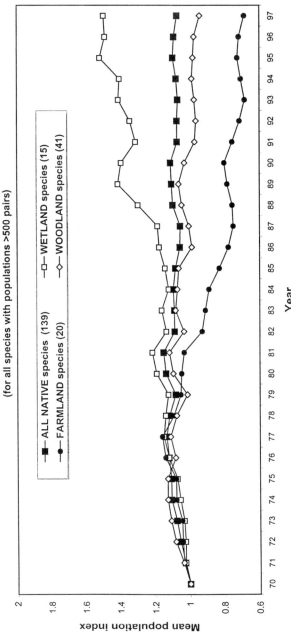

Indicator of wild bird populations
(for all species with populations >500 pairs)

ALL NATIVE species (139)
FARMLAND species (20)
WETLAND species (15)
WOODLAND species (41)

Mean population index

Year

The index for all native species together shows populations to have been relatively stable since 1970, with a slight upward trend (see figure). However, woodland birds have declined moderately, and farmland birds rapidly, in the last twenty years. Based as it is on the summed effects of many species, this indicator has limitations. However, the significant decline for farmland birds is confirmed by analyses of population trends in individual species such as Kestrel, Corn Bunting and Bullfinch.These trends suggest that farmland is being seriously degraded from the perspective of common countryside birds and there may be even worse effects on rarer farmland specialists not well monitored by these schemes.

The contrast between the farmland and woodland species declines and the upward trends for wetland species (see figure) and 33 rarer (excluded from the headline indicator) is interesting. This suggests that although focused conservation efforts have been effective, many birds are facing serious problems in the wider countryside.

I have not so far mentioned the most recent use of birds - as indicators of global warming. As described later (pages 229-234), long-term data held by the BTO's Nest Record Scheme, reveal that the egg laying dates of many British birds are increasingly early, in line with increases in temperatures. Following this finding, the British Government included the laying dates of Chaffinch and Robin, counts of Wrens in CBCs, and the arrival date of Swallows at coastal bird observatories in its recently announced set of indicators of climate change.

Since ancient history, birds have symbolized the changing of seasons and climatic events such as storms, so at the start of a new millennium it is very fitting that birds are again providing valuable information on this particular aspect of our environment.

THE CHANGING
BIRD COMMUNITIES
OF OUR GARDENS

by

David Glue and Andrew Cannon*

Agriculture is the largest single land-use category in lowland Britain. Hence it is farmland that historically has supported the lion's share of our common songbird populations. Recent changes in the management of both arable and pastoral farms appear, however, to have reduced the numbers of birds that farmland can support. The work of BTO survey volunteers shows that the numbers of some typical birds of woodland are also declining. Other types of habitat are therefore becoming increasingly important as refuges for the species concerned.

With the growing interest in 'wildlife gardening' and the availability of more appropriate supplementary foods, suitable for feeding birds all year round, gardens are potentially a very important resource for birds that may be in trouble elsewhere. More than ever we need to monitor and try to understand changes in the birds using gardens, as they may well be linked to changes of conservation significance in the wider countryside.

What the BTO has done is to launch a mass-participation nationwide garden bird survey. With the support of CJ Wildbird Foods, the project began in 1995. Anyone with access to a garden can take part in the

---

* David Glue is Senior Research Officer with the BTO, running the Garden Bird Feeding Survey and the Raptor Research Register; he is also involved in the Nest Record Scheme and Common Birds Census.
* Andrew Cannon organises the BTO's Garden BirdWatch project, for which he produces the magazine *Bird Table*; he is also the author of the *Garden BirdWatch Handbook*.

BTO Garden BirdWatch which can be joined at any time of year and is self-funded by a volunteers' annual contribution of £10. Already it has produced some unique and fascinating data. In particular it has given us a great deal of new information about how birds vary their use of gardens through the seasons. Of course it will be some time before we can extract genuine long-term trends from the results.

However, thanks to a few stalwart volunteers, we are fortunate enough to have a small but precious long-term record of some of the most interesting changes. Participants in another and longer-running BTO project, the Garden Bird Feeding Survey (GBFS), keep a weekly record of all the birds taking food in their gardens between October and March. Sites are now selected from among those covered by Garden BirdWatch, where participants are willing and able to make an extra commitment. The selection is made according to garden type and location, and sites include city flats, town houses, suburban semis and rural farmsteads. The idea is to sample as broadly representative and geographically widespread a cross-section of gardens as possible from those available. This is the thirtieth consecutive winter of GBFS recording, so although very small (about 250 gardens are monitored each winter) the project is revealing some very interesting long-term changes.

Garden Bird Feeding Survey records from the most recently analysed winter (1998/99) show twelve relatively abundant species taking supplementary foods or water provided in at least 70% of all gardens. Robin, Blue Tit and Blackbird vie for 'Top Spot' at feeding stations and in fact this has been the case over all three decades with remarkably little change. However, moving down the rankings we start to see some fascinating increases and a few striking decreases in the reporting rates of some species at bird tables in winter since the 1970s.

Obviously, more birds tend to resort to gardens for help in colder winters than in milder ones, but despite this it is not unreasonable to make a simple comparison between the 1970s and 1990s. Both decades were essentially mild in character, apart from the relatively cold winters of 1978/79 and 1990/91. Fifty-nine different bird species were recorded at one per cent or more of all the feeding stations over the combined decades. Forty species increased their use of gardens between one decade and the other and eighteen species were seen less often, while in each of the two decades Blackbirds took food at more than ninety-nine per cent of GBFS sites.

Comparing two single winters, both similarly mild, shows how the variety of species has tended to increase. GBFS sites in town and country settings attracted averages of only 15 and 16 different species respectively in 1977/78 compared to 20 and 21 species in 1997/98. Whether gardens have tended to provide richer, more varied winter habitat in recent years or whether this simply reflects the fact that more birds are having trouble finding winter food in the countryside is not yet clear. Both factors are probably involved, affecting the different species to varying degrees. Despite the general upward trend, species richness at feeding stations continues to vary greatly. Some gardens in city, coastal and bleak open country situations may attract just half a dozen species over a full winter, while others in rural hamlets with a mosaic of habitats and those in the warm microclimate of suburbia can support up to fifty species or even more in exceptional locations.

The forty species which appear to have increased their use of supplementary foods over the last three decades include some spectacular 'climbers'. Siskins, Long-tailed Tits and Goldfinches have learned how to employ new feeding methods and to exploit novel types of foods, notably peanuts, fats and improved seed mixtures with higher

Long-tailed Tits on peanut feeder
(photograph by Derek Toomer)

quality and more appropriate constituents such as black sunflower seeds. These are smaller, thinner-skinned and richer in oil than the traditional 'hamster food' striped varieties and are hence much more suitable for finches and other garden-feeder users. Better quality and more regular feeding, allied to reduced persecution and a consequent greater tolerance of humans, will have contributed to the spectacular increases in feeding station use by Magpie, Woodpigeon and Carrion Crow. The overall populations of all four species have increased significantly over the survey period, but nonetheless they would not previously have been considered typical garden birds in most areas. It has also to be said that the increases have resulted in richer pickings for hunting Sparrowhawks.

The number of gardens feeding Collared Dove and Great Spotted Woodpecker has also risen, reflecting the population increases of these birds over the same period and their versatility in exploiting new foods. A further five species now patronize an additional ten percent or more of gardens compared to the 1970s: Coal Tit, Blackcap, Jay, Jackdaw and Pheasant. Some have probably been drawn to gardens initially by improvements in their semi-natural resources. More trees and shrubs, nuts, seeds and berries are available in our increasingly wildlife-friendly gardens, attracting typical scrub and woodland birds which then discover supplementary foods and learn to exploit them.

Just eighteen species have tended to visit fewer winter feeding stations in the 1990s than in the 1970s, but these 'sliders' include many well-known garden favourites that will be sorely missed if declining trends continue. The Song Thrush shows the most worrying decline with more than twenty-two per cent fewer gardens visited. The reasons for the population decrease are not yet fully understood but some conservationists now believe that gardens provide a refuge habitat that will be critical in enabling any recovery of the species.

House Sparrow and Starling feeding flocks have fallen markedly in size, although disappearing completely from only a small numbers of gardens. Neither can be considered ubiquitous or abundant any longer in many parts of the British Isles. Fewer records of Willow Tit, Bullfinch and Reed Bunting reflect substantial breeding population reductions, but most of the other garden feeders which appear to have decreased, including Pied Wagtail, Mistle Thrush, Redwing, Fieldfare and Black-headed Gull, are in any case to varying degrees cold weather 'specialists' in gardens. The unusually mild and snow-free (albeit often wet and stormy) winters of the 1990s have enabled these birds to find plenty of food in their natural habitats without having to resort to artificial feeding stations.

Scarce species that turn up in gardens and exploit the supplementary foods provided by GBFS observers are a constant source of amazement. Gardens in open countryside or in highland, coastal or island settings consistently attract birds such as Chough (Gwynedd), Raven (Dyfed), Cirl Bunting (Devon) and Crested Tit (Highland) in winter. The 1998/99 recording season brought the first record of Glaucous Gull, feeding alongside Herring Gulls in West Glamorgan and bringing the tally to 159 species over 29 winters. Mediterranean Gull (Suffolk), Mandarin Duck (Surrey), Hoopoe (Dyfed), Jack Snipe (Devon) and Whinchat (Yorks) have all been observed at garden feeding sites in recent years.

As we enter the new millennium, it is intriguing to speculate about new species that might appear and about future trends in garden feeding behaviour. Could Monk's Parakeets follow Ring-necked Parakeets on to feeders, as has happened in North America? Might Ring Ouzels and Lesser Whitethroats linger in our winter gardens and learn to benefit from supplementary foods as Blackcaps have done with such success? There have already been a handful of confirmed winter garden records of Lesser Whitethroat. Will the worrying slide in Song Thrush and House Sparrow numbers be arrested, and hopefully even reversed, perhaps with a major contribution coming from improvements to their garden habitats?

Careful, consistent recording of garden birds by BTO volunteers will help us to understand what is happening in a habitat of ever-increasing importance, and to obtain new insights into that importance by comparing trends in gardens with those in the wider countryside. It will also help us to focus garden management on providing resources for the species most likely to benefit and to quantify the value of new or improved artificial foods.

BIRDS OF THE
WIDER COUNTRYSIDE

by

Andy Wilson*

While global conservation issues such as pollution, climate change and the destruction of native forests grab the news headlines, local issues like urbanisation, road developments and, on a brighter note, the establishment of nature reserves are perhaps closest to the hearts of most birdwatchers. However, the largest challenge facing most of the birds in Britain is how to adapt to an ever changing countryside. The majority of the 300 million or more birds breeding and wintering in Britain live in farmland and woodland, which make up well over half the surface area of the country.

Of course, farmland and woodland in Britain are man-made habitats, or at the very least have been radically altered by humans over the last few thousand years. As a result, the bird communities found in most of our countryside are in a sense artificial - made up of the species that have adapted successfully to a changing landscape.

Farmland was colonised by birds once found in natural habitats such as open woodland or forest edges, at a time when these habitats were being lost. The character of farmland has changed over the centuries. Enclosure of fields, increased mechanisation, depopulation of the countryside and agricultural depression must all have had major impacts on bird populations in the past. There can be little doubt, however, that the pace of change in agriculture has accelerated greatly since the second world war, and the resulting impact on birds and other wildlife has been enormous. Changes in land use and farming practices will always have resulted in some birds decreasing, but such losses may have been

---

* Andy Wilson has worked for the BTO for five years, four of them as Common Birds Census analyst and one in the Terrestrial Ecology Unit. He is bird recorder for the Brecks and editor of the *Breckland Bird Report*.

compensated for by increases in other species. Enclosure of fields and common land in the 16th century may have led to massive losses among species preferring the open countryside, such as Great Bustard, Lapwing and Corn Bunting, but the sudden increase in hedgerows undoubtedly benefited many others.

Some of the recent changes in the British countryside are obvious - almost half of our hedgerows have been removed during the last fifty years, resulting in a huge loss of available habitat for many species. Other changes have been rather more subtle but their impacts on bird populations have been enormous, and in the vast majority of cases detrimental.

The BTO first became concerned about the effects of changes in farmland during the late 1950s and early 1960s, a time when large numbers of birds were killed by organochlorine seed-dressings. A major outcome was the establishment of the Common Birds Census (CBC), which has monitored population trends of our commoner farmland and woodland birds since the early 1960s. Those who pioneered the CBC should be applauded for their foresight. The CBC has provided sound evidence of changing bird populations and, importantly, it has documented the massive declines in some farmland bird species. The figures are staggering; between 50% and 90% of Grey Partridge, Snipe, Turtle Dove, Skylark, Song Thrush, Tree Sparrow, Yellowhammer, Reed Bunting and Corn Bunting populations were lost between 1972 and 1996. Without the backing of data from schemes such as the CBC, the arguments for promoting wildlife-friendly farming practices would be significantly weaker.

While the scale and breadth of decreases among farmland birds has been astonishing, the CBC has shown that some woodland birds have also shown marked population changes. Some, such as Blackcap and Nuthatch have increased steadily over the last twenty to thirty years while others, such as Willow Tit and Redpoll have decreased alarmingly. The reasons for these changes are little understood, partly as their does not appear to be a common thread between the species involved in terms of their habitat requirements or their breeding biology. Most of the woodland in Britain is managed for one reason or another - for timber, leisure, game interests or conservation, and as in farmland, management practices have changed over time. Woodlands have also borne the brunt of foreign invaders introduced by Man - mammals such as Grey Squirrel and Muntjac and plants such as sycamore and rhododendron have spread at a worrying rate and caused major changes to the structure of woodlands and the wildlife within them.

The CBC has been highly successful in showing population changes in farmland and woodland bird numbers in lowland England but due to the intensive nature of the fieldwork - our volunteers make around ten visits to their plot each breeding season, relatively few people are able to contribute, especially in north and west Britain where there are fewer birdwatchers. To overcome this, the Breeding Bird Survey (BBS), a joint venture with the RSPB and Joint Nature Conservation Committee, was launched in 1994. BBS requires just two visits to a randomly selected 1km square each spring and therefore many more people can get involved. In fact, well over 2000 squares are now surveyed each year, enabling the BTO to monitor the populations of many more bird species throughout their British range.

Of course, merely being able to show the rate that bird populations are changing does not provide solutions to the problems that face birds in a changing environment. It is vital that the reasons behind the population changes are understood, only then can measures be suggested to improve the lot of species that are losing-out to the ever increasing demands of the human populace. The BTO organises many one-off or periodically repeated surveys to investigate more specific issues or examine the fortunes and requirements of individual species in more detail.

BTO Lapwing surveys showed a 49% decrease in breeding Lapwing numbers between 1987 and 1998. Many other species have shown similar declines in recent years. (photograph by Mike Weston, courtesy BTO)

In recent years, BTO surveys have shown that organic farms hold more birds than conventional farms, while a survey of birds on set-aside demonstrated the importance of this new habitat within farmland. A range of surveys of beleaguered farmland birds such as Lapwing, Skylark and Corn Bunting have provided valuable information not just on numbers and distribution, but also on habitat use - a key to understanding what may be causing the decreases shown by the CBC and BBS. Common threads among the declines of farmland birds are the loss of diversity of crop and farming types, loss of over-winter stubbles and a general reduction in food supply due to the ever increasing efficiency of farming operations, including, importantly, the application of herbicides and pesticides. Many of these changes are here to stay. We cannot hope for the return of the countryside as it was a hundred years ago. We must strive to find ways of making the modern farming landscape more accommodating for birds and capitalise on increasing environmental awareness for the benefit of all wildlife.

The constantly growing number of farmland birds showing steep population decreases is one of the major conservation issues in Britain. It is recognised that birds are excellent indicators of the health of the environment. As such they provide overwhelming evidence that huge areas of the British countryside are now unsuitable for all but the most adaptable of animals and plants. While farmland issues are likely to be at the forefront of BTO research for many years to come, we must remember that other habitats such as woodlands and uplands are also changing. The BTO has always conducted a varied research programme; in 1999 it organised a national Nightingale Survey while in recent years it has conducted surveys on species whose numbers are increasing, such as Little Egret, Canada Goose, sawbills, Woodlark (jointly with the RSPB) and Rook. A rolling programme of single-species surveys will ensure that gaps in our knowledge of bird populations are plugged. But with an ever increasing number of species showing rapid and sustained population changes, we must ensure that our surveys are driven by important conservation issues.

At the same time, the continued success of the CBC and BBS in monitoring populations of a wide range of species is essential - who knows what unforseen trials and opportunities birds of the British countryside may face in years to come?

AN ATLAS OF
BIRD MIGRATION

by

Mike Toms*

Birdwatchers have long been fascinated by the movements of birds. Many of the scarce passerines to have reached our shores unexpectedly have done so because of a navigational failure on their part or because of the interruptive effects of weather. There are many different types of bird movements, some of which have a pronounced seasonal basis. The most widely recognised of these is 'migration' where a species moves between two distinct areas, typically breeding in one area and then migrating to a different area in which to spend the winter. Of course, the scale of the migrational movement differs between species; some are long-distance migrants, others may move only a short way.

   While such movements have a tremendous biological interest, they also have important implications for the conservation and management of bird populations. To implement an effective conservation strategy for a migratory species, where the species winters and how it gets to and from the wintering area need to be known. Threats to the future of the species on its wintering grounds, or *en route* back to its breeding sites, will ultimately affect the health of the population of that species. This is where the collation of data on bird movements is all important. While we begin to take a more global view of bird populations as the new millennium approaches, so the value of ringing data becomes more widely appreciated.

   Such data have been gathered in Britain and Ireland since 1909, under the Ringing Scheme co-ordinated by the BTO. Birds are fitted with individually numbered rings by specially trained and licensed volunteers.

* Written by Mike Toms, Research Officer, on behalf of the Migration Atlas Team: Dr Chris Wernham (Senior Populations Biologist, Ringing), John Marchant (Migration Atlas principal editor) and Jacquie Clark (Head of Ringing Unit).

Subsequent recaptures of live birds or recoveries of dead ringed individuals are used to establish patterns of seasonal movement. There have now been more than 25 million birds ringed and more than half a million subsequently reported, potentially providing a great deal of information.

Until relatively recently the analysis of movements using ringing data has been somewhat piecemeal, with studies concentrating on individual species and published data scattered across many different publications. To allow implementation of effective conservation strategies, this information needs to be brought together, with additional analyses carried out to provide data on those species for which little previous work has been done. The BTO has set up a Migration Atlas project to do just this, providing data in a suitable format for virtually all of the bird species using Britain and Ireland in any numbers. Although this project is currently ongoing, some feeling for its conservation value can be seen by examining one or two examples.

Sedge Warblers provide a good example of a trans-Saharan migrant, with the entire breeding population wintering in Africa to the south of the Sahara Desert (Map 1). Pre-migratory movements begin in late July when the birds seemingly seek those sites with high densities of Plum-reed Aphids. These form an important but short-lived food source as the birds fatten up in readiness for the long journey south. From the ringing data it appears that some birds move to France in order to exploit this food resource, while others remain in Britain & Ireland. After fattening, most Sedge Warblers move rapidly south, crossing Iberia, North Africa and the Sahara Desert. Once over the Sahara, progress south seems to slow down, with most birds arriving in their main winter quarters during October. Interestingly, individuals ringed in Ireland and the south west of Britain appear to winter further west in West Africa, with birds from the eastern side of Britain wintering further east.

The wintering areas of migrants can be very important for their conservation, as can be seen from ring-recovery data for Sandwich Terns, Roseate Terns and Common Terns. All three species winter along the west coast of Africa and many recoveries are reported from Ghana, the Ivory Coast, Liberia and Sierra Leone. Here the terns exploit the large shoals of sardines and anchovies that periodically occur. In those years when the fish populations are high, the number of recoveries reported would be expected to decline, as terns are able to exploit the abundant food resource. However, this is not the case. In those years when small fish are abundant, the recovery rate actually increases. While this may seem counter-intuitive, it does have a simple explanation. Local people catch terns using baited noose-traps or lines of baited hooks, and in those years when small fish are abundant, the terns are more readily caught coming close inshore to catch the fish. Tern populations

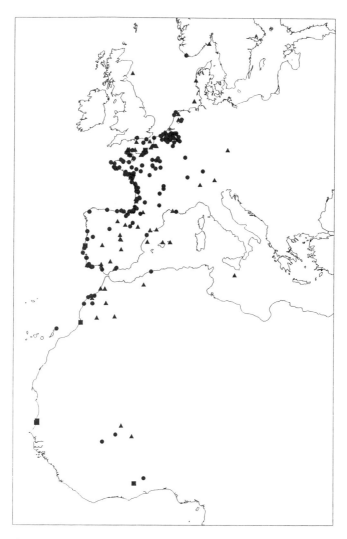

Map 1. *Recovery locations (outside the breeding season) of*
Sedge Warblers ringed in Britain and Ireland
(circles = autumn; squares = winter; triangles = spring)

wintering further south and exploiting different fisheries appear to be at
less risk from such catching. This clearly has implications for the future
of tern populations breeding in Britain and Ireland.

Just as some terns exploit fisheries as staging areas *en route* to wintering grounds further south, so too many wader species have clearly defined staging areas. Some of these have been revealed from ring-recovery data. Two distinct breeding populations of Knot use Britain and Ireland; birds breeding in Siberia stop-over on estuaries *en route* to wintering grounds in Africa, while birds breeding in Arctic Canada and Greenland actually winter here. Approximately 90% of Knot wintering in Europe do so on UK estuaries, and while the importance of such estuaries is apparent from counts of birds, it is the ringing data that actually show from which breeding populations they originate.

Map 2. *Movements of Knot between the British Isles and abroad. Each line links a ringing with a recovery location but does not imply the route taken by the bird.*

It is exactly this sort of information that is important for the development of international conservation strategies. By bringing together available data on bird movements, as revealed by ring-recoveries, into an atlas of bird migration, it should be possible to provide the developers of conservation policies with the information they need. The role of the ringers and the BTO Ringing Scheme in this is therefore of considerable importance.

CLIMATE CHANGE AND
BIRDS IN THE UK

by

Humphrey Crick*

Global warming is a fact: over the last 150 years, average temperatures on the earth have risen by 0.6°C. The last two decades of the millennium are the two warmest since recording began in the 1850s. Two questions immediately spring to mind: (1) Is such an apparently trivial change really important? And (2) Can this change be laid at the door of Man?

It's getting hotter
0.6°C sounds pretty small when we face a temperature change of 10-30°C each day in our so-called British summer! But this is the difference between climate and weather. A one degree centigrade shift in average temperature moves us about 250km southwards: a two degree shift would really upset the new Scottish Parliamentarians, because it would move Edinburgh right back down to London again! Other evidence suggests that this trivial change is already having major effects: glaciers are retreating worldwide, coral reef bleaching has increased (hot water kills the coral), Arctic sea-ice has shrunk and the Antarctic ice shelves are breaking up.

  Are all these changes caused by man? There is a wonderful organisation, a real achievement for mankind, called the Intergovernmental Panel on Climate Change, or IPCC. This was set up by the World Meteorological Organisation and United Nations Environmental Programme in 1988. It exists to assess the evidence for climate change and calls on the expertise

---

* Dr Humphrey Crick is Senior Ecologist in the Populations Research Department of the BTO. Before settling in the temperate climate of the British Trust for Ornithology, where he has led the Nest Record Scheme, he experienced more extreme climates in Scotland, studying pesticide side-effects, and has been globally warmed in Africa where he studied co-operative breeding among Red-throated Bee-eaters.

of hundreds of scientists worldwide, the majority of whom give their time freely. In its 2nd report in 1995 it made the statement that: *'The balance of evidence suggests a discernible human influence on global climate'.* These were very carefully chosen words that took months of discussion because of their import. They were very cautious about this, but the world scientific consensus is that there is about an 80-90% chance that we are an important cause of global warming. There are a few scientists who disagree, but they are very much in the minority.

The mechanics of global warming are outlined in the box opposite, but the IPCC estimates that world temperatures will have risen by 2°C by the year 2100 (with a range of between 1°C and 3.5°C). The increases in temperature will be greatest near the poles. Again, this rise sounds quite small and slow but, to put it into context, the change out of the last ice age involved a rise in temperature of about 5-7°C at a rate of 1°C per 1000 years. In contrast, we are currently aiming to move things along at a rate of 1°C per 70 years. The change will be incredibly rapid and plants and animals are going to find it hard to keep up.

Birds are laying earlier

Here at the BTO we are lucky enough to have some of the best sets of long-term data in the world - thanks to all our members. One, the Nest Record Scheme, provides unparalleled information for a large number of species, gathered over the whole country. It is a goldmine of information, which is why it is part-funded under the BTO/JNCC Partnership.

During the annual monitoring process, we noticed that there was a surprisingly large number of species which appeared to be laying earlier. On further investigation we found that 20 (31%) of 65 species showed statistically significant trends towards earlier laying over the past 25 years. The average advancement was 9 days (Crick *et al* 1997).

I have since followed this up, in collaboration with Tim Sparks at the Institute of Terrestrial Ecology, by looking at the full 57 years of data that we have available and seeing how the changes are related to temperature and rainfall. A very clear image has emerged. Most species show a pattern of early laying dates in the 1940s and 1950s, later laying dates in the 1960s and 1970s and then earlier laying dates in the 1980s and 1990s. This pattern matches well with changes in average spring temperatures: these have become cooler and then warmer over the last half century. In fact, when we analyse the data statistically, we find that for seven of the most widespread species, the trends in laying dates can be accounted for purely by the trends in temperatures, and for 10 others temperature and rainfall account for many of the changes. Overall, these results from the Nest Record Scheme constitute one of the strongest pieces of evidence, to date, for the widespread effect of climate change on wildlife (Crick & Sparks 1999).

THE GREENHOUSE

The greenhouse effect is a good thing. Without the blanketing effect of our atmosphere, we would have an average surface temperature of minus 6°C, not plus 15°C. (The famous scientist Fourier first pointed this out in 1827).

It works by visible light entering the atmosphere from the sun, hitting the ground and being re-radiated as heat (infra-red). This does not bounce back out into space but is intercepted by the 'greenhouse gases', especially water and carbon dioxide, which absorb it and re-radiate it. As a result, only part of it gets back into space, the rest carries on bouncing around in the atmosphere warming up the air.

Carbon dioxide, by its sheer volume, is the most important greenhouse gas. It has increased dramatically since the industrial revolution in the 1850s by about a third. (We know this from air bubbles trapped inside ice cores taken from the Antarctic). Carbon dioxide levels are set to continue increasing due to fossil fuel burning (coal, oil, gas).

The other greenhouse gases are (a) water, which is increasing because of greater evaporation due to warming; (b) methane, which has increased by 150%, comes mainly from rice paddies and oil or gas fields and is equivalent to 20 carbon dioxide molecules; (c) nitrous oxide, which has increased 15%, is released by agricultural fertilizers and from industrial process and is equivalent to 200 carbon dioxide molecules; and (d) chlorofluorocarbons (CFCs), which also destroy the ozone layer, each molecule is equivalent to 10,000 carbon dioxide molecules in terms of the greenhouse effect.

We don't know yet whether these changes will be good, bad or indifferent to the birds. They may be good, because early fledglings often survive better than later nestlings. However, if they get out of synch with their food supply or if they get hit by bad weather later in the spring, then the early nesters will suffer. There is some good evidence that caterpillars are speeding up their development faster than the birds can keep up with - resulting in a lack of food for any but the earliest birds. This is a subject that we hope to pursue over the coming years.

Changing distributions and migration

Not only is there evidence for changes in laying dates of birds, but also spring migrants appear to be arriving earlier and the distributions of breeding and wintering birds appear to be shifting in response to climate changes.

Tim Sparks has been accumulating data on the arrival dates of migrants with a variety of co-workers from within Britain. In particular, he has been analysing data from the network of Bird Observatories that exists around the British Isles. Since the 1970s, the average first arrival dates of Chiffchaff have advanced from 21 to 11 March, of Swallow from 6 April to 31 March, of Willow Warbler from 7 April to 30 March, of Blackcap from 15 to 3 April, of Swift from 1 May to 26 April and of Garden Warbler from 4 May to 20 April. Changes in arrival dates are certainly linked to warmer spring temperatures in the UK and in southern Europe and are probably determined by the earlier availability of insect food supplies (Sparks 1999).

Jack Lennon and Chris Thomas at the University of Leeds have analysed changes between the two BTO breeding bird atlases that covered 1968-72 and 1988-91. They have been able to show that birds with southern distributions have shifted the northern edge of their distributions further north by, on average, 19 km between the two atlases (Thomas & Lennon 1999).

Another new piece of evidence has come from BTO analysis of Wetland Bird Survey (WeBS) data by Mark Rehfisch and Graham Austin. They have shown that most of the UK's internationally important wintering populations of waders have been shifting the centres of their distributions eastwards. So far, they have looked at the Ringed Plover in detail and tested whether these changes might be related to climate warming. Their analyses have shown that the distributions of wintering Ringed Plovers are affected by the numbers of days with ground frost, such that under warmer conditions the birds can winter more on the productive eastern coastline compared with the less productive west coast. Such changes may have important implications for the placement of the UK's network of protected sites for wintering wildfowl (Rehfisch & Austin 1999).

Government Climate Change Indicators

In June 1999, the Minister of State for the Environment, the Rt Hon Michael Meacher, announced a new set of Government *Indicators of Climate Change in the UK*. The aim is to help raise awareness of how our climate is changing and how it is changing both the man-made and natural worlds in which we live. The evidence for climate change is mounting and it is beginning to become obvious even to us, here in the UK. In order to track these changes as they happen across the UK, the Government has gathered together a first set of indicators that are influenced by climate.

There are three bird indicators among those that have been chosen. The first is from the BTO's Nest Record Scheme: the laying dates of Chaffinch and Robin, both of which are strongly related to spring temperatures. The second is the population change of the Wren, as measured by the BTO's Common Birds Census. Wren numbers fluctuate widely, mainly due to high mortality in severe winters. Small bodied birds are particularly prone to prolonged spells of cold, wet, snowy or frosty weather because they cannot obtain enough food to maintain body temperatures. Big population declines have occurred after severe winters such as 1962/63, 1978/79 and so on. It is expected that Wren populations will not increase indefinitely if winters become progressively milder, but they will tend to stabilise at a relatively high level. The third bird indicator is the arrival date of Swallows, as measured by the daily records of birds seen at British coastal Bird Observatories. Tim Sparks and Dick Loxton have extracted and analysed information from four Observatories (Dungeness, Portland, Bardsey and Calf of Man) to show that arrival dates have become earlier with our warmer springs.

It is very important that BTO data have been chosen to be used in such Government statistics. It is data from such long-running schemes that are going to be vital in monitoring the impacts of climate change as it develops over the next few decades and centuries. Currently the world appears not to be taking sufficient action to limit the speed of climate change and it is quite likely that more dramatic and potentially damaging effects will be observed in our birdlife in the not too distant future. Among climatologists and others who study global systems, it is pretty much an axiom that the faster the change the greater the likelihood of (nasty) surprises.

References

Crick H Q P & Sparks T H (1999). Climate change related to egg-laying trends. *Nature* 399: 423-424.

Crick H Q P, Dudley C, Glue D E & Thomson D L (1997). UK birds are laying eggs earlier. *Nature* 388: 526.

Rehfisch M M & Austin G E (1999). Ringed Plovers go east. *BTO News* 223: 14-15.
Sparks T H (1999). Phenology and the changing pattern of bird migration in Britain. *Int J Biometeorology* 42: 134-138.
Thomas C D & Lennon J J (1999). Birds extend their ranges northwards. *Nature* 399: 213.

CHALLENGES FOR 2000
AND BEYOND

by

Jeremy Greenwood*

In the course of the last half century, ornithology has transformed itself. Formerly something of a Cinderella among the biological sciences, it has more recently been at the heart of dramatic developments in the study of ecology, behaviour and evolution. The BOU has shed its decidedly dusty image to play its full part in this transformation. BTO, through the dedicated work of its members, other birdwatchers and professional staff, is producing much more (and higher quality) information about our bird populations and their habitats; it is, furthermore, making significant contributions to leading-edge ecology and providing the firm base of knowledge that effective conservation demands. RSPB, no doubt seen as a band of a few thousand rather cranky bird protectionists fifty years ago, is now a major political force, both nationally and internationally. Bird clubs have flourished, not only making their contributions to knowledge and conservation at local levels but also, in collaboration with others, at the national level. Whether we call ourselves birdwatchers or ornithologists, we can feel proud of what has been achieved.

Laurels should not, however, be cushions but spring-boards. What are the challenges for the future and how does the BTO fit into this wider picture?

First, there is the challenge of maintaining the high quality of work that we have come to expect. We work in an increasingly competitive

---

* Dr Jeremy Greenwood became Director of the British Trust for Ornithology in 1988. He is a former President of the Scottish Ornithologists' Club, has served on the Councils of the Royal Society for the Protection of Birds and the British Ornithologists' Union, and edited *Bird Study* for three years.

environment, in which the measures used to judge the winner may bear little relation to true quality. Academics are judged on the number of papers they publish on trendy topics; in-depth scholarship is increasingly old-fashioned. Research contracts are too often won on price alone, rather than on real value for money. Politicians demand quick fixes and simple solutions. Bureaucrats just want the designated hoops to be jumped through, even if this produces no real progress. This is a challenge to the integrity of researchers and the ingenuity of managers (who have to find a way of using the system to deliver truly good work). BTO is fortunate in not being wholly dependent on a single source of funding and in having an independent Council to be the ultimate guardians of its standards.

Standards are about how we work. What about the subjects that we work on? What are the big issues? For those interested in the environment, one of the biggest is the simultaneous growth of the human population and of its *per capita* use of resources: Man is demanding more and more of what the earth has to offer, leaving less and less for other creatures. As long ago as 1986, some American ecologists calculated that *Homo sapiens* utilised or diverted up to 40% of global potential net primary productivity for himself and his domestic animals; the figure must be substantially higher today. This is fundamentally why so many once-common birds are declining: we are leaving them too little to live on. The birdwatchers' contribution to dealing with this problem is that, through surveys and research, we can document the impact that Man is having on other creatures and suggest measures to ameliorate the problem.

A second major issue is that of global climate change. Ornithology has a role here, not only in carrying out research that will allow the proper planning of measures to minimize the impact on bird populations, but also in reporting on changes that are apparently already being driven by climate change. To the average citizen, news that birds are breeding earlier or retreating northwards seems more relevant to their own lives than technical reports on global atmospheric circulation. Our wild bird populations are today's large-scale equivalent of the miner's canary.

Data from collaborative surveys such as the Common Birds Census and distribution atlases have emphasised the need to think about conservation in terms of the wider countryside, for recent decades have seen substantial declines in many formerly widespread and common species. The importance of the countryside outside nature reserves and other special places has yet to get through to some politicians and administrators, especially at the EU level. Sites of Special Scientific Interest and Natura 2000 sites are very important but the countryside in between must not be forgotten - nor will it be if birdwatchers continue to participate in national monitoring as they have done in the past.

Farmland is the dominant habitat in most of Britain. BTO has been at the forefront of revealing the losses of many farmland bird populations and in researching their causes. Given that the Common Agricultural Policy remains largely unreformed, this work must continue, so that the problems are not forgotten and so that we can give the best advice on what changes are needed to restore at least some of what we have lost. We must not however, neglect other habitats. We already know that woodland birds, for example, are not faring as well as those in some other habitats; we must look at this issue in more detail and unravel what is happening. No doubt other problems will emerge with time. We can, for example, expect increasing demands on water resources to interact with changing rainfall patterns in ways that may affect birds. What might be the effects on the food supply of farmland birds if the extent of crop irrigation were to change? Given the continuing and ever-changing demands of the human population, we must, indeed, be ready to expect the unexpected - we still know too little to make many predictions about the state of our bird populations over the coming decades.

The programme of bird population monitoring that we have in Britain, and the associated research, is currently surpassed in few other countries. It continues to develop. It is, however, a long-term programme which must be protected against the vagaries of short-termism and fashion. Everyone, be they the people who do the work or those who cover the inevitable costs, must accept that a commitment to the environment is a commitment for ever.

Fortunately, the national effort on bird conservation research is underpinned by the dedication of birdwatchers, who have demonstrated their commitment over many decades. Some of it is directed at local concerns, some at national issues. There is perhaps a challenge here, to draw the local and national together more effectively, to the benefit of both. A clear challenge is for us in Britain to expand the scale upwards, lending our support to the efforts to establish bird monitoring throughout all European countries and to draw the results together so that we can see the big picture.

One lesson of recent decades has been the value of more focused work. Bird ringers, for example, have put more and more of their time into schemes such as Constant Effort Sites and Retrapping Adults for Survival. Such studies produce information on breeding success and survival, which is essential if we are to understand the causes of population declines. Today, surveys are not organised simply because 'it would be interesting to ...' or because 'we do it every ten years', but in order to address particular problems. We have, for example, surveyed habitat use by Skylarks in order to understand the causes of their population decline and what might be done to reverse it. Such clear focus must be our watchword if we are to get the most out of the efforts that are mounted. Some of the special projects may not be suitable for blanket surveys, so we can look forward to more projects like that on organic farming, in which a fairly small team of volunteers worked closely with the professional organiser.

The collaboration between amateurs and professionals remains the outstanding feature of British ornithology. One sometimes hears views (mostly from people who are not much involved in collaborative studies themselves) that 'it's all being taken over by the professionals'. This is simply untrue. The partnership remains, stronger than ever, and is a source of continual inspiration to me and, I am sure, to many others.

British birdwatchers and ornithologists can reflect with pride that their work on farmland birds ranks alongside global climate change and the hole in the ozone layer as one of the three areas in which environmental research has had a major impact on policy. That is a good base on which to build efforts in the years to come.

Acknowledgements

Many of the projects referred to by authors in this collection of articles receive financial support from other bodies, due acknowledgement of which is made here.

The Constant Effort Sites scheme, Retrapping Adults for Survival project, Common Birds Census and Ringing Scheme are funded through a partnership of the British Trust for Ornithology and the Joint Nature Conservation Committee.*
The Wetland Bird Survey is funded through a partnership of the BTO, The Wildfowl and Wetlands Trust, the Royal Society for the Protection of Birds and the JNCC.*
The Breeding Bird Survey is funded through a partnership of the BTO, JNCC* and RSPB.
The Waterways Bird Survey is funded by the Environment Agency's research and development programme with additional sponsorship from waterways companies (currently Anglian Water, Severn Trent Water, Northumbrian Water and Essex and Suffolk Water plc).
The Garden BirdWatch Survey is funded by the BTO and CJ Wildbird Foods.

* Funding by the Joint Nature Conservation Committee (JNCC) is on behalf of English Nature, Scottish Natural Heritage, the Countryside Council for Wales, and also on behalf of the Environment & Heritage Service in Northern Ireland.

PART EIGHT
BOOKS AND ARTICLES

(Actual size 239 x 294 mm)

Towards the Sea, by Robert Greenhalf, Pica Press, 1999, 128p plus pictures on endpapers, £45.00. ISBN 1 873403 89 5. Hbk.

Birdwatching involves observation, so too do drawing and painting birds. To some, the excitement is in the chase, to the artist the experience is more holistic: it lies in absorbing the whole scene and interpreting it in a pictorial record. This requires different skills - ones that Greenhalf possesses and reveals here in good measure. The Barn Owl is not just *in* the picture, it is *of* the picture; the delicate Swallows pose a contrast to the solid sea rocks. Extracts from the artist's diary are another manifestation of his reflective nature, unlike the language of the typical birder's field notebook. This beautiful volume shows that other side of birdwatching in a way that draws the reader back to it again and again to savour its evocative images. If you only purchase one example of this kind of bird art, you will never regret choosing *Towards the Sea* by Robert Greenhalf.

A BIRDWATCHER'S LIBRARY

Reviews by John Pemberton of selected recent books appear on the title pages of Parts 1-6 and 8-9. See previous page for example.

ARTICLES
IN BIRD REPORTS

This list is based on information supplied by recorders and bird report editors. Systematic lists of species recorded and ringing records are not detailed here as their inclusion in reports is assumed. See County Directory for details of where to obtain copies of reports.

ARGYLL BIRD REPORT 1997
Increases in Fulmars breeding on Colonsay 1975-1997, by David C Jardine. Recent mink-related declines of gulls and terns in west Scotland and the beneficial effects of mink control, by J C A Craik.

AVON BIRD REPORT 1997
The diet of urban Peregrines, by J Tully.
Species new to Avon - Desert Wheatear, by R Hunt.
Avon Breeding Bird Survey 1997, by J Tully.
Obituary: George Sweet.

AYRSHIRE BIRD REPORT 1998
Marsh Harrier breeding in Ayrshire, by A Hogg.
The Kestrel in Ayrshire - 1998, by G S Riddle.
The Sparrowhawk in Ayrshire - 1998, by I Todd.

BIRDS OF BERKSHIRE 1995
'Sea-watching' at Queen Mother Reservoir, by Chris Heard.

BRECONSHIRE BIRDS 1998
Birds of the Sennybridge Range, by M Peers.

BUCKINGHAMSHIRE BIRD REPORT 1997
Recording Buckinghamshire's Birds [inc. List of Birds Recorded in Buckinghamshire], by Mike Wallen.
The River Warbler at Linford: a first for Buckinghamshire, by Rob Andrews and Jenny Wallington.
The Icterine Warbler at Aylesbury [first for county] by David Glue.

CAMBRIAN BIRD REPORT 1998
The Isabelline Shrike at Cemlyn: fourth for Wales, by Stephen Culley.
Nutcracker at Beddgelert in 1968 (sic): first for Caernarfonshire, by Rhion Pritchard.

CAMBRIDGESHIRE BIRD REPORT 1997
A guide to birdwatching on the Nene Washes, by Jonathan Taylor.
Shore Lark - a new species for Cambridgeshire, by Ian Barton.

CEREDIGION BIRD REPORT 1997
Breeding birds at Denmark Farm, by N Taylor and R Williams.
Predation and breeding Lapwings, by R Bamford.

CHESHIRE & WIRRAL BIRD REPORT 1998
Buzzard Survey, by Richard Hargreave.
Dark-eyed Junco, by A M Broome.
Breeding Bird Survey, by Charles Hull.

CLEVELAND BIRD REPORT 1998
New to Cleveland: King Eider and Little Swift, by M A Blick; Red-breasted Goose, by T Bell; Hume's Warbler in 1994, by B Beck; Snow Goose, by G Joynt.
Long-term changes in Peregrine numbers, by R M Ward.

BIRDS IN CORNWALL 1997
Birds of St Austell Sewage Works, by R Lane.
Henry Mewburn of St Germans (1780-1834), an early 19th century ornithologist, by R D Penhallurick.

BIRDS IN CORNWALL 1998
Hume's Leaf Warbler - first for Cornwall.

DERBYSHIRE BIRD REPORT 1998
Breeding Hen Harriers in the Goyt Valley, by G W Hudson.
Chiffchaff of the race *tristis* at Carr, by M A Beevers.
Serin at Combs Reservoir: a new species for Derbyshire, by R W Key.
Black-throated Thrush at Hollingwood: a new species for Derbyshire, by R W Key.
Arrival and departure dates of breeding summer migrants, by S Shaw.

DEVON BIRD REPORT does not contain articles as these are published in the magazine *Devon Birds*.

DORSET BIRD REPORT 1997
Siberian Rubythroat - new to Dorset.
Little Egrets - breeding at Brownsea - the first breeding record for Britain.
Status of Cormorant and Shag in Poole Harbour.
Woodlarks in Dorset in 1997.

BIRDS IN DURHAM 1997
Bird watching by numbers: five years of the Durham Bird Club coordinated migrant count, by K Bowey.
Waterfowl populations along the Durham coast and their importance, by R M Ward.

ESSEX BIRD REPORT 1997
The Naze wheatear - what was it? by Adrian Dally.
East Mersea in winter, by Dougal Urquhart.
Status of the Marsh Warbler in Essex, by Ken Barratt.
Large gulls in Essex, by Mike Dennis.
Old Hall Marshes RSPB Reserve 1997, by Chris Tyas.
Bradwell Bird Observatory, by Graham Smith.

FAIR ISLE BIRD OBSERVATORY REPORT 1998
Fulmar research on Fair Isle in 1998, by Catherine Gray.
The Isabelline Wheatear on Fair Isle, 20th-30th September 1998, by Charlie Holt.
Fair Isle Heligoland trap renovation and plantation improvements in 1998, by Paul Baker.
Report on causes of death in birds on Fair Isle in 1998, by Jason Waine.

EASTERN GLAMORGAN BIRD REPORT 1997
Special report/rarity descriptions: Woodlark at Cardiff Heliport on 8 Feb 1997, by John D Wilson and W L Middleton; Woodlark at Rhoose Quarries on 15 May 1997, by N W Phillips; Caspian Tern at Kenfig Pool on 6 Aug 1997, by N Donaghy; Richard's Pipit at Lavernock Point on 19 Oct 1997, by Maurice Chown.

FIFE BIRD REPORT 1997
Mediterranen Gulls in Fife, by D Fotheringshaw.
Climate in Fife, by N Elkins.
Bee-eater (1st record).
Nuthatch (1st record).
Yellow-breasted Bunting (2nd record).
Bonaparte's Gull (2nd record).

FORTH AREA BIRD REPORT 1996 (in Forth Naturalist & Historian 1997, Vol 20)
Current status of the Raven as a breeding species in Central Scotland, by P Stirling-Airds.

GLOUCESTERSHIRE BIRD REPORT 1998
Two-barred Crossbill: new to Gloucestershire, by A M Heaven.

GOWER BIRDS 1998
Some observations from 30 years of *Gower Birds*, by D K Thomas.
The status of the Reed Warbler at Oxwich National Nature Reserve 1997, by Barry Stewart.

GWENT BIRD REPORT 1997
Dunlop Semtex Pond: an ornithological appraisal, by Steve Williams.

HAMPSHIRE BIRD REPORT 1997
Obituary: E E H Jones, by G Rowland.
Breeding censuses in Hampshire 1997, by Peter Morrison.
The birds of Boniley Common - a 20-year persepective, by J Eyre.
The 1997 Woodlark Survey, by J Eyre.
Wintering Wildfowl in the lower Avon: conservation aspects of recent counts, by N Pratt.

HERTFORDSHIRE BIRD REPORT 1997
BTO Breeding Censuses in 1997, by C Dee.
Common Rosefinch at Wilstone Reservoir, by J Taylor.

Barn Owls in mid-Hertfordshire, by R A Cooke and E M Cooke.
Yellow-browed Warbler - second record for Hertfordshire, by P Burton.
Breeding waders of wet meadows in 1997, by K Smith.
The increase of the Collared Dove in Herts: can it continue? by M Russell.
A partially hepatic Cuckoo, by A Harris.
Leucistic Lesser Whitethroat, by A Harris.
Crossbills in Herts, winter 1997-8, by L Marshall and T Fletcher.

ISLE OF WIGHT BIRD REPORT 1997
Phenological report for 1997.
Escaped birds, 1997, by J M Cheverton and J Stafford.
The Wetland Bird Survey, 1996/1997, by J M Cheverton.
New Island species: Red-breasted Goose, by J C Gloyn; Lesser Yellowlegs, by D
and G Brazier; Little Swift, by K Turner; Hume's Warbler, by I Ridett; Collared

The *Isle of Wight*
Bird Report 1997

A joint publication of the
Isle of Wight Ornithological Group
and the
Isle of Wight Natural History and Archaeological Society

Flycatcher, by K V Thompson and J Stafford.
Colour-ringed Mediterranean Gulls in the Isle of Wight, by J C Gloyn.

ISLES OF SCILLY BIRD REPORT 1997
Review of migrants and scarce birds recorded during 1997, by Will Wagstaff.
Selected 1997 rarity descriptions: Blackpoll Warbler, by D L Acfield; American
Herring Gull, by Will Wagstaff; Paddyfield Warbler, by M S Scott.
Blast from the past [texts of reports]: Scarlet Tanager at Gimble Porth, Tresco
in 1975, by G C Hearl; Yellow-bellied Sapsucker at Great Pool, Tresco in 1975
by D B Hunt.

KENT BIRD REPORT 1997
Birds of Great Chattenden Woods, by Murray Orchard.
Corn Buntings on the Hoo Peninsula, by Murray Orchard.
Marsh Harriers on Sheppey, by Adam Rowlands.
Wigeon at Elmley, by P J Oliver.
Golden Plover Survey 1996, by Tim Hodge.
The BTO Rook Survey 1997, by Jim Martin.

LANCASHIRE BIRD REPORT 1998
New checklist of county birds, compiled by Steve White.
Seawatching off Lancashire coast, by Steve White.

LEICESTERSHIRE AND RUTLAND BIRD REPORT 1998
A Leicestershire Hawfinch in Norway, by Jim Fowler.
Bird populations in Leicestershire woodlands, by Dr D A C McNeill.
Ringing at Eye Brook Reservoir, by Dean Roizer.
The Bean Goose in Leicestershire and Rutland, by Andrew Harrop.
The Nightjar in Leicestershire and Rutland, by Andy MacKay.
Blue-winged Teal - new to the County List, by Matthew Berriman.
Spotted Sandpiper - new to the County List, by Dave Summerfield.

LINCOLNSHIRE BIRD REPORT 1996
Rookery Survey 1996.
Results of monitoring projects 1995-96: Breeding Bird Survey, Garden Bird
Feeding Survey, Wetland Bird Survey.
Accounts of Lincolnshire rarities: White-billed Diver, Lanceolated Warbler.

LONDON BIRD REPORT 1998
Year listing in London, 1997, by S Connor.
Crossbill invasion in London, 1997, by P J Oliver.
The Breeding Bird Survey in London, 1998, by D A Coleman.

LOTHIAN BIRD REPORT 1997
1997 Turnhouse Constant Effort Scheme Report, by Alan Hilton.
Breeding Bird Survey Lothian, 1994-97, by Ian J Andrews.
Marsh Sandpiper at Musselburgh, May 1997, by Guy Thompson.
Western Sandpiper at Musselburgh, August 1997, by Ian J Andrews.
Desert Wheatear at Dunglas and Thorntonloch, November 1997, by Keith
Gillon.

BIRDS IN GREATER MANCHESTER 1998
The 1998 BTO Breeding Lapwing Survey in the Manchester Region, by A J
Smith.
The dispersal of juvenile Starlings and their longevity at four ringing locations,
1977-1986, by Ray Yates.
The Wetland Bird Survey (WeBS) on rivers in Greater Manchester, 1998-99 - a
new venture, by A J Smith.
The Whitehead Landfill, Astley, by Pete Berry.
Hope Carr Reserve, Leigh, by Judith Smith.
The Breeding Bird Survey in the Manchester Region, 1998, by A J Smith.
Notes on sightings of particular interest, by various authors.
Directory of Greater Manchester birding.

MONTGOMERYSHIRE BIRD REPORT 1995-1997
Vexed arguments and difficult decisions, by Roger Lovegrove.
The Kestrel in Wales, by Michael Shrubb.

MORAY & NAIRN BIRD REPORT 1998
Birds new to Moray & Nairn: Bearded Tit, by Martin Cook; Yellow-browed
Warbler, by Bob Proctor; Terek Sandpiper, by Dave Pullen; Reed Warbler, by
Martin Cook.
A census of cliff nesting seabirds in Moray in 1998, by Martin Cook.

NORFOLK BIRD & MAMMAL REPORT 1997
Canvasback, an addition to the County List, by John Kemp.
Calandra Lark, an addition to the County List, by Tom Brown *et al.*
White Wagtails nesting in Norfolk, by Richard Millington.
Fea's/Zino's Petrel in Norfolk, by Stefan McElwee.
The Yarmouth Little Tern colony, by Mark Thoms and Jenny Atkins.
The birds of Felbrigg Park, by Moss Taylor.
The birds of the Wash, 1971-1996, by Paul Fisher.

NORTHAMPTONSHIRE BIRD REPORT 1999 (1998 records)
Caspian Gulls at Welford tip, by John Wright.

NORTHERN IRELAND BIRD REPORT 1997
A List of the Birds of Northern Ireland (1997)
Species new to Northern Ireland: Great White Egret, by George Gordon; Rustic
Bunting, by L J McFaul; Little Bunting, by Eric Randall.
Scaup - a new Irish breeding species, by Dave Allen and Matthew Tickner.
Short-eard Owl breeding in Northern Ireland, by Don Scott.
Hen Harrier records from Copeland Bird Observatory, by Don Scott.

BIRDS IN NORTHUMBRIA 1997
Historical status of the Honey Buzzard in Northumberland, by N Rossiter.
Sawbill Survey 1997, by T and M Cadwallender.
Birding Sites I: Newbiggin, by J G Steele.
Birding Sites II: Arcot Pond, by L McDougall.
Desert Wheatear, an addition to the County List, by S Bloomfield.

ORKNEY BIRD REPORT 1998
Breeding Mute Swans on the Harray and Stenness Lochs, by Eric Meek.
North Ronaldsay Bird Observatory Report 1998, by A Duncan.
Papa Westray Migration Report 1998, by S Wellock.
A study of a Bonxie colony on Hoy 1973-1998, by G Booth.

OUTER HEBRIDES (WESTERN ISLES) BIRD REPORT 1998
The winter range of Redshank breeding in the Outer Hebrides, by Digger
Jackson.
White's Thrush at North Tolsta, Lewis, by Alastair Henderson.

BIRDS IN OXFORDSHIRE 1997
The Yellow-legged Gull in Oxfordshire, by Jon Baker.
National Wetland Bird Survey, by John Brucker.

PEMBROKESHIRE BIRD REPORT 1998
Hume's Leaf Warbler at Strumble Head, first for Pembrokeshire, by S Berry.
Bonaparte's Gull at Strumble Head, second for Pembrokeshire, by G H Rees.
Kumlien's Gull at Llys y Fran Reservoir, first for Pembrokeshire, by D J Astins.
Survey of wintering birds at sewage treatment works in Pembrokeshire, Jan-Feb
1996 and Feb 1997, by D J Astins.

SCOTTISH BIRD REPORT 1996
Soft-plumaged Petrel: a first record for Scotland, by Richard W White.
A review of the status of the Little Ringed Plover in Scotland, by R D Murray.

SHROPSHIRE BIRD REPORT 1997
The Peregrine Falcon in Shropshire, by J Tucker.
The Long Mynd Breeding Bird Project, by L Smith.
Shropshire Raven Study Group, by L Smith.
Breeding Skylarks in Shropshire, by A Dawes.
Venus Pool 1997, by G Holmes.
Gull-billed Tern at Venus Pool, by A Matthews.
Woodchat Shrike near Mainstone, by S O'Donnell.
White Stork near Minsterley, by G Holmes.

SOMERSET BIRDS 1998
Breeding birds of Crewkerne, by A J Parsons.

SUFFOLK BIRDS 1998
Seabird movements and abundance off Covehithe, Suffolk 1994-98: III Sooty and
Manx Shearwaters, by P J Dare.
The Breeding Bird Survey - an update, by Garry Lowe.

SURREY BIRD REPORT 1997
Red-rumped Swallow at Stoke Lake, by Jeremy Gates.
Red-footed Falcon in Surrey, by Dave Harris.
Squacco Heron at Walton Reservoirs, by Dave Harris.
Great White Egret at Vachery Pond, by Robin Stride.
The 1997 Woodlark Survey in Surrey, by Jeffery Wheatley.
Grey Herons in Surrey, by Roger Suckling.

SUSSEX BIRD REPORT 1998
The current status of the Common Buzzard in Sussex, by Martin Kalaher.
A Semi-palmated Sandpiper in Sussex, by Alan Kitson.
A survey of Sussex gamebirds during the 1998/99 season, by Tony Cocks.

WEST MIDLAND BIRD CLUB ANNUAL REPORT 1997
European Nightjars and other breeding birds of Cannock Chase 1997, by
Richard Harbird.
Short articles on hybrid Whooper x Mute Swans (Bradnock's Marsh/Packington
Park), by Brian Kington and Nick Barlow. Breeding Northern Lapwings on the
North Staffordshire Moors, by J A Lawrence. Citrine Wagtail at Brandon Marsh
- a new bird to the region, by Loyd (sic) Berry and Jim Rushforth. Icterine
Warbler (Napton Hill) - the first Warwickshire record, by P D Hyde.

WILTSHIRE BIRD REPORT 1997 (in Hobby)
Does the nominate race of Lesser Black-backed Gull occur in Wiltshire? by P
Combridge and S King.
The origins and movements of colour-ringed large gulls recorded in Wiltshire,
by J Grearson.
Year 3 of the Wiltshire Tetrad Atlas, by G Pictor and R Turner.
Pied-billed Grebe at the Cotswold Water Park, by G Buchanan.
Squacco Heron at the Cotswold Water Park, by J Grearson.

PART NINE

RESERVES AND OBSERVATORIES

(Actual size 240 x 160 mm)

Birds of the West Indies, by Herbert Raffaele, James Wiley, Orlando Garrido, Allan Keith and Janis Raffaele, Helm (A&C Black), 1998, 510p, £35.00. ISBN 0 7136 4905 4. Hbk.

Some of the species in this volume are on the British list, and to anyone who has visited North America many more will be familiar. This still leaves a goodly number of special birds which attract visitors annually to the West Indies. The book itself conforms to the well-tried format and consistent quality of the 'Helm Identification Guides', which bodes well for its success. There have been many advances in ornithological knowledge of the region since the original James Bond's book with the same title appeared in 1930, and travel facilities have improved in like measure. This inviting volume is essential to the preparation of any birdwatcher's visit to these bird-rich countries - and later back home.

IMPORTANT NOTES

There is an Index of Reserves and Observatories on pages 315-320

In the interests of bird protection this directory has been compiled in consultation with the appropriate national, regional and county conservation organisations, management bodies and wardens.

The sites described are well distributed throughout Britain and Ireland; they provide good examples of most kinds of habitat and afford excellent opportunities for observing and studying a wide range of bird species. As to which birds may be encountered at each reserve it is possible to give only general indications, along with some specialities. Care should always be taken to note the seasons in which particular species may occur; when in doubt, it is advisable to consult a good field guide.

It is only with the co-operation of landowners that many of the reserves have been established, and it is therefore essential that visiting birdwatchers do nothing to endanger good relations. Prior permission should always be obtained when it is proposed to visit parts of a reserve away from public rights of way or nature trails, or to use the hides provided at certain reserves. Dogs are not usually welcome, and there are sometimes restrictions on photography. Motor vehicles are a not infrequent source of irritation: inconsiderate parking can upset local residents.

Charges are made for parking and/or entering many reserves, but actual fees have not been included as they are subject to change. Enquiries, including requests for permits and descriptive leaflets, should be made to the addresses given in the entries or to the respective management authorities. Addresses for offices of BirdWatch Ireland, Countryside Council for Wales, Department of the Environment for Northern Ireland (Environment and Heritage Service), English Nature, Royal Society for the Protection of Birds, Scottish Natural Heritage, Wildfowl & Wetlands Trust and other national bodies will be found in the National Directory, and those for clubs and county wildlife trusts in the County Directory.

While details of access are provided, it must be stressed that no rights of way are implied. All information has been carefully checked, but no guarantee can be given as to its accuracy; changes occurring between compilation and publication will in all probability have caused certain of the facts to be superseded.

ABBREVIATIONS

ASSI	Area of Special Scientific Interest (N Ireland)	EN	English Nature
		LNR	Local Nature Reserve
BC	Borough Council	NCT	Nature Conservation Trust
CBC	County Borough Council	NNR	National Nature Reserve
CCW	Countryside Council for Wales	SNH	Scottish Natural Heritage
		SPA	Special Protection Area
DANI	Dept of Agriculture Northern Ireland	SSSI	Site of Special Scientific Interest
EHS	Environment and Heritage Service (DoE N Ireland)	TNC	Trust for Nature Conservation
		WT	Wildlife Trust

ENGLAND

BEDFORDSHIRE

HARROLD ODELL COUNTRY PARK. (144a) Bedfordshire CC SP960570. 10 miles NW of Bedford off the Harrold to Carlton road. Open at all times. Visitor centre. Restaurant and cafe open W-Su 1000-1630. Hide. Lakes (one with island), lagoons, osier beds, meadows adjacent River Great Ouse, woodland. Breeding Reed and Sedge Warblers, Lesser Whitethroat; passage waders, Common and Black Terns; late summer Hobby; winter wildfowl, Water Rail. Bill Thwaites, Country Park, Carlton Road, Harrold, Bedford MK43 7DS. 01234 720016

MARSTON VALE MILLENNIUM COUNTRY PARK. (318a) Marston Vale Trust TL010420. SSW of Bedford. Via A421 off Green Lane. Opening Easter 2000. Visitor centre. Lakes, reedbeds, scrub, newly planted forest. Wide range of species, esp. winter wildfowl, passage terns and waders; large winter gull roost can inc. Glaucous & Iceland. Ranger, Forest Centre, Station Road, Marston Moretaine, Bedford MK43 0PR. 01234 767037

PRIORY MARINA COUNTRY PARK. (300a) Bedford BC TL071495. Barkers Lane, Bedford (off A428). Open at all times. Hides, nature trail, car parks, toilets, visitor centre; disabled facilities. Lakes, scrub, plantations, riverside meadows, rough grassland, Over 200 species recorded. Breeding warblers, woodpeckers, Sparrowhawk, Kingfisher, Common Tern. Good spring and autumn passages, inc. waders, gulls, terns, chats, wagtails. Winter wildfowl, plus grebes on the lakes and river; winter finch, bunting and corvid roosts in conservation area. Errol Newman, Wardens Office, Visitor Centre, Priory CP, Barkers Lane, Bedford MK41 9SH. 01234 211182

BERKSHIRE

DINTON PASTURES COUNTRY PARK. (230a) Wokingham DC SU784718. Off B3030 between Hurst and Winnersh. Open all year, dawn to dusk. Hides, information centre; car park, cafe, toilets. Suitable for wheelchairs. Mature gravel pits and banks of River Loddon. Kingfisher, Water Rail, Little Ringed Plover, Common Tern, Nightingale; winter wildfowl (inc. Goldeneye, Wigeon, Teal, Gadwall). Dave Webster, Ranger, Dinton Pastures Country Park, Davis Street, Hurst, Berks. 0118 934 2016

LAVELL'S LAKE. (32a) Wokingham DC SU781729. Via Sandford Lane off B3030 between Hurst and Winnersh. Dawn to dusk. No permit required. Hides. Gravel pits, 2 wader scapes, rough grassland, marshy area, R. Loddon, Emm Brook. Sparrowhawk; summer Garganey, Common Tern, Little Ringed Plover, Redshank, Lapwing, Hobby; passage waders; winter Green Sandpiper, ducks. Contact as Dinton Pastures.

MOOR GREEN LAKES. (90a) RMC (Southern) Ltd SU805626. NW of Camberley. Off Lower Sandhurst Road which runs between B3016 at Finchampstead and Little Sandhurst. Also accessible from Mill Lane at SU819619. Access limited to public footpath along W and S boundaries. 2 hides normally open to public 0900-1600 Su and also when in use by the Moor Green Lakes Group. Car park. Gravel pit with 3 lakes and islands, grassland, scrub. Wader scrape. Ducks (inc. wintering Goosander); passage and breeding waders; breeding Common Tern, Stonechat and warblers; hunting Hobby. Hide opening times from Blackwater Valley Recreation & Countryside Management Service on 01276 686615.

BUCKINGHAMSHIRE

COLLEGE LAKE WILDLIFE CENTRE. (100a) Berks, Bucks & Oxon NT with Castle Cement (Pitstone) Ltd SP935139. On B488 Tring/Ivinghoe road at Bulbourne. Open daily 1000-1700. Permits available on site or from Trust HQ. Hides, nature trails, visitor centre, toilets. Marsh area, lake, islands, shingle. Breeding Lapwing, Redshank, Little Ringed Plover; summer Hobby; passage waders inc. Green Sandpiper. Graham Atkins, College Lake Wildlife Centre, Upper Icknield Way, Bulbourne, Tring, Herts HP23 5QG. H: 01296 662890

HANSON ENVIRONMENTAL STUDY CENTRE. (95a) Milton Keynes DC SP842429. Entrance almost opp. Black Horse on Wolverton Road SW of Newport Pagnell. Open daily dawn to dusk. Day or annual permit from Warden. 3 hides. Lake, ponds, marsh, wood, scrub, willow carr, meadows. Breeding warblers, wildfowl and waders; passage waders; winter wildfowl and gulls. Andrew Stevenson, Hanson Environmental Study Centre, Wolverton Road, Great Linford, Milton Keynes MK14 5AH. 01908 604810

WESTON TURVILLE. (12a) Berks, Bucks & Oxon NT SP859095. From Wendover take A413 north; R after 1 mile opp Marquis of Granby PH; park in layby after 500m and reserve is on R. Public access on perimeter path. Reservoir, large reed fen. Water Rail; breeding wablers; winter wildfowl and gulls. Contact: Trust HQ.

CAMBRIDGESHIRE

BRAMPTON WOOD. (327a) WT for Cambs TL185698. 2 miles E of Grafham village on N side of road to Brampton. Car park, interpretative shelter. SSSI. Ash and field maple with hazel coppice. Breeding Grasshopper Warbler, Nightingale, Spotted Flycatcher, Woodcock; all 3 woodpeckers; winter thrushes. Contact: Trust HQ.

FOWLMERE. (87a) RSPB TL407461. Turn off A10 Cambridge to Royston road by Shepreth and follow sign. Access at all times along marked trail. Boardwalk for wheelchairs. 4 hides. Reedbeds, meres, woodland, scrub. 9 breeding warblers; Corn Bunting roost; Water Rail, Kingfisher all year; wintering Snipe, raptors. Doug Radford, RSPB Fowlmere, Manor Farm, High Street, Fowlmere, Royston, Herts SG8 7SH. 01763 208978

GRAFHAM WATER. (370a) Anglian Water & WT for Cambs TL148680. Park at Mander car park off B661. Open all year round. Wildlife cabin (information centre). 7 hides, nature trails, wildlife garden. Large reservoir with sheltered creeks, deciduous woods, mixed plantations, rough grassland. Reservoir attracts winter wildfowl inc. divers (occasional), rarer grebes, Scoter, Scaup, Goldeneye, Long-tailed Duck, Smew, Goosander. Elsewhere in reserve Nightingale, Grasshopper Warbler and Turtle Dove breed. Passage (esp. autumn) Little Gull, Black Tern, waders. Jo Calvert, c/o Fishing Lodge, Grafham Water, West Perry, Huntingdon, Cambs PE18 0BX. 01480 812660 daytime

HAYLEY WOOD. (120a) WT for Cambs TL292529. Between Cambridge and Sandy. Take B1046 W out of Longstowe for 1.5 miles and park opposite water tower. Walk up old track to wood. Open at all times. Interpretative centre. Ancient semi-natural woodland. Active coppice cycle and derelict coppice. Woodland species inc. Nightingale, Blackcap, Garden Warbler, Nuthatch, Treecreeper, Marsh Tit, Woodcock, woodpeckers.

NENE WASHES. (710a) RSPB TL277992. Near Peterborough. Off B1040 to Thorney 1 mile N of Whittlesey. Open access along drove. Parties and coach parking by prior arrangement. Wet meadows. Breeding Spotted Crake, Black-tailed Godwit, Snipe, Lapwing, Garganey, Shoveler, Gadwall, Shelduck; summer Marsh Harrier and Hobby; wintering Bewick's Swan, Wigeon, Pintail, Teal, Short-eared Owl. Charlie Kitchin, 21A East Delph, Whittlesey, Peterborough PE7 1RH. W:01733 205140

OUSE WASHES. (2850a) RSPB/WT for Cambs TL471861. Near Chatteris. Signposted from Manea village. Access at all times from information centre (open every day except 25 & 26 Dec) at Welches Dam to public hides approached by marked paths behind boundary bank. Flood meadows. Breeding Black-tailed Godwit, Shoveler, Gadwall, Garganey, Redshank, Snipe, Spotted Crake. Large numbers of winter Bewick's Swan (also Whooper), Wigeon, Teal, Shoveler, Pintail; Merlin, Hen Harrier regularly winter. Cliff Carson, Ouse Washes Reserve, Welches Dam, Manea, March, Cambs PE15 0NF. 01354 680212; fax 01354 688036

PAXTON PITS. (142a) Hunts DC (LNR) TL197629. At end of High Street, Little Paxton. Open at all times on marked paths. Hides (always open), visitor centre open most weekends. Group visits by prior arrangement. SSSI. Heronry, large Cormorant breeding colony and winter roost; also large Stock Dove roost. 70 species breed annually, inc. Little Ringed Plover, Redshank, Common Tern, Kingfisher, warblers (inc. Grasshopper, Reed, Sedge, Lesser Whitethroat), Nightingale, Yellow Wagtail, Sparrowhawk; Hobby summer visitor; passage terns (inc. Black), Little Gull, chats, waders; winter grebes and wildfowl (inc. Goosander, Smew, Gadwall). Bird club/group enquiries to the Ranger at the visitor centre on 01480 406795, or to: Tony How, 63 Gordon Road, Little Paxton, Cambs PE19 4NH. 01480 474159

WICKEN FEN. (800a) National Trust (NNR) TL563705. S of A1123, 3 miles SW of Soham. Open daily by ticket (charge) or NT card. Parties by arrangement. Information centre, hides, waymarked trails. Self-catering accommodation available. Open water, reedbeds, wet meadows, scrub. Breeding Lapwing, Snipe, Woodcock, Redshank, Marsh Harrier, Bearded Tit, warblers; wintering wildfowl, Hen Harrier roost, occas. Bittern. Martin Lester, Wm Thorpe Visitor Centre, Lode Lane, Wicken, Ely, Cambs CB7 5XP. Tel/fax 01353 720274; e-mail awnmdl@smtp.ntrust.org.uk

CHESHIRE

FIDDLERS FERRY. (200a) Powergen SJ552853. Off A562 between Warrington and Widnes; parking at main gate of power station. Summer 0800-2000; winter 0800-1700. Permit (free); apply in advance with sae to Manager, Fiddlers Ferry Power Station,

Warrington WA5 2UT. Hide, nature trail. Lagoons, tidal and non-tidal marshes with phragmites and great reedmace, meadow grassland with small wooded areas. Breeding Oystercatcher, Ringed and Little Ringed Plovers; winter Glaucous, Iceland and Yellow-legged Gulls, Short-eared Owl, Peregrine. Nationally important for Teal, Pintail, Pochard; internationally for Shoveler. Recent rarities inc. Black-necked Grebe, Little Egret, Marsh Harrier, Little Crake, Red-necked Phalarope, Mediterranean Gull, Hoopoe, Savi's Warbler, Bearded Tit. Warden: Keith Massey, 4 Hall Terrace, Great Sankey, Warrington WA5 3EZ. 01925 721382

GAYTON SANDS. (5040a) RSPB SJ274789. By Neston. Take B5135 to Parkgate off A540 Chester-Hoylake Road, then R at Boathouse Restaurant. Good views (esp. at high tide) from Old Baths car park, Parkgate and adjacent public footpath. Intertidal mudflats, saltings. Dangerous tides. Passage waders; winter wildfowl (esp. Pintail, Shelduck), Water Rail, Peregrine, Merlin, Hen Harrier, Short-eared Owl. High tide birdwatching event programme available from Warden (sae 9x6"): Colin Wells, Burton Point Farm, Station Road, Burton, Nr Neston, South Wirral CH64 5SB. 0151 336 7681

MARBURY NATURE RESERVE. (15a) Cheshire WT/RSNC SJ651768. N of Northwich. Access to public bird hide from adjacent country park; access to woodland by permit from Trust. Reedbeds, open water, mixed woodland. Waterfowl, warblers. Contact Trust HQ.

MOORE NATURE RESERVE. (186a) 3C Waste Management Ltd SJ577854. W of Warrington. Take A56 towards Chester; at Higher Walton follow signs for Moore village; R down Moore Lane to swing bridge and park beyond crossroads. Open at all times. Wetland and woodland hides, nature trails. Breeding wildfowl and waders (inc. Little Ringed Plover), also Sparrowhawk. Winter wildfowl (inc. Wigeon, Gadwall, Goldeneye); waders (inc. Snipe, Jack Snipe, Green Sandpiper); excellent for gulls (inc. Iceland, Glaucous, Mediterranean). Miss Estelle Linney, c/o Arpley Landfill Site, Forest Way, Sankey Bridge, Warrington WA4 6YZ. 01925 444689

ROSTHERNE MERE. (377a, mere itself 120a) English Nature (NNR) SJ744843. View from Rostherne churchyard and lanes; no public access, except to A W Boyd Observatory (permits from D A Clarke, 1 Hart Avenue, Sale M33 2JY, tel 0161 973 7122). Deep lake, woodland, willow bed, pasture. Good range of wintering duck including Ruddy Duck and Pintail; gull roost in winter (inc. occasional Iceland and Glaucous); passage Black Terns. Tim Coleshaw, Site Manager, English Nature, Attingham Park, Shrewsbury SY4 4TW, 01743 709611

SANDBACH FLASHES. (130a) Management Committee SJ720590. Elton Hall Flash from new road at SJ716595; Foden's Flash from road at SJ730614; Watch Lane Flash from car park at SJ728608. Fresh and brackish water, reedbed, carr woodland, inland saltmarsh. Passage waders; nesting and wintering wildfowl; many rarities occur. Patrick Whalley, 3 Barracks Lane, Ravensmoor, Nantwich, Cheshire CW5 8PR. 01270 624420

WOOLSTON EYES. (850a) Woolston Eyes Conservation Group. E of Warrington. S of A57 at Woolston, down Weir Lane. Lagoons, marsh, scrub, river. Access only by annual permit, from Warden. Breeding wildfowl (inc. Shoveler, Gadwall, Pochard, Ruddy Duck, Garganey), Black-necked Grebe now a speciality, warblers. Passage waders inc. regular rarities; passage and wintering raptors (Merlin, Peregrine, harriers). Goshawk, Hobby in late summer/autumn. SSSI status for wintering wildfowl. Brian Ankers, 9 Lynton Gardens, Appleton, Cheshire WA4 5ED. 01925 267355

CORNWALL

BRENEY COMMON. (135a) Cornwall WT SX054610. Minor road off A390 1 mile W of Lostwithiel, through Lanlivery Village to Lowertown; track leads into reserve. Keep to paths. Extensive wetland complex inc. willow carr, scrub, heath and pools. Eric Higgs, Crift Farm, Lanlivery, Bodmin, Cornwall PL30 5DE. 01208 872702

BUDE MARSHES. (15a) LNR SS208057. By public footpath beside Bude Canal. Keep to paths. Public hide. Reedbed, grassland and pools. Breeding Reed, Sedge and Cetti's Warblers; winter wildfowl (inc. Shoveler, Teal, Goosander), Snipe amd occas. Bittern; Little Egret late summer/autumn. R Braund, 36 Killerton Road, Bude, Cornwall EX23 8EN. 01288 353906

DRIFT RESERVOIR. (90a) Cornwall Birdwatching & Preservation Society SW436288. From lane to Sancreed off A30 at Lower Drift (SW of Penzance). For CBWPS hide, park at dam car park and walk along bank. No permit. No dogs. Open water surrounded by fields; extensive areas of mud exposed in autumn. Largely gulls and waders; possibility of American vagrants in autumn.

HAYLE ESTUARY. (355a) RSPB SW550370. At town of Hayle. Best vantage points from new hide and car park at Ryan's Field behind The Causeway and the car parks at Old Quay House Inn at Lelant and Commercial Road at Copperhouse. Intertidal mudflats and seawater lagoon ('Carnsew Pool'). Important as a cold weather refuge for wildfowl and waders inc. Wigeon, Teal, Dunlin, Grey Plover, Curlew, Great Northern Diver most winters. Rare migrants in spring (eg Spoonbill, Osprey, Little Egret) and autumn (eg Pectoral and White-rumped Sandpipers). Dave Flumm, Manor Office, Marazion, Penzance TR17 0EF. 01736 711682

LOVENY RESERVE - COLLIFORD RESERVOIR. (317a) Cornwall Birdwatching & Preservation Society with Cornwall WT SX183744. By foot from SW Water Deweymeads car park, A30 E of Bodmin. Open at all times; access restricted to SW edge of reserve. Wetlands, moorland. Wildfowl (inc. Shoveler, Wigeon, Smew); passage waders can inc. N American species. David Conway, Tregenna, Cooksland, Bodmin, Cornwall PL31 2AR. 01208 77686

MAER LAKE, BUDE. Cornwall Birdwatching & Preservation Society with Cornwall WT SS208075. View from private road next to Maer Lodge Hotel, heading N. Wetland meadows. Wildfowl and waders (inc. rarities eg. Temminck's Stint, Wilson's Phalarope).

MARAZION MARSH. (132a) RSPB SW510315. On seafront road between Penzance and Marazion. Public footpath through reserve from Ropewalk car park half mile W of Marazion. Reedbeds and open water. Spring migrants (inc. Wheatear, Yellow Wagtail, Garganey); breeding warblers (inc. Cetti's, Reed, Sedge), Grey Heron, Water Rail; autumn noted for Spotted Crake and Aquatic Warbler; Mediterranean Gull regular in winter. Dave Flumm, Manor Office, Marazion, Penzance TR17 0EF. 01736 711682

NANSMELLYN MARSH. (11a) Cornwall WT SW762543. E edge of Perranporth, 6 mi SW of Newquay. Open at all times. Access to hide via boardwalk (keys from Trust HQ). Reedbed, willow carr. Snipe, warblers (inc. Reed), Water Rail, Reed Bunting. C Easton, 6 Eureka Vale, Perranporth, Cornwall TR6 0BS. 01872 573612

PENDARVES WOOD. (44a) Cornwall WT SW641377. 2 mi S of Camborne off B3303. Open at all times. Dogs prohibited. Nature trails. Broadleaved woodland, conifers, lake. Woodland species, wintering duck. Malcolm Perry, 7 Relistian Park, Reawla, Gwinear, Hayle, Cornwall TR27 5HF. 01736 850612

STITHIANS RESERVOIR. (273a) Cornwall Birdwatching & Preservation Society. SS715365. From B3297 S of Redruth. Good viewing from causeway. Key to hides from Debbie Melarickas, 20 Midway Drive, Truro TR1 1NQ. 01872 241558. Open water, marshland. Wildfowl and waders (inc. rarities, eg. Lesser Yellowlegs).

TAMAR ESTUARY. (6 miles of foreshore) Cornwall WT SX434612. Lanes from A388 N of Saltash to (a) Cargreen; (b) Landulph, at end of lane to S enter gate on right and go to E end of sea wall on N shore of Kingsmill Lake; (c) Botusfleming and Moditonham Quay. Mudflats; saltmarsh at Kingsmill Lake and N of Moditonham Quay. Autumn/winter waders (inc. Avocet). Contact: Victoria Scott, Trust HQ.

TAMAR LAKES. (100a) South West Water PLC SS295115. Near Kilkhampton. Car park off minor road running between upper and lower lakes. Hide open all year round. New birdwatching centre on lower Tamar. Cafe, toilets (Apr-Sep). Migrant waders (inc. North American vagrants); spring Black Tern; wintering wildfowl (inc. Goldeneye, Wigeon, Pochard). Ranger, Tamar Lakes Water Park, Kilkhampton, N Cornwall. 01288 321262

CUMBRIA

CAMPFIELD MARSH. (200a) RSPB. W of Bowness-on-Solway. View from road (do not venture on to marsh). Saltmarsh. Autumn-spring: high tide roosting sites for waders at West Herdhill (NY207620) and Maryland Farm (NY195616), eg. Curlew, Bar-tailed Godwit, Dunlin, Knot; winter geese (inc. Pink-footed, Barnacle). Escorted parties by written application to Warden. Norman Holton, North Plain Farm, Bowness on Solway, Carlisle CA5 5AG. Tel/fax 01697 351330 office hours only.

HAWESWATER. (23222a) RSPB NY470108. Off A6 at Shap, follow signs to Bampton and turn L in village; car park at S end of reservoir. Access at all times. Observation point open daily Apr-Aug 0900-1800. Fells with rocky streams, steep oak and birch woodlands. Breeding Golden Eagle, Peregrine, Raven, Ring Ouzel, Curlew, Redshank, Snipe, Pied Flycatcher, Wood Warbler, Tree Pipit, Redstart, Buzzard, Sparrowhawk. Bill Kenmir, 7 Naddlegate, Burn Banks, Penrith, Cumbria CA10 2RL.

HODBARROW. (227a) RSPB SD174791. Millom. Along track which forks left off Mainsgate Road, Millom. Lagoon, slag bank, scrub, marshy areas. Breeding Great Crested and Little Grebes, Red-breasted Merganser, Shelduck on lagoon; Oystercatcher, Ringed Plover, Sandwich, Common, and Little Terns on slag bank; warblers in scrub. Barn Owl, Sparrowhawk, Peregrine regular. Winter wildfowl concentrations (inc. Wigeon, Goldeneye, Merganser) and wader roost. Norman Holton, North Plain Farm, Bowness-on-Solway, Carlisle CA5 5AG. Tel/fax 01697 351330 office hours only.

ST BEES HEAD. (55a) RSPB. Near Whitehaven. Public footpath, with observation points 1.8 mi N from St Bees beach car park NX962118. Toilet. Sandstone cliffs. Raven; Black Guillemot and other auks; Kittiwake; Rock Pipit. Norman Holton, North Plain Farm, Bowness-on-Solway, Carlisle CA5 5AG. Tel/fax 01697 351330 office hours only.

SIDDICK POND. (48a) Allerdale BC/EN/Cumbria WT NY001305. 1 mile N of Workington, adjacent to A596. Access to hide by arrangement with Iggesund Paperboard (Workington) Ltd on site. Shallow pond with reedbeds. Winter wildfowl (inc. Goldeneye, Shoveler, Whooper Swan); 35 nesting species; occasional visitors inc. Black-necked Grebe, Black-tailed Godwit, Black Tern, Ruff, Osprey. Patrick Joyce, Parks Development Officer, Allerdale BC, Allerdale House, Workington, Cumbria CA14 3YJ. 01900 326412; fax 01900 326346

SOUTH WALNEY. (250a) Cumbria WT SD212623. S tip of Walney Island, Barrow-in-Furness. Open daily 1000-1700, closed Mondays exc Bank Hols. Permits required, available on reserve. 6 hides (1 with wheelchair access); 2 nature trails; disabled-access toilets. Mudflats, saltmarsh, sandy beaches and dunes, freshwater and brackish pools. Large colony breeding Herring, Lesser and Great Black-backed Gulls plus southernmost Eider colony in Britain. Passage migrants and seabirds in spring and autumn; wintering waders and wildfowl. Cottage accommodation. Warden, Coastguard Cottages, South Walney Nature Reserve, Walney Island, Barrow-in-Furness, Cumbria LA14 3YQ. 01229 471066

WALNEY BIRD OBSERVATORY. Location as above. Monitoring and ringing of breeding and migrant birds. Cottage and caravan accommodation plus facilities for qualified ringers. Uncommon and rare species on spring and autumn migration. For bookings write to Walney Bird Observatory, South End, Walney Island, Barrow-in-Furness, Cumbria LA14 3YQ.

DERBYSHIRE

DRAKELOW WILDFOWL RESERVE. (77a) Powergen PLC SK227207. Entrance at Drakelow C power station, 1 mile NE of Walton-upon-Trent. Permit by post from Drakelow Power Station, Burton-on-Trent. Open daily 0930-2145 (on wildfowl count Sundays opens at 1100); closed all June. Parties, by special arrangement, limited to 10. 7 hides. Water-filled gravel pits. Breeding Little Ringed Plover, Reed and Sedge Warblers; passage waders; winter waterfowl (inc. Goldeneye, Pintail, Shoveler, Gadwall). Regular sightings of Peregrines on the station towers. Tom Cockburn, 1 Dickens Drive, Swadlincote, Derbys DE11 0DX. 01283 217146

OGSTON RESERVOIR. (208a) Severn Trent Water plc. From A61 S of Clay Cross take B6014. View from roads, car parks or hides (3 for Ogston BC members, 1 public). Toilets. Open water, pasture, mixed woodland. All 3 woodpeckers, Little and Tawny Owls, Kingfisher, Grey Wagtail, warblers. Passage raptors (inc. Osprey), terns and waders; winter gull roost, wildfowl, tit and finch flocks. Contact: Ogston Bird Club; information pack on request.

DEVON

AYLESBEARE COMMON. (530a) RSPB. Access at all times along paths only. Car park at SY057898 beside A3052, 6 miles from Exeter. Lowland heath, mires and woodland. Dartford Warbler, Nightjar, Stonechat, Curlew. Toby Taylor, Hawkerland Brake Barn, Exmouth Road, Aylesbeare, Exeter EX5 2JS. 01395 233655

CHAPEL WOOD. (14a) RSPB SS483413. Off minor road to Georgeham, W of A361 2 miles N of Braunton. Permit required (send sae). Mixed woodland. Sparrowhawk, Buzzard, Raven, all 3 woodpeckers, Grey Wagtail, Dipper, warblers, Pied Flycatcher. Cyril Manning, 8 Chichester Park, Woolacombe, North Devon EX34 7BZ. 01271 870713

DART VALLEY. (717a) Devon WT SX680727. Dartmeet. Follow riverside paths. Open at all times. Oakwood, birchwood, moorland, fast flowing river. Summer: Pied Flycatcher, Redstart, Wood Warbler, Tree Pipit, all 3 woodpeckers, Buzzard, Peregrine, Dipper, Grey Wagtail.

DAWLISH WARREN LNR. (505a) Teignbridge DC & Devon WT SX983788. From A379 NE of Dawlish. Visitor centre beyond N end of N car park. Hide reached from seaward edge of dunes (no access to golf course or mudflats). All visiting parties should book with Warden. Guided walks throughout year. Exe estuary, saltmarsh, mudflats, dunes, seashore, grassland, scrub, reedbed, ponds. Passage and winter waders (inc. occasional Spotted Redshank, Curlew Sandpiper, Little Stint); winter wildfowl (inc. Brent Geese, Wigeon, Eider, Scoter), divers and grebes; gulls, terns, passerines. Keri Walsh, Teignbridge DC, Forde House, Brunel Road, Newton Abbot, Devon TQ12 4XX. Visitor Centre: 01626 863980

EXMINSTER MARSHES. (250a) RSPB. Car park at SX955872. Access via A379 to Swans Nest roundabout, over the railway bridge and sharp right. Breeding Lapwing, Redshank; warblers (inc. Cetti's, Sedge and Reed). Birds from Exe Estuary during periods of high tide and flooding. Estuary and whole of marshes are an SSSI and SPA Ramsar Site; important for winter concentrations of wildfowl (inc. Wigeon, Dark-bellied Brent Geese, Red-breasted Merganser) and waders (inc. Black and Bar-tailed Godwits, Grey Plover, Dunlin, Curlew, Oystercatcher). Passage Whimbrel, Ringed Plover, Greenshank. RSPB South West Regional Office organises boat trips to view wintering Avocets. Malcolm Davies, RSPB Exe Estuary Reserves Office, The Victory Hall Annexe, Main Rd, Exminster, Exeter EX6 8DB. 01392 833632

OLD SLUDGE BEDS. (13a) Devon WT SX952888. S of Exeter. Park at Countess Wear wharf (SX941895) and follow canal. Reserve lies beyond sewage works between canal and river. Path with board walks. Former sludge settlement lagoons, now reverted to reedbed and willow carr. Warblers (inc. Garden, Cetti's, Sedge, Reed); Water Rail.

OTTER ESTUARY. (57a) Devon WT SY076822. E of Budleigh Salterton. Paths along W & E sides of estuary. No restrictions. Hide on E side. Saltmarsh, mudflat, shingle beach. Summer Shelduck, Rock Pipit, Stonechat. Winter wildfowl (inc. Brent Goose, Wigeon), waders.

PRAWLE POINT. Devon Birdwatching & Preservation Society. SE of Salcombe. 2 acres by NT car park & 2 quarter acre plots in Pigs Nose Valley. Coastal migration watch point. Strictly DBW&PS members only. Over 230 species recorded in area. Noted for seabird movements. Good list of raptors. Breeding Cirl Bunting. American vagrants inc. Red-eyed Vireo, Black-and-white Warbler, Blackpoll Warbler. Also Pallas's and Yellow-browed Warblers.

RACKENFORD AND KNOWSTONE MOORS. (302a) Devon WT SS858211. Unrestricted access. The moors straddle the A361 between Tiverton and South Molton. Turn off road at picnic site (SS833219). Unique combination of heath, fen and mire called 'culm grassland'. Summer: Curlew, Stonechat, Whinchat, Grasshopper Warbler. Winter: Hen Harrier, Merlin, Short-eared Owl, Snipe, Jack Snipe, Fieldfare, Redwing.

SOUTH MILTON LEY. (40a) Devon Birdwatching & Preservation Society. South coast near Thurlestone. Second largest freshwater reedbed in Devon. Strictly DBW&PS members only, but can be overlooked from public footpath. Breeding Reed and Sedge Warblers, and usually Cetti's Warbler. Good area for observing spring and autumn passages: Aquatic Warbler most years. Cirl Buntings close by.

YARNER WOOD. (372a) English Nature SX786788. Part of East Dartmoor Woods and Heaths NNR. Off B3344 W of Bovey Tracey at Reddaford Water. Reserve open from 0830-2000 or dusk if earlier. Visiting groups should book in advance. Two nature trails, hide. Mainly oak woodland, small area of heathland. Pied Flycatcher, Redstart, Dartford and Wood Warblers, Grey Wagtail, Raven, Buzzard, Lesser Spotted Woodpecker, Nightjar. Site Manager, Yarner Wood, Bovey Tracey, Newton Abbot, Devon TQ13 9LJ. 01626 832330

DORSET

ARNE. (1296a) RSPB SY973882. Turn off A351 at Stoborough just S of Wareham. Shipstal Point nature trail and hide open all year, with access from Arne car park. Coaches and escorted parties by prior arrangement. Dorset heathland, woods, carr, reedbeds, saltmarsh. Resident Dartford Warbler, Stonechat, Sparrowhawk, Little Egret; passage waders (inc. Black-tailed Godwit, Spotted Redshank, Whimbrel); summer Nightjar, warblers; winter Hen Harrier, Goldeneye, Red-breasted Merganser. Neil Gartshore, RSPB Nature Reserve, Syldata, Arne, Wareham, Dorset BH20 5BJ. 01929 553360

BROWNSEA ISLAND. (250a) Dorset WT SZ025882. By boat from Poole Quay or Sandbanks. 1 Apr-30 Sep. Guided tours pm 1445 daily in July & Aug. Self-guided trails 1030-1300 (last entry) at other times. Woodland, reedbed, lakes, lagoon. Ducks, waders, nesting colonies of Common and Sandwich Terns, large heronry. Kevin Cook, The Villa, Brownsea Island, Poole, Dorset BH13 7EE. 01202 709445

DURLSTON COUNTRY PARK. (260a) Dorset CC SZ032774. One mile S of Swanage (signposted). Visitor centre in car park open weekends during winter and daily in other seasons (phone for times). Guided walks. Cliff-nesting seabird colonies; good variety of scrub and woodland breeding species; spring and autumn migrants; seawatching esp. Apr/May & Aug/Nov. Hamish Murray, Durlston Country Park, Swanage, Dorset BH19 2JL. 01929 424443

GARSTON WOOD. (84a) RSPB SU004194. Small car park on Sixpenny Handley to Bowerchalke minor road, off B3081 midway between Salisbury and Blandford Forum. Open at all times; keep to paths. Remnant of Cranborne Chase mixed woodland. Breeding Great Spotted Woodpecker, Turtle Dove, Garden Warbler, Blackcap, Spotted Flycatcher, Nuthatch, Treecreeper, Bullfinch. Sparrowhawk and Buzzard frequent. Warden: c/o Arne (above).

HOLT HEATH. (1200a) English Nature (NNR) SU052046. W of Ringwood. From minor roads between Three Legged Cross and Holt. Open at all times. Mainly lowland heath, some woodland. Dartford Warbler, Stonechat, Nightjar, Curlew; winter Hen Harrier, Merlin. Contact: Ian Nicol, 3 Saddle Close, Colehill, Wimborne, Dorset BH21 2UN. 01202 841026

LODMOOR. (165a) RSPB SY686807. Adjacent Lodmoor Country Park, in Weymouth, off A353 to Wareham. Marsh, shallow pools, reeds and scrub, remnant saltmarsh. Breeding Common Tern, warblers (inc. Reed, Sedge, Grasshopper, Cetti's), Bearded Tit. Winter wildfowl and waders. Passage waders and other migrants. Martin Slater, 52 Goldcroft Avenue, Weymouth, Dorset DT4 0ES. 01305 778313

PORTLAND BIRD OBSERVATORY. S end of Portland Bill. Self-catering accommodation for up to 20 in 6 bedrooms, plus 6 in small self-contained flat. Blankets provided; take own towels, sheets/sleeping bags. Electric fires in all bedrooms; lounge. Equipped kitchen. Laboratory. Good seabird movements. Migration watch point. Many rare warblers. Breeding auks, Fulmars, Kittiwakes. Over 300 species. Ringing, esp. spring and autumn. Martin Cade, Bird Observatory, Old Lower Light, Portland Bill, Dorset DT5 2JT. 01305 820553

RADIPOLE LAKE. (222a) RSPB SY677796. From Swannery car park (Weymouth) on footpaths. Visitor centre open every day 0900-1700. Nature trail and hide open in daylight hours; permit (from Centre) required by non-RSPB members. Lake, reedbeds. Winter wildfowl; breeding reedbed warblers (inc. Cetti's), Bearded Tit; passage waders and other migrants. Garganey regular in spring. Good for rarer gulls. Information centre 01305 778313. Warden as Lodmoor above.

SOPLEY COMMON. (85a) Dorset WT SZ129971. NW of Christchurch. Access from parking area on S side of 'Avon causeway' road E of Hurn. Heathland, some secondary woodland. Sparrowhawk, Buzzard, Dartford Warbler, Nightjar, Woodlark.

STANPIT MARSH. (150a) Management Committee (LNR) SZ169921. From car park in Stanpit Lane, Christchurch. Information caravan. Public access (with some restrictions). SSSI. Estuary, mudflats, salt/freshwater marshes, reedbeds, scrub. On Avon valley migration route; over 200 species recorded. Passage wildfowl and waders; Bearded Tit. Peter Holloway, Christchurch Countryside Service, Steamer Point Woodland, Highcliffe, Christchurch, Dorset BH23 4XX. 01425 272479

STOBOROUGH. (130a) RSPB SY929847. 2 miles from Wareham (bus to Stoborough). Restricted roadside parking. Keep to permitted and public paths, to which there are several entrances. Lowland heath. Dartford Warbler, Nightjar, Stonechat, Linnet. Warden: c/o Arne (above).

STUDLAND & GODLINGSTON HEATHS. (1558a) English Nature and National Trust (NNR) SZ030846. From Ferry Road N of Studland village. Hides, nature trails. Woodland, heath, dunes, inter-tidal mudflats, saltings, freshwater lake, reedbeds, carr. Water Rail, Reed and Dartford Warblers, Nightjar, Stonechat; winter wildfowl. (Studland Bay, outside the reserve, has winter Black-necked and Slavonian Grebes, Scoter, Eider). Contacts: English Nature, Slepe Farm, Arne, Wareham, Dorset BH20 5BN. 01929 556688. National Trust, Countryside Office, Studland, Dorset BH19 3AX. 01929 450259.

DURHAM

CASTLE EDEN DENE. (550a) English Nature (NNR) NZ427389. From junction of A19 and A181. Footpath access. Education groups (subject to booking). Woodland, shingle coast, winter lagoon. Kittiwake, terns; autumn Little Gull passage; winter Snow Bunting. Site Manager, Oakerside Dene Lodge, Stanhope Chase, Peterlee, Co Durham SR8 1NJ. 0191 586 0004

TEESMOUTH. (876a) English Nature (NNR). S of Hartlepool, E of A178. Route to north part of reserve from car park at NZ534282, with no restrictions over dune slack and most of N Gare Sands. For south part proceed E along S bank of Greatham Creek from NZ510254; access restricted to hides at NZ516255 (disabled users by arrangement) overlooking Seal Sands and at NZ516253 overlooking intertidal pool. Passage and wintering wildfowl and waders; wintering Merlin, Peregrine, Snow Bunting, Twite, divers, grebes; passage terns and skuas in late summer; scarce passerine migrants and rarities. Mike Leakey, English Nature, Visitor Centre, British Energy, Tees Road, Hartlepool TS25 2BZ. Tel/fax 01429 853325

WITTON-LE-WEAR (Low Barns). (84a) Durham WT NZ160315. Off unclassified road between Witton-le-Wear (signposted on A68) and High Grange. 3 hides (2 with disabled access), observation tower above visitor centre (manned), nature trail. Former gravel workings, lake, ponds, riverbank. Resident Greylag Geese, Kingfisher; Goosander, Grey Wagtail, Redpoll have bred; winter wildfowl (inc. Goldeneye, Shoveler). Visitor Centre Manager. Low Barns Nature Reserve, Witton-le-Wear, Bishop Auckland, Co Durham DL14 0AG. 01388 488728

ESSEX

ABBERTON RESERVOIR. (9a on edge of 1200a reservoir) Essex WT TL963185. Six miles SW of Colchester on B1026. Tu W Th F Sa Su 0900-1700 except 25 & 26 Dec. Visitor centre, toilets, nature trail, 5 hides (disabled access). Also good viewing where roads cross reservoir. Nationally important for Mallard, Teal, Wigeon, Shoveler, Gadwall, Pochard, Tufted Duck, Goldeneye (most important inland site in Britain). Smew regular. Passage waders, terns, birds of prey. Tree-nesting Cormorants (largest colony in Britain); raft-nesting Common Tern. Summer: Yellow Wagtail, warblers, Nightingale, Corn Bunting; Autumn: Red-crested Pochard, Bearded Tit, Water Rail; large numbers of waders in winter. Annette Adams, Essex Wildlife Trust, Abberton Reservoir Visitor Centre, Layer-de-la-Haye, Colchester CO2 0EU. 01206 738172

BRADWELL BIRD OBSERVATORY. 100 yards S of St Peter's Chapel, Bradwell-on-Sea. Accommodation for 8 in hut; 2 rooms each with 4 bunks; blankets, cutlery, etc. supplied. Mouth of Blackwater estuary, between Maldon and Foulness. Winter wildfowl (inc. Brent Geese, Red-throated Divers, Red-breasted Mergansers), large numbers of waders; Twite, Snow Buntings and occasional Shore Larks on beaches, also Hen Harriers, Merlins and Peregrines. Good passage of migrants usual in spring and autumn. Small breeding population of terns and other estuarine species. Graham Smith, 48 The Meads, Ingatestone, Essex CM4 0AE. 01277 354034

COLNE POINT. (673a) Essex WT TM108125. W of Clacton, via B1027 to St Osyth then Lee Wick Lane. Car park just inside reserve on seaward side of sea wall (liable to flood at very high tides). Day permit for non-Trust members. Mudflats, shingle pools. On major migration route for finches and chats; spring and autumn birds of prey; breeding Little Tern, Ringed Plover, Oystercatcher, Redshank; winter divers, grebes, ducks, and feeding ground for Brent Geese. Contact: Trust HQ.

FINGRINGHOE WICK. (125a) Essex WT TM041195. From unclassified road at Fingringhoe (E of B1025 at Abberton). Visitor centre, toilets (inc disabled); nature trails, 8 hides. Freshwater lake, foreshore, saltmarsh, scrape, heath, woodland. Large winter flock of Dark-bellied Brent Geese; passage waders; breeding Little Grebe, warblers, Nightingale stronghold. Laurie Forsyth, Fingringhoe Wick Nature Reserve, South Green Road, Fingringhoe, Colchester CO5 7DN. 01206 729678

HANNINGFIELD RESERVOIR. (100a on edge of 870a reservoir). Essex WT TQ737976. Giffords Lane, off South Hanningfield Road, S of the village, leads down to the fishing lodge and public car park. Reserve is along SE shore. M-Su 0800-sunset Apr-Oct. Visitor centre opens early 2000. 4 hides. SSSI. Breeders include Gadwall, Pochard, Common Tern; woodland birds include Crossbill, 3 species of woodpecker, Firecrest. Winter Goosander, Goldeneye, Wigeon, Teal, Smew, Pintail. Contact: Warden 01245 212032.

LEIGH. (634a) Essex WT and English Nature NNR TQ824852. Two Tree Island, approached from Leigh on Sea. Important to keep to marked footpaths. Hide, nature trail. Intertidal mudflats, saltmarshes. Autumn Dark-bellied Brent Geese.

OLD HALL MARSHES. (1134a) RSPB TL950117. From minor road N of Tollesbury. Open all days except Tu; obtain permit in advance from Warden. Walk *below* sea wall. Grazing marsh, reedmarsh, meres, saltings on shore of Blackwater estuary. Breeders include Avocet, Redshank, Lapwing, Pochard, Shoveler, Gadwall, Common Tern. Winter wildfowl include large numbers of Brent Geese, Wigeon, Teal; divers, Goldeneye and Red-breasted Merganser in channels; passage and wintering waders. Short-eared Owl, Hen Harrier, Barn Owl and Merlin also regular. Chris Tyas, 1 Old Hall Lane, Tolleshunt D'Arcy, Maldon, Essex CM9 8TP.

STOUR ESTUARY. (956a) RSPB TM189309. Near Harwich. Car park at Stour Wood off B1352 from Manningtree to Ramsey, 1 mile E of Wrabness village. Access at all times. 3 hides overlook bay. Ancient coppice-with-standards woodland, mainly oak and sweet chestnut. Woodpeckers, Nightingale, warblers in wood. Nearby foreshore has winter Brent Geese, Shelduck, Pintail and Black-tailed Godwit. Russell Leavett, 24 Orchard Close, Great Oakley, Harwich, Essex CO12 5AX. Tel/fax 01255 886043

TOLLESBURY WICK NATURE RESERVE. (599a) Essex WT TL970104. E of Maldon. B1023 runs out to Tollesbury via Tiptree, leaving A12 at Kelvedon. Parking at Woodrolfe Green (toilets open Apr-Oct), walk 350m past Marina to entrance. Public footpath at top of sea wall. SSSI. Breeding Dabchick, Little Tern, Redshank, Oystercatcher, Reed and Sedge Warblers, Skylark, Meadow Pipit, Corn and Reed Buntings. Contact: Warden 01621 868628.

GLOUCESTERSHIRE

ASHLEWORTH HAM AND MEEREND THICKET. (101a) Glos WT SO830265. Leave Gloucester N on A417; R at Hartpury and follow minor road through Ashleworth towards Hasfield. Access prohibited at all times but birds may be viewed from hides in Meerend Thicket. Low lying grassland flood plain. Winter wildfowl (inc. 4000 Wigeon, 1500 Teal, Pintail, Goldeneye, Bewick's Swan); passage waders; Peregrine, Hobby. Contact: Trust HQ.

HIGHNAM WOODS. (300a) RSPB SO778190. W of Gloucester. Entry via car park beside A40. Open at all times. Large parties by prior arrangement. Keep to waymarked paths. Mainly broadleaved woodland, scattered scrub, small ponds. Breeding Tawny Owl, Sparrowhawk, warblers, Nightingale, all 3 woodpeckers; winter Siskin, Redpoll. Winter feeding project in front of hide. Ivan Proctor, The Puffins, Parkend, Lydney, Glos GL15 4JA. 01594 562852

NAGSHEAD. (378a) RSPB SO612078. From B4431 road to Coleford after leaving Parkend. Waymarked path always open across part of reserve. Hides. Information centre open Sun Apr-Aug. Mature oak woodland. Pied Flycatcher, Redstart, Wood Warbler, woodpeckers, Hawfinch, Grey Wagtail. Ivan Proctor, The Puffins, Parkend, Lydney, Glos GL15 4JA. 01594 562852

SLIMBRIDGE. (800a) WWT Centre SO723048. Signposted from M5 (exit 13 or 14). Daily except 25 Dec, 0930-1730 (1700 in winter). Hides, observatory, exhibition, tropical house, facilities for disabled. Reedbed, saltmarsh, freshwater pools, mudflats. Kingfisher, waders, raptors. Winter wildfowl esp. Bewick's Swans, White-fronted Geese, Wigeon, Teal. Neil Woodward, Centre Manager, The Wildfowl & Wetlands Trust, Slimbridge, Gloucester GL2 7BT. 01453 890333

WHELFORD POOLS. (31a) Glos WT SU174995. SE of Fairford. Leave Fairford E on A417, turn R towards Whelford and reserve is on left (just before Whelford sign). Open at all times. 2 hides, 1 with wheelchair access. Flooded gravel pits in eastern section of Cotswold Water Park. On main passage flight route (Yellow Wagtail, Black Tern, Osprey, waders); breeding Common Tern; summer Hobby; winter wildfowl. Contact: Trust HQ.

WOORGREENS LAKE AND MARSH. (22a) Glos WT SO630127. Forest of Dean. W of Cinderford, N of B4226 Cannop road. Marsh, lake, heath on reclaimed opencast coalmine. Open at all times. Whinchat, Stonechat, Tree Pipit, Hobby, Nightjar; passage waders (inc. Greenshank, Spotted Redshank, Green Sandpiper). Contact: Trust HQ.

HAMPSHIRE

FARLINGTON MARSHES. (300a) Hants WT (LNR) SU685045. Track from flyover where A2030 joins A27 NE of Portsmouth. Open at all times. Keep to paths; dogs on lead. Information building. Coastal grazing, pools, reedbed, scrub, saltings. Waders and wildfowl; passage includes large numbers of Black-tailed Godwit, Greenshank, Spotted Redshank; rarities also occur. Bob Chapman: 02392 214683

HOOK-WITH-WARSASH LNR. (560a) Hants CC SU490050. W of Fareham. Car parks by foreshore at Warsash. Reserve includes Hook Lake. Public footpaths. Shingle beach, saltings, marsh, reedbed, scrape. Winter Brent Geese on Hamble estuary; waders; Stonechat; Cetti's Warbler. Warden: as Titchfield.

LANGSTONE HARBOUR. (1370a) RSPB. View from footpath along N shore off junction of A27/A2030, Farlington Marshes (qv), and car park off Hayling Island road by Esso garage (SU718029). Mudflats. Breeding Little, Sandwich and Common Terns, gulls and waders. Passage/winter waders (inc. Black-tailed and Bar-tailed Godwits); winter wildfowl (inc. Shelduck, Goldeneye, Merganser and c7,000 Dark-bellied Brent Geese), Black-necked Grebe, Short-eared Owl, Peregrine. RSPB Warden, 46 Stein Road, Southbourne, Emsworth, Hants PO10 8LD. 01243 376010

LOWER TEST. (400a) Hants WT SU364150. M271 S to Redbridge. Open at all times; keep to paths. Hides. Saltmarsh, brackish grassland, wet meadows, reedbed, scrape, meres. Breeding Cetti's Warbler, waders. Passage/winter waders (inc. Green and Common Sandpipers). Wintering wildfowl, Bearded Tit, Water Pipit, Jack Snipe. Contact: Jess Pain, 02380 667919

LYMINGTON REEDBEDS. (80a) Hants WT SZ325963. E of Lymington town centre, 5 mins walk from rail station. Good views from adjacent roads to S and E of reserve;

otherwise access only on public paths. One of largest reedbeds on S coast. Breeding Cetti's Warbler and Bearded Tit. One of highest concentrations of Water Rail in the country; resident but most evident in winter. Contact: Michael Boxall, 01590 622708

LYMINGTON-KEYHAVEN NNR. (454a) Hants CC SZ315920. S of Lymington along seawall footpath; car parks at Bath Road, Lymington and at Keyhaven Harbour. Coastal marshland and lagoons. Spring passage of waders (inc. Knot, Sanderling, Bar-tailed and Black-tailed Godwits, Whimbrel, Spotted Redshank), Pomarine and Great Skuas; breeding Oystercatcher, Ringed Plover, and Sandwich, Common and Little Terns; autumn passage of raptors, waders and passerines; winter wildfowl (inc. Brent Geese, Wigeon, Pintail, Red-breasted Merganser), waders (inc. Golden Plover), Little Egret, gulls.

MARTIN DOWN. (830a) English Nature (NNR) SU057192. SE of Salisbury. Car park on road W of Martin. Groups contact Warden in advance. Chalk grassland and scrub mix. Nightingale, warblers, Grey Partridge. Winter Short-eared Owl, Hen Harrier. David Burton, English Nature, Parsonage Down NNR, Cherry Lodge, Shrewton, Salisbury SP3 4ET. 01980 620485

NORTH SOLENT. (2024a) EN/Bealieu Estate/Cadland Estate (NNR) SZ425980. Part of reserve viewed from public footpath from Beaulieu to Bucklers Hard. Several footpaths/bridleways criss-cross Cadland Estate heathland. Access over designated routes (apply for permit to the Resident Agent, John Montagu Building, Beaulieu, Brockenhurst, Hants SO42 7ZN). 5 hides (1 for disabled). Coastal shingle/saltmarsh, brackish and freshwater lagoons, reedbeds, grazing marshes, heathland, woodland. Sandwich and Little Terns, Nightjar; passage waders (inc. Spotted Redshank); winter wildfowl (inc. Brent Geese). Bob Lord, English Nature, 1 Southampton Road, Lyndhurst, Hants SO43 7BU. 01703 283944

PILSEY ISLAND. (45a) RSPB SU770006. Approach via coastal footpath around Thorney Island. No access on to island but good views from surrounding areas at low tide. Saltmarsh and shingle. Major wader roost at high tide. Wintering waterfowl. Warden c/o Langstone Harbour above.

TITCHFIELD HAVEN NNR. (330a) Hants CC SU535025. From A27 W of Fareham; public footpath follows derelict canal along W of reserve and road skirts S edge. Open W-Su all year, plus Bank Hols. Centre has information desk, toilets, tea room and shop. Guided tours (book in advance). Hides. Reedbeds, freshwater scrapes, wet grazing meadows. Bearded Tit, waders (inc. Black-tailed Godwit, Ruff), wildfowl, Common Tern, breeding Cetti's Warbler, Water Rail. Bittern in winter. Barry Duffin, Haven House Visitor Centre, Cliff Road, Hill Head, Fareham, Hants PO14 3JT. 01329 662145; fax 01329 667113

HERTFORDSHIRE

LEMSFORD SPRINGS. (9a) Herts & Middx WT TL223123. Off roundabout leading to Lemsford Village, W of A1(M) near Welwyn Garden City. Keep to paths. Hides. Access by arrangement with Warden. Former water-cress beds. Open shallow lagoons, stretch of River Lea, marsh, hedgerows. Sparrowhawk, Snipe, Jack Snipe, Water Rail, Grey Wagtail, Kingfisher, Heron. Noted for winter Green Sandpiper. Barry Trevis, 11 Lemsford Village, Welwyn Garden City, Herts AL8 7TN. 01707 335517

RYE HOUSE MARSH. (62a) RSPB TL387099. E of Hoddesdon, near Rye House railway station. Marsh, willow scrub, pools, scrapes, lake and reedbed. Open every day 1000-1700. Hides. Breeding Tufted Duck, Gadwall, Common Tern, Kestrel, Kingfisher, 9 species of breeding warblers; winter Bittern, Shoveler, Water Rail, Teal, Snipe, Jack Snipe, Redpoll and Siskin. Mike Pollard, RSPB Rye House Marsh Reserve, Rye Meads Sewage Treatment Works, Stanstead Abbotts, Herts SG12 8JY. 01279 793720; fax 01279 793721

RYE MEADS. (43.4a) Herts & Middx WT TL387106. Through RSPB Rye House Marsh Reserve (above). Open daily except 25 & 26 Dec 0900-1700, free to RSPB and Trust members. Hide. Ancient flood meadows and tall mixed fen vegetation. Breeding Snipe; Grasshopper, Sedge and Reed Warblers. Winter Bittern, wildfowl (inc. Gadwall, Shoveler, Teal), Water Rail, Snipe. Contact: Trust HQ.

STOCKER'S LAKE. (93a) Herts & Middx WT (LNR) TQ044931. Rickmansworth, off A412 into Springwell Lane (TQ043932) L after bridge, or via Bury Lake Aquadrome (parking). Mature flooded gravel pit with islands. 50 species breed; over 200 recorded. Heronry. Breeding Pochard, Gadwall, Common Tern. Large numbers of migrants and winter duck (inc. Goldeneye and nationally significant numbers of Shoveler). Contact: Trust HQ.

TRING RESERVOIRS. (49a) British Waterways Board SP918137. From B489 which leaves the A41 at Aston Clinton. Hides. Reservoirs, reedbeds, woodland. Heronry, breeding Reed and Sedge Warblers; Hobby, Marsh Harrier, Osprey regular on migration; passage terns and waders; winter wildfowl (inc. Goldeneye, Goosander) and occasional Bittern.

KENT

BLEAN WOODS. (222a) English Nature (NNR) TR120609. NW of Canterbury on A290. Road opposite Chapel Lane at Blean. Keep to paths. Mixed coppice with standard sessile oak, glades, rides. Some 70 breeding species, inc. Woodcock, all 3 woodpeckers, Tree Pipit, Redstart, Nightingale, Wood Warbler, Hawfinch. David Maylam, Coldharbour Farm, Wye, Ashford, Kent TN25 5DB. 01233 812525

BLEAN WOODS. (765a) RSPB TR126592. From Rough Common (off A290, 1.5 miles NW of Canterbury). Open 0800 to 2100, along public footpaths and 4 waymarked trails. Woodland (mainly oak and sweet chestnut), relics of heath. Nightingale, Redstart, Hawfinch, 3 species of woodpecker. Michael Walter, 11 Garden Close, Rough Common, Canterbury, Kent CT2 9BP. 01227 462491

BOUGH BEECH RESERVOIR. (45a NE corner) Kent WT TQ495489. Viewed from road between B2027 (W of Tonbridge) and Winkhurst Green. Entry permit only granted for scientific studies. Facilities for school parties - contact Education Officer, Kent WT. Information centre in oast house (open W Sa Su & bank hol M Apr-end Oct). Passage waders, Osprey, Hobby, terns; Great Crested Grebe; winter wildfowl (including Goosander, Smew, Scaup).

BURHAM MARSHES. (100a) Kent WT TQ712624. From Burham Court via minor road W of A229 N of Maidstone. Essential to keep to footpath. River, freshwater marsh, reedbed. Water Rail, waders, ducks. Contact Kent WT.

DUNGENESS. (2219a) RSPB TR063196. SE of Lydd. Visitor centre, toilets. Open daily 0900-2100 or sunset when earlier; visitor centre 1000-1700 (1600 Nov-Feb). Parties over 10 by prior arrangement. Shingle, flooded gravel pits, sallow scrub. Resident Corn Bunting; breeding gulls, terns; winter wildfowl (inc. Wigeon, Goldeneye, Goosander, Smew), divers and grebes; migrant waders; landfall for passerines. Manager, Boulderwall Farm, Dungeness Road, Lydd, Romney Marsh, Kent TN29 9PN. 01797 320588

DUNGENESS BIRD OBSERVATORY. Founded 1952. N of two lighthouses on Dungeness Point. Self-catering for 10 visitors in 2 dormitories. Take own sheets/sleeping bag, pillow cases, food. Meals bought locally. Spring passage inc. Little and Mediterranean Gulls, Pomarine Skua. Gulls, terns, Black Redstart breed. Both passages have large numbers of passerines, inc. rarities; winter duck, divers, grebes. Daily collection of migration data. David Walker, Dungeness Bird Observatory, Dungeness, Romney Marsh, Kent TN29 9NA. 01797 321309

ELMLEY MARSHES. (3364a) RSPB TQ926705. SW Isle of Sheppey. Open every day except Tu and 25-26 Dec 0900-2100 (or sunset when earlier). Car park 2 miles along farm track from A249 to Sheerness 1 mile beyond Kingsferry Bridge. Hides 1.25 miles walk from car park. Grazing marsh, saltings, foreshore. Winter wildfowl (inc. 1800 White-fronted Geese); passage waders; breeding wildfowl and waders. Bob Gomes, Kingshill Farm, Elmley, Sheerness, Isle of Sheppey, Kent ME12 3RW. 01795 665969

HAMSTREET WOODS. (240a) English Nature (NNR) TR003337. E on B2067 from Hamstreet, car park first L at green. Keep to paths. Damp oak woodland, coppice/standards. Over 90 species recorded. Woodcock, Great & Lesser Spotted Woodpeckers, Nightingale, Redstart, warblers, Hawfinch. Contact English Nature, David Maylam, Coldharbour Farm, Wye, Ashford, Kent TN25 5DB. 01233 812525

NOR MARSH. (190a) RSPB TQ811689. Park at Riverside CP just E of Gillingham on B2004. No access to island but good views of reserve and Medway estuary from Horrid Hill causeway. Channels, saltings, mudflats. Gulls and terns in summer; winter wildfowl, waders, divers and rarer grebes. Warden: A Parker at Northward Hill (below); or contact Ranger Service, Riverside CP, tel 01634 378987.

NORTHWARD HILL. (615a) RSPB TQ784759. From car park off Northwood Ave, High Halstow. Mixed woodland, scrub, adjacent N Kent marshes. Largest UK heronry (viewing by prior arrangement with Warden), Nightingale, warblers; wintering wildfowl and raptors. A Parker, RSPB Office, Bromhey Farm, Eastborough, Cooling, Rochester, Kent ME3 8DS. 01634 222480

SANDWICH & PEGWELL BAY LNR. (1507a) Kent WT. N side TR340632, Country Park off A256 Ramsgate/Sandwich road. S side TR354605, from Sandwich via Sandwich Bay Estate (toll road). Inter-tidal mudflats, saltmarsh, salt dune and coastal scrub. Breeding Ringed Plover, Cuckoo, warblers (inc. Reed and Sedge), scrubland species. Passage waders, wildfowl and passerines. Winter waders (esp. Sanderling, Dunlin, Redshank), Hen Harrier, Short-eared Owl, Snow Bunting. Contact: Kent WT.

SANDWICH BAY BIRD OBSERVATORY. E of Sandwich. Open all year; Apr/May, Aug/Nov best. Hostel for 4. Training for ringers. Mist nets used at observatory and on ringing expeditions to the reedbeds, etc. Migration research centre. Kentish Plover, Mediterranean Gull, Golden Oriole, Avocet, Short and Long-eared Owls regular; rarities. The Secretary, Sandwich Bay Bird Observatory, Old Downs Farm, Guilford Road, Sandwich, Kent CT13 9PF. 01304 617341

STODMARSH. (620a) English Nature (NNR) TR220610. Car park down track leaving Stodmarsh village by Red Lion. Public access on Lampen Wall (flood protection barrier), also from Grove Ferry along river wall. 3 hides (disabled access). Toilets. Lagoons, reedbeds, marsh, partially flooded meadows, damp alder/willow woodland. Shelduck, Garganey, Marsh Harrier, Bittern; Cetti's, Grasshopper Warblers; Bearded Tit; passage and winter wildfowl, waders, harriers. Paul Burnham, English Nature, Grove Road, Preston, Canterbury, Kent CT3 1EF. 01227 728382

SWALE. (1000a) Kent WT. (1) South Swale Nature Reserve (LNR) TR035647, from minor road off B2040, N of Brenley Corner roundabout at M2/A2/A299 junction. (2) Oare Marshes TR011645, from Oare village NW of Faversham. Tidal mudflats, grazing marsh, reedbed. Winter wildfowl (inc. Brent Goose); birds of prey (inc. Merlin, Hen Harrier, Peregrine, Short-eared Owl); waders (inc. Knot, Grey Plover, Black-Tailed Godwit, Turnstone); flocks of Linnet, Twite, Goldfinch, etc. with occasional Lapland and Snow Buntings. Breeding Redshank, Lapwing, duck species, Bearded Tit. Spring and autumn duck (inc. Pintail, Gadwall, Shoveler); waders (inc. Greenshank, Black-tailed Godwit). Contact: Kent WT.

SWALE. (543a) English Nature (NNR) TR052682. From Leysdown-on-Sea (Isle of Sheppey) along sea front to Muswell Manor; rough track for 1 mile to car park. Permissive track to Shellness Point, may be closed. Keep to pathways. Hides, 1 tower hide overlooking flood areas. Coastal saltmarsh, freshwater grazing marsh, shell/shingle beach. Seawatching during autumn: large seabird movements viewed from Shellness inc. Gannet, skuas, divers, grebes. Winter: large numbers of wildfowl and waders (roosts of Oystercatcher, Black-tailed Godwit, Knot, Dunlin, Grey Plover), Hen Harrier, Short-eared Owl. Breeding birds inc. Gadwall, Teal, Garganey, Pochard, Avocet, Snipe, Lapwing, Redshank, Yellow Wagtail. Contact: English Nature, Coldharbour Farm, Wye, Ashford, Kent TN25 5DB. 01233 812525

TUDELEY WOODS. (708a) RSPB TQ616433. Beside A21 S of Tonbridge; entered off minor road to Capel. Open every day except 25 Dec. No dogs. 3 nature trails, car park. Semi-natural ancient woodland, softwood plantation, lowland heath, old pasture. Breeders inc. all 3 woodpeckers, Nuthatch, Marsh Tit, Blackcap, Garden Warbler, Whitethroat, Nightingale, Spotted Flycatcher, Turtle Dove, Hobby, Tree Pipit, Nightjar, Redpoll, Sparrowhawk. Martin Allison, Crown House, Petteridge Lane, Matfield, Tonbridge, Kent TN12 7LT.

WYE. (326a) English Nature (NNR) TR079454. From Wye up hill towards Hastingleigh, car park at roadside. Keep to paths. Nature trail. Downland, scrub, woodlands, grazing meadows. Breeding Sparrowhawk, Tawny Owl, Nightingale, Spotted Flycatcher, Lesser Whitethroat, Hawfinch. David Maylam, Coldharbour Farm, Wye, Ashford, Kent TN25 5DB. 01233 812525

LANCASHIRE

HEYSHAM NATURE RESERVE & BIRD OBSERVATORY. (25a) Lancs WT SD408601. New A683 from Lancaster to Heysham, L at Moneyclose Inn lights, R after quarter mile. Open access, car park (daylight hours). Reedbed, pools, scrub/woodland; nearby power station outfalls and rocky shore. Breeding warblers; migrant passerines in scrub; well recorded visible migration; gulls and terns on outfalls; large seabird passage (esp. Arctic Tern in spring); winter Water Rails and wader roost. Pete Marsh, 17 Albion Street, Lancaster LA1 1DY. 01524 66775

LEIGHTON MOSS. (321a) RSPB SD478751. Near Carnforth. Off Yealand Redmayne-Silverdale road near station. Daily 0900-2100 or sunset when earlier. Toilet. 5 hides. Public hide on causeway always open. Reedmarsh, meres, willow and alder carr. Breeding Bittern, Marsh Harrier, Water Rail, Bearded Tit; Black Tern, Osprey; wildfowl (inc. Gadwall, Garganey). Warden, Myers Farm, Silverdale, Carnforth, Lancs LA5 0SW. 01524 701601

MARTIN MERE. (376a) WWT Centre SD430144. From M6 exit 27; signposted on A59 at Burscough Bridge and A565 at Mere Brow. Daily except 25 Dec, 0930-1730 (dusk if earlier); parties book in advance. Hides, education centre, visitor centre, and facilities for disabled. Lake, marsh. Winter wildfowl esp. Pink-footed Geese (max 27,500), Whooper and Bewick's Swans, Wigeon (max 25,500). Breeding Little Ringed Plover and Tree Sparrow. Pat Wisniewski, Centre Manager, The Wildfowl & Wetlands Trust, Martin Mere, Burscough, Ormskirk, Lancs L40 0TA. 01704 895181

MARTON MERE. (96a) Blackpool BC SD345352. Signposted from Blackpool Zoo car park (free) and De Veres Hotel car park. Open at all times. Dogs on lead. Hides. Open water surrounded by patchwork of grassland, scrub and reedbed. Breeding warblers; migrant waders (inc. Little Ringed Plover, Jack Snipe), Black Tern; good range of winter duck, also Bittern annual; regular Mediterranean and Little Gulls. David McGrath, Community & Tourism Services, 125 Albert Road, Blackpool FY1 4PW.

MERE SANDS WOOD. (259a) Lancs WT SD448157. From B5246 W of Rufford. Visitor centre, 6 hides. Oak woodland, coniferous plantation, reclaimed sand pits forming lakes, marsh, wader scrape, heath. Breeding Great Crested and Little Grebes, Pochard, Little Ringed Plover, Turtle Dove; wintering Teal, Gadwall, Tufted Duck, Redpoll, Siskin; passage waders, Osprey. Dominic Rigby, Mere Sands Wood Nature Reserve, Holmeswood Road, Rufford, Ormskirk, Lancs L40 1TG. 01704 821809; e-mail lancswtmsw@cix.co.uk

MORECAMBE BAY. (4000a) RSPB SD468666. Near Carnforth. Good views of waders at high tide from Hest Bank signal box, off A5105 Morecambe-Carnforth road. Dangerous channels and quicksands on foreshore. Large numbers of waders (up to 40,000 in spring) inc. Bar-tailed Godwit; Red-breasted Merganser; winter Goldeneye, Peregrine, Merlin. Access at all times to saltings lagoon hides, reached from car park off Carnforth road near Leighton Moss (SD476737). Warden (who can advise on times), c/o Leighton Moss Reserve (above).

RIBBLE ESTUARY. (11,314a) English Nature (NNR) SD380250. No formal visiting facilities. High water wader roosts (of Knot, Dunlin, Black-tailed Godwit, Oystercatcher and Grey Plover) are best viewed from Southport, Marshside, Lytham and St Annes. Pink-footed Geese and wintering swans are present in large numbers from Oct-Feb on Banks Marsh and along R Douglas respectively. The large flocks of Wigeon, for which the site is renowned, can be seen on high tides from Marshside but feed on saltmarsh areas at night. Good numbers of raptors also present in winter. English Nature, Pier House, Wallgate, Wigan WN3 4AL. 01942 820342

UPPER COLDWELL RESERVOIR. Lancs WT SD905360. 3 miles SE of Nelson. Public footpath along N perimeter wall; access to reserve area by permit. Upland reservoir, coniferous woodland, moorland. Breeding Tufted Duck, Little Ringed Plover, Whinchat; moors have Twite, Short-eared Owl, Golden Plover. Contact: Trust HQ.

LEICESTERSHIRE & RUTLAND

EYEBROOK RESERVOIR. (400a trout fishery, season Apr-Oct) Corby Water Co. SP853964. Reservoir built 1940. Fom unclassified road W of A6003 at Stoke Dry. Bird sanctuary; SSSI since 1955. Access to 150 acres private grounds granted to members of Leics and Rutland Ornithological Society, and Rutland Nat Hist Soc. Organised groups with written permission (from Corby Water Co, PO Box 101, Weldon Road, Corby NN17 5UA). Good viewing from public roads. Open water, plantations and pasture. Good populations of breeding birds, passage waders and Black Tern; winter wildfowl (inc. Goldeneye, Goosander, Bewick's Swan).

RUTLAND WATER. (350a) Leics and Rutland WT SK866676072. Ramsar site & SPA. Egleton Reserve: from Egleton village off A6003 S of Oakham, daily 0900-1700; Lyndon Reserve: south shore E of Manton village off A6003 S of Oakham, winter: Sa Su 1000-1600, summer: daily except M 1000-1600. Day permits available for both reserves. 21 hides (inc. 10 for disabled), nature trail, interpretative centre at Lyndon. Birdwatching Centre, 4-seat electric buggy and conference facilities at Egleton. Reservoir, lagoons, scrapes, woods, meadows, plantations. Outstanding for spring/autumn wader passage and winter wildfowl (inc. Goldeneye, Goosander, rare grebes, all divers); also harriers, owls, passerine flocks, terns (Black, Arctic, breeding Common, occasional Little and Sandwich); wintering Ruff flock. Tim Appleton, Fishponds Cottage, Stamford Road, Oakham, Rutland LE15 8AB. 01572 770651; fax 01572 755931; e-mail awbc@rutlandwater.u-net.com; http://www.rutlandwater.u-net.com

LINCOLNSHIRE

DONNA NOOK-SALTFLEETBY. (2425a) Lincs TNC TF422998. Off A1031 coastal road. Normally unrestricted, but no access when red flags flying during bombing practice. Dunes, slacks, intertidal mudflats, saltmarsh, open lagoons. Uncommon passage migrants, with over 250 species recorded; late summer congregations of terns (esp. Sandwich); migrant waders, ducks; winter Woodcock, Hen Harrier, Short-eared Owl, Brent Geese, Twite, Lapland Bunting, Shore Lark.

FAR INGS. (75a) Lincs TNC TA010233. Barton-upon-Humber. Car park. Visitor centre off Ings Lane, Barton. Access from A1077 W of A15 Humber Bridge roundabout, or from B1218 in Barton. Open during daylight hours. Keep to waymarked route. Permit required for groups of over six. 7 public hides. Reedbeds, open water, wader scrape. Breeding Water Rail, Bearded Tit, warblers (inc. Grasshopper and Lesser Whitethroat); passage waders; winter wildfowl. North Lincs Warden, 01652 634507.

FRAMPTON MARSH. (921a) RSPB TF364385. 4 miles SE of Boston. Signposted from Frampton village off A16 S from Boston. Open at all times. One of the oldest and most extensive areas of saltmarsh on the Wash. High density of breeding Redshank; regular Marsh Harrier in spring and summer; large numbers of wintering Brent Geese; passage and winter waders; regular Hen Harrier, Merlin, Short-eared Owl, Twite and Lapland Bunting. Lewis James, 157 Frieston Road, Boston, Lincs PE21 0JR. Tel/fax 01205 359064.

GIBRALTAR POINT NNR & BIRD OBSERVATORY. (1500a) Lincs TNC TF556580. S of Skegness at NW corner of the Wash. Access via road signposted Skegness; no public transport. No permit, but sanctuary areas restricted. Hides, nature trail, toilets, visitor centre (guided walks in summer). Day parties of 10 and over by prior booking. Foreshore, saltmarsh, mudflats, dune grassland and scrub, freshwater marsh and mere. Nesting Little Terns; good migration point; winter waders, wildfowl (inc. Brent Goose), Short-eared Owl, Hen Harrier, Snow Bunting, Shore Lark. Field Station provides residential facilities all year; full-board accommodation Mar-Nov (max 28); self catering in winter and school holidays. Field Station Warden (bookings) Rachel Breeds. Nature Reserve Warden: Kevin Wilson, Gibraltar Point Field Station, Skegness, Lincs PE24 4SU. 01754 762677

SALTFLEETBY-THEDDLETHORPE DUNES. (1088a) English Nature and Lincs TNC (NNR) TF480900. Public access (inc. 'easy access' trail for disabled from car park at TF468918), but heed warning signs when out. Dunes, foreshore, mudflats, freshwater marsh. Over 270 species on list. 48 regular breeding species inc. 9 warblers. Migrants. Autumn and winter Merlin. Winter Hen Harriers; passage and winter wildfowl and waders. Simon Smith, English Nature, The Maltings, Wharf Road, Grantham, Lincs NG31 6BH. 01476 568431; fax 01476 570927

SNIPE DALES NATURE RESERVE. (150a) Lincs TNC TF320683. Access down track off A1115, 2.1 miles from junction with A158 close to telephone box. Keep to marked route. Wooded valleys, stream, marshy areas. Woodcock, Short-eared Owl; breeding warblers (inc. Grasshopper). Separate entrance to Country Park, which has toilets, information, picnic area. Warden: 01507 588401.

TETNEY MARSHES. (3111a) RSPB TA345025. Near Cleethorpes. Via gate or river bank E of Tetney Lock, which is 2 miles E of A1031 at Tetney. Access at all times. Visitors are asked to keep to the seawalls, especially during the breeding season (Apr-Aug). Saltmarsh, sand-dunes and inter-tidal sandflats. Breeding Little Tern, Redshank, Shelduck; winter Brent Goose, Common Scoter, Wigeon, Bar-tailed Godwit, Knot, Grey and Golden Plovers; all 3 harriers recorded on passage; migrant Whimbrel. Tetney Warden RSPB, 4 Benton Terrace, Sandyford Road, Newcastle upon Tyne NE2 1QU.

WHISBY NATURE PARK. (145a) Lincs TNC SK912662. SW of Lincoln. Moor Lane off Lincoln by-pass. Open during daylight hours. Visitor centre, 2 public hides. Keep to waymarked route. Old sand and gravel pits, copses, scrub. Breeding Great Crested Grebe, Great Spotted Woodpecker, Willow Tit, Nightingale, warblers; passage waders, Black Tern; winter wildfowl (inc. Wigeon, Goosander, Goldeneye). Warden: 01522 500676.

LONDON, GREATER

BEDFONT LAKES COUNTRY PARK. London Borough of Hounslow. TQ079729. From J13 on M25 take A30 towards London; at roundabout take Clockhouse Lane to Ashford (Country Park signposted). Winter 0800-1630; summer 0800-2100. Extensive reedbeds, lakes and rough grassland. Summer Sedge and Reed Warblers, Skylark, Common Tern, Pochard, Ruddy Duck, Hobby; winter Smew, Woodcock, Water Rail, Bittern; passage Wheatear, Whinchat, Redstart, Meadow Pipit. Paths good for wheelchairs. Strict dogs on leads by-law. Nick Butcher, Ranger, Bedfont Lakes Country Park, Clockhouse Lane, Bedfont, Feltham, Middx TW14 8QA. 01784 423556.

CHASE (THE). (120a) London Wildlife Trust. Via Chase Road from Dagenham Road, and Upper Rainham Road. 3 lakes, marsh, scrub, woodland. Heron, Teal, Lapwing, Water Rail, all 3 woodpeckers. Bruce Edwards. 0181 593 8096

SYDENHAM HILL WOOD. (26a) London Wildlife Trust TQ346726. Via Crescent Wood Road, London SE26. Open at all times. Nature trail. Typical woodland and fringe species, inc. Treecreeper, Nuthatch, Long-tailed Tit, warblers, all 3 woodpeckers, Hawfinch. Warden. 0181 699 5698

MANCHESTER, GREATER

ASTLEY MOSS. (85a) Lancs WT SJ692975. S of A580 at Astley; follow Higher Green Lane to Rindle Farm. Permit from Trust required. Remnant peat bog, scrub, oak/birch woodland. Breeding Turtle Dove, Tree Pipit; winter raptors (inc. Merlin, Hen Harrier), finch flocks, thrush flocks; Long- and Short-eared Owls. Dave Woodward, 54 Windermere Road, Leigh, Lancs WN7 1UZ. No tel

AUDENSHAW RESERVOIRS. NW Water SJ915965. Access and parking on Audenshaw Road B6390 at N end of site. No disabled access. Hide (contact R Travis on 0161 330 2607). Permit (free) from D Tomes, NWW Bottoms Office, Woodhead Road, Tintwistle, Glossop SK13 1HS. Major migration point; notable winter gull roost inc. regular Mediterranean Gull; large Goosander roost; many rarities.

ETHEROW COUNTRY PARK. (242a) Stockport MBC SJ965908. B6104 into Compstall near Romiley, Stockport. Open at all times; permit required for conservation area. Keep to paths. Hide, nature trail, visitor centre, scooters for disabled. River Etherow, woodlands, marshy area. Sparrowhawk, Buzzard, Dipper, all 3 woodpeckers, Pied Flycatcher, warblers; winter Brambling, Siskin, Water Rail. John Rowland, Etherow Country Park, Compstall, Stockport, Cheshire SK6 5JD. 0161 427 6937; fax 0161 427 3643

HOLLINGWORTH LAKE COUNTRY PARK. (116a lake with 20a designated nature reserve) NW Water/Rochdale MBC SD942147. 3 miles NE of Rochdale, B6225 to Littleborough, M62 junct 21. Hide, trails, visitor centre, education services. Marsh, open water, willow scrub. Wildfowl, waders and passage birds. Ranger, Hollingworth Lake Country Park, Visitor Centre, Rakewood Road, Littleborough, Lancs OL15 0AQ. 01706 373421

HOPE CARR NATURE RESERVE. NW Water. SJ664986. From A580 E Lancs Road turn N at Greyhound Motel roundabout, L at first lights, first L at mini roundabout. Free parking, disabled access. Hide. Purpose-built scrapes and lake adjoining sludge lagoons of Leigh ETW. Wide variety of breeding and wintering wildfowl; excellent for passage waders; wintering Water Pipit, Green Sandpiper. Joe Grima, Leigh Environmental Education Centre, Hope Carr, Hope Carr Lane, Leigh WN7 3XB. 01942 269027; fax 01942 269028

PENNINGTON FLASH COUNTRY PARK. SJ640990. Signposted from A580 E Lancs Road. Car park, disabled access, toilets, information point, mobile cafe, 7 hides. Wide variety of breeding and wintering wildfowl; passage and breeding warblers, waders and terns; wintering Long-eared Owls; finches, tits etc. attracted to feeding station all year. Recent rarities inc. American Wigeon, Blue-winged Teal, Arctic Redpoll, Black-faced Bunting. Peter Alker, Pennington Flash Country Park, St Helens Road, Leigh WN7 3PA. Tel/fax 01942 605253

MERSEYSIDE

DEE ESTUARY. (10000a) Wirral MBC SJ253815. Beach viewpoint 500 metres along shore N of Banks Road, Lower Heswall. Large passage and winter wader roosts (from 2.5 hours before time of high water) inc Dunlin, Redshank, Spotted Redshank, Greenshank, Curlew, Knot, Black-tailed Godwit, Golden Plover. Large numbers of winter duck (inc. Shelduck, Teal, Wigeon, Pintail, Red-breasted Merganser); also winter Peregrine, Merlin, Hen Harrier, Short-eared Owl. Senior Area Ranger, Wirral Country Park Centre, Station Road, Thurstaston, Wirral CH61 0HN. 0151 648 4371/3884; www.wirral.gov.uk/leisure/ranger.htm

HILBRE ISLAND. (14a) Wirral MBC (LNR) SJ184880. Tidal island at mouth of Dee estuary. Reached by 2 mile walk across sands from West Kirby. Do not cross either way within 3 hours of high water (tide times and suggested safe route on noticeboard at Dee Lane slipway by N end of Marine Lake). Prior booking for parties of 6 or more. Passage migrants. Flocks of waders at high water; Purple Sandpiper; raptors; autumn Gannet, terns, skuas, seaduck, divers, grebes, also Leach's Petrel in numbers after 2/3 days of NW winds. Dee Estuary Ranger, 0151 632 4455. Access information and bookings from Wirral Country Park Centre, Station Road, Thurstaston, Wirral CH61 0HN. 0151 648 4371/3884. **HILBRE BIRD OBSERVATORY.** Established in 1957 as Ringing Station. Heligoland traps in private ground, some mist-netting. Visitors and use of seawatch hide by prior appointment. No accommodation. For birdwatching information on the island (inc. Obs) contact C J Williams, 17 Bridge Road, West Kirby, Wirral (0151 625 5848); for up-to-date news and Annual Report contact S J Williams (0151 625 2146); otherwise Ringing Secretary, John Gittins, 17 Deva Road, West Kirby, Wirral CH48 4DB (0151 625 5428).

MARSHSIDE. (272a) RSPB SD355202. From Southport take coast road N; car park by sand-winning plant at SD352204. Open access. Keep to paths; also keep to pavement along Marine Drive south of car park to avoid disturbing birds. Hide 300m N of car park; second planned. Coastal grazing marsh, saltmarsh, sand-flats on S shore of Ribble estuary. Breeding Lapwing, Redshank, Snipe. Wintering Pink-footed Geese (10,000), Wigeon (7,000), Black-tailed Godwit (1,000), Ruff, Golden Plover, Peregrine, Merlin, Short-eared Owl. Tony Baker, Beechwood, Cat Tail Lane, Scarisbrick, Southport, Merseyside PR8 5LW. Tel/fax 01704 233003; mobile 0589 386008

SEAFORTH NATURE RESERVE. (50a) Lancs WT SJ318973. 5 miles NNW from Liverpool city centre. From A565 through Freeport entrance at Crosby Road South. Pedestrian access only. Parties by arrangement. Visitor centre, 3 hides. Fresh- and saltwater lagoons, marsh, scrub. Breeding Common Tern, Ringed Plover; spring and autumn migrants, up to 500 Little Gulls in April; passage/winter waders, Mediterranean, Iceland and Glaucous Gulls. Steve White, Seaforth Nature Reserve, Port of Liverpool L21 1JD. 0151 920 3769; e-mail lwildlife@cix.co.uk

NORFOLK

BERNEY MARSHES. RSPB TG465055. W of Great Yarmouth. Public footpath by Berney Arms Station on the Norwich to Yarmouth railway line NE of Reedham. Boat service to reserve departs from Burgh Castle Marina first Su of month at 1000 & 1400, returning 1300 & 1600 (phone 01493 700645 to book). In the Halvergate

Marshes. Winter Bewick's Swan, Wigeon, birds of prey (inc. Hen Harrier, Merlin, Peregrine, Short-eared Owl). Spring migrants can include Spoonbill, Little Egret, Ruff. Warden, Ashtree Farm, Goodchild Marine, Butt Lane, Burgh Castle, Great Yarmouth, Norfolk NR31 9PE.

BLAKENEY POINT. (1100a) National Trust (NNR) TG000465. By boat from Morston or Blakeney Quays (car parks), or by walking W for 3.5 miles from Cley beach. Main nesting areas wired off during breeding season. Guide books and information at Lifeboat House; interpretative display, public hides. Shingle spit, dunes, saltmarsh. Breeding terns (Common, Little, Sandwich); autumn migrants, waders, skuas; winter duck and large numbers of Dark-bellied Brent Geese. Joe Reed, 35 The Cornfields, Langham, Holt, Norfolk NR25 7DQ. Tel/fax 01263 740241

CLEY MARSHES. (423a) Norfolk WT TG055441. Permits obtainable from visitor centre on S side of A149, half mile E of Cley village. 1 Apr-31 Oct daily except M; 1 Nov-31 Mar permits from Warden's House (NWT members free). Hides, observation hut with telescope, interpretative centre. Reedbeds, freshwater and saltmarsh, scrapes, grazed saltings, shingle ridge. Bittern, Bearded Tit, Ruff, Black-tailed Godwit, Black Tern, Spoonbill, Avocet, Spotted Redshank, many species of duck. Bernard Bishop, Watcher's Cottage, Cley, Holt, Norfolk NR25 7RZ. 01263 740008

EAST WRETHAM HEATH. (362a) Norfolk WT TL913887. On A1075. Open all year 1000-1700. Nature trail. Breckland heath, meres, pine woodland. Crossbill, Long-eared Owl, Hawfinch and Hen Harrier in winter; wildfowl and waders on fluctuating meres.

HICKLING BROAD. (1360a) Norfolk WT (NNR) TG428222. Follow tourist signs from Hickling village. NWT members free. Open all year 1000-1700. Winter closing at dusk. Visitor centre open Apr-Sep; nature trails. Water trail May-Sep, booking essential. Open water, reed and sedge beds, oak woodland. Bearded Tit, Marsh Harrier, Bittern, Gadwall, Garganey; migrant waders (esp. Black-tailed Godwit, Ruff, Little Stint); Black Tern, Osprey, Little Gull, Spoonbill. John Blackburn, Warden's House, Hickling NNR, Stubbs Mill, Hickling, Norwich NR12 0BW. 01692 598276

HOLKHAM. (9700a) English Nature (NNR) TF890450. From Holkham village turn N off A149 down Lady Ann's Drive; parking. Sandflats, dunes, marshes, pinewoods. Access unrestricted, but keep to paths and off grazing marshes and farmland. Passage migrants and winter wildfowl, inc. Brent, Pink-footed and White-fronted Geese; breeding Little Tern. R Harold, Hill Farm Offices, Main Road, Holkham, Wells-next-the-Sea NR23 1AB. 01328 711183; fax 01328 711893

HOLME BIRD OBSERVATORY. Founded 1962. Norfolk Ornithologists' Assocn (NOA). In 10 acres of diverse habitat: sand dunes, Corsican pines, scrub and reed-fringed lagoon, making this a migration hot spot. Several hides (seawatch hide reserved for NOA members). Reserve open daily to members dawn to dusk; non-members 0900-1700 by permit from the Observatory. Parties by prior arrangement. Species list over 320; ringed species 141; recent rarities have included Laughing Gull, Collared Pratincole and Woodchat Shrike. Jed Andrews, Holme Bird Observatory, Broadwater Road, Holme, Hunstanton, Norfolk PE36 6LQ. 01485 525406

HOLME DUNES. (700a) Norfolk WT (NNR) TF697438. By car from Holme village (turn R before golf course and beach) or walk along Thornham sea wall. Open all year round 1000-1700. Permit required (NWT members free). Foreshore, dunes, saltmarsh, fresh marsh. Water Rail, Green Sandpiper, Avocet, Greenshank, Snow Bunting, 'chats', warblers, Marsh Harrier, Arctic Skua. Gary Hibberd, The Firs, Broadwater Road, Holme-next-Sea, Hunstanton, Norfolk PE36 6LQ. 01485 525240

NUNNERY LAKES. (200a) BTO TL872834. Thetford. Via footpath along E bank of Little Ouse from Nuns' Bridge, or footpath along S bank of R Thet from Arlington Way near Melford bridge roundabout. Open during daylight hours. Keep to marked paths; keep dogs on lead. Groups welcome by prior arrangement with BTO. Waymarked paths; site information boards and observation hide. Flood meadows, fen, open water, woodland, grass heath, scrub. Breeding birds: Egyptian Goose, Kingfisher, Gadwall, Lapwing, Little Ringed Plover, Willow Tit, Nightingale, Grasshopper and Sedge Warblers. Passage waders, Wheatear. Winter Water Rail, Jack Snipe, Hawfinch, Siskin. Chris Gregory, BTO, The Nunnery, Thetford, Norfolk IP24 2PU. 01842 750050

REDWELL MARSH. (35a) Norfolk Ornithologists' Association TF702436. View from public footpath from centre of Holme village to Broadwater Road. Open at all times. Hide due 2000 (subject to planning). Wet grazing marsh with ditches, pond and large wader scrape. Wildfowl and waders (inc. Avocet, Black-tailed Godwit, Curlew/Green/Wood Sandpipers). Recent Marsh Harrier, Ring-necked Parakeet, Waxwing. Jed Andrews, Holme Bird Observatory, Broadwater Road, Holme, Hunstanton, Norfolk PE36 6LQ. 01485 525406

SCOLT HEAD ISLAND. (1821a) English Nature (NNR) TF820460. Boat from Brancaster Staithe on A149. Walking at low tide is dangerous. Ternery closed during breeding season. Nature trail Apr-Sep. Mudflats, saltmarsh, shingle. Common, Little and Sandwich Terns; passage/winter wildfowl (esp. Pink-footed and Dark-bellied Brent Geese), waders, skuas. Contact: Michael Rooney, English Nature, Hill Farm Offices, Main Road, Holkham, Wells-next-the-Sea NR23 1AB. 01328 711166

SNETTISHAM. (3250a) RSPB TF647335. Near Hunstanton. Beach is signposted from A149 King's Lynn-Hunstanton. Along beach overlooking reserve. Park in car park signposted from beach road. Disabled visitors should contact Warden re arrangements. 4 hides. Flooded pits, saltmarsh, shingle beach, mudflats. Terns, huge numbers of waders (inc. 100,000 Knot, 5000 Bar-tailed Godwit, 800 Sanderling) and winter wildfowl (inc. 30,000 Pink-footed Geese, 1400 Brent). Jim Scott, 43 Lynn Road, Snettisham, King's Lynn, Norfolk PE31 7LR. 01485 542689

STRUMPSHAW FEN. (599a) RSPB TG342066. Near Norwich. Entrance across level-crossing from car park reached by turning sharp right and right again into Low Road from Brundall, off A47 to Great Yarmouth. Toilet. Mixed fen, broads, woodland and marshes. Start at car park reception hide. Summer Marsh Harrier, Bearded Tit, Cetti's Warbler, Water Rail; winter Hen Harrier, Bean and White-fronted Geese. Warden, Staithe Cottage, Low Road, Strumpshaw, Norwich NR13 4HS. 01603 715191

SURLINGHAM CHURCH MARSH. (68a) RSPB TG304066. 6 miles E of Norwich, S of R Yare, N of A146 Norwich to Lowestoft road. Footpaths from Surlingham church run around reserve. Open at all times (NB nearby shooting W Su). Two hides. Broadland marsh with dykes, shallow pools, reedfen and sedge beds, alder and willow carr. Breeding Reed, Sedge & Grasshopper Warblers; Cuckoo, Marsh Harrier; passage waders (inc. Green Sandpiper); winter Hen Harrier, wildfowl (inc. Gadwall, Teal, Shoveler, Shelduck, geese) and waders (inc. Snipe and Jack Snipe). Contact: as Strumpshaw Fen (above).

TITCHWELL MARSH. (937a) RSPB TF749436. Near Hunstanton. Footpath along sea wall from A149 between Thornham and Titchwell. Reserve and hides open at all times. Visitor centre, shop and servery open every day 1000-1700, but 1000-1600 Nov-Mar (closed 25 & 26 Dec). Reedbed, brackish & freshwater pools, saltmarsh, dunes, shingle. Nesting Avocet, Bearded Tit, Water Rail, Marsh Harrier, Reed and Sedge Warblers, Little Tern; flocks of Knot in autumn; winter Brent Geese, Goldeneye,

Scoter, Eider, Hen Harrier roost, Snow Bunting and Shorelark on beach. Warden, Titchwell Marsh Reserve, King's Lynn, Norfolk PE31 8BB. 01485 210432

WALSEY HILLS. (2a) Norfolk Ornithologists' Association TG062441. Up footpath and steps from A149 at Cley. Open daily throughout year. Wardened visitor centre providing up-to-date birding information. Short walk through scrub and beside Snipe's Marsh (Norfolk WT). Excellent views across adjoining reserves between Cley and Salthouse. Important migration watchpoint. Recent sightings include Bittern, Short-eared and Long-eared Owls, White Stork, Rough-legged Buzzard, Osprey, Merlin, Crane, Red-necked Phalarope, Marsh Warbler, Bluethroat, Rustic Bunting. Tom Fletcher, 01263 740875

WEETING HEATH. (343a) Norfolk WT (NNR) TL756881. On L of Hockwold Road W of Weeting. Permit from Warden (Apr-Aug). Information hut in car park. 4 hides. Stone Curlew, Woodlark, Hobby. Parties must book in advance: 01842 827615 (Apr-Aug) or 01842 755010.

THE WASH NNR. (21,168a) English Nature TF540270. Access at TF613203 from Peter Scott Walk along sea wall, West Lynn; or at TF493256, east bank of River Nene, Lincs. Unrestricted. Visitors should keep to sea wall footpath due to dangerous nature of the site. Saltmarsh and intertidal mud. Wintering and passage Grey Plover, Knot, Dunlin, Oystercatcher, Bar-tailed Godwit, Pink-footed and Brent Geese, Shelduck, Wigeon. Breeding Redshank. Simon Smith, English Nature East Midlands, The Maltings, Wharf Road, Grantham, Lincs NG31 6BH. 01476 568431

WELNEY. (922a) WWT Centre TL548946. All visitors please report at reception, tourist signposted from the A10 and A1101. Open daily except 25 Dec, 1000-1700. Also evening visits to view swans under floodlights Nov-end Feb. Parties must book in advance. Two-mile trail across Ouse Washes throughout summer months. Observatory, hides. Winter wildfowl esp. Bewick's and Whooper Swans, Wigeon, Pintail. Breeding Garganey, Black-tailed Godwit. Carl Mitchell, Centre Manager, The Wildfowl & Wetlands Trust, Hundred Foot Bank, Welney, Wisbech, Cambs PE14 7TN. 01353 860711

NORTHAMPTONSHIRE

DAVENTRY RESERVOIR COUNTRY PARK. (137a) Daventry DC SP577642. Signposted from B4036 Daventry to Welton road. Open at all times. 2 hides (combinations for locks from Rangers - bring proof of identity), cafe, visitor centre. Open water, wetlands, reed, meadows, woodland. Autumn passage waders inc. Dunlin, Ruff, Greenshank, Green Sandpiper; Common Terns nest, Arctic and sometimes Black on passage; gull roost; rare species inc. Pacific Swift, Baird's Sandpiper, Wilson's Phalarope, Sabine's Gull. Over 180 species recorded; 60 have bred. Dewi Morris, Daventry Country Park, Reservoir Cottage, Northern Way, Daventry, Northants NN11 5JB. 01327 877193

PITSFORD RESERVOIR. (480a) (N section) WT for Northants SP780708. View from causeway on Holcot to Brixworth road. Permits to enter reserve and use the 8 hides from fishing lodge by causeway or by writing to Warden. Large reservoir with grassland and woodland surrounds. Passage waders and terns. Winter wildfowl (inc. Pintail, Goldeneye, Goosander); less common divers and grebes. 224 species recorded. Warden: Cliff Christie.

SHORT WOOD. (62a) WT for Northants TL015913. Via bridle path from road between Glapthorn and Southwick. Park on roadside verge. Primary and secondary mixed woodland (oak, ash, field maple, hazel), coppiced. Woodcock, Marsh Tit, warblers, Redpoll.

STANFORD RESERVOIR. (169a) WT for Northants/Severn Trent Water SP605805. View from the South Kilworth/Thornby road where it crosses the R Avon. Hides. Migrant waders and terns; winter duck, inc. Ruddy Duck, Goldeneye and Goosander. Phil Richardson, 10 Bedford Cottages, Great Brington, Northampton NN7 4JE. 01604 770632

SUMMER LEYS LNR. (117a) Northants CC SP885634. 2 miles S of Wellingborough. Signposted off Great Doddington to Wollaston road. Open at all times. Keep to waymarked perimeter path. Dogs on leads. No permit required. Car park, hides with wheelchair access. Flooded gravel pit with islands; scrape, ponds, grassland, marsh. Summer: breeding Gadwall, Common Tern, Little Ringed and Ringed Plovers, Redshank, Tree Sparrow, plus regular Garganey, Hobby, Kingfisher. Passage waders (inc. Wood, Green and Curlew Sandpipers, Little Stint), Black Tern, Little Gull, Marsh Harrier. Winter: wildfowl (inc. Smew, Goldeneye), waders (inc. Dunlin and nationally important numbers of Golden Plover), Little Grebe. Steve Brayshaw. 01604 236633

THRAPSTON GRAVEL PITS & TITCHMARSH LNR. (190a) WT for Northants TL008804. Public footpath from layby on A605 N of Thrapston. Alder/birch/willow wood; old duck decoy. Breeding Heron (no access to Heronry), warblers; migrants, inc. Red-necked and Slavonian Grebes; summer Common Tern, Little Ringed Plover; Bittern and Marsh Harrier recorded.

NORTHUMBERLAND

ARNOLD RESERVE, CRASTER. (3a) Northumb WT NU255197. SW of Craster village. Public footpath from car park in disused quarry. Semi-natural woodland and scrub near coast. Migrant passerines can inc. Bluethroat, Red-breasted Flycatcher, Barred and Icterine Warblers, Wryneck; moulting site for Lesser Redpoll.

BRIARWOOD BANKS. (59a) Northumb WT NY791620. At Plankey Mill 3 miles SW of Haydon Bridge. Footpaths open to public. Ancient woodland along steep valley. Pied Flycatcher, Wood Warbler, Redstart, Dipper, Woodcock, Treecreeper, Nuthatch.

COCKLAWBURN DUNES. (14a) Northumb WT NU033481. SE of Scremeston off A1 4 miles S of Berwick. Open access. Dunes, rocky shore. Eider, waders, good seawatching.

COQUET ISLAND. (16a) RSPB NU294046. Boat trips around island arranged with Dave Gray 01665 711975. No landings. Colonies of Eider, Puffin, terns (inc. Roseate). RSPB Warden, c/o RSPB North of England Office.

DRURIDGE BAY RESERVES. Northumb WT. S of Amble. HAUXLEY (67a) NU285023 approached by track from road midway between High and Low Hauxley. Visitor centre, 5 hides (1 suitable for disabled). Disabled toilet. Lake with islands behind dunes. Good for spring and autumn passage (inc. divers, skuas). Summer for coastal birds, esp. terns (inc. Roseate). DRURIDGE POOLS (61a) NZ274965.

3 hides. Deep lake and wet meadows with pools behind dunes. Especially good in spring. Winter and breeding wildfowl; passage and breeding waders. CRESSWELL POND (49a) NZ283943. Half mile N of Cresswell. Hide. Shallow brackish lagoon behind dunes fringed by saltmarsh and reedbed, some mudflats. Good for waders, esp. on passage. Day permits for all 3 reserves from: Jim Martin, Hauxley Nature Reserve, Low Hauxley, Amble, Morpeth, Northumberland. 01665 711578

FARNE ISLANDS. National Trust (NNR). Opposite Bamburgh (NU180355). Only Inner Farne and Staple Island are open to visitors. Apr-Sep. Weather permitting, there are daily boat excursions from Seahouses (contact Billy Shiel 01665 720308). School parties by prior booking with Warden. Breeding Eider, Kittiwake, terns (inc. Roseate and Sandwich), auks. John Walton, 8 St Aidan's, Seahouses, Northumberland NE68 7SR. 01665 720651

GRINDON LOUGH. (220a) Northumb WT NY806677. View from unclassified road W of Grindon Hill, 3 miles NW of Haydon Bridge. No access to lakeside. Noted for geese (esp Greylag and Pink-footed) and Whooper Swans.

HOLYWELL POND. (35a) Northumb WT NZ319752. N of Holywell near Seaton Delaval on A192. Public hide (suitable for disabled) accessed from public footpath leading from housing estate. Good for winter wildfowl (inc. Goldeneye, Greylag Geese).

LINDISFARNE. (8101a) English Nature (NNR) NU094428. Several roads E of A1(T); to Holy Island via causeway (impassable at high tide) from Beal. Hide at Holy Island Lough. Dunes, saltmarshes, mudflats. Passage/winter wildfowl and waders; only regular British wintering ground of Svalbard Pale-bellied Brent Goose; Long-tailed Duck, Whooper Swan; migrants (inc. Yellow-browed Warbler, Red-breasted Flycatcher). Phil Davey, English Nature, Beal Station, Berwick-on-Tweed TD15 2SP. 01289 381470

NOTTINGHAMSHIRE

ATTENBOROUGH GRAVEL PITS. (240a) RNC Aggregates with Notts WT SK525350. From A6005 S of Beeston. Essential to keep to footpaths. Gravel pits, reeds, alder and willow along R Trent. Breeding Common Tern; Cormorants regular; passage waders and Black Tern; winter duck and sawbills.

COLWICK COUNTRY PARK. (250a) Nottingham City Council SK610395. Off A612 3 mi E of Nottingham city centre. Open at all times, but no vehicle access after dusk or before 0700. Nature trails. Sightings log book in Fishing Lodge. Lakes, pools, woodlands, grasslands, new plantations, River Trent. Summer warblers, Hobby, Common Tern (15+ pairs); winter wildfowl and gulls; passage migrants. Mark Dennis, The Fishing Lodge, Colwick Country Park, River Road, Colwick, Nottingham NG4 2DW. 0115 987 0785; http://www.colwick2000.freeserve.co.uk

LOUND. (1200a) Powergen, with Notts WT and Idle Valley Society. SK690856. 2 miles N of Retford off A638 adjacent to Sutton village. Open at all times. Use public rights of way only. Working gravel quarries, fish ponds, river valley, infilled and disused fly ash tanks, farmland, scrub, open water. Summer gulls and terns; passage waders and raptors; winter wildfowl; rarities inc. Ring-billed Gull, Caspian and White-winged Black Terns; Lesser Scaup, Richard's Pipit, Baird's Sandpiper. Lound Bird Club, c/o 23 Milne Road, Bircotes, Doncaster DN11 8AL. 01302 742779

OXFORDSHIRE

ASTON ROWANT. (320a) English Nature (NNR) SU731966. Leave M40 at Junction 5 or 6 on to old A40 then Christmas Common Road (look for signs to reserve car park). Open access but groups contact Site Manager in advance. Chalk grassland, scrub, mature beech woodland. Red Kite, Woodcock, Little and Tawny Owls, Green and Great Spotted Woodpeckers, warblers, Hawfinch. Ring Ouzel, Wheatear on spring passage. Winter Brambling, Siskin, Redpoll. Contact English Nature 01844 351833.

OTMOOR NATURE RESERVE. (543a) RSPB SP569126. From Beckley village (NE of Oxford) follow road to E of Abingdon Arms (marked as dead end); turn R into Otmoor Lane, then L at end of road (1 mile). Take care: narrow lane used by children, walkers, horse riders. Open during daylight hours, but call Warden before visiting as site still under development. Do not park outside car park. Mainly grassland with small reedbed. Breeding Shoveler, Gadwall, Redshank, Lapwing, Curlew, Snipe, Grasshopper Warbler, Bullfinch; wintering birds include Wigeon, Pintail, Golden Plover, Peregrine, Merlin. Neil Lambert, RSPB, c/o Lower Farm, Noke, Oxford OX3 9TX. 01865 848385; mobile 07801 030392

VICARAGE PIT. (23a) Berks, Bucks & Oxon NT SP400057. The whole reserve is visible from the road, one mile W of Stanton Harcourt. Open water with reed margins. Wildfowl and passage migrants. Contact: Trust HQ.

SHROPSHIRE

CLUNTON COPPICE. (56a) Shrops WT SO343806. Park in Clunton village and walk S into the woodland. Open at all times. Access along road and public rights of way only. Oak coppice. Buzzard and Raven regular; wide range of woodland birds, inc. Redstart, Wood Warbler and Pied Flycatcher in summer. Contact: Trust HQ.

LLYNCLYS HILL. (102a) Shrops WT SJ273237. SSW of Oswestry. Park in layby on A495 at SJ277242 and walk up Turner's Lane. Open at all times. Old mixed limestone woodland and scrub. Sparrowhawk, Green Woodpecker, Goldcrest, large warbler population. Occasional Peregrine, Buzzard. Contact: Trust HQ.

WOOD LANE. Shrops WT SJ425327. Turn off A528 at Spurnhill near Ellesmere. Open at all times. Car parks. Hides (access by permit). Gravel pit. Breeding Sand Martins. Popular staging post for waders (inc. Redshank, Greenshank, Ruff, Dunlin, Little Stint, Green and Wood Sandpipers). Wintering Lapwing and Curlew. Contact: Trust HQ.

SOMERSET

AVON GORGE. (154a) National Trust (NNR) ST555730. Entrance in North Road, Leigh Woods between Clifton Suspension Bridge and A369 (M5 J19 to Bristol). Open at all times. Keep to paths. Mixed broadleaved woodland, open grassland, scrub on limestone cliffs. Specialities: Hawfinch, Lesser Spotted Woodpecker, Wood

Warbler; Peregrine (best seen from Clifton side of gorge). The National Trust, 1 Rangers Cottage, Valley Road, Leigh Woods, Bristol BS8 3PZ. 0117 973 1645

AVONMOUTH SEWAGE WORKS. (25a) Avon WT/Wessex Water ST533797. Lane connecting Kings Weston and Lawrence Weston Lanes near Avonmouth. Hide. Some of reserve visible from road. Permits from Wildlife Trust (members only). Artificial pools, rough grassland. Winter wildfowl (inc. Gadwall, Shoveler, Pochard); autumn waders (inc. Common and Green Sandpipers); occasional terns; one of very few sites in area for Tree Sparrow.

BLAGDON LAKE. (440a) Bristol Water plc. ST510600. Reservoir between Butcombe and Blagdon, 11 miles SW of Bristol. Overlooked from A368, with a mile of public footpath (outside the reservoir enclosure) along SE side from E tip of lake near Ubley westwards to Holt Farm; also public access to wooded N tip, from N end of dam wall carrying Blagdon/Butcombe byway. Birds and permits as Chew (below), though birds fewer; permits give access to private paths and 2 hides.

BRIDGWATER BAY. (6000a) English Nature (NNR) ST280465. N of A39 at Cannington. Permit required for Stert Island; access on Fenning Island restricted to hides (closed 25 Dec). Car park. Tidal mudflats (can be treacherous), saltmarsh. Mainly wintering wildfowl and waders, spring and autumn passage migrants, moulting Shelduck in mid-summer. R M Prowse, Dowells Farm, Steart, Bridgwater, Somerset TA5 2PX. 01278 652426

CATCOTT LOWS. (127a) Somerset WT ST400415. Off A39 about 7 miles W of Street. Car park, 2 hides. Seasonally flooded grassland, scrapes all year. Winter ducks, swans, waders, raptors; spring wader passage, esp. Whimbrel. D E Reid, c/o Trust HQ.

CHEW VALLEY LAKE. (1200a) Bristol Water plc/Avon WT ST570600. Reservoir (partly a Trust reserve) between Chew Stoke and West Harptree, crossed by A368 and B3114, 9 miles S of Bristol. Permit for access to hides (5 at Chew, 2 at Blagdon). Best roadside viewing from causeways at Herriott's Bridge (nature reserve) and Herons Green Bay. Day and year permits from Bristol Water, Recreation Department, Woodford Lodge, Chew Stoke, Bristol BS18 8SH. Tel/fax 01275 332339. Autumn/winter concentrations of wildfowl (inc. Bewick's Swan, Goldeneye, Smew, Ruddy Duck), gull roost (inc. regular Mediterranean, occasional Ring-billed). Migrant waders and terns (inc. Black). Recent rarities inc. Blue-winged Teal, Spoonbill, Alpine Swift, Citrine Wagtail, Little Bunting, Ring-necked Duck, Kumlien's Gull.

EBBOR GORGE. (101a) English Nature (NNR) ST523485. Access from car park on Wookey Hole to Priddy road, NW of Wells, from 0830 to dusk. Display centre, waymarked paths. Woodland, some grassland & scrub, limestone cliffs. Buzzard, Woodcock, Sparrowhawk, Lesser Spotted Woodpecker, Lesser Whitethroat; occasional Merlin. R G Corns, English Nature, Roughmoor, Bishop's Hull, Taunton, Somerset TA1 5AA. 01823 283211; fax 01823 272978

HURSCOMBE-WIMBLEBALL LAKE. (46a) Somerset WT SS974317. Four miles NE of Dulverton. Nature trail. Reservoir, mud, woodland, scrub, grassland. Wintering wildfowl. Miss Joan Loraine, Greencombe, Porlock, Minehead, Somerset TA24 8NU. 01643 862363

LANGFORD HEATHFIELD. (226a) Somerset WT ST106227. Oak/ash woodland, birch/willow scrub, wet heath. Lesser Spotted Woodpecker, Marsh Tit; warblers (inc. Wood, Garden), Barn Owl, Redstart, Tree Pipit. Contact: Trust HQ.

SAND POINT/MIDDLE HOPE. National Trust ST326660. N of Weston-super-Mare. Footpaths from car park at N end of Sand Bay. Second car park near Woodspring Priory at Huckers Bow. Coastal scrub, grassland. Migration watchpoint. Ring Ouzel, Wheatear, Redstart, Pied Flycatcher, Grasshopper and other warblers in spring. Finches, Yellow Wagtail, visible migration in autumn. Occasional seabirds (Gannet, Manx Shearwater, Fulmar) and sea duck off Sand Point.

STEEP HOLM ISLAND. (50a) Kenneth Allsop Memorial Trust ST228607. Day trips on boats from Weston-super-Mare, generally Sa, W, Bank Hol M, Apr-Oct. Nature trail. Limestone cliffs. Breeding Cormorant, Shelduck, Great Black-backed, Lesser Black-backed and Herring Gulls; autumn passerines. For boat, booking and other details tel: Joan Rendell 01934 632307.

WALBOROUGH. (40a) Avon WT ST315579. Access from Uphill boatyard. Special access trail suitable for less able visitors. Limestone grassland, scrub, saltmarsh, estuary. The Axe Estuary holds good numbers of migrant and wintering wildfowl (inc. Teal, Shelduck) and waders (inc. Black-tailed Godwit, Lapwing, Golden Plover, Dunlin, Redshank). Other migrants inc. Little Stint, Curlew Sandpiper, Ruff. Little Egrets occur each year, mostly in late summer. Contact: Trust HQ.

WEST SEDGEMOOR. (1400a) RSPB ST361238. Entrance down by-road off A378 Taunton-Langport road, 1 mile E of Fivehead. Access at all times to woodland car park, heronry hide, and moor viewpoint. Part of the Somerset Levels wet grasslands. Breeding Grey Heron, Curlew, Lapwing, Redshank, Snipe, Buzzard, Sedge Warbler; passage Whimbrel and Hobby in spring; large flocks of wintering waders and wildfowl (inc. Lapwing, Golden Plover, Shoveler, Teal, Wigeon). John Leece, Dewlands Farm, Redhill, Curry Rivel, Langport, Somerset TA10 0PH. 01458 252805

WESTHAY MOOR NNR. (283a) Somerset WT ST458438. NW of Glastonbury. Along drove from Westhay to Godney minor road. 3 hides open at all times. Lakes, reedbeds with typha and phragmites, islands. Winter wildfowl (inc. Goosander); spring/summer Black Tern, Hobby, warblers (inc. Reed, Sedge, Cetti's, Grasshopper). D E Reid, c/o Trust HQ.

WILLSBRIDGE MILL. (20a) Avon WT ST665708. Turn N off A431 at Longwell Green along Long Beach Road, park after quarter mile in car park overlooking valley. Unrestricted access; visitor centre, nature trail. Broadleaved woodland, grassland, scrub, stream, pond. High densities of birds of woodland and scrub. Kingfisher and Dipper regular in winter. Ruth Worsley, Willsbridge Mill, Willsbridge Hill, Bristol BS15 6EX. 0117 932 6885

STAFFORDSHIRE

BELVIDE RESERVOIR. (182a) British Waterways Board and West Midland Bird Club SJ865102. Near Brewood, 7 miles NW of Wolverhampton. Access only by permit from the West Midland Bird Club. Hides. Important breeding, moulting and wintering ground for wildfowl; passage terns and waders. Miss M Surman, 6 Lloyd Square, 12 Niall Close, Edgbaston, Birmingham B15 3LX.

BLACK BROOK. (300a) Staffs WT SK020645. N of Leek, W of A53. West of road from Royal Cottage to Gib Tor. Access is via public footpath from Gib Tor to Newstone Farm; this first passes through a conifer plantation which is outside the reserve. Heather and bilberry moorland, and upland acidic grassland. Merlin, Kestrel,

Red Grouse, Golden Plover, Snipe, Curlew, Dipper, Ring Ouzel, Wheatear, Whinchat, Twite. Contact: Trust HQ.

BLITHFIELD RESERVOIR. (800a) South Staffs Waterworks Co. SK058237. View from causeway on B5013 (Rugeley/Uttoxeter). Access to reservoir and hides by permit from West Midland Bird Club. Good populations of wintering wildfowl (inc. Bewick's Swan, Goosander, Goldeneye, Ruddy Duck), large gull roost (can inc. Glaucous, Iceland), passage terns (Common, Arctic, Black) and waders, esp. in autumn (Little Stint, Curlew Sandpiper, Spotted Redshank regular). Miss M Surman, 6 Lloyd Square, 12 Niall Close, Edgbaston, Birmingham B15 3LX.

CASTERN WOOD. (51a) Staffs WT SK119537. E of Leek. Unclassified road SE of Wetton. Limestone grassland and woodland. All 3 woodpeckers, warblers, Pied Flycatcher, Sparrowhawk. Contact: Trust HQ.

COOMBES VALLEY. (370a) RSPB SK009534. S of A523 (Leek-Ashbourne), 1 mile along minor road to Apesford. Open each day 0900-2100, or sunset if earlier. Information centre. Wooded valley, stream. Breeding Sparrowhawk, Tawny and Long-eared Owls, Kingfisher, Dipper, Redstart, Pied Flycatcher, Wood Warbler, Tree Pipit. Maurice Waterhouse, Six Oaks Farm, Bradnop, Leek, Staffs ST13 7EU. 01538 384017

DOXEY MARSHES. (260a) Staffs WT SJ904252. Stafford, NW of town; keep to footpaths. Hide, observation platform. Marshes, large pools, wet meadows, scrape. Breeding Redshank and Snipe; Sedge, Reed and Grasshopper Warblers. Breeding and wintering duck. Passage migrants, inc. rarities. Contact: Trust HQ.

LONGSDON WOODS. (240a) Staffs WT SK965555. Reserve lies off A53 Leek road. Can be approached from Ladderedge near Leek; City Lane, Longsdon; or Rudyard Station. Access restricted to public rights of way. Woodland and wet grassland. Heronry; Sparrowhawk; Curlew, Snipe, Jack Snipe, Woodcock; Little and Tawny Owls; all 3 woodpeckers; Redstart, Blackcap, Garden Warbler. Contact: Trust HQ.

SUFFOLK

BRADFIELD WOODS. (170a) Suffolk WT (NNR) TL935581. 7 miles SE of Bury St Edmunds. Open during daylight hours. Hide. Visitor centre open Su 1300-1700 Easter to end Sep, also Bank Hol Mondays. Ancient coppiced working woodland. Wide range of breeding woodland species (inc. Nightingale). Warden: Peter Fordham, Felsham Road, Bradfield St George, Bury St Edmunds, Suffolk IP30 0HU. W:01449 737996; H:01284 810379

CARLTON MARSHES. (114a) Suffolk WT TM508920. SW of Lowestoft. Open during daylight hours. Keep to marked paths. Wide range of wetland and Broadland birds. Nick Sanderson, Suffolk Broads Wildlife Centre, Carlton Colville, Lowestoft, Suffolk NR33 8HU. 01502 564250

DINGLE MARSHES. (630a) Suffolk WT and RSPB. Between Dunwich and Walberswick. Park at Dunwich Beach car park; keep to designated footpaths; dogs under control. Open during daylight hours. Coastal wetland, inc. grazing marsh, salty lagoons, shingle and reedbed. Breeding waders (inc. Avocet), Bittern. Passage waders and wintering wildfowl. Warden: Alan Miller 01728 748292.

HAZELWOOD MARSHES. (148a) Suffolk WT TM435575. 4 miles W of Aldeburgh. Small car park on A1094. Mile walk down sandy track. Open dawn to dusk. Hide. Estuary, marshes. Marshland and estuary birds; spring and autumn migrants. Rodney West, Flint Cottage, Stone Common, Blaxhall, Woodbridge, Suffolk IP12 2DP. 01728 689171; fax 01728 688044; e-mail rodwest@ndirect.co.uk

HAVERGATE ISLAND. (267a) RSPB TM425496. Open Apr-Aug 1st & 3rd weekends and every Th; Sep-Mar 1st Sa every month. Book in advance, in writing. Shallow brackish water, lagoons with islands, saltmarsh, shingle beaches. Breeding Avocet, Arctic, Common and Sandwich Terns; migrants; winter wildfowl. John Partridge, 30 Mundays Lane, Orford, Woodbridge, Suffolk IP12 2LX. 01394 450732

LACKFORD WILDFOWL RESERVE. (200a) Suffolk WT TL803708. Via track off N side of A1101 between Lackford and Flempton. Open daytime. Access to hides (8) and visitor hut only. Restored gravel pit with open water, lagoons, islands, willow scrub. Wide range of waders and wildfowl (inc. Goosander); good in spring and autumn for migrants, inc. raptors; large winter gull roost. Colin Jakes, 7 Maltward Avenue, Bury St Edmunds IP33 3XN. 01284 702215

LANDGUARD. (40a) Suffolk WT TM285315. Open at all times. Nesting Little Tern, Ringed Plover, Wheatear and Black Redstart. Prime migration route (see next entry). Both for reserve and observatory all group visits and guided walks are arranged via the Ranger: Paul Holmes, Landguard Bird Observatory, View Point Road, Felixstowe, Suffolk IP11 8TW. 01394 673782; mobile 0850 427928

LANDGUARD BIRD OBSERVATORY. TM283317. Road S of Felixstowe to Landguard Nature Reserve and Fort. Visiting by appointment. Close grazed turf, raised banks with holm oak, tamarisk, etc. Migration watch point and ringing station. Contact: as previous entry. Paul Holmes, Landguard Bird Observatory, View Point Road, Felixstowe, Suffolk IP11 8TW. 01394 673782; mobile 0850 427928

MINSMERE. (2300a) RSPB. Near Saxmundham. Signposted off B1125 from Westleton to Leiston or, for cars only, via East Bridge N from Leiston (TM452680). Open all days except Tu 0900-2100 or sunset if earlier (visitor centre, shop and tearoom 0900-1700); closed 25-26 Dec. Always advisable to check times etc. when planning to visit this popular reserve. Public viewing platform on shore overlooking reserve, approached from NT Dunwich Cliffs car park (TM475680). Reedmarsh, lagoons, woodland, grazing marsh, heath. Breeding Bittern, Marsh Harrier, Avocet, terns, Bearded Tit, Nightingale; passage waders; winter wildfowl. Geoff Welch, Minsmere Reserve, Westleton, Saxmundham, Suffolk IP17 3BY. 01728 648281

REDGRAVE AND LOPHAM FENS. (315a) Suffolk WT (NNR) TM046797. W of Diss between South Lopham and Botesdale. Open during daylight hours. Keep to paths, dogs on lead. Fenland. Wetland breeding species include Snipe, Water Rail, Grasshopper Warbler; others seen include Nightingale, Sparrowhawk, Hobby. Harry Barnett, Suffolk WT, Low Common Road, Bressingham, Diss, Norfolk. 01379 687618

TRIMLEY MARSHES. (208a) Suffolk WT TM360268. Near Felixstowe. From A45 to Trimley St Mary. Park at end of Station Road. 2 mile walk to reserve. 5 hides open at all times. Visitor centre open M, W, Sa, Su 1000-1600. Freshwater lagoons, wet meadows, reeds. Breeding and passage waders; winter wildfowl. Mick Wright, 15 Avondale Road, Ipswich IP3 9JT. 01473 710032

NORTH WARREN & ALDRINGHAM WALKS. (1050a) RSPB TM467575. Near Aldeburgh. Car park on coast road just N of Aldeburgh. Open access along footpaths at all times. Grazing marsh, reedbeds, woodland, heath. Breeding Lapwing,

Redshank, Marsh Harrier, Hobby, Bearded Tit, Water Rail, Nightingale, Nightjar, Woodlark. Passage waders and raptors; wintering wildfowl (inc. White-fronted and Bean Geese). Snow Bunting on beach. Rob Macklin, Racewalk, Priory Road, Snape, Suffolk IP17 1SD. 01728 688481

WALBERSWICK. (1604a) English Nature (NNR) TM475733. Good views from B1387 and from lane running W from Walberswick towards Westwood Lodge; elsewhere keep to public footpaths. Parties and coach parking by prior arrangement. Hide on S side of Blyth estuary, E of A12. Tidal estuary, fen, freshwater marsh and reedbeds, heath, mixed woodland, carr. Marsh Harrier, Bearded Tit, Water Rail, Bittern, Nightjar; passage/winter wildfowl, waders and raptors. English Nature, Regent House, 110 Northgate Street, Bury St Edmunds IP33 1HP. Or: Adam Burrows. 01502 742229

SURREY

FRENSHAM COMMON AND COUNTRY PARK. (998a) Waverley BC and National Trust SU855405. Common lies on either side of A287 between Farnham and Hindhead. Open at all times. Car park (locked 2130-0900). Keep to paths. Information rooms, toilets and refreshment kiosk at Great Pond. Dry and humid heath, woodland, 2 large ponds, reedbeds. Dartford Warbler, Woodlark, Hobby, Nightjar, Stonechat; winter wildfowl (inc. occasional Smew), Bittern, Great Grey Shrike. Mike Coates, Rangers Office, Bacon Lane, Churt, Surrey GU10 2QB. 01252 792416

NOWER WOOD EDUCATIONAL RESERVE. (81a) Surrey WT TQ193546. B2033 Leatherhead to Headley road. Open days Apr-Oct (call for dates and times). Refreshments. Hide, nature trail, visitor centre. Ancient deciduous woodland with ponds. Breeding Sparrowhawk, all 3 woodpeckers, Tawny Owl, Spotted Flycatcher, Woodcock, common warblers, Mandarin Duck. Education Department, Surrey Wildlife Trust, Nower Wood, Mill Way, Leatherhead KT22 8QA. 01372 379509; fax 01372 363964

RIVERSIDE PARK, GUILDFORD. (230a) Guildford BC TQ005515. From car park at Bowers Lane, Burpham (TQ011527). Open at all times. Follow marked paths. Access to far side of lake and marshland area via boardwalk. Water Rail all year; summer Sedge, Reed and Garden Warblers, Common Tern, Hobby; winter ducks and Snipe; passage migrants; speciality: Water Pipit in winter and early spring (up to 12 most years).

THURSLEY COMMON. (825a) English Nature (NNR). The Moat car park SU900417. From Elstead/Churt road S of B3001. Open access. Parties must obtain prior permission. Wet and dry heathland, woodland, bog. Winter Hen Harrier and Great Grey Shrike; summer Hobby, Woodlark, Dartford Warbler, Stonechat, Curlew, Snipe, Nightjar. Simon Nobes, English Nature, Uplands Stud, Brook, Godalming, Surrey GU8 5LA. 01428 685878

SUSSEX, EAST

FORE WOOD. (135a) RSPB TQ756126. Half mile up hill from car park at village hall by church in Crowhurst, W of A2100 Battle-Hastings road. Access at all times.

Managed coppice, pond, streams. Sparrowhawk, Woodcock, Great and Lesser Spotted Woodpeckers, Spotted Flycatcher, Nightingale, warblers, Hawfinch. Martin Allison, Crown House, Petteridge Lane, Matfield, Tonbridge, Kent TN12 7LT.

LULLINGTON HEATH. (155a) English Nature (NNR) TQ525026. W of Eastbourne, 6 miles on A259 turn N on minor road to Lullington Court for parking, then 1 mile up hill (bridleway). Chalk downland and heath, dense woodland scrub and areas of gorse. Breeding Nightingale, Nightjar and Grasshopper Warbler, Turtle Dove. Winter raptors (inc. Hen Harrier), Woodcock. Malcolm Emery, English Nature, Howard House, 31 High Street, Lewes, E Sussex BN7 2LU. 01273 476595

PETT POOLS. (6.5a) Sussex WT TQ903145. Good views from Rye/Hastings coast road. Man-made shallow pools. Good autumn wader passage; wintering Bearded Tit.

PEVENSEY LEVELS. (128a) English Nature (NNR) TQ665054. NE of Eastbourne. S of A259, 1 mile along minor road from Pevensey E to Norman's Bay. Good views from road. Freshwater grazing marsh, subject to light flooding after rains. Breeding Reed and Sedge Warblers, Yellow Wagtail, Snipe, Redshank, Lapwing. Winter: large numbers of wildfowl (inc. some Bewick's and Whooper Swans) and waders (inc. Golden Plover). Birds of prey (inc. Merlin, Peregrine, Hobby, Short-eared Owl). Malcolm Emery, English Nature, Howard House, 31 High Street, Lewes, E Sussex BN7 2LU. 01273 476595

RYE HARBOUR. (825a) Management Committee. From unmanned information centre at Rye Harbour car park (TQ942189). Keep strictly to footpaths. Permission required for parties over 10. 4 hides (1 adapted for wheelchair access). Shingle, saltings, sand/mud shore at low tide, gravel pits, meadow, arable, scrub. Seabirds, waders, wildfowl, migrants. Dr Barry Yates, 2 Watch Cottages, Nook Beach, Winchelsea, E Sussex TN36 4LU. 01797 223862

SUSSEX, WEST

ADUR ESTUARY. (25a) RSPB TQ211050. Good views from riverside paths between footbridge in Shoreham town centre and A259 Norfolk bridge (car park). Mudflats and saltmarsh. Small area but good for easy viewing of waders.

ARUNDEL. (80a) WWT Centre TQ020081. N of Arundel off A27. Daily except 25 Dec, 0930-1730 (or 1630 in winter). Hides, activity stations, visitor centre, observatory, disabled facilities. Water meadows, ponds, reedbeds, scrapes. Ducks, Kingfisher, Green Sandpiper, Water Rail, Cetti's Warbler. breeding Redshank, Lapwing, Common Tern. David Julian, Centre Manager, The Wildfowl & Wetlands Trust, Mill Road, Arundel, W Sussex BN18 9PB. 01903 883355

KINGLEY VALE. (360a) English Nature (NNR) SU825088. N from Chichester on A286 turn L at Mid Lavant to West Stoke where R into lane to park, cross stile and along footpath for 0.75 mile. Open access. Field museum, nature trail. Chalk downland, dense scrub, large yew forest. Warblers, Tawny Owl, Hobby (on migration), Tree Pipit. Autumn migrants (inc. Black Redstart, flycatchers, Siskin, Redpoll). Winter Buzzard, Woodcock, Fieldfare, Redwing. Site Manager, Gamekeeper's Lodge, West Stoke House Farm, Downs Road, West Stoke, Chichester, W Sussex PO18 9BN. 01243 575353

PAGHAM HARBOUR. (1600a) W Sussex CC (LNR) SZ857965. From the B2201/B2145 Chichester/Selsey road. Part prohibited during breeding season. Visitor centre (open Sa Su all year). Pre-booking required for coach parties. Nature trails at Sidlesham and Pagham Spit. Saltmarsh, shingle banks, farmland. Migrant and winter waders (inc. Avocet); winter wildfowl (inc. Brent Goose, Smew). Hides at Ferry Pool, Church Norton and Pagham Spit. Ferry Field, Sussex WT (SZ855964) has marshy pasture with permanent water, good for spring and autumn passages. Rob Carver, Pagham Harbour LNR, Selsey Road, Sidlesham, Chichester, W Sussex PO20 7NE. 01243 641508; fax 01243 641568; e-mail pagham.nr@westsussex.gov.uk

PULBOROUGH BROOKS. (423a) RSPB. Entrance from A283 Pulborough to Storrington Road. Nature trail and hides open daily exc 25 Dec 0900-sunset. Visitor centre open daily exc 25-26 Dec 1000-1700. Also shop, tearoom (1000-1645, 1500 M), toilets. Wet meadows, woodland, hedgerows, grassland, scrub. Breeding Teal, Shoveler, Lapwing, Redshank, Snipe, Woodcock, Little and Barn Owls, Nightingale. Summer visitors inc. Hobby and Lesser Whitethroat. Common and unusual passage waders; also passage Wheatear, Whinchat, Stonechat, Redstart. Wintering waterfowl (inc. Wigeon, Pintail, White-fronted Goose, Bewick's Swan) and Ruff; Peregrine, Merlin, Hen Harrier possible. Uppertons Barn Visitor Centre, Wiggonholt, Pulborough, W Sussex RH20 2EL. 01798 875851

WARNHAM NATURE RESERVE. (95a) Horsham DC TQ167324. From A24, car park on B2237 into Horsham. All year Th F Sa Su 1000-1800. Hides, nature trail, visitor centre, cafe. 20-acre millpond, reedbeds, marsh, meadow, woodland. Breeding Great Crested Grebe, Heron, Pochard, Nuthatch, Treecreeper, Green and Great Spotted Woodpeckers, Kingfisher, Grey Wagtail, warblers (9 species); special viewing arrangements for winter wildfowl (inc. Pintail, Gadwall). Julia Hargeaves, Warnham Nature Reserve, Warnham Road, Horsham, W Sussex RH12 2RA. 01403 256890

WOODS MILL. (15a) Sussex WT TQ218137. On A2037 1.5 miles S of Henfield. Open Easter-early Oct, telephone for details as times subject to change. Nature trail, exhibition, information centre. Woodland, meadow, marsh, lake, stream. Breeding woodpeckers, Treecreeper, Nightingale, Grey Wagtail. Steve Tillman, Woods Mill, Henfield, W Sussex BN5 9SD. 01273 492630

TYNE & WEAR

BIG WATERS. (37a) Northumb WT NZ227734. S along track off Wideopen/ Dinnington road. View from public hide (suitable for disabled) at E end of recreation area; permit for further access from NWT. Pond, fen/wet grassland. Breeding & winter wildfowl; Swallow roost.

BOLDON FLATS. (80a) South Tyneside MBC NZ377614. View from Moor Lane on minor road NE of East Boldon station towards Whitburn. Meadows, part SSSI, managed flood in winter, pond, ditches. Passage/winter wildfowl and waders; winter gull roost may inc. Mediterranean, Glaucous, Iceland; Merlin fairly regular.

DERWENT WALK COUNTRY PARK. (400a) Gateshead MBC. Access via Thornley Woodland Centre NZ178604 on A694 between Winlaton Mill and Rowlands Gill; also via Swalwell Visitor Centre NZ198620 off A1. Mixed woodland, meadows, riverside, pond, wader scrape. Nature trail. Hides (purchase or hire key from Centre). Breeding Kingfisher, Dipper, Grey Wagtail; warblers (inc. Wood Warbler); Pied Flycatcher, Great Spotted and Green Woodpeckers, Nuthatch, Woodcock. Autumn wildfowl. Winter Water Rail, Jack Snipe; feeding station with over 40 species annually. Countryside Management Team, Thornley Woodland Centre, Rowlands Gill, Tyne & Wear NE39 1AU. 01207 545212

RYTON WILLOWS. (65a) Gateshead MBC NZ155650. S of River Tyne at old village of Ryton-upon-Tyne. Pond, marsh grassland, riverside. Nature trail. Breeding warblers (inc. Sedge, Grasshopper, Lesser Whitethroat), Water Rail, Great Spotted Woodpecker, Tawny Owl, Sparrowhawk, Hawfinch. Wintering wildfowl (inc. Goldeneye, Goosander). Passage waders in small numbers. Thornley Woodland Centre, as above.

SHIBDON POND. (30a) Durham WT and Gateshead MBC NZ195628. E of Blaydon on N side of Shibdon Road (B6317) S of Scotswood Bridge, close to A1. Large pond, reedbeds, marsh, scrub, wet grassland. Nature trail. Hide (purchase key at Centre). Wintering wildfowl (inc. diving ducks, Teal, Shoveler); Water Rail, Lesser Whitethroat, Reed Warbler, Grasshopper Warbler breed; passage waders in autumn; the large gull flocks in winter may include Mediterranean, Glaucous. Thornley Woodland Centre, as above.

WALLSEND SWALLOW POND. (35a) Northumb WT NZ301693. S off A191 by garden centre. View from public hide on bridleway. Pond, mixed woodland. Breeding & winter wildfowl.

WASHINGTON. (105a) WWT Centre NZ3156. On N bank of R Wear, W of Sunderland. Daily except 25 Dec; 0930-1700 in summer; 0930-1600 in winter. Visitor centre, hides. Lake, ponds, woods. Waders, wildfowl and woodland birds. Migrants. Breeding Little Ringed Plover, Oystercatcher, Common Tern, Heron. Chris Francis, Centre Manager, The Wildfowl & Wetlands Trust, Washington, Tyne & Wear NE38 8LE. 0191 416 5454

WASHINGWELL WOOD. (30a) Gateshead MBC NZ219599. NW of A692 Gateshead/Consett road, near Sunniside. Close to Marquis of Granby. Nature trail. Deciduous woodland, open grassland, and conifer plantation. Grey Wagtail, Chiffchaff, Whitethroat, Wood Warbler, Goldcrest, Willow Tit, Hawfinch; winter finch flocks (inc. Siskin, Redpoll, Goldfinch, Linnet, Brambling, Crossbill). Thornley Woodland Centre, as above.

WHITBURN BIRD OBSERVATORY. National Trust/Durham Bird Club NZ414633. Cliff top location. Esp. seawatching but also passerine migrants inc. rarities. Access details from Recorder. Tony Armstrong, 39 Western Hill, Durham City DH1 4RJ. 0191 386 1519

WARWICKSHIRE

ALVECOTE POOLS. (93a) Warwicks WT SK251043. SSSI. Access by Alvecote Priory along Pooley Fields Nature Trail (open access). Shallow pools, marsh, bog. Spring and autumn waders and terns (inc. Black); summer Little Ringed Plover, Redshank, Kingfisher, Reed Warbler, Lesser Whitethroat; winter duck. Contact: Reserves Team, Trust HQ, 01203 308979.

BRANDON MARSH. (228a) Warwicks WT SP386761. SE of Coventry on minor road E of A45 towards Brandon. Park in nature centre car park. Open 0900-1700 weekdays, 1000-1700 Sa, Su. Toilets, refreshments. 5 hides. Nature trail for wheelchairs with access to hide. No dogs. SSSI. Subsidence pools and flooded gravel pits, marsh and reed beds, willow carr, woodland, grassland. Breeding Common Tern, warblers (inc Cetti's), waders (inc. Little Ringed Plover, Redshank) and wildfowl, good for passage waders; non-breeding birds of prey inc. Short-eared Owl, Sparrowhawk, Hobby. Nature Centre 01203 302912. Ken Bond. 01203 328785

HARTSHILL HAYES COUNTRY PARK. (136a) Warwickshire CC. SP317943. Signposted as 'Country Park' from B4114 W of Nuneaton. 3 waymarked walks. Mixed woodland, grassland hillside. Warblers, woodpeckers, tits, Goldcrest. Manager as Kingsbury, below.

KINGSBURY WATER PARK. (650a) Warwickshire CC. SP203960. Signposted 'Water Park' from A4097 NE of Birmingham. Closed on Christmas Day. Hides, interpretative centre, waymarked walks. Open water; numerous small pools, some with gravel islands; gravel pits; silt beds with reedmace, reed, willow and alder; rough areas and grassland. Breeding warblers (9 species), Little Ringed Plover, Great Crested and Little Grebes; Shoveler, Shelduck and a thriving Common Tern colony; passage waders (esp. spring); winter wildfowl, Short-eared Owl. Country Park Manager's Office, Kingsbury Water Park, Bodymoor Heath Lane, Sutton Coldfield, West Midlands B76 0DY. 01827 872660

UFTON FIELDS. (77a) Warwicks WT & Warwicks CC (LNR) SP378615. S of A425 Leamington Spa to Southam Road. Open at all times. Easy-going nature trail, 2 hides. SSSI. Colonising limestone quarry with pools, grass, scrub and woodland. Willow Tit, Goldcrest, Reed Bunting, up to 9 warblers, Little Grebe, Green Woodpecker. Contact: Trust HQ, 01203 302912.

WHITACRE HEATH. (109a) Warwicks WT SP209931. Car park off Lea Marston/Whitacre Heath road. Trust members and permit holders only. SSSI. Keep to paths, no dogs. 4 hides. Open water, reedbed, young woodland, flood meadow adjacent to River Tame. Passage migrants; wildfowl, waders and warblers. Contact: Trust HQ, 01203 302912.

WEST MIDLANDS

PLANTS BROOK. (26a) Birmingham City Council (LNR) SP140922. Eachelhurst Road, Walmley, Birmingham. Open at all times. Nature walk. Pools, marsh, willow carr, scrub, meadow. Great Crested and Little Grebes, duck species, occasional Water Rail. Leo McKevitt. 0121 382 0898

SANDWELL VALLEY. (1700a) Sandwell MBC SP012918 & SP028992. Access and car park from Dagger Lane or Forge Lane, West Bromwich. Nature reserve, lakes, woods and farmland. Mainly public open space. Also 25-acre RSPB reserve with nature centre at SP036931: access and car park off Tanhouse Avenue, Great Barr. Nature trails, hides. Lake, freshwater marsh, woodland. Breeding Lapwing, Little Ringed Plover, Sparrowhawk. All 3 woodpeckers, Tawny Owl, Reed Warbler; passage waders. For RSPB reserve contact Warden, 20 Tanhouse Avenue, Great Barr, Birmingham B43 5AG, tel 0121 358 3013. For Sandwell Valley: Senior Ranger, Sandwell Valley Nature Centre, Salters Lane, West Bromwich, W Midlands B71 4BG. 0121 553 0220 or 2147

SMESTOW VALLEY LOCAL NATURE RESERVE. (155a) Wolverhampton Council SJ895005. Main entrance at Henwood Road, Tettenhall near junction of A41 and A454. Open at all times. Visitor centre (Neil Parsons, 01902 552351). Woodland, meadowland, canal. Breeding Nuthatch, Great Spotted and Green Woodpeckers, Treecreeper, Reed Bunting, Skylark, Warblers (7 species); winter Little Grebe, Siskin, Redwing, Fieldfare, Snipe, Water Rail. Chris Jones. 01902 552197

WILTSHIRE

COATE WATER COUNTRY PARK. (114a) Swindon BC SU179821. From M4 exit 15, approx 2 miles towards Swindon. Open during daylight hours. Daily or annual permit available on site. 2 hides. Open water, reedbed, damp scrub. Passage waders; breeding Sparrowhawk, Heron, warblers; Hobby regular on summer evenings; winter duck. Rangers, Coate Water Country Park, Marlborough Road, Swindon SN3 6AA. 01793 490150

SWILLBROOK LAKES. (64a) Wilts WT SU018934. 1 mi S of Somerford Keynes on Cotswold Water Park spine road; turn off down Minety Lane (parking). Open at all times. Footpath along N and E sides of lakes. Gravel pits with shallow pools, rough grassland and scrub around edges. Winter wildfowl (inc. Gadwall, Pochard, Smew, Goosander); breeding Reed and Sedge Warblers; best site for Hobby in Cotswold WP. Contact Wilts WT HQ, 01380 725670.

WORCESTERSHIRE

KNAPP AND PAPERMILL. (62a) Worcs WT SO749522. Take A4103 SW from Worcester; R at Bransford roundabout then L towards Suckley and reserve is approx 3 miles (do not turn off for Alfrick). Park at Bridges Stone layby (SO751522), cross road and follow path to the Knapp House. Open daily exc 25 Dec. Large parties contact Warden. Hide, nature trail, small visitor centre, wildlife garden. Broadleaved woodland, unimproved grassland, fast stream. Breeding Grey Wagtail, Kingfisher, Pied Flycatcher, all 3 woodpeckers. Redstart also occurs. Warden, The Knapp, Alfrick, Worcester WR6 5HR. 01886 832065

TRENCH WOOD. (106a) Worcs WT SO931585. NE of Worcester. Car park. Open daily exc 25 Dec. (NB mature trees to SW and SE of wood are not part of reserve). Young broadleaved woodland, mixed scrub. Very good for warblers; Woodcock. Contact: Trust HQ.

UPTON WARREN. CHRISTOPHER CADBURY WETLAND RESERVE (65a) Worcs WT SO936677. From A38 Bromsgrove/ Droitwich by AA box. Trust permit required. 7 hides. Series of freshwater and saline ponds, marsh, rough grassland. Breeding and winter wildfowl; passage waders and terns; good variety of passerines, esp. warblers. Parties contact: Arthur Jacobs, 3 The Beeches, Rectory Lane, Upton Warren, Bromsgrove, Worcs B61 7EL. 01527 861370

WYRE FOREST. (1060a) EN (NNR) also areas run by Worcs WT SO750760. A456 out of Bewdley. Observe reserve signs and keep to paths. Forestry Commission visitor centre at Callow Hill. Fred Dale Reserve (57a) is reached by footpath W of B4194 (parking at SO776763). Facilities for disabled (entry by car) if Warden telephoned in advance. Oak forest, conifer areas, birch heath, stream. Buzzard, Pied

Flycatcher, Wood Warbler, Redstart, all 3 woodpeckers, Woodcock, Crossbill, Siskin, Hawfinch, Kingfisher, Dipper, Grey Wagtail, Tree Pipit. Michael Taylor, Lodge Hill Farm, Bewdley, Worcs DY12 2LY. 01299 400686

YORKSHIRE

ANGLERS COUNTRY PARK. NCB & Wakefield MDC SE380160. SE of Wakefield. Leave A638 at signpost for Crofton. Turn left in village on road to Ryhill, turning just past Anglers pub in Wintersett hamlet. Open at all times. 2 hides. 3 lakes. Winter wildfowl (inc. Wigeon, Goosander), large gull roost with regular Iceland, Glaucous, Mediterranean. Passage waders and passerines. Breeding Little Ringed Plover, Redshank, Lapwing, and warblers (inc. Grasshopper and Lesser Whitethroat).

BEMPTON CLIFFS. RSPB TA197738. Near Bridlington. Take cliff road N from Bempton Village off B1229 to car park and visitor centre. Public footpath along cliff top with observation points. Four miles of chalk cliffs. Best to visit May to mid-July for eg Puffin, Gannet (only colony on English mainland), Fulmar, Kittiwake; also nesting Tree Sparrow, Corn Bunting; good migration watchpoint. Summer Warden, RSPB Visitor Centre, Cliff Lane, Bempton, Bridlington, E Yorks YO15 1JF. 01262 851179

BLACKTOFT SANDS. (460a) RSPB SE843232. Car park half mile E of Ousefleet, off A161 from Goole. Open daily 0900-2100 or sunset when earlier. 6 hides. Reedbed, saltmarsh, artificial brackish lagoons. Breeding Bearded Tit, Grasshopper Warbler, Water Rail, Marsh Harrier, Avocet; winter Hen Harrier, waders, wildfowl. Andrew Grieve, Hillcrest, High Street, Whitgift, Goole, E Yorks DN14 8HL. 01405 704665

BOLTON ON SWALE LAKE. (27a) Yorks WT SE248985. From B6721 Northallerton/Catterick road turn left to Ellerton at Ellerton Cross. Former gravel workings. Breeding Shelduck, Oystercatcher, Ringed Plover; winter wildfowl inc. 1300 Wigeon, 400 Greylag, Bewick's and Whooper Swans. Contact Trust HQ.

CARLTON MARSH. (198a) Barnsley MBC (LNR) SE379103. Small car park off Weet Shaw Lane, Cudworth, Barnsley. Access only along public rights of way and disused railway. 2 hides. Marsh with reed and sedge, some open water. Breeding Water Rail, Little Ringed Plover, Sedge, Reed and Grasshopper Warblers; autumn Swallow roost; Barn Owl, Jack Snipe. Nigel Labdon, Leisure Services, Berneslai Close, Barnsley, S Yorks S70 2HS. 01226 774478; fax 01226 773599; e-mail nigellabdon@barnsley.gov.uk

COATHAM MARSH. (134a) Tees Valley WT NZ586247. W of Redcar. Car park off Tod Point Road past old railway bridge. Open at all times. 2 hides (inc. 1 for disabled). Freshwater marsh on old saltings, developing spoil tips. Breeding Sedge Warbler, Yellow Wagtail; wintering Smew, Lapland Bunting, Water Rail, Kingfisher, Jack Snipe; passage waders (inc. Wood Sandpiper, Greenshank, Ruff); also passage Garganey and Wheatear; occasional rarities. Contact Trust HQ.

FAIRBURN INGS. (680a) RSPB SE452278. Near Castleford. On W side of A1 2 miles N of Ferrybridge. Access at all times to public hides off causeway below Fairburn village. Car park, walkway and hide one mile W of village open daily 0900-dusk, also information centre open Sa Su 1000-1700. Shallow lakes, marshy depressions, floodpools. Breeding Gadwall, Shoveler, Little Ringed Plover, Common Tern; large hirundine roosts in autumn; winter wildfowl (inc. Goldeneye, Goosander,

Whooper Swan), Glaucous Gull; noted for spring passage of terns and Little Gulls and autumn passage of waders. RSPB Fairburn Ings, Visitor Centre, Newton Lane, Castleford, W Yorks WF10 2BH. 01977 603796

FILEY BRIGG ORNITHOLOGICAL GROUP BIRD OBSERVATORY. Recording area includes Filey Dams, a 15-acre Yorks WT freshwater nature reserve (TA106807). Access through Wharfedale Estate, off Muston Road, Filey. Open at all times. 2 hides. Main ringing site is the 'Top Scrub' to the N of the Country Park caravan site. Whole of Filey Bay is included, as far as Speeton. Keys to the seawatch hide on the Brigg can be hired from the Country Park cafe. No accommodation. Migrant seabirds and passerines, inc. rarities, in spring and autumn; winter divers, grebes, ducks (inc. Eider, Long-tailed Duck), waders (inc. Purple Sandpiper), gulls, Lapland and Snow Buntings. Syd Cochrane, 4 Pinewood Avenue, Filey, N Yorks YO14 9NS. 01723 515480.

HUNTCLIFF. Tees Valley WT NZ674215. Along Cleveland Way footpath from Saltburn or Skinningrove. Strip of coastal grassland and cliff face. Large colony of Kittiwakes and some Cormorants.

LOWER DERWENT VALLEY. English Nature/Yorks WT (NNR) SE698367, SE694444. Off Wheldrake to Thorganby road, SE of York, off A163 between North Duffield and Bubwith. Open dawn to dusk daily except Dec 25. Permit (from Warden) required for areas away from hides. Lowland flood meadow, swamp and alder woodland. Breeding wildfowl (inc. Black-necked Grebe, Shoveler, Garganey) and waders (inc. Redshank, Snipe); wintering wildfowl (inc. wild swans, Wigeon), waders (inc. Golden Plover, Ruff), birds of prey (inc. Short-eared Owl, Hen Harrier, Merlin, Peregrine, Goshawk). Tim Dixon, English Nature, Genesis 1, University Road, Heslington, York YO10 5ZQ. 01904 435500; fax 01904 435520; e-mail york@english-nature.org.uk

OLD MOOR WETLAND CENTRE. (250a) Barnsley MBC SE422022. Access from MI J36 then A6195, or from A1 then A635 and A1695; follow brown signs. Entry fee with membership scheme. 5 hides. Lakes and flood meadows, wader scrape and reedbeds. Breeding waders and wildfowl. Migrant waders. Rare vagrants recorded annually. Large number of wintering wildfowl (inc. Whooper Swans). Contact: Debra Bushby, Manager, Old Moor Wetland Centre, Old Moor Lane, off Manvers Way, Broomhill, Wombwell, Barnsley S73 0YF. 01226 751593; fax 01226 751617

POTTERIC CARR. (320a) Yorks WT SE589007. From M18 junction 3 take A6182 (Doncaster) and at first roundabout take third exit; entrance and car park are on R after 50m. Access by permit only (01302 364142, answerphone). Parties must obtain prior permission. Field Centre (light refreshments, toilet) open 1000-1500 Su all year. 8 hides (3 for disabled). Reed fen, open water, woodland. Nesting waterfowl (inc. Shoveler, Gadwall, Pochard); Water Rail, Little Ringed Plover, Snipe, Kingfisher, all 3 woodpeckers, Lesser Whitethroat, Reed and Sedge Warblers also breed. Passage/winter: wildfowl, Bittern, Marsh Harrier, Black Tern, waders.

PUGNEYS COUNTRY PARK. (60a) Wakefield MDC SE330180. Leave M1 at J29 towards Wakefield; reserve signposted from first roundabout. Open daily 0900 to one hour before sunset. 2 hides. 3 lakes, one of which is in reserve area. Winter: large gull roost, Bittern, good range of wildfowl (inc. Smew), Short-eared Owl. Breeding Common Tern, Sedge and Reed Warblers. Passage waders. 01924 302360.

SALTBURN GILL. (52a) Tees Valley WT NZ673210. Public footpath runs through wood from Saltburn to Brotton. Keep to path. Deciduous woodland. Breeding warblers (inc. Lesser Whitethroat), Grey Wagtail, Spotted Flycatcher, Sparrowhawk, Great Spotted Woodpecker. Contact: Trust HQ.

SKIPWITH COMMON. (888a) Yorks WT, English Nature & Escrick Park Estate SE645375. Two miles down King Rudding Lane, E off A19 at Riccall between York & Selby. Open at all times. Keep dogs under close control. Nature trail. Lowland heath. Breeding Nightjar, Grasshopper Warbler, Curlew, Long-eared Owl, Water Rail, Teal, Shoveler, Little Grebe. Winter Goshawk, Wigeon, Teal. Contact Trust HQ.

SPURN BIRD OBSERVATORY. Est. 1946 by Yorkshire Naturalists' Union. N end of Spurn Head, 200 yards inside main entrance to Spurn National Nature Reserve (access at TA417151 - no dogs, not even in cars). From Hull via A1033 to Hedon and Patrington, and from latter on the B1445 to Kilnsea and Spurn. Open throughout the year, but bookings for parties over 6 not accepted Apr/May, Aug/Nov. Self-catering accommodation for 17 with cooking facilities, mattresses and blankets; sheets/sleeping bags and pillow slips must be taken. Meals obtainable in a local pub. Notable for autumn migrants; rarities often recorded. Warden, Spurn Bird Observatory, Kilnsea, Patrington, Hull HU12 0UG.

TOPHILL LOW NATURE RESERVE. (272a) Yorkshire Water TA071482. Midway between Beverley and Driffield on A164; turn off at Watton and follow signs for 4 miles. Open W-Su (also bank hol Mondays) summer 0900-1800, winter 0900-1600. No dogs. Permit from machine on entry. 12 hides, nature trails, visitor centre. 2 reservoirs (SSSI), lagoons, marshes, woods, scrub, grassland. Breeding Pochard, Gadwall, Shelduck, Reed Warbler; passage waders (up to 25 Green Sandpipers); winter wildfowl. Peter Izzard, Tophill Low Nature Reserve, Watton Carrs, Hutton Cranswick, Driffield YO25 9RH. 01377 270690

WORSBROUGH COUNTRY PARK. (148a) Barnsley MBC SE345034. From CP car park off A61. Open access at all times. Hide, toilets. Open water, willow carr, phragmites and typha reedbed, deciduous wood and meadow land. Breeding Ruddy Duck, Sparrowhawk, Sedge and Reed Warblers, Kingfisher, Common Tern; autumn Swallow roost; winter gulls. Cultural Services, Worsborough Mill, Barnsley, S Yorks S70 5LJ. 01226 774527

SCOTLAND

A note on headings. The regional nomenclature of Scotland remains confused. SOC Branch Areas differ from the Recording and Bird Report Areas. SNH Areas are different again and the RSPB uses only eight areas, including the defunct Strathclyde. It would clearly be impractical to use all thirty-two of the administrative authorities here, and though some requests have been received from readers in Scotland for certain changes to be made to the headings we use, most people appear to find them familiar and convenient. Hence they are retained for this edition.

BORDERS

BEMERSYDE MOSS. (67a) Scottish WT NT614340. 4 miles E of Melrose on minor road. Shallow Loch and marsh with large Black-headed Gull colony, Black-necked Grebe, wintering wildfowl, waders on migration, raptors. Hide with parking nearby.

DUNS CASTLE. (185a) Scottish WT NT778550. Duns (W of Berwick upon Tweed). Access from Castle Street. Loch and woodland. Woodland birds, waterfowl.

PEASE DEAN. (75a) Scottish WT NT790705. W of St Abb's Head. Park at Pease Bay Caravan Park off A1107. Valley woodland. Valuable landfall, feeding and sheltering site for migrants.

ST ABB'S HEAD. (190a) National Trust for Scotland (NNR) NT914688. Visitor centre and car park at S of reserve, or by foot from St Abbs. Seabird cliffs with large numbers of Kittiwake, auks, Shag, Fulmar. Unusual migrants in spring and autumn. Good seawatching in autumn. Parties must contact Ranger in advance. All dogs must be kept on a lead. Kevin Rideout, Ranger's Cottage, Northfield, St Abbs, Eyemouth, Berwickshire TD14 5QF. 0189 07 71443

YETHOLM LOCH. (65a) Scottish WT NT803279. Off B6352, turning to Lochtower (unmetalled road). Hide. Breeding and winter wildfowl.

CENTRAL

CAMBUS POOLS. (15a) Scottish WT NS846937. Park by river in Cambus village, cross R Devon by bridge at NS853940 and walk down stream on R bank past bonded warehouses. Wet grassland and pools. Used extensively by migrants, inc, wildfowl and waders.

GARTMORN DAM. (215a) Clackmannanshire (LNR) NS920943. Access road leaves A908 N of Alloa between Keilarsbrae and New Sauchie. Hide, visitor centre (01259 214319). Reservoir with small wooded island. Breeding Great Crested and Little Grebes, Tufted Duck, Heron. Winter wildfowl (inc. Whooper Swan, Greylag & Pink-footed Geese, Shoveler, Teal, Goldeneye, Wigeon, Gadwall, Goosander); large winter thrush flocks, occasional Waxwing and Brambling flocks. Countryside Ranger Service, Clackmannanshire Council, Lime Tree House, Alloa, Clackmannanshire FK10 1EX. 01259 452409

INVERSNAID. (923a) RSPB NN337088. On E side of Loch Lomond. Via B829 W from Aberfoyle, then along minor road to car park by Inversnaid Hotel. Deciduous woodland rises to craggy ridge and moorland. Breeding Buzzard, Blackcock, Grey Wagtail, Dipper, Wood Warbler, Redstart, Pied Flycatcher, Tree Pipit. The loch is on a migration route, especially for wildfowl and waders. Contact via RSPB South & West Scotland Regional Office.

DUMFRIES & GALLOWAY

CAERLAVEROCK. (18532a) SNH (NNR) NY040645. From B725 and Caerlaverock Castle. Open all year. Visitors may enter most of the reserve, except sanctuary area. The saltmarsh (local: merse) can be dangerous at high tides; visitors should consult the Area Officer for advice. No permit, but organised groups should apply to Area Officer well in advance. Research and surveys require approval of SNH Area Manager. Wintering grounds for Barnacle, Pink-footed and Greylag Geese, Whooper and Bewick's Swans, ducks, waders and raptors. Wally Wright, SNH Office, Hollands Farm Road, Caerlaverock, Dumfries DG1 4RS. 0138 770 275

CAERLAVEROCK. (1400a) WWT Centre NY051656. From B725 at Bankend. Open daily except 25 Dec. 20 hides, heated observatory, 3 towers, sheltered picnic area. Self-catering accommodation and camping facilities. Nature trails in summer. Winter wildfowl esp. Barnacle Geese (max 13,700), Whooper and Bewick's Swans. John Doherty, Centre Manager, The Wildfowl & Wetlands Trust, Eastpark Farm, Caerlaverock, Dumfries DG1 4RS. 01387 770200

CARSTRAMON WOOD. (205a) Scottish WT NT592605. 2 miles N of Gatehouse of Fleet on minor road off B796. Car parking alongside road. Network of paths. Ancient deciduous oak woodland. Typical woodland birds (inc. Pied Flycatcher).

KEN/DEE MARSHES. (326a) RSPB. Between New Galloway and Castle Douglas. Good views from A762, A713 and minor road N of Glenlochar & W of River Dee.

Access from the car park at entrance to farm Mains of Duchrae (NX699684). Marshes, meadows, farmland, deciduous woods. Winter wildfowl (inc. Greenland White-fronted Geese, Pintail), Hen Harrier, Merlin, Peregrine; Buzzard & Sparrowhawk are common residents; breeding Goosander, Redshank, Shoveler, Barn Owl, Redstart, Pied Flycatcher, Willow Tit; Crossbill and Siskin also occur. Paul N Collin, Gairland, Old Edinburgh Road, Minnigaff, Newton Stewart, Wigtownshire DG8 6PL. 01671 402861

MERSEHEAD. (2,500a) RSPB NX925560. From A710 near Caulkerbush. Open at all times. Hide, nature trails, information centre and toilets. Wet grassland, arable farmland, saltmarsh, inter-tidal mudflats.Winter: up to 9,500 Barnacle Geese, 4,000 Teal, 2,000 Wigeon, 1,000 Pintail, waders (inc. Dunlin, Knot, Oystercatcher). Breeders include Lapwing, Redshank, Skylark. Eric Nielson, Mersehead, Southwick, Mersehead, Dumfries DG2 8AH. 01387 780298

MULL OF GALLOWAY. (12a) RSPB NX156304. Near Stranraer. From A716 S of Drummore then minor road to lighthouse by cliffs. Largest land-based seabird colony in the region. Access at all times. May-Jul best. Breeding auks (inc. Black Guillemot), Fulmer, Shag, Kittiwake; Stonechat, Wheatear, Twite. Manx Shearwaters and Gannets regular off headland. Contact via Paul Collin at Wood of Cree.

WOOD OF CREE. (657a) RSPB NX382708. NW of Newton Stewart on minor road from Minnigaff parallel to A714. Access at all times. Broadleaved woodland, scrubland, burns, riverside marsh. Breeding Buzzard, Sparrowhawk, Oystercatcher, Woodcock, Common Sandpiper, Dipper, Grey Wagtail, Redstart, Pied Flycatcher, Wood and Garden Warblers, Great Spotted Woodpecker. Paul N Collin, Gairland, Old Edinburgh Road, Minnigaff, Newton Stewart, Wigtownshire DG8 6PL. 01671 402861

FIFE

Fife Bird Club

CAMERON RESERVOIR. Fife Council & Scottish WT NO479114. SW of St Andrews on A915. Car park at NE corner of reservoir. Open access. Hide (SOC & SWT members), key and information from Ian Cumming, 11 Canongate, St Andrews, Fife KY16 8RT. 01334 473773

EDEN ESTUARY. (2200a) Fife Council (LNR) NO480190. Views from layby car park on A91 (T) at Guardbridge. Path from NO466188 to Balgove Bay. Also from West Sands, St Andrews. Permits to parts of N shore (and information) from Cupar address below. Hide at Balgove Bay (enquire of Ranger Service, St Andrews) and Fife Bird Club hide at Edenside Stables (contact Club). Reserve Centre open every day 0900-1700 at Guardbridge (NO452194). Estuary, mudflats. Waders include Bar-tailed and Black-tailed Godwits, Golden Plover, large wintering flock of Grey Plover, spring passage of Ringed Plover;

wildfowl (inc. Shelduck, Wigeon, Eider, large nos. of Scoter, Greylag and Pink-footed Geese); sometimes Velvet Scoter and Long-tailed Duck. Reserve Advisory Committee, Fife Council, County Buildings, St. Catherine Street, Cupar, Fife KY15 4LS. 01334 412200. Countryside Ranger, Craigtoun Country Park, by St Andrews, Fife KY16 8NX. 01334 472151

ISLE OF MAY NNR. (140a) NT655995. This small island lying 6 miles off Fife Ness in the Firth of Forth is a National Nature Reserve owned by the SNH. Contact boatman for day trips: J Reaper tel 01333 310103. Keep to paths. No dogs; no camping; no fires. Prior permission required if scientific work is to be carried out. Sea cliffs, rocky shoreline. Breeding auks and terns, Kittiwake, Shag, Eider, Fulmar. SNH Warden usually resident Apr-Sep.

ISLE OF MAY BIRD OBSERVATORY. Hostel accommodation in disused lighthouse (the Low Light) for up to 6, Apr-Oct; usual stay is one week. No supplies on island; visitors must take own food and sleeping bag. Fishing boat from Anstruther, arranged by the Observatory. Rock landings mean that delays are possible, both arriving and leaving, because of weather. Weather-related autumn/spring migrations include rarities each year. 5 Heligoland traps used for ringing migrants when qualified personnel present. Bookings: Mike Martin, 2 Manse Park, Uphall, W Lothian EH52 6NX, tel 01506 855285. Information: Ian M Darling, 579 Lanark Road West, Balerno, Edinburgh EH14 7BL. Tel/fax 0131 449 4282

KILMINNING COAST. (19a) Scottish WT NO633090. Off minor road 1.5 miles NE of Crail; turn R past disused airfield. Coastal footpath. Scrub, grassland, rocky shoreline. Eider, waders; terns, Gannet. Excellent for passage migrants in spring and autumn.

GRAMPIAN

CULLALOE. (67a) Scottish WT NT188877. On loop of B9157 just N of Aberdeen, Car parking on reserve. Loch, scrub willow, woodland, meadow. Good for wildfowl (inc. Teal) and passage waders.

FORVIE. (2472a) SNH (NNR) NK020275. From car parks on A975 N of Newburgh. Interpretative centre. Keep to paths; dogs on leads only. S end of reserve fenced off in breeding season. Foreshore, sand dunes, sea cliffs, moorland, estuary. Largest concentration of breeding Eider in UK; colonies of Kittiwakes, Fulmars, terns (4 species); autumn/winter grey geese flocks; waders on Ythan estuary. Area Officer, SNH Forvie NNR, Grampian Area, Little Collieston Croft, Collieston, Ellon, Aberdeenshire AB41 8RU. 01358 751330

FOWLSHEUGH. (1.5 miles) RSPB NO876805. Unrestricted. Cliff top path N from car park at Crawton, signposted from A92 3 miles S of Stonehaven. Large seabird colony: Kittiwake, auks. Boat trips Tu & F evgs May-Jul from Stonehaven Harbour. Contact: RSPB Aberdeen Office.

LEIN (THE), SPEY BAY. (64a) Scottish WT NJ335657. Immediately W of Kingston at end of B9015. Shingle, rivermouth and coastal habitats. Summer Osprey, waders, wildfowl. Wintering seaduck and divers offshore (esp. Long-tailed Duck, Common and Velvet Scoters, Red-throated Diver).

LOCH OF STRATHBEG. (2261a) RSPB NK057581. Loch near sea between Fraserburgh and Peterhead. Open at all times. Centre at Starnafin Farm. Hides. Breeding Eider, Shelduck, Sandwich Tern, Water Rail; large numbers of wintering duck, grey geese, Whooper Swan. Warden, Starnafin Farm, Crimond, Fraserburgh, Aberdeenshire AB43 8QN. 01346 532017

LONGHAVEN CLIFFS. (112a) Scottish WT NK114394. Access from car park at Blackhills quarry or Bullers of Buchan. Seabird colony, inc. Kittiwake, Shag, Guillemot, Razorbill, Puffin.

ST CYRUS. (227a) SNH (NNR). N of Montrose. Main access at NO743635, or N end at NO752646. Interpretative centre open Apr-Oct. S part of reserve closed May-Aug for breeding birds, otherwise open access. Coastal dunes, relict saltmarsh, scrub, pasture, basalt cliffs. Breeding Stonechat, Whinchat, Grasshopper and Sedge Warblers, Fulmar. Shelduck often seen on saltmarsh. Eider, Arctic, Sandwich and Common Terns near R Esk; Gannets, Great and Arctic Skuas occas. passage out at sea. SNH, Old Lifeboat Station, Nether Warburton, Montrose, Angus DD10 0DG. Tel/fax 01674 830736

HIGHLAND

ABERNETHY FOREST RESERVE - LOCH GARTEN. (4384a) RSPB NH978184. SW of Nethy Bridge; follow 'RSPB Osprey' road signs. Reserve open at all times. Osprey centre open daily 1000-1800 1 Apr-end Aug, provided Ospreys nest. Pine forest, lochs. Osprey, Redstart, Crested Tit, Siskin, Scottish Crossbill; Goldeneye, Goosander, Greylag on Loch Garten in winter. Richard Thaxton, Grianan, Nethy Bridge, Inverness-shire PH25 3EF. 01479 831694

BEINN EIGHE. (11757a) SNH (NNR) NG960600. From car park at Loch Maree side. No dogs. Nature trails, visitor centre (open May-Sep). Native Scots pine forest, mountains, moorland. Red-throated Diver, Golden Eagle, Merlin, Ptarmigan, Siskin, Crossbill. SNH Reserve Manager, Anancaun Field Station, Kinlochewe, Ross-shire IV22 2PD. 01445 760 254

BEN MORE COIGACH. (14278a) Scottish WT NC075065. N of Ullapool. Access at several points from minor road off A835 to Achiltibuie. Loch, bog and moorland. Upland birds (inc. Ptarmigan, Raven).

CAIRNGORM NNR. (61728a) SNH, RSPB, NTS, Rothiemurchus & Glen Feshie Estates NJ010010. Mountain, moorland, pine woodland and lochs. Goosander, Crested Tit, Siskin, Redstart, Crossbill, Capercaillie, Black Grouse, Ptarmigan, Dotterel, Golden Eagle. SNH, Achantoul, Aviemore, Inverness-shire PH22 1QD. 01479 810477; fax 01479 811363

CULBIN SANDS. (2130a) RSPB NH901573. Kingsteps (1 mile E of Nairn) past golf course. Saltmarsh, sandflats, dunes. Esp. winter for waders (inc. Knot, Bar-tailed Godwit) and wildfowl (inc. Common and Velvet Scoters, Long-tailed Duck, Red-breasted Merganser). Kenna Chisholm, Brochruben Cottage, Torness, Inverness IV2 6TY. 01463 751329; e-mail kenna.chisholm@rspb.org.uk

FORSINARD. (18,752a) RSPB NC905465. Visitor centre at Forsinard railway station (active) on A897 open every day 0900-1800 Easter-end Oct. Regular guided walks. Access restricted to paths and roads Apr-end Jun. Blanket peatland in 'flow country', bog pools (trail), lochs. Breeding Hen Harrier (nest watch May-Jul), Merlin, Buzzard, Short-eared Owl, Golden Plover, Greenshank, Dunlin, native Greylag, Curlew, wildfowl. Norrie Russell, Forsinard Station, Forsinard, Sutherland KW13 6YT. 01641 571225

GLENMORE. (290a) Scottish WT/Forest Enterprise NJ998104. Park at Glenmore 7 miles E of Aviemore. Access over a comprehensive network of paths. Visitor centre at Glenmore. Native Caledonian pinewood, moorland. Crossbill, Crested Tit, Redstart.

HANDA. (897a) Scottish WT NC130480. Day visits (except Su) by local boatman from Tarbet, 15 Apr-1 Sep (tel 01971 502340). Visitors may arrange to stay in bothy through SWT. Cliffs, moorland, lochans. Nesting auks, Fulmar, Kittiwake, skuas; passage Greenshank, Sanderling and Whimbrel; winter Barnacle Geese. SWT Summer Warden, c/o S MacLeod, 15 Scouriemore, Scourie, Lairg, Sutherland.

INSH MARSHES. (2105a) RSPB NH775998. Near Kingussie. From car park on B970. Hides and information building open at all times. Marshes and woodland along River Spey. Breeding Goldeneye, Wigeon, Greylag, Snipe, Curlew, Redshank, Sedge and Grasshopper Warblers, Dipper, Grey Wagtail, Redstart, Tree Pipit. Winter wildfowl inc. Whooper Swans and Greylag Geese. Hen Harrier, Osprey, Buzzard regular. Dr Tom Prescott, Ivy Cottage, Insh, Kingussie, Inverness-shire PH21 1NT. 01540 661518

ISLE OF EIGG. (3640a) Scottish WT NM474875. Ferry from Mallaig or Arisaig. Guided walks with Warden in summer. Hazel scrub, coastal cliff, moorland, bog, lochans. Often excellent for offshore seabirds. Breeding species include Manx Shearwater, Black Guillemot, Red-throated Diver. Raven and Golden Eagle. John Chester, SWT Warden, Isle of Eigg PH42 4RL. 01687 482477

ISLE OF RUM. (26531a) SNH (NNR) NM370970. Steamer from Mallaig. Prior booking needed to stay overnight. General store and Post Office. Restrictions due to deer stalking/research, check access with Reserve Office. Self-guided trails. Coast, moorland, woodland restoration, montane. Large Manx Shearwater colonies on hill tops; breeding auks (inc. Black Guillemot), Kittiwake, Fulmar, Eider, Golden Plover, Merlin, Red-throated Diver, Golden Eagle. SNH Reserve Office, Isle of Rum PH43 4RR. 01687 462026

LOCH FLEET. (1750a) Scottish WT NH794965 (NNR). View across tidal basin from A9 or unclassified road to Skelbo. Important feeding place for wintering ducks and waders. The sea off the mouth of Loch Fleet is a major wintering area for Long-tailed Duck, Common and Velvet Scoters, Eider Duck. Pinewood off minor road S from Golspie to Little Ferry, with Crossbill, occasional Crested Tit.

LOCH RUTHVEN. (211a) RSPB NH638281. Take B851 SW off A9, turn off on minor road NE at Croachy; car park 1 mile. Open at all times. Freshwater loch and woodland. Best breeding site in Britain for Slavonian Grebe. Teal, Wigeon and other wildfowl breed. Black Grouse, Peregrine, Hen Harrier and Osprey often seen. Kenna Chisholm as Culbin Sands above.

LOTHIAN

ABERLADY BAY. (1439a) East Lothian Council (LNR) NT472806. From reserve car park; also from public car park at Gullane. No dogs Apr-Jul. Mudflats, saltmarsh, sandbars, sand dunes, grassland, and the small freshwater Marl Loch. Breeding birds include Shelduck, Eider, Reed Bunting and up to 8 species of warbler. Passage waders inc. Green, Wood and Curlew Sandpipers, Little Stint, Greenshank, Whimbrel, Black-tailed Godwit. Divers (esp. Red-throated), Red-necked and Slavonian grebes and geese (large numbers of Pink-footed roost) in winter; sea-ducks, waders. Organised parties should apply to the Warden well in advance. Ian M Thomson, 4 Craigielaw, Longniddry, East Lothian EH32 0PY. 01875 870588

BASS ROCK. NT602873. The spectacular cliffs hold a large Gannet colony. Private property. Regular daily sailings from N Berwick around Rock; local boatman has owner's permission to land individuals or parties by prior arrangement. For details contact Fred Marr, N Berwick on 01620 892838.

BAWSINCH & DUDDINGSTON LOCH. (64a) Scottish WT NT284725. Centre of Edinburgh below Arthur's Seat. Loch with breeding and wintering wildfowl. Bitterns in winter. Marsh, ponds, trees and scrub. Open access to N shore of loch; to remainder of site and hide by prior arrangement with Colin McLean, 27 Manse Road, Roslin, Midlothian.

ORKNEY

BIRSAY MOORS. (5781a) RSPB. Cottasgarth hide along track left off A966 3 miles N of Finstown (HY368187). Separate access to hide at Burgar Hill, signposted from A966 at Evie (HY346247). Birsay Moors viewed from B9057 NW of Dounby. Nesting Hen Harrier, Merlin, Great and Arctic Skuas, Short-eared Owl, Golden Plover, Curlew, Red-throated Diver. No regular warden.

COPINSAY. (375a) RSPB HY610010. Breeding Kittiwake, auks, Shag, Fulmar, Rock Dove, Eider, Twite, Raven and Greater Black-backed Gull; passage migrants esp. during periods of E winds.

HOBBISTER. (1875a) RSPB HY396070 or HY381068. Near Kirkwall. Open access between A964 and the sea. Orkney moorland, bog, fen, saltmarsh. Breeding Hen Harrier, Merlin, Short-eared Owl, Red Grouse, Red-throated Diver, Eider, Merganser, Black Guillemot. Wildfowl and waders at Waulkmill Bay.

HOY. (9700a) RSPB HY223034. Island. Passenger ferry from Stromness to Moaness Pier; car ferry from Houton to Lyness. Moorland: Red-throated Diver, Great Skua, Red Grouse, Golden Plover, Dunlin, Curlew, Hen Harrier, Merlin, Short-eared Owl, Twite. Cliffs: Fulmar (22,500 pairs on reserve), Guillemot, Razorbill, Kittiwake, Shag, Buzzard, Peregrine, Raven, Manx Shearwater. Warden, Ley House, Hoy, Orkney KW16 3NJ. 01856 791298

LOONS (THE). (90a) RSPB HY246242. Access to hide (only) via minor road from A986, 3 miles N of Dounby. Marsh. Breeding duck (inc. Pintail, Red-breasted Merganser) and waders (inc. Snipe, Redshank, Black-tailed Godwit), Common and Black-headed Gulls, Arctic Tern; regular flock of Greenland White-fronted Geese in winter.

MARWICK HEAD. (46a) RSPB HY229242. Near Dounby. Path N from Marwick Bay, or from car park at Cumlaquoy at HY232252. May-Jul best. Rocky bay, sandstone cliffs. Large numbers of Kittiwakes and auks, also nesting Fulmar, Rock Dove, Raven, Rock Pipit.

NORTH HILL, PAPA WESTRAY. RSPB HY496538. N end of island's main road. Access at all times; during breeding season report to summer warden at Rose Cottage, 500m S of reserve entrance. Ferry and flights from Kirkwall (Loganair 01856 872494). Close views of colony of Puffins, Guillemots, Razorbills and Kittiwakes. Black Guillemots nest under flagstones around reserve's coastline. One of UK's largest colonies of Arctic Terns, also Arctic Skuas. RSPB Summer Warden, c/o Rose Cottage, Papa Westray KW17 2BU. 01857 644240

NORTH RONALDSAY BIRD OBSERVATORY. (1800a) HY760540. Flights by Loganair from Kirkwall, Orkney twice daily Mon-Sat (subsidised) 01856 872494; sea transport Fri (and some Sunday excursions in summer) from Kirkwall harbour 01856 872044. Open all year. Guest house and dormitory accommodation for up to 28 offered on half or full board basis. Advance booking essential. Daily ringing. Low lying arable land with several areas of marsh and maritime heath; rocky and sandy shores. Area of stunted trees attracts migrants. 308 species recorded to date. Important migration station in both spring and autumn. Annual occurrence of national rarities. Vast seabird movements in autumn. Lighthouse attractions. Alison Duncan or Dr Kevin Woodbridge, Twingness, North Ronaldsay, Orkney KW17 2BE. 01857 633200

NOUP CLIFFS. (35a) RSPB HY392500. Westray. No restriction; minor road from Pierowall to Noup Farm then track NW to lighthouse. May-Jul best. 1.5 miles of sandstone cliffs. Huge seabird colony; breeding Rock Dove, Raven, Shag, auks, Rock Pipit.

TRUMLAND, ROUSAY. (1070a) RSPB HY427276. Ferry from Tingwall in NE Mainland to Rousay. Reserve and nature trail (access at all times) from entrance to Taversoe Tuick Cairn. Dry heather moorland interspersed with wetter areas of rushes and ferns. Breeding Hen Harrier, Merlin, Short-eared Owl, Red-throated Diver, Golden Plover, Great and Arctic Skuas, Common Gull.

SHETLAND

FAIR ISLE BIRD OBSERVATORY. Between Orkney and Shetland. Access either by boat from Grutness, Shetland (Tu Th Sa May-Sep; Tu only Oct-Apr - weather permitting) or by Loganair scheduled flight from Tingwall Airport, Shetland (M W F Sa). Hotel-type accomm. for 34; single and twin rooms and dormitories. All meals, sheets and towels provided. Obs. open mid Apr-31 Oct; advance booking essential. (Friends of Fair Isle have preferential advance booking period of 1 month prior to opening of standard booking season. No staff available to take bookings Dec-mid

Jan.) Important migration station with 354 species recorded; many rarities annually. Continuous ringing programme. Large seabird colonies with 17 species inc. Arctic and Great Skuas, Storm Petrel. Deryk Shaw/Hollie Craib, Fair Isle Bird Observatory, Fair Isle, Shetland ZE2 9JU. 01595 760258: email fairisle.birdobs@zetnet.co.uk

FETLAR. (1700a) RSPB HU603917. Car ferry from Gutcher, north Yell. Booking essential, tel 01957 722259/722268. Part of RSPB reserve (Vord Hill) closed mid-May to end July; entry to this area during this period is only by arrangement with Warden. Serpentine heath/rough hill land. Island has breeding Red-throated Diver, Eider, Shag, Whimbrel, skuas, Manx Shearwater, Storm Petrel; Red-necked Phalarope on Loch of Funzie (HU655899) viewed from road or RSPB hide overlooking Mires of Funzie. RSPB North Isles Officer Shetland, Bealance, Fetlar, Shetland ZE2 9DJ. 01957 733246

ISLE OF NOSS. (774a) SNH (NNR) HU542405. Boat crosses Noss Sound Tu, W, F, Sa, Su in summer (reserve closed Sep-May). Avoid centre of island. Visitor room with exhibition. Moorland, rough pasture, sea cliffs, rocky shore. Breeding auks, Great and Arctic Skuas, Kittiwake, Fulmar, Gannet, Shag, Arctic Tern. Summer Warden. SNH Shetland Office, Ground Floor, Stewart Building, Lerwick, Shetland ZE1 0LL. 01595 693345

SUMBURGH HEAD. (39a) RSPB HU407079. S tip of mainland Shetland. Open all year but seabirds best May-mid Aug. Breeding Puffin, Guillemot, Razorbill, Kittiwake, Shag. RSPB Shetland Office, East House, Sumburgh Head Lighthouse, Virkie, Shetland ZE3 9JN. 01950 460800.

STRATHCLYDE

AYR GORGE WOODLANDS. (115a) Scottish WT NS457249. At Failford, off B743 Mauchline to Ayr road. Park in lay-by in Failford village. Access by path along west bank of River Ayr. Gorge woodland. Woodland and riverside birds.

BARONS HAUGH. (265a) RSPB NS755552. Motherwell. Via Adele Street, then lane off North Lodge Avenue. 4 hides. Marshland, flooded areas, woodland, parkland, meadows, scrub, river. Breeding Gadwall, warblers (inc. Garden, Grasshopper); Whinchat, Common Sandpiper, Kingfisher. Excellent for autumn waders (22 species). Winter: Whooper Swan. Contact via Lochwinnoch.

FALLS OF CLYDE. (170a) Scottish WT NS882425. At New Lanark, S of Lanark. Valley woodland along River Clyde by Falls of Clyde, including river and spectacular falls. Visitor centre open daily from Easter to October. Woodland and riverside species. Apr-Jun 'Operation Peregrine' (public viewing of breeding Peregrines and 24-hr surveillance/protection). Ranger Service, SWT Wildlife Centre, New Lanark, Lanark ML11 9DB. 01555 665262

KNOCKSHINNOCK LAGOONS. (244a) Scottish WT NS776113. Car park off B741 new Cumnock to Dalmelling road, or from Kirkbrae in New Cumnock. Mining spoil, lagoons, meadows, woodland. Breeding Redshank, Lapwing, Snipe, Curlew, Shoveler, Teal, Pochard and Garganey. Whooper Swans and large number of ducks in winter. Good for migrating waders in spring and autumn.

LOCH GRUINART, ISLAY. (4087a) RSPB. Good views from B8017 on S and W sides of loch. Car park. Visitor centre at Aoradh Farm (NR275672) open daily 1000-1700. New hide in flooded fields gives good views of waterfowl in winter and waders in summer. Pasture, saltmarsh, moorland, woodland, hill lochs. Major wintering site for Greenland race of Barnacle Goose (Oct-Apr); also large flocks of White-fronted Geese. Other winter birds include Golden Eagle, Peregrine, Merlin, Whooper Swan. Summer Buzzard, Wigeon, Shoveler, Teal, Redshank, Snipe, Curlew, Corncrake, Stonechat. Hen Harrier all year. Also Barn Owl, Chough. Clive McKay, RSPB Office, Bushmills Cottages, Gruinart, Bridgend, Isle of Islay PA44 7PS. 01496 850505

LOCHWINNOCH. (388a) RSPB NS358582. 18 miles SW of Glasgow, adjacent to A760. Open every day (except Xmas & New Year bank hols) 1000-1700. Special facilities for schools and disabled. Refreshments available. Nature centre, hides. Shallow lochs, marsh, mixed woodland. Winter wildfowl (esp. Whooper Swan, Greylag, Goosander, Goldeneye); occasional passage migrants inc. Whimbrel, Greenshank; breeding Great Crested Grebe, Water Rail, Sedge and Grasshopper Warblers. RSPB Nature Centre, Largs Road, Lochwinnoch, Strathclyde PA12 4JF. 01505 842663

MACHRIHANISH SEABIRD OBSERVATORY. NR628209. B843 just W of Machrihanish village at Uisaed Point. Parking for 3 vehicles only. Open at dawn during main migration periods, otherwise by appointment. Hide with access for people with mobility difficulties. Open sea, rough grazing, uplands. Storm and Leach's Petrels, Sooty, Manx and Mediterranean Shearwaters, Gannet, skuas, Golden Eagle, Twite. Eddie Maguire, 25B Albyn Avenue, Campbeltown, Argyll PA28 6LX. 01586 554823

POSSIL MARSH. (70a) Scottish WT NS585700. On A879 on outskirts of Lambhill in N of Glasgow, next to Forth and Clyde Canal. Parking in Skirsa Court, off Skirsa Street, Lambhill. Loch, rich marshland. Breeding and wintering wildfowl. Good area for waterbirds and warblers on migration.

TAYSIDE

BALGAVIES LOCH. (114a) Scottish WT NO534508. From car park on A932, 5 miles E of Forfar. Wintering wildfowl and wetland breeding birds. Hide open at weekends.

KILLIECRANKIE. (640a) RSPB NN907627. W of A9 Pitlochry-Blair Atholl road, B8079 to Killiecrankie, then minor road SW to reserve. Upland birchwood, crags and moorland. Buzzard, Crossbill, Wood Warbler, Redstart, Tree Pipit; Black Grouse and Whinchat on moorland fringe; occasional Golden Eagle, Peregrine, Raven. Contact RSPB East Scotland Regional Office.

LOCH LEVEN. (3946a) SNH (NNR) NO150010. Leave M90 at exit 5. Public access restricted to three short stretches of shoreline. Most birdwatchers visiting the reserve go to the RSPB nature centre at Vane Farm (qv) overlooking the loch. Lowland loch with islands. Wintering flocks of geese (over 20,000 Pinkfeet), ducks, Whooper Swan; breeding ducks (10 species) and grebes; passage waders. Extensive ornithological research programme. Alan Lauder/Paul Brooks, SNH, Loch Leven Laboratory, The Pier, Kinross KY13 7UF. 01577 864439

LOCH OF KINNORDY. (200a) RSPB NO361539. From B951 W of Kirriemuir. Open every day 0900 to dusk. Hides. Shallow loch, fen, swamp and carr. Breeding Great Crested and Black-necked Grebes, Wigeon, Gadwall, Shoveler, Pochard, Water Rail, regular Osprey; passage Greenshank, Ruff; winter roosting Pink-footed and Greylag Geese, also wintering wildfowl inc. Goosander. Summer Warden, The Flat, Kinnordy Home Farm, Kirriemuir, Angus DD8 5ER. 01575 574553; winter 01250 881496

LOCH OF LINTRATHEN. (400a) Scottish WT NO278550. View from road N of loch. Hide available on open days (key from Warden). Winter wildfowl, inc. 2000-5000 Greylag, 600-700 Wigeon, 10-15 Goosander. Karen Spalding, as Montrose Basin (below).

LOCH OF LOWES. (242a) Scottish WT NO050440. 2 miles E of Dunkeld. Hide open all year, visitor centre Mar-Oct. Advance booking necessary for groups. Loch with wooded fringe. Water birds; winter goose roost; breeding Osprey. Dr Alan Barclay, SWT Loch of Lowes Centre, Dunkeld, Perthshire PH8 0HH. 01350 727337; fax 01674 678773

MONTROSE BASIN. (2500a) Scottish WT (LNR) NO690580. Views from A934 (extensive), A935 and A92 (esp. from visitor centre). Footpath from Old Montrose (NO675572) to Bridge of Dun (NO663584) along river. Hides. Information boards at numerous points around basin. Tidal mudflats. Waders (esp. Redshank, Knot, Dunlin, Curlew, Oystercatcher); important wintering ground for wildfowl (inc. Greylag and Pink-footed Geese, Wigeon, Mallard, Eider, Pintail). Summer: 300 moulting Mute Swan and 150 Goosander; over 500 Eider nest; regular Osprey, terns, passage migrants. Karen Spalding, Montrose Basin Wildlife Centre, Rossie Brae, Montrose, Angus DD10 9TJ. 01674 676336; fax 01674 678773

SEATON CLIFFS. (26a) Scottish WT NO667416. Car parking at N end of promenade at Arbroath. Red sandstone cliffs with nature trail. Seabirds inc. Eider, auks, terns; Rock Dove and House Martin breed.

VANE FARM. (600a) RSPB NT160993. Near Kinross. From B9097 E of M90 (exit 5). Open at all times; nature centre open Apr-Dec 1000-1700; Jan-Mar 1000-1600. New Loch Leven centre now open with observation facilities, shop, coffee shop. New wetland trail with hides overlooking flooded areas and wet grassland. Special facilities for schools by arrangement. Farmland and hillside beside Loch Leven. Birds: see Loch Leven, above; also Tree Pipit, Buzzard, Peregrine, Redpoll. Ken Shaw, Vane Farm Nature Centre, Kinross KY13 7LX. 01577 862355; fax 01577 862013

WESTERN ISLES

BALRANALD. (1625a) RSPB NF706707. North Uist. Turn off main road 3 miles NW of Bayhead at signpost to Hougharry. Reserve visitor centre and toilets open at all times. Machair, beaches, marshland and lochs. Corncrake, wildfowl, waders, terns, Corn Bunting; skua passage. Gwen Evans, Druidibeg Cottage, Stilligarry, South Uist HS8 5RR. 01870 620369

LOCH DRUIDIBEG. (4145a) SNH (NNR) NF782378. South Uist. Restricted access during breeding season. Loch, machair, coast. Breeding Greylag, waders. SNH Area Officer, 135 Stilligarry, South Uist HS8 5RS. 01870 620238

WALES

NORTH WALES

BARDSEY BIRD OBSERVATORY. On a private 444 acre island in the Irish Sea, 2 miles off the tip of the Lleyn Peninsula. Boat from Aberdaron. Farmhouse accommodation; 6 bedrooms, common room, dining room, library, ringing room, cooking facilities; chemical toilets; electric lighting. Weekly bookings, Sat-Sat only, for up to 12 persons; ringers very welcome. Chough and 10 species of seabird breed (Manx Shearwater colony). Large numbers of migrants recorded every spring and autumn; good chance of vagrants from N America and S Europe. Well known for attracting birds to its lighthouse beams. 300 species recorded. Bookings to Mrs Alicia Normand, 46 Maudlin Drive, Teignmouth, Devon TQ14 8SB, tel 01626 773908. Volunteers apply to Warden. Steven Stansfield, Bird Observatory, Bardsey Island, off Aberdaron, Pwllheli LL53 8DE. 08312 55569

BWLCHCOEDIOG NATURE RESERVE. (25a) SH878149. Half mile E of Mallwyd turn L into Cwm Cewydd, then 1.25 mi up valley and park at Bwlchcoediog House. Open all year. No dogs; in fenced areas keep to paths. Farmland, woodland, streams, 2 ponds, lake. Breeding Tree Pipit, Redstart, Garden and Wood Warblers, Pied and Spotted Flycatchers; winter Woodcock, Brambling; Raven, Buzzard, Sparrowhawk, Siskin all year; occasional Peregrine, Red Kite, Dipper. Owner: Dr R J Banham, Bwlchcoediog Isaf, Cwm Cewydd, Mallwyd, Machynlleth, Powys. 01650 531243

CADAIR IDRIS. (969a) CCW (NNR) SH728116. 3 miles SW of Dolgellau. Permit for enclosed woodland. Cliffs, heath. Breeding Raven, Wheatear, Ring Ouzel, Pied Flycatcher. Contact: CCW North West Area. Rhodri Evans. Tel/fax 01766 780937; mobile 0378 373879

CEMLYN. (44a) North Wales WT SH337932. Unclassified road N of A5025 at Tregele, W of Cemaes Bay, Anglesey. Keep on seaward side of shingle ridge during nesting season. Brackish lagoon, shingle spit. Breeding terns. Passage waders; winter wildfowl (inc. Little Grebe, Goldeneye, Shoveler).

COEDYDD ABER. (419a) CCW (NNR) SH660710. From car park at Bont Newydd, SE of Aber. Permit required for places away from designated routes. Small visitor centre. Upland valley, deciduous woodland, river. Dipper, Grey Wagtail, Buzzard, Raven, woodland birds. Duncan Brown. Tel/fax 01286 650547; mobile 0421 869263

COEDYDD MAENTWROG. (169a) CCW (NNR) SH667416. From car park on B4410 Maentwrog/Rhyd road. Coed Llyn Mair Nature Trail. Oak woodland; views over lake. Summer: Redstart, Wood Warbler, Pied Flycatcher; winter: Goldeneye, Pochard. Doug Oliver. Tel/fax 01766 530461; mobile 07771 925888

CONNAHS QUAY POWERGEN RESERVE. (300a) Deeside Naturalists' Society SJ275715. Take A548 from Queensferry towards Flint, 2 miles. Advance permit required. Field studies centre, 4 hides. Saltmarsh, mudflats, grassland scrub, open water, wetland meadow. High water roosts of waders, inc. Black-tailed Godwit, Oystercatcher, Redshank, Spotted Redshank; also passage waders; winter wildfowl (inc. Teal, Pintail, Goldeneye), Merlin, Peregrine. R A Roberts, 38 Kelsterton Road, Connahs Quay, Flints CH5 4BJ.

CONWY. (116a) RSPB SH799771. Leave A55 at exit to Conwy and Deganwy (entrance off roundabout). Car park, visitor centre (open daily exc. 25 Dec, 1000-1700 or dusk if earlier) with toilets, shop and refreshments. 4 hides. Keep to trails. Coastal lagoons, island, reedbeds, grassland, estuary. Breeding waders inc. Little and Ringed Plovers, Redshank, Lapwing, Sand Martin. Large flocks of roosting Curlew and Oystercatcher. Up to 1000 wildfowl in winter (esp. Teal, Mallard, Wigeon). Good for raptors and passage waders. Recent rarities inc. Terek and Broad-billed Sandpipers, Wryneck, Hoopoe, Marsh Warbler, Ortolan Bunting. Ian Higginson, Conwy RSPB Nature Reserve, Llandudno Junction LL31 9XZ. 01492 584091

CWM IDWAL. (984a) CCW (NNR) SH648603. Access from the Snowdonia National Park car park on A5 between Bethesda and Capel Curig. Do not enter experimental enclosures. Mountain, river, shallow lake. Heron, gulls, Dipper, Ring Ouzel, Wheatear, Common Sandpiper. Hywel Roberts. Tel/fax 01248 362312; mobile 0468 918573

GORS MAEN LLWYD. North Wales WT SH975580. N of Llyn Brenig. Hide next to lake. Heather moorland, blanket bog. Red and Black Grouse, Wheatear, Whinchat, Merlin, Hen Harrier.

LLYN ALAW. (1000a) Hyder plc/Hamdden SH374855. Near Llanerchymedd, Anglesey. Open access, except to sanctuary at NE end. 2 hides, visitor centre. Lake, mixed woodland. Winter wildfowl (inc. Bewick's and Whooper Swans, Long-tailed Duck, White-fronted & Pink-footed Geese); passage waders (inc. Spotted Redshank, Little Stint, and Wood, Curlew & Pectoral Sandpipers); birds of prey (inc. Hen Harrier, Peregrine, Merlin, Short-eared Owl). Jim Clark, Head Ranger, Visitor Centre, Llyn Alaw Reservoir, Llantrisant, Holyhead, Anglesey LL65 4TW. 01407 730762; fax 07070 711660

LLYN CEFNI. (150a) Hyder plc/Hamdden SH451782. N of Llangefni on B5111 Llanerchymedd road. Open at all times. Hide. Lake, coniferous woodland. Crossbill, Siskin, Redpoll, owls, warblers; grebes, diving ducks, Whooper Swan. Jim Clark, Head Ranger, Visitor Centre, Llyn Alaw Reservoir, Llantrisant, Holyhead, Anglesey LL65 4TW. 01407 730762; fax 07070 711660

MAWDDACH VALLEY. (1288a) RSPB. 1. Coed Garth Gell (SH687191). Park in lay-by on A496 Barmouth/Dolgellau road opposite Borthwnog Hotel. Broadleaved woodland. Breeding Buzzard, Raven, Pied Flycatcher, Wood Warbler, Redstart, Lesser Spotted Woodpecker, Grey Wagtail, Dipper. 2. Arthog Bog (SH630138). Park at Morfa Mawddach station. Willow and alder scrub, raised mire. Whitethroat, Sedge and Grasshopper Warblers, Redpoll. 3. Penmaenpool Information Centre (SH695186, next to Penmaenpool toll bridge), with information video, open daily from late May-Sep and weekends in Apr & May. Graeme Stringer, Abergwynant Lodge, Penmaenpool, Dolgellau LL40 1YF. 01341 422071

NEWBOROUGH WARREN. (3842a) CCW (NNR) SH406670/430630. A4080 S of Malltraeth, Anglesey. Permit required for places away from designated routes. Sandhills, estuaries, saltmarshes, dune grasslands. Wildfowl and waders at Malltraeth

Pool (visible from road), Braint and Cefni estuaries (licensed winter shoot on marked areas of Cefni estuary administered by CCW); waterfowl at Llyn Rhosddu (public hide). Contact: W Sandison, CCW North West Area. Tel/fax 01248 716422; mobile 0468 918572

POINT OF AIR. (6200a) RSPB SJ113833. Near Prestatyn. View from end of Station Road off A548 at Talacre. Hide overlooking roost reached from embankment leading towards colliery. Shingle, saltmarsh, mudflats. 20,000 wintering waders, esp. Oystercatcher, Knot, Dunlin, Redshank; also passage waders, inc. Sanderling; many terns in summer and autumn; Shelduck, Red-breasted Merganser, Snow Bunting, Twite in winter. Warden, c/o Gayton Sands (see Cheshire).

SOUTH STACK CLIFFS. (780a) RSPB SH205823. W of Holyhead, Anglesey. Car parks. Information centre (Ellin's Tower) with windows overlooking main auk colony open daily 1100-1700 Easter-Sep, with live TV of the seabirds. Public footpaths. Sea cliffs, maritime heath. Chough, Fulmar, auks, migrant warblers. Alastair Moralee, Plas Nico, South Stack, Holyhead, Anglesey LL65 1YH. 01407 764973

SPINNIES. (7a) North Wales WT SH613721. Adjacent to Traeth Lafan (see below). Hide with disabled access. Brackish lagoon, woodland. Summer Little Grebe, Sedge Warbler; winter Kingfisher, Water Rail, Greenshank.

TRAETH LAFAN. (6000a) Gwynedd Council & Conwy CBC (LNR). Minor road from old A55 near Tal y Bont (SH610710) to Aber Ogwen car park by coast (SH614723). Also access from minor road from Aber village to Morfa Aber LNR (SH646731), car park and bird hide, track to Morfa Madryn LNR (SH667743), bird hides, and Llanfairfechan promenade (SH679754). Toilets and cafes. Public paths. Intertidal sands and mudflats, wetlands, streams. SPA and SSSI. Third most important area in Wales for wintering waders; of national importance for moulting Great Crested Grebe and Red-breasted Merganser; internationally important for Oystercatcher and Curlew; passage waders; winter concentrations of Goldeneye and Greenshank, and of regional significance for wintering populations of Black-throated, Red-throated & Great Northern Divers and Black-necked & Slavonian Grebes. Director, Planning and Economic Development Dept, Gwynedd Council, Council Offices, Caernarfon LL55 1SH. 01286 679381; fax 01286 673324; e-mail ruralservices @gwynedd.gov.uk

SOUTH WALES

ABERTHAW SALTMARSH. (20a) Glamorgan WT ST045657. E of Aberthaw Power Station. Park in layby on main road. Open access. Lias limestone cliffs, saltmarsh (very mobile), pebble beach. Whimbrel in spring; migrant waders and passerines in autumn; Peregrine in winter. Good seawatching. Contact: Trust HQ.

CWM CLYDACH. (213a) RSPB SN685026. Car park 2 miles N of Clydach opp side of river to New Inn pub in Craig-cefn-Parc. Access at all times; keep to marked public path along river. Oak woodlands with some areas of birch and beech; ash and alder on wetter ground; heather and bracken slopes. Nesting Buzzard, Sparrowhawk, Raven, Pied Flycatcher, Redstart, Wood Warbler, all 3 woodpeckers, Nuthatch, Treecreeper, Tawny Owl, Dipper, Grey Wagtail, Tree Pipit, Wheatear; winter Snipe, Woodcock, Redpoll, Siskin. Martin Humphreys, 2 Ty'n y Berllan, Craig-cefn-Parc, Swansea SA6 5TL. 01792 842927

CWM COL-HUW. Glamorgan WT SS957674. Follow beach road from Llantwit Major village. Unimproved grassland, woodland, scrub and lias cliff. Cliff-nesting House Martin colony, breeding Fulmar, Grasshopper Warbler. Large autumn passerine passage. Peregrine. Seawatching vantage point. Contact: Trust HQ.

KENFIG. (1240a) Bridgend CBC (NNR) SS802811. From car park at Kenfig on unclassified road between North Cornelly and Porthcawl. Avoid reedswamp on W shore of pool during breeding season (Mar-Jul). Interpretative centre (check hours), 2 hides. Mobile and fixed dunes, low lying wetland (slacks), pool (70a), river, grassland, adjacent rocky shore. Winter Whooper and Bewick's Swans (though both now irregular), Goldeneye, Short-eared Owl, Merlin; July & Aug large numbers of Manx Shearwaters; autumn Black Tern, waders. David G Carrington, Kenfig Reserve Centre, Ton Kenfig, Pyle, Bridgend CF33 4PT. 01656 743386

LAVERNOCK POINT. (15a) Glamorgan WT ST182680. Public footpaths S of B4267 between Barry & Penarth. Cliff top, unimproved grassland, scrub. Seawatching in late summer; Glamorgan's best migration hotspot in autumn. Contact: Trust HQ.

LLYN FACH. (40a) Glamorgan WT SN905038. From car park off A4061 1.8 miles S of Hirwaun. Lake, bog, cliff and scree, surrounded by plantations. Nesting Raven, Ring Ouzel; Buzzard, Sparrowhawk. Contact: Trust HQ.

OXWICH. (750a) CCW (NNR) SS875505. Off A4118 W of Swansea. Open at all times. Hide, trails. Marshes, dunes, woodland, foreshore. South Gower Coast NNR (SS85390) near Rhossili. Co-operation of visitors essential when in Worms Head area during breeding season. Seabirds, waders.

PARC SLIP NATURE PARK. (247a) Glamorgan WT SS880840. Tondu, half mile W of Aberkenfig. Open dawn to dusk. 3 hides, nature trail, interpretation centre. Restored opencast mining site, wader scrape, lagoons. Breeding Tufted Duck, Lapwing, Skylark. Migrant waders (inc. Little Ringed Plover, Green Sandpiper), Little Gull. Contact: Trust HQ.

EAST WALES

BRECHFA POOL. (16a) Brecknock WT SO118377. Lane off A470, 1.5 miles SW of Llyswen; on Brechfa Common, pool is on right after cattle grid. Marshy grassland, large shallow pool. Teal, Wigeon, Bewick's Swan, Redshank, Lapwing, Dunlin. Contact Trust HQ.

DOLYDD HAFREN. (104a) Montgomeryshire WT SJ206005. S of Welshpool on A483 then A490 to Forden. Follow road through Forden and 2 miles on turn R at SO209996 down track at Gaer Farm to the reserve. Open all year. River Severn flood plain with scrapes and enlarged oxbow lakes. 2 hides. Waders and wildfowl. Contact: Trust HQ.

ELAN VALLEY. (45,000a) Hyder plc & Elan Valley Trust. Visitor centre at SN927646. 3 miles W of Rhayader. Open access, marked trails. Reservoirs, oak woodland, moorland. Red Kite, Peregrine, Merlin, Golden Plover. Pete Jennings, Elan Valley Visitor Centre, Rhayader, Powys LD6 5HP. H:01597 811522; W:01597 810880

GILFACH. (418a) Radnorshire WT SN965717. 2 miles N of Rhayader, turn E off A470 to St Harmon. Open at all times. Visitor centre open F-Su from Easter to 30 Sep. Nature trail. River, oak woodland, open moorland, fields. Buzzard, Red Kite, Peregrine, Merlin, Dipper, Grey Wagtail, Pied Flycatcher, Redstart, Wood Warbler, Stonechat, Tim Thompson, Gilfach Farm, St Harmon, Rhayader, Powys CD6 5LF. 01597 870301

GLASLYN, PLYNLIMON. (535a) Montgomeryshire WT SN825945. NW of Llanidloes, on minor road between Staylittle and Machynlleth. Access via gate at SN837952 along single track road. Public access, keep dogs on lead. Heather moorland, ravine, scree slopes, upland oligotrophic lake. Red Grouse, Wheatear, birds of prey, Golden Plover, Raven.

LLYN MAWR. (30a) Montgomeryshire WT SO007972. Minor 'no through' road N of Clatter. Stay close to shore. Upland lake, wetland, scrub. Breeding Great Crested Grebe, Snipe, Curlew, Whinchat. Winter: occasional Goldeneye, Goosander, Whooper Swan.

MAGOR MARSH. (65a) Gwent WT ST425867. Leave M4 at exit 23. S of Magor village; gate on Whitewall Common on E side of reserve. Keep to path. Parties give advance notice. Hide. Marsh, reens, pond, willow and alders, scrub. Waterfowl (inc. breeding Garganey); reedbed warblers; Water Rail. Derek Upton, 14 Westfield, Caldicot, Newport, Gwent NP6 4HE. 01291 420137

MAGOR PILL TO COLDHARBOUR PILL. (0.6 mile) Gwent WT ST437847. Access from Magor Pill Farm track down to sea wall. Foreshore. Passage and winter waders. Derek Upton, 14 Westfield, Caldicot, Newport, Gwent NP6 4HE. 01291 420137

PETERSTONE WENTLOOGE. (2a) Gwent WT ST269800. Public footpaths to sea wall off B4239 NE of Cardiff. Foreshore, grazing. Passage waders and winter wildfowl.

PWLL-Y-WRACH. (21a) Brecknock WT SO165327. Half mile SE of Talgarth, access is from the minor road. Small car park. Keep to public footpaths (inc. one for disabled). Steep valley woodland, stream. Dipper, Grey Wagtail, woodland species (inc. Pied Flycatcher, Wood Warbler).

ROUNDTON HILL. (80a) Montgomeryshire WT SO293947. SE of Montgomery. From Church Stoke, take minor road to Old Church Stoke, R at phone box, then first R. Car park. Open access. Ancient hill grassland, woodland, streamside wet flushes, scree, rock outcrops. Buzzard, Raven, Wheatear, all 3 woodpeckers, Tawny Owl, Redstart, Linnet, Goldfinch. Contact: Trust HQ.

STRAWBERRY COTTAGE WOOD. (16a) Gwent WT SO315214. N of Abergavenny. Leave A465 at Llanvihangel Crucorney on minor road to Llanthony, about 1.25 miles. Open at all times. Keep to waymarked trail. Mixed woodland on valley side. Buzzard, Redstart, Pied Flycatcher, Wood Warbler. Jerry Lewis, Y Bwthyn Gwyn, Coldbrook, Abergavenny, Monmouthshire NP7 9TD. 01873 855091

TAF FECHAN RESERVOIR (UPPER). (182a) Brecknock WT SO056145. N of Merthyr Tydfil, off Ponticill to Talybont road over dam to Dolygaer entrance by stile. Park before crossing dam. Permit required; BWT members only. Overwintering Goosander, Whooper Swan, Goldeneye; Teal and Wigeon, Redshank, Common Sandpiper.

TALYBONT RESERVOIR. (490a) Brecon Beacons National Park SO100190. Views from minor road off B4558 S of Talybont. Displays at the Glyn Collwm information centre at Aber, between the reservoir and Talybont. Reservoir, woodland. Winter wildfowl (inc. Goldeneye, Goosander, Whooper Swan); migrant waders; winter Redpoll and Siskin.

VYRNWY (LAKE). (24392a) RSPB SJ020193. Near Llanfyllin. Access along public roads and footpaths. Information centre open daily 1030-1730, but weekends only Xmas-Mar. Toilet, shop. 3 nature trails; 4 hides. Lake, woodlands, uplands. Nesting Goosander, Sparrowhawk, Common Sandpiper, Dipper, Kingfisher, Redstart, Pied Flycatcher, Crossbill, Siskin. Mike Walker, Bryn Awel, Llanwddyn, Owestry, Shrops SY10 0LZ. 01691 870278

WEST WALES

CASTLE WOODS. (62a) WT West Wales SN615217. Open all year by footpath from Tywi Bridge, Llandeilo (SN627221). Old mixed deciduous woodlands. All woodpeckers, Buzzard, Raven, Sparrowhawk, Pied and Spotted Flycatchers, Redstart, Wood Warbler. Steve Lucas, 35 Maesquarre Road, Betws, Ammanford, Carmarthenshire SA18 2LF. 01269 594293

CORS CARON. (2016a) CCW (NNR) SN690635. Reached from B4343 N of Tregaron. Access along old railway track (inc. observation tower) quarter mile N of Maesllyn farm entrance. Permit required for all areas except railway track: access restricted between 1 Oct-31 Jan on certain days (usu. F or Sa) due to sporting rights. Peat bogs, flashes, river. Sparrowhawk, Redpoll, Grasshopper Warbler, Water Rail; winter wildfowl, waders and raptors (esp. Hen Harrier, Red Kite). Paul Cullyer, Neuaddlas, Tregaron, Ceredigion SY25 6LG. 01974 298480

DINAS & GWENFFRWD. (1711a) RSPB SN749460. N of Llandovery. Off minor road to Rhandirmwyn from Llandovery or Pumpsaint; Dinas car park off road to Llyn Brianne reservoir at SN788472. Public nature trail at Dinas open at all times. For access to Gwenffrwd trails for RSPB members only (Good Friday-Aug) obtain details at Dinas car park. Hillside oakwoods, streams, bracken slopes, moorlands. Buzzard, Raven, Pied Flycatcher, Redstart, Woodcock; Red Kite in area.

DYFI. (5595a) CCW (NNR) SN610942. Public footpaths off A493 E of Aberdyfi, and off B4353 (S of river); minor road from B4353 at Ynyslas to dunes and parking area. Ynyslas dunes and the estuary have unrestricted access. No access to Cors Fochno (raised bog) for casual birdwatching; permit required for study and research purposes. Good views over the bog and Aberleri marshes from W bank of Afon Leri. Public hide overlooking marshes beside footpath at SN611911. Sandflats, mudflats, saltmarsh, creeks, dunes, raised bog, grazing marsh. Wintering flock of Greenland White-fronted Geese; passage and wintering wildfowl, waders and raptors. Breeding wildfowl and waders (inc. Teal, Shoveler, Merganser, Lapwing, Curlew, Redshank). Ynyslas Visitor Centre 01970 871640. Mike Bailey, CCW Warden, Plas Gogerddan, Aberystwyth, Ceredigion SY23 3EE. 01970 828100

LLANELLI. (220a) WWT Centre SS533984. Signposted from A484, E of Llanelli. Open daily 0930-1730 in summer, earlier in winter (except 24 & 25 Dec). Visitor centre, restaurant, hides, education facilities, disabled access. Overlooks Burry Inlet.

Large flocks of Curlew, Oystercatcher, Redshank on saltmarsh. Wintering Pintail, Wigeon, Teal. Also Little Egret, Short-eared Owl, Peregrine. Dr Geoff Proffitt, Centre Manager, The Wildfowl & Wetlands Trust, Penclacwydd, Llwynhendy, Llanelli SA14 9SH. 01554 741087

PENGELLI FOREST. (160a) WT West Wales SN123396. Minor road off A487 from Felindre Farchog/Eglwyswrw. Open all year. No permit. Trails. 40a sessile oak wood, 120a mixed oak/ash wood (inc. scrub, rides). Pied Flycatcher, Redstart, Wood Warbler, Buzzard, Raven, woodpeckers. Lin Gander, Welsh Wildlife Centre, Cilgerran, Cardigan SA43 2TB. 01269 621600

RAMSEY ISLAND. (625a) RSPB SM702240. Boats from Lifeboat Station, St Justinian's, nr St David's, leave daily except Tu at 1000 & 1300 (also 1030 Jul/Aug), returning 1315 & 1600. Limited to 40 visitors a day normally, but 80 mid Jul-Aug. Advance boat bookings 01437 721686 & 0800 163621. Breeding auks, Kittiwake, Manx Shearwater, Peregrine, Buzzard, Chough, Raven, Lapwing, Wheatear. Warden, Ramsey Island, St David's, Pembs SA62 6QA. Mobile 0836 535733

SKOKHOLM ISLAND. WT West Wales SM738037. Day visits, M only Jun-Aug from Martinshaven. Weekly accomm. Apr-Oct, tel 01437 765462 for details and booking. Cliffs, bays and inlets. Large colonies of Razorbill, Puffin, Guillemot, Manx Shearwater, Storm Petrel, Lesser Black-backed Gull; migrants inc. rare species.

SKOMER ISLAND. WT West Wales (NNR) SM725095. By boat Apr-late Oct daily except M (but inc. Bank Hols) 1000-1800. Photographers using hides should apply to Trust; researchers apply to CCW. Some limited self catering accommodation. Cliffs, rocky beaches. One of finest seabird colonies in NW Europe with Fulmar, Shag, Kittiwake, Razorbill, Puffin, Guillemot, Manx Shearwater. Also Buzzard, Short-eared Owl, Raven, Chough, and good migrants in spring and autumn.

WELSH WILDLIFE CENTRE. (264a) WT West Wales SN188451. Access by car from minor road near Cilgerran to the Centre car park. Shop, information area and restaurant. Many observation hides, trails. Open all year. Wetland with reedbeds, grazing marshes, pools and estuary, woodland and river gorge. Cetti's Warbler breeds. Winter wildfowl, passage waders; scarce visitors have inc. Little Egret, Little Bittern, Night Heron, Osprey, Marsh Harrier, Temminck's Stint. Mary Davies, Manager, Welsh Wildlife Centre, Cilgerran, Cardigan SA43 2TB. 01239 621600; fax 01239 613211

YNYS-HIR. (1360a) RSPB SN686956. Off A487 Aberystwyth/Machynlleth road in Eglwys-fach village. Reserve open every day 0900-2100 or sunset when earlier; visitor centre & toilet Mar-Oct 0900-1700 and w/e in winter. Woodland, farmland, freshwater marsh, saltmarsh, estuary. 74 species breed on the reserve inc. Buzzard, Sparrowhawk, Pied Flycatcher, Sedge and Grasshopper Warblers. Winter wildfowl inc. Wigeon, Greenland White-fronted Geese; non-breeding raptors inc. Peregrine, Merlin, Red Kite, Hen Harrier. Dick Squires, Cae'r Berllan, Eglwysfach, Machynlleth, Powys SY20 8TA. 01654 781265

CHANNEL ISLANDS

GUERNSEY

COLIN McCATHIE RESERVE (VALE POND). (20a) La Société Guernesiaise. Open at all times. Hide on road to Vale church must be used. Avoid lake edge. Brackish tidal pond, reed fringes. Migrant waders. Julian Medland, Clyne, Rue de la Ronde Cheminée, Castel, Guernsey GY5 7GE. 01481 55411

LA CLAIRE MARE. La Société Guernesiaise. Open at all times. Hide down concrete track off the Rue de la Rocque road. Reedbeds, pasture, willow thickets, scrape. Avoid venturing further than hide. Good winter site, also migrant waders and passerines. Julian Medland, Clyne, Rue de la Ronde Cheminée, Castel, Guernsey GY5 7GE. 01481 55411

ISLE OF MAN

CALF OF MAN BIRD OBSERVATORY. Small island off the SW tip of the Isle of Man. Local boat from Port Erin or Port St Mary. Accommodation Apr-Oct for 8 in 3 bedrooms. Daily ringing and recording of migrants and complete census of the breeding birds. Hen Harrier and Peregrine most of year; breeding seabirds (9 species inc. Storm Petrel, Manx Shearwater), Raven, Chough. Excellent autumn seabird passage. Many rarities. Bookings: Administration Dept, Manx National Heritage, Manx Museum, Douglas, Isle of Man IM1 3LY.

CLOSE SARTFIELD. (31a) Manx NCT SC358956. On fringe of Ballaugh Curragh. Hide with disabled access. Damp meadows, willow carr and bog myrtle/purple moor-grass bog. Water Rail, Hen Harrier, Lesser Redpoll, Grasshopper Warbler. Contact: Manx NCT.

CRONK Y BING. (15a) Manx NCT NX377015. Sand dunes with single foreshore, S of the Lhen Trench. Open throughout the year. Terns, divers, Gannet. Contact: Manx NCT.

DALBY MOUNTAIN. (69a) Manx NCT SC232766. Heather moorland both sides of the A27. Parking. Open throughout the year. Hen Harrier, Red Grouse, Curlew, Snipe. Contact: Manx NCT.

NORTHERN IRELAND

CO ANTRIM

BREEN OAKWOOD. (40a) DANI (Forest Service) & EHS (NNR) D125338. Off the Armoy-Glenshesk-Ballycastle road. Oak and birch woodland. Wood Warbler. Ian Irvine, Portrush Countryside Centre, 8 Bath Road, Portrush, Co Antrim BT56 8AP. 01265 823600

GLENARM. (840a) Ulster WT D304110. By gate on B97 half mile SW of Glenarm. Private demesne. Permit required. Glen with hazel coppice and oakwood. Buzzard, Sparrowhawk, Peregrine, Raven, Dipper, Grey Wagtail, Woodcock, Heron. Contact: UWT HQ.

KEBBLE. (303a) EHS (NNR) D095515. W end of Rathlin Island. Scheduled ferry service from Ballycastle. Major cliff nesting colonies of auks (inc. Puffin), Fulmar and Kittiwake; also Buzzard and Peregrine; remainder grass and heath with a lake and marsh. Ian Irvine, Portrush Countryside Centre, 8 Bath Road, Portrush, Co Antrim BT56 8AP. 01265 823600

LAGAN MEADOWS. (33a). Ulster WT J335703. From Bladon Drive (off Malone Road) or from River Lagan towpath upriver from Stranmillis. Within Lagan Valley Regional Park where Crossbill, Siskin breed and Goshawks reported breeding. Open all year. Grazed and ungrazed pastures with a pond, some wet drains and willow scrub. In summer Sedge, Grasshopper and Willow Warblers abundant; Kingfisher and Dabchick on adjacent river; Snipe, Water Rail breed. Wide range of winter passerines. Contact: UWT HQ.

LOUGH NEAGH ISLANDS. EHS (NNR). On most of the 80 islands within the reserve there are breeding wildfowl (inc. Gadwall, Shelduck), gulls, terns. Landing is only by arrangement with Warden. Judith Montgomery-Watson, Lough Neagh Nature Reserves, Oxford Island, Craigavon, Co Armagh BT66 6NJ. 01762 322398

PORTMORE LOUGH. (154a) RSPB J017685. Follow brown signs from Aghalee village. Damp grassland, alder/willow carr, reedbed. Reception area with shelter and toilets. Best visited in winter when Greylag Geese (4000), Whooper Swans (60+) and other waterfowl frequent the meadows. The lough can hold massive numbers of diving ducks, viewable from hide. Warden: Eddie Franklin, 01846 652406

RANDALSTOWN FOREST. (22a) DANI (Forest Service) & EHS (NNR) J088872. 2 miles S of Randalstown. Lough Neagh shore and scrub. Public hide. Wildfowl. Judith Montgomery-Watson, Lough Neagh Nature Reserves, Oxford Island, Craigavon, Co Armagh BT66 6NJ. 01762 322398

RATHLIN ISLAND CLIFFS. (2.5 miles) RSPB. Crossings from Ballycastle: daily scheduled sailings with Caledonian MacBrayne; for times call 01265 769 299. Access to seabird viewpoint only under supervision of Warden. Booking essential. Nesting auks, Fulmar, Shag, Kittiwake; Buzzard, Peregrine, Raven occur. Liam McFaul, South Cleggan, Rathlin Island, Co Antrim BT54 6RT. 01265 763948

REA'S WOOD. (65a) DANI (Forest Service) & EHS (NNR) J142855. 1 mile S of Antrim. Lough Neagh shore and scrub. Wildfowl and woodland species (inc. Blackcap, Siskin). Judith Montgomery-Watson, Lough Neagh Nature Reserves, Oxford Island, Craigavon, Co Armagh BT66 6NJ. 01762 322398

CO ARMAGH

OXFORD ISLAND. (128a) Craigavon BC (NNR) J053616. On Lough Neagh shore N of Lurgan. Signposted from junction 10, M1. Open at all times except 25 Dec. 5 hides. Lough shore, reedbed, wet grassland, ponds, woodland, scrub. Wide variety of breeding and wintering wildfowl. Lough Neagh Discovery Centre with café and shop open daily Apr-Dec and W-Su Oct-Mar. Mrs P Davidson, Lough Neagh Discovery Centre, Craigavon, Co Armagh BT66 6NJ. 028 383 22205

CO DOWN

BELFAST LOUGH RESERVE. (272a) RSPB. Take A2 N from Belfast and follow signs to Belfast Harbour Estate. Both entrances to reserve have checkpoints. From Dee Street 2 miles to reserve, from Tillysburn entrance 1 mile. Mudflats, wet grassland, freshwater lagoon. Latter is overlooked by observation room (check for opening hours) and 2 view points. Noted for Black-tailed Godwit numbers and excellent variety of waterfowl in spring, autumn and winter, with close views. Rarities have included Buff-breasted, Pectoral, White-rumped and Semi-palmated Sandpipers, Spotted Crake, Amerian Wigeon, Laughing Gull. Warden: Anthony McGeehan, 01247 479009

CASTLE ESPIE. (50a) WWT Centre J474672. On Strangford Lough 10 miles E of Belfast, signposted from A22 in the Comber area. Open daily (except 25 Dec) from 1030 Mon-Sa, from 1130 Su. Visitor centre, educational facilities, views over lough, 3 hides, woodland walk. Winter wildfowl esp. Pale-bellied Brent Geese, Scaup. Summer warblers. Wader scrape has attracted Little Egret, Ruff, Long-billed Dowitcher, Killdeer. Reedbed filtration system with viewing facilities. James Orr, Centre Manager, The Wildfowl & Wetlands Trust, Castle Espie, Ballydrain Road, Comber, Co Down BT23 6EA. 01247 874146

COPELAND BIRD OBSERVATORY. Situated on a 40-acre island 4 miles N of Donaghadee. Access is by chartered boat from Donaghadee. Observatory open Apr-Oct most weekends and some whole weeks. Hostel-type accommodation for up to 20. Daily ringing, bird census, sea passage recording. Large colony of Manx Shearwaters; Black Guillemot, Eider, Water Rail also nest; Storm Petrels visit during summer nights; moderate passage of passerine migrants. General bookings: Neville McKee, 67 Temple Rise, Templepatrick, Co. Antrim BT39 0AG, tel 01849 433068. Hon Sec: Dr Peter Munro, Talisker Lodge, 54B Templepatrick Road, Ballyclare, Co Antrim BT39 9TX. 01960 323421

CRAWFORDSBURN COUNTRY PARK. (280a) EHS J467826. Signposted off A2 Belfast-Bangor road. Open at all times. Car parks. Sea, shore (rocky and sandy), woodland, glen, open fields. Woodland and grassland species; Dipper; Eider, gulls, divers, terns, shearwaters can all be seen offshore, esp. in autumn. D C T Drew, Crawfordsburn Country Park, Bridge Road South, Helen's Bay, Co Down BT19 1LD. 01247 853621

DORN. (1952a) EHS (NNR) J593568. Near Ardkeen on Kircubbin to Portaferry coastal route. Waders; wildfowl (inc. Pale-bellied Brent Goose). Access only by arrangement with Warden. Shaun D'Arcy-Burt, Quoile Countryside Centre, 5 Quay Road, Downpatrick, Co Down BT30 7JB. 01396 615520

KILLARD. (167a) EHS (NNR) J610433. Access from Millquarter Bay on coastal road 4 mi S of Strangford village. Varied rocky and sandy shoreline. Waders (inc. Purple Sandpiper in winter); good seawatching (esp. shearwaters, skuas); breeding Fulmar, Shelduck, Stonechat and Sand Martin. Shaun D'Arcy-Burt, Quoile Countryside Centre, 5 Quay Road, Downpatrick, Co Down BT30 7JB. 01396 615520

MURLOUGH. (699a) National Trust (NNR) J394338. Between Dundrum and Newcastle. Sand dunes, heathland. Visitor centre. Waders and wildfowl occur in Inner Dundrum Bay adjacent to the reserve; divers and large numbers of Scoter (inc. regular Surf Scoter) and Merganser in Dundrum Bay. Head Warden, Murlough NNR, The Stable Yard, Keel Point, Dundrum, Newcastle, Co Down BT33 0NQ. 01396 751467

NORTH STRANGFORD LOUGH. (2482a) National Trust (NNR) J510700. View from adjacent roads and car parks; also from hide at Castle Espie (J492675). Extensive tidal mudflats, limited saltmarsh. Major feeding area for Pale-bellied Brent Goose, also Pintail, Wigeon, Whooper Swan. Waders (inc. Dunlin, Knot, Oystercatcher, Bar-tailed Godwit). Head Warden, National Trust, Strangford Lough Wildlife Scheme, Strangford Lough Wildlife Centre, Castle Ward, Strangford, Co Down BT30 7LS. 01396 881411

QUOILE PONDAGE. (475a) EHS (NNR) J500478. 1 mile N of Downpatrick on road to Strangford. Freshwater pondage with many vegetation types on shores. Hide (J505489), visitor centre (J496470). Many wildfowl species, woodland birds; migrant and wintering waders including Spotted Redshank, Ruff and Black-tailed Godwit. Shaun D'Arcy-Burt, Quoile Countryside Centre, 5 Quay Road, Downpatrick, Co Down BT30 7JB. 01396 615520

CO FERMANAGH

LOWER LOUGH ERNE ISLANDS. (605a) RSPB & EHS H009603. 42 islands on Lower Lough Erne with access from adjacent roads, esp A47 Beleek/Pettigoe, and by boat to Lusty More Island H105615. Lakeside scrub provides good habitat for warblers. Breeding waders (inc. Curlew, Lapwing, Redshank, Snipe), Red-breasted Merganser, Sandwich and Common Terns; Long-eared Owl, Garden Warbler, Siskin and Crossbill in forest; winter wildfowl inc. Whooper Swan. Brad Robson, Lower Lough Erne Islands Reserve, Garvary, Leggs PO, Enniskillen, Co Fermanagh BT93 2BY.

CO LONDONDERRY

LOUGH FOYLE. (3300a) RSPB C545237. Minor roads off Limavady-Londonderry road to view-points (choose high tide) at Longfield Point, Ballykelly, Faughanvale. Staging-post for migrating wildfowl (eg. 15,000 Wigeon, 4,000 Pale-bellied Brent Geese in Oct/Nov); winter Slavonian Grebe, divers, Bewick's and Whooper Swans, Bar-tailed Godwit, Golden Plover, Snow Bunting; autumn waders (inc. Ruff, Little Stint, Curlew Sandpiper, Spotted Redshank). Contact: RSPB N Ireland HQ (01232 491547).

ROE ESTUARY. (1170a) EHS (NNR) C640295. Access off A2 coast road between Castlerock and Limavady. Mudflats and saltings (beware soft mud). Pale-bellied Brent Goose, many wildfowl and wader species. Darrell Stanley, NW Nature Reserves Office, The Cornstore, Dogleap Road, Limavady, Co Londonderry BT49 9NN. 01504 763982

ROE VALLEY COUNTRY PARK. (200a) EHS C678203. Signposted off Belfast-Londonderry and Limavady-Dungiven roads. Open at all times. Car parks, visitor centre, nature trail, pathways. Mixed woodland and gorge. Typical woodland and river species, inc. Wood Warbler, Dipper, Grey Wagtail. Ciaran McLarnon, Roe Valley Country Park, 41 Dogleap Road, Limavady, Co Londonderry BT49 9NN. 01504 722074

UMBRA. (70a) Ulster WT C724355. Entrance on A2 between Coleraine and Limavady coast road beside automatic railway crossing about 1.5 miles W of Downhill. Permit required (available to Trust members only). ASSI. Part of large area of unspoilt dunes; thickets of sea buckthorn, pine and some deciduous woodland. Hunting Buzzard, Peregrine, Raven from nearby cliffs; numerous warblers in scrub; Gannet, shearwaters, skuas seen from dunes in autumn and Great Northern Diver in Winter. Contact: UWT HQ.

CO TYRONE

KILLETER BOG. (55a) DANI (Forest Service) & EHS (NNR) H086821, H090808. 6 miles W of Killeter. Greenland White-fronted Geese in area in winter. Ronnie Thompson, District Forest Office, Sperrin House, Sedan Avenue, Omagh, Co Tyrone BT79 7AQ. 01662 251020 ext 34477

REPUBLIC OF IRELAND

CO CORK

ALLEN'S POOL, BALLYCOTTON. (20a) BirdWatch Ireland W989667. View from sand dunes (hide). This brackish pool forms the eastern extremity of the complex of marshes, beach and lake that make up the prime birdwatching area of Ballycotton. Reedbed, marsh, sand dunes. Good diversity of waders (inc. American); autumn passerine migrants.

CUSKINNY MARSH. BirdWatch Ireland W8269. Small brackish lagoon 1.25 miles E of Cobh on Great Island in Cork Harbour. Good viewing conditions for a wide range of birds inc. ducks, waders, and woodland birds nearby.

KNOCKADOON HEAD & CAPEL ISLAND. BirdWatch Ireland. Situated on the east Cork coast, the headland attracts autumn passerine migrants (rarities inc Yellow-browed and Sardinian Warbler, Pied Wheatear). The 13 acre island and its environs hold Chough, Pergerine and a Cormorant colony; winter divers.

LOUGH BEG. (12a) BirdWatch Ireland W7963. Small brackish lagoon beside Cork Harbour. Hide. High tide wader roost especially for Black-tailed Godwit, Dunlin, Curlew, Redshank, Golden Plover; occasional American waders; Shelduck.

MIZEN LIGHTHOUSE. Located at the most south-westerly point of Ireland, this is a superb site for watching sea passage inc. autumn Manx, Sooty and Great Shearwaters, Great and Arctic Skuas. It incorporates a BirdWatch Ireland seawatching room.

CO DONEGAL

SHESKINMORE LOUGH. (66a) BirdWatch Ireland and Wildlife Service G7096. Shallow freshwater coastal lagoon, located midway between Portnoo and Ardara. An internationally important wetland renowned for wintering White-fronted and Barnacle Geese and breeding waders.

CO DUBLIN

NEWHAGGARD, ROGERSTOWN ESTUARY. (30a) BirdWatch Ireland. Grassland site bordering the inner estuary and susceptible to flooding at high tide. Regularly used by Brent Geese, Wigeon and Short-eared Owls in winter, the pools also attract a variety of passage waders inc. American vagrants.

CO KERRY

LITTLE SKELLIG. (16a) BirdWatch Ireland V2762. A rocky island located 6.8 miles SW of Valentia Island. Of international importance, it regularly holds 20,000 pairs of breeding Gannets, one of the largest colonies in the world. Landing is not permitted, though good views can be had from a boat.

PUFFIN ISLAND. (130a) BirdWatch Ireland V3473. A precipitous island 4.5 miles SW of Valentia. It has an internationally important seabird breeding colony, esp for Puffins and Manx Shearwaters. Day visits arranged from Valentia by contacting Des Lavelle (0667 6124). A visiting permit from BWI is required for longer stays.

CO OFFALLY

BULLOCK ISLAND. (47a) BirdWatch Ireland N022175. Located at Shannon Harbour, 2 miles N of Banagher. The flat, low-lying grasslands (or Callows) are subject to flooding in winter and spring. The area is best known for its concentration of breeding Corncrakes. Breeding waders inc. Lapwing, Snipe, Curlew, Redshank; Whimbrel occur on spring migration; winter wildfowl (inc. Wigeon). Visiting by arrangement with BWI.

TERMONCARRAGH LAKE. BirdWatch Ireland F6634. Coastal lake and reedbed located 4.5 miles W of Belmullet in NW Mayo. Nationally important for wintering waterfowl (inc. Whooper Swan) and breeding waders.

CO WEXFORD

WEXFORD WILDFOWL REFUGE. (509a) BirdWatch Ireland and National Parks & Wildlife Service T0824. Open daily 16 Apr-30 Sep 0900-1800; 1 Oct-15 Apr 1000-1700. An area of reclaimed slobland located 3 miles NE of Wexford town. Visitor centre, hides, observation tower. An internationally important wetland. Winter flocks of up to 10,000 Greenland White-fronted Geese, 2,000 Pale-bellied Brent, 15,000 Wigeon and 200 Bewick's Swans. Also almost annual occurrence of Blue-phase Lesser Snow Goose and small races of Canada Goose.

CO WICKLOW

KILCOOLE. (16a) BirdWatch Ireland. Off R671 N of Wicklow. Lowland, wet grassland site running parallel to the sea and separated from it by a shingle and marram bank. Breeding waders inc. Snipe, Redshank and Lapwing; also Water Rail. Little Terns breed nearby.

INDEX OF RESERVES AND
OBSERVATORIES

320 INDEX OF RESERVES & OBSERVATORIES